Seek and Strike

Jacket Images

Front cover: Tornadoes of 14 Squadron. (RAF News)

Rear cover: Phantoms of 14 Squadron on their return to QRA. (RAF Brüggen)

By the same author

Swift Justice: The Full Story of the Supermarine Swift. Astonbridge
Publishing, Gloucester, 2000

Seek and Strike: RAF Brüggen in War and Peace.
Astonbridge Publishing, Gloucester, 2001

Swift Justice: Supermarine Low Level Reconnaissance Fighter.
Pen & Sword Books, Barnsley, 2004

Best of Breed: The Hunter in Fighter Reconnaissance, An Operational
History of the Hawker Hunter FR10. Pen & Sword Books, Barnsley, 2006

Voodoo Warriors: The Story of the McDonnell Voodoo Fast Jets.
Pen & Sword Books, Barnsley, 2007

Dragon Rampant: The Story of No.234 Fighter Squadron. Merlin Massara
Publications, Dunstable, 2007

Built to Endure: The RAF Airfield Construction Branch in the Cold War.
Old Forge Publishing, Peterborough, 2009

From the Cockpit No.14: Swift. Ad Hoc Publications, Suffolk, 2011

Thinking the Unthinkable: The Lives of RAF and East German Pilots in
the Cold War. Astonbridge Publishing, Gloucester, 2012

Hitler's Revenge Weapons: The Last Blitz of London.
Pen & Sword Books, Barnsley, 2018

Seek and Strike

RAF Brüggen in War and Peace

Nigel Walpole

AIR WORLD

First published in Great Britain in 2020 and reprinted in 2020 by
Air World
An imprint of
Pen & Sword Books Limited
Yorkshire - Philadelphia

ISBN 978 1 52675 8 422

A CIP catalogue record for this book is available from the British Library

Printed and bound in the UK by CPI Group (UK) Ltd, Croydon, CR0 4YY

Pen & Sword Books Limited incorporates the imprints of Atlas, Archaeology,
Aviation, Discovery, Family History, Fiction, History, Maritime, Military,
Military Classics, Politics, Select, Transport, True Crime, Air World, Frontline
Publishing, Leo Cooper, Remember When, Seaforth Publishing, The
Praetorian Press, Wharncliffe Local History, Wharncliffe Transport,
Wharncliffe True Crime and White Owl.

For a complete list of Pen & Sword titles please contact
PEN & SWORD BOOKS LIMITED
47 Church Street, Barnsley, South Yorkshire S70 2AS, United Kingdom
E-mail: enquiries@pen-and-sword.co.uk
Website: www.pen-and-sword.co.uk

Or
PEN AND SWORD BOOKS
1950 Lawrence Rd, Havertown, PA 19083, USA
E-mail: Uspen-and-sword@casematepublishers.com
Website: www.penandswordbooks.com

Dedicated to all those who helped make
RAF Brüggen what it was

Contents

Glossary   viii

Preface   xiii

Foreword   xv

Acknowledgements   xvi

Chapter One   Before the Beginning   1
Chapter Two   Starting from Scratch   6
Chapter Three   No. 135 Fighter Wing   20
Chapter Four   Multi-Role Station   51
Chapter Five   Brüggen Phantoms   91
Chapter Six   Jaguar Strike Wing   134
Chapter Seven   Tornado – Change and Continuity   187
Chapter Eight   The Gulf War   221
Chapter Nine   The Last Ten Years   252
Chapter Ten   Marching Out   318

Epilogue   339

Appendix One   Station Commanders   340

Appendix Two   Resident Operational Squadrons and Aircraft   341

Bibliography   343

Index   344

Glossary

AOC	Air Officer Commanding
ACB	Airfield Construction Branch
AAFCE	Allied Air Forces Central Europe
AAA	Anti-Aircraft Artillery
AM	Air Ministry/Air Marshal
ATC	Air Traffic Control
AEW	Airborne Early Warning
AVM	Air Vice-Marshal
AMQ	Airman's Married Quarter
AAM	Air-to-Air Missile
ACM	Air Chief Marshal
AAR	Air-to-Air Refuelling
ASP	Aircraft Servicing Platform
ATOC	Allied Tactical Operations Centre
APC	Armament Practice Camp
AMWD	Air Ministry Works Department
AFC	Air Force Cross
ALARM	Air Launched Anti-Radiation Missile
ACMI	Air Combat Manoeuvring Instrumentation
ASM	Airfield Survival Measures
Air Cdre	Air Commodore
ARRC	Allied Rapid Reaction Corps
AWACS	Airborne Warning and Control System
ADR	Airfield Damage Repair
AFCENT	Allied Forces Central Europe
AB	Air Base
ARRC	Allied Rapid Reaction Corps
BDT	Brüggen Drawdown Team
BEM	British Empire Medal
BCDU	Bomber Command Development Unit
BDR	Battle Damage Repair
BAD	Base Ammunition Depot
BAF	Belgian Air Force
BAOR	British Army of the Rhine
CINCENT	C-in-C Central Europe
CT	Chief Technician

GLOSSARY

CAP	Combat Air Patrol
C-in-C	Commander-in-Chief
CBU	Cluster Bomb Unit
COMAO	Combined Air Operations
CAS	Chief of the Air Staff
COC	Combat Operations Centre
CCF	Combined Cadet Force
CFE	Conventional Forces Europe
C3I	Command, Control, Communications and Intelligence
CAOC	Combined Air Operations Centre
Dep Cdr	Deputy Commander
DSO	Distinguished Service Order
DFCS	Day Fighter Combat School
DFLS	Day Fighter Leaders School
DF/GA	Day Fighter/Ground Attack
DME	Distance Measuring Equipment
DZ	Drop Zone
ECM	Electronic Counter-Measures
ECR	Electronic Combat Reconnaissance
EO	Electro-Optical
EOD	Explosives Ordnance Demolition
ESA	Explosives Storage Area
EW	Electronic Warfare
FLIR	Forward Looking Infra-Red
FOD	Foreign Object Damage
FB	Fighter Bomber
FGA	Fighter Ground Attack
Flt Lt	Flight Lieutenant
Fg Off	Flying Officer
FBSA	Fighter Bomber Strike Attack
FRG	Federal Republic of Germany
FOB	Forward Operating Base
FSC	Field Standard 'C' (Rapier)
FJTF	Fast-Jet Turnround Facility
GCA	Ground Controlled Approach
GEP	General Equipment Park
GCI	Ground Controlled Interception
GGS	Gyro Gunsight
Gp Capt	Group Captain
GEF	General Engineering Flight
GAF	German Air Force
GPS	Global Positioning System

GSO	General Service Organisation
HAS	Hardened Aircraft Shelter
HF	High Frequency
HMG	Her Majesty's Government
HUD	Head-Up Display
INAS	Inertial Navigation System
IFF	Identification Friend or Foe
IRLS	Infra-Red Linescan
ILS	Instrument Landing System
IP	Initial Point
IFOR	Implementation Force
JHQ	Joint Headquarters
JP	Junior Pilot
Kg	Kilogram
LAA	Light Anti-Aircraft
LFA	Low Flying Area
LABS	Low Angle Bombing System
LGB	Laser-Guided Bomb
LAAD	Local Anti-Aircraft Defence
LFS	Low Flying System
MTSU	Motor Transport Servicing Unit
MTO	Mechanical Transport Officer
MCAG	Mobile Civilian Artisan Group
MU	Maintenance Unit
MFPU	Mobile Field Processing Unit
MPC	Missile Practice Camp
MRCA	Multi-Role Combat Aircraft
MRAF	Marshal of the RAF
MOD	Ministry of Defence
MACC	Main Access Control Centre
MBE	Member of the British Empire
NDT	Non-Destructive Testing
NBC	Nuclear, Biological and Chemical
NVG	Night Vision Goggles
NFZ	No-Fly Zone
NMS	New Management Strategy
NAVWASS	Navigation and Weapons Aiming Sub-System
NATO	North Atlantic Treaty Organisation
OMQ	Officer's Married Quarter
OTR	Operational Turn-Round
OCU	Operational Conversion Unit
OLF	Operational Low Flying

GLOSSARY

ORP	Operational Readiness Platform
OMB	Office of Management and Budgets
OCA	Offensive Counter Air
PSA	Public Services Agency
PI	Photograph Interpreter
PSP	Perforated Steel Plate
PGM	Precision Guided Munitions
PSI	Public Services Institute
PD	Pulse Doppler
PBF	Pilot Briefing Facility
Plt Off	Pilot Officer
PROM	Property Management
QGH	Controlled Descent through Cloud
QRA	Quick Reaction Alert
QWI	Qualified Weapons Instructor
RRR	Rapid Runway Repair
RHWR	Radar Homing Warning Receiver
RE	Royal Engineers
RIC	Reconnaissance Intelligence Centre
RFC	Royal Flying Corps/Rugby Football Club
RRF(Air)	Rapid Reaction Force (Air)
SOC	Sector Operations Centre
SAM	Surface-to-Air Missile
SHORAD	Short Range Air Defence
SLAR	Sideways Looking Airborne Radar
SEngO	Senior Engineering Officer
SIF	Services Institute Fund
SACEUR	Supreme Allied Commander Europe
SEAD	Suppression of Enemy Air Defences
Sqn Ldr	Squadron Leader
SAC	Senior Aircraftsman
SATCO	Senior Air Traffic Control Officer
Sgt	Sergeant
SSA	Special Storage Area
TWU	Tactical Weapons Unit
TAF	Tactical Air Force
TLP	Tactical Leadership Programme
TFM	Tactical Fighter Meet
TKL	Target of Known Location
TAM	Tactical Air Meet
TBC	Tactical Bombing Competition
TFR	Terrain Following Radar

TIALD	Thermal Imaging Airborne Laser Designator
UHF	Ultra High Frequency
USMC	US Marine Corps
USN	US Navy
WVS	Women's Voluntary Service
Wg Cdr	Wing Commander
WGF	Western Group of Forces
WP	Warsaw Pact
WEWO	Wing Electronic Warfare Officer
WOC	Wing Operations Centre

Preface

I first landed at Brüggen one Friday afternoon in 1957, leading a pair of Hunters from RAF Oldenburg on a 'routine training exercise'; Lieutenant Mike Maina was on my wing and we would spend much of our time until Monday playing golf. Mike, an RN exchange pilot, came to Oldenburg when Brüggen's Hunter Wing disbanded almost overnight, just after he had ejected on take-off, leaving his aircraft on 'Hill 60' to add a little realism to an RAF Regiment exercise taking place there (more of which later). He had waxed lyrically over this huge base, part of a new NATO breed so different from standard RAF and Luftwaffe stations, with its own golf course of 'eighteen aircraft dispersals and a reserve hospital'. I wanted to see all this for myself – and when I did I was impressed.

NATO was established in 1949, as a defensive alliance against the growing threat of communism, and RAF Brüggen was built as part of this expansion; it was one of a 'Clutch' of four new airfields built for the RAF between the Ruhr and the German/Dutch border, and was ready for operations in 1953. RAF Brüggen was at war for most of its life, the greater part devoted to the Cold War, preparing for the unthinkable, but we who were there certainly had the feeling that we were at war, albeit without the physical pain. We learned what we could about our potential adversaries, and proved to a very demanding NATO Tactical Evaluation (Taceval) team that we were as ready as we could be for anything.

During the Cold War came the Falklands conflict, and although Brüggen aircraft were not committed many of its personnel were deployed to support the 'teeth' arms. Brüggen squadrons were, however, at the forefront of action in the 1991 war with Iraq, bringing much credit upon themselves, and they retained a presence in the Gulf thereafter. They were also actively involved in the Balkans in 1999, and hit the headlines again as the only RAF Tornado station to launch operational missions directly to Kosovo.

The Station Crest, approved by Her Majesty the Queen in 1963, depicts a crossbow symbolising a weapon from which missiles can be launched, with the roundel representing a fortress which could cause fire and destruction by day and night. This, and the motto 'To Seek and Strike' was very appropriate.

I have dealt with each phase of Brüggen's history in turn, as NATO evolved with ever-changing political scenarios and military concepts. The day fighter/ground-attack wing, Canberra, Phantom and Jaguar eras belong exclusively to the Cold War, as the strategy changed from that of massive nuclear retaliation to 'tripwire' and 'flexible response', while the Tornados came in at the tail end of this East/West confrontation and then saw action against different enemies.

The front line takes precedence in Seek and Strike, but much space is also given to the collective and individual efforts in its support, and to the domestic, sport, social and charitable activities which contributed so much to that special spirit and quality of life at Brüggen. This is a tribute to everyone who helped make Brüggen RAF Germany's 'jewel in the crown'.

Seek and Strike is not a definitive history of RAF Brüggen. The factual framework, drawn from official records, is overlaid with anecdotes of all sorts, but I am deeply conscious that there are many players who have not been given the credit they deserve. Likewise, some events of significance may not have been covered, or covered adequately. For all this I apologise. To give full and proper cover would have been an endless task; moreover, for diverse reasons, some primary sources have not been available to me – and the later chapters have less of the human stories than I would have wished. In most cases I have used only that material which has had some corroboration, and every part of the text has been vetted by at least one key player of the time. That said, I am sure that some anomalies remain, and that there will be other versions of many of the events and anecdotes I have recounted. Finally, the views offered in this book have no official standing, so I cannot vouch for the veracity of all that is written here; the result is only as good as the inputs, but I do hope I have done enough to stimulate memories of hard-earned achievement and some happy days at RAF Brüggen. In Jaguar times, one Brüggen station commander greeted new arrivals with the message:

> You are joining the largest operational wing in the Royal Air Force and the largest of the four major stations in the front line command of the Service, Royal Air Force Germany. In fulfilling our assigned role in NATO alongside our allies we face impressive military odds. Our task is to help balance the odds by providing from the aircraft, missiles and other equipment we have here the finest fighting quality we can achieve. That balance is the key to the security of Europe and to the deterrence of war. If you have ever in the past doubted the worth of your contribution you will have little cause to doubt it here. You are at the 'sharp end' and it does not come much sharper! You will work hard at Brüggen but the other side of the coin is that you will have the facilities and opportunities to play hard as well. Make the most of them, the local area has its interests and we are conveniently situated on an excellent autobahn system which allows us to travel swiftly throughout Western Europe. Our relationships with our German and Dutch neighbours are excellent and they will remain so if we behave as we would expect them to if they were guests in our country. Do try to learn something of the language; it will make a great difference to the enjoyment of your tour.

Enough said, for those who did not have the privilege and pleasure of serving at Brüggen, this is the story of those who did. To those who did – welcome back!
NJRW

Foreword

This is an unpretentious and amusing, factual and anecdotal history of one of the most important overseas flying stations in the Royal Air Force's history, and of its people. Above all, it is a story of success, of an amalgam of colourful and talented individuals working in concert within the framework of a NATO Alliance that provided a resolute bulwark against a real and significant communist threat in the Cold War. Indeed, Brüggen's success in that endeavour epitomized the spirit of the Alliance throughout this pivotal period. Much of that recorded here could be read across to other like bases, which in itself makes 'Seek and Strike' a useful piece of primary evidence in the story of the Cold War. However, Brüggen was 'special', and the author does not hide his pride in a base which excelled in all that it did, at work and play, in its operational expertise and inventiveness, extraordinary contribution to myriad charities, its prowess in sport and its enduring and meaningful relationships with a variety of local communities of different nationality.

Nigel Walpole is supremely qualified to tell the story. He started the first of six tours in Germany in 1955 as the Cold War gathered pace and was part of Brüggen's growth in scale and importance, ending his active flying career on Jaguars while the Officer Commanding Operations Wing at Brüggen in 1979. In six years at Rheindahlen he was Group Captain Offensive Operations in HQ RAF Germany and then Assistant Chief of Staff Offensive Operations in 2ATAF, throughout which Brüggen's every Cold War interest was one of his primary concerns. On retirement from the Service, he became the air weapons advisor to British Aerospace and remained close to those Brüggen Tornado crews committed to the Gulf War armed with the laser-guided bomb and ALARM missile. Moreover, in spending time at Brüggen drafting this history, he gained a good insight into the wing's continuing involvement in the Gulf, and into its latter day operations in the Balkans.

Sensibly, the author has avoided the peculiar and ever-changing vernacular, so beloved by those of us who inhabit the flight line, in favour of plain English and clarity, but he has undoubtedly captured the enduring spirit and moods of the times in a fascinating story of a great airbase which should appeal to both the initiated and interested layman.

5 September, 2001

Group Captain T.M. Anderson DSO
MA MRAeS RAF Officer Commanding
Royal Air Force Brüggen

Acknowledgements

This book could not have been written without the co-operation of RAF Brüggen in its busy, final days. With too many to name, I hope that all those who contributed from there will accept my thanks through the last three station commanders: Air Commodore Iain McNicoll, Group Captain Tim Anderson and Wing Commander Julian Andrews – from whom I welcomed inputs, guidance and encouragement. However, I must give all those involved with the Brüggen Circuit a special mention and thank the station for helping to fund the project.

For their guidance, I thank Tony Stephens, Steve Clarke and Clive Richards of the MOD Air Historical Branch, and David Belson, the Crown Copyright Administrator, for authorising the use of Crown Copyright/MOD photographs, reproduced with the permission of the Controller of Her Majesty's Stationery Office. I am greatly indebted to Andrew Wise, Editor of the RAF News, for access to past copies of that excellent newspaper, and to him and his staff for making our frequent visits there so agreeable.

My sincere appreciation also goes to Air Commodore Mike Allisstone and David Baron, both ex-Brüggen men, who toiled through the manuscript and helped with the written word, and the following who offered personal testimony or secondary evidence: Alan Arber, Peter Arthur, Air Commodore 'Tinkle' Bell, Tony Buttler, Air Marshal Sir Ivor Broom, Eddie Brown, Air Commodore Jack Broughton, Robin Brown, John Burns, Jack Campling, Dick Carrey, Air Commodore John Chandler, John Chick, Clive Compton, Bob Copping, Bob Creer, Air Vice-Marshal Eddie Crew, Alan Curry, Don Curson, Air Marshal Sir John Curtiss, Air Vice-Marshal Tony Dudgeon, Ed Durham, Gerry Dwyer, Bill Floydd, Peter Foster, Jerry Gegg, Sid Geoghegan, Air Vice-Marshal Mike Gibson, Bert Gledhill, Jack Gordon, Steve Griggs, Ian Hall, Bill Hannah, Bill Hansford, Don Hanson, Sir Peter Harding, John Hare, David Hattersley, Air Vice-Marshal David Henderson, Air Chief Marshal Sir Patrick Hine, Air Vice-Marshal Bob Honey, Air Commodore John Houghton, Richard Howard, Mike Hudson, Frank Hulse, Les Hutchinson, Bob Jones, David King, Bob Knight, Frank Leeson, Air Vice-Marshal Tim Lloyd, Malcolm Lovett, Air Commodore Nigel Maddox, 'Pop' Miles, Dick Milsom, Air Commodore Frank Mitchell, 'Murph' Morrison, Anthony Mumford, Alex Muir, Terry Nash, Mavis Newstead, Ben Nicol, Tony Pearson, Jim Peters, Ray Pixley, Neil Pollock, Arthur Porter, Tom Redley, Keith Reyner, Ray Roberts, Tom Robertson, Alec Robinshaw, Bill Rose, Les Rowe, Dick Smerdon, Mel Smith, Dave Spink, Ian Stanway, Air Marshal Sir Tom Stoner, Bill Taylor, Lady Thomson, Frank Turner, Gerry Tyack, Del Williams, Air

ACKNOWLEDGEMENTS

Vice-Marshal Graham Williams, MRAF Sir Keith Williamson, Ted Willis, Jerry Wilmot, Simon and Jenny Wilmshurst-Smith, Air Chief Marshal Sir 'Sandy' Wilson, Air Commodore Jerry Witts, Geoff Woolston, Air Chief Marshal Sir Bill Wratten, Air Vice-Marshal Rob Wright.

It has also been a great pleasure to work with Miles Bailey and his helpful staff within Action Publishing Technology of Gloucester.

All profits from the sale of this book will be donated to 'Combat Stress', The Ex-Services Mental Welfare Society committed to meeting the needs of ex-Service men and women who suffer from Post Traumatic Stress and related conditions.

Chapter One

Before the Beginning

It was in a vast tract of flat, conifer covered, low-lying and sandy ground on the German/Dutch border, close to the Dutch town of Roermond, that this piece of history was made; this was the Elmpt Forest or Elmpter Wald. With the B230 bisecting the forest it had some strategic importance as one of the main road arteries between central Germany and southern Holland. Touched by two world wars and the defeat of Germany in both, it escaped the ravages suffered elsewhere on the continent before playing its part in a successful conclusion to the Cold War.

In 58 BC this area of Germany west of the Rhine was occupied by Julius Caesar's Roman army, and it was then that the route between Roermond and Mönchengladbach was first established through the village and forest named after the Von Elmpt family. The French arrived in 1792, during the Napoleonic Wars, and left in 1815 with the bells from the Elmpt Parish Church; the area around Elmpt, Niederkruchten and Wegberg was then ceded to the Prussian crown. Farming and forestry supported a frugal life, briefly enhanced with the introduction of a cottage industry in velvet weaving, circa 1840, which peaked with 350 hand-looms before declining in the 1880s.

Traditional livelihoods suffered greatly when much of the Elmpter Wald was destroyed by fire in 1911, then during the hard winter of 1916–17 and from the many effects of the First World War which ultimately cost the lives of fifty-one of the local men. Between the wars the fortunes of the area mirrored those of the new Weimar Republic as a whole, with rampant inflation and unemployment, the impact of the American economic crisis and the humiliation of the Versailles Settlement of 1918, all helping Hitler and his Nazi party to take power in the mid-1930s. Generally, the Nazis found little favour in the strongly Catholic district of Elmpt but two prominent head teachers managed to muster an enthusiastic Hitler Youth Group, when the village was joined administratively with Niederkruchten.

In prophetic anticipation of what was to come, the Germans built static defences along the 'Westwall', better known as the Siegfried Line, from Kleve in the north 300 miles south to Basle in Switzerland. Construction began in 1936, providing work for 500,000 by 1938 and consuming one third of Germany's annual output of cement. Passing just east of the villages of Brüggen and Niederkruchten, some evidence of these defences remain today.

German troops stationed in the area decamped westwards at the start of the Second World War, after which the relative calm of the area was broken only by steadily increasing allied bombing which caused major fires in the Elmpter Wald. In August 1944, with the allied armies approaching rapidly from the west and air raid sirens now sounding day and night, the schools were closed and the local women and children ordered to evacuate the area. Old men and boys, not fit for service at the front, were drafted into the Volkssturm (home guard), while many Dutch men were taken into military service or forced to work in Germany; others melted into the forest to escape deportation, surviving as best they could and risking death if found. The Dutch were also forced to hand over their cattle to the Germans, which were then herded eastwards.

In September, further north across the border in Holland, Montgomery's planned thrust towards the Rhineland stalled with the failure of Operation Market Garden, the battle of Arnhem and virtual destruction of the British First Airborne Division. The Germans were far from spent and it was clear that they would not give ground easily. They continued to shore up their static defences on a line which ran roughly along the Maas river in southern Holland, the Elmpter Wald to the east offering a natural defensive position.

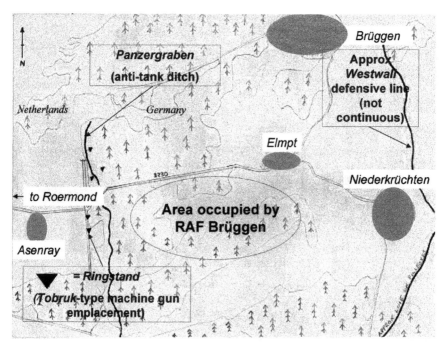

Location of Second World War German defences in the local area.

The Germans made full use of every resource available, including forced labour with Russian women helping to build or strengthen gun positions, anti-tank ditches, dugouts and revetments on the western edge of the forest. Long lines of trenches still snake through the woods around RAF Brüggen, and some concrete machine-gun pits and earth revetments are still visible. Elmpter Wald defences included 'Tabruk' or 'Ringstand' machine-gun emplacements, sited directly ahead of or behind a 'Panzergraben' (tank ditch). The Ringstand derived its name from the rail which surrounded the neck on which a machine gun could traverse through 360°. Ammunition was stored below the entrance.

These defences were never put to the test. During the winter of 1944–45 fighting in the area was confined largely to artillery exchanges and some patrol activity; there were no major actions on the ground. The Germans then retreated behind the Rhine and the Americans entered Roermond and Elmpt in March 1945. The German evacuees returned to their homes to face the inevitable wrath of their Dutch neighbours, who immediately retrieved all the cattle they could find. During the whole conflict Elmpt had lost fifty-two men on active service and suffered many of its incidental effects, but for them the war was over and calm descended on the forest as the village began to recover once more. Little did it know what the future had in store.

Second World War German 'Ringstand' machine gun bunker, still visible at the western end of the airfield in 2000. (*Author*)

In the wake of war the British Air Forces of Occupation (BAFO) took over many old Luftwaffe bases, among them Fassberg, Wunstorf, Bückeburg, Celle, Jever and Gütersloh. This was to have been a temporary expedient but as the Cold War developed from 1949 so did the demand for greater defensive measures within the newly formed NATO Alliance. Specifically for BAFO, plans were laid for less vulnerable airfields to be constructed well to the west of those already in use and optimised for second generation jet fighters and fighter-bombers. Although built to NATO standards, these were to be 'utility' airfields with finite lives; they would be known as the 'Clutch airfields' and one of the sites chosen for this purpose would be on Gemeindeland (Parish Land) in the Elmpter Wald – the peace and calm of which was about to be shattered.

Opposition to the new base by those who saw their whole lifestyle now at risk, particularly from noise pollution, was strident; local records from that time claimed 'A new catastrophe has overtaken the woods at Elmpt, worse than the fire of 1911: an airfield is to be built.' It was to be of no avail: politico-military imperatives, economic attractions and the seduction of compensation won the day.

The road past what would be RAF Brüggen, circa 1900, the Main Gate just beyond and to the right of the cottage – which still stands today. (*RAF Brüggen*)

4

Councils were required to give up 650 hectares and private owners 350 hectares of the forest, but they were compensated by two million D-Marks to fund much needed local investment and infrastructure. In addition, 5,000 men and women would find work building an airfield which would ultimately provide jobs for 800, with all the knock-on benefits to the surrounding economies.

In the spring of 1952 the Gemeinde Director of the Elmpt District, Herr Heinkiss, was given nine days to clear the trees from land requisitioned for the airfield and a veritable army of German workers descended on the site with axe and saw. An airfield was about to be born.

Chapter Two

Starting from Scratch

Although the intended airfield was on the fringe of the village of Elmpt and was known initially by the Germans as 'Flugplatz Elmpt', it would be named formally after the nearest railhead, the two syllable: Brüggen.

The operational and domestic, but not sports facilities at RAF Brüggen would be funded by the Germans as part of the reparations agreement and built by them in liaison with the Airfield Construction Branch (ACB) of the RAF. Married quarters would be paid for by Kreis Erkelenz and handed over to the local authority when no longer required by the Service.

The ACB, which at its peak numbered some 30,000 men, already had a fine record for innovation, ingenuity and industry from its invaluable service in the Second World War. This reputation grew in the aftermath with widespread evidence of its work as far afield as Hong Kong, the Far East, The Azores, Iceland and St. Kilda in the Hebrides, and it played a major part at both ends of the Berlin Airlift. The ACB was about to add another feather to its cap.

The more senior ACB officers tended to have been seconded from or started their professional life with the Air Ministry Works Directorate (AMWD), while junior officers were invariably graduates, recently qualified civil engineers or surveyors on national service or short-service commissions. The latter were guaranteed transfer to the AMWD at the end of five years' active service, seduced by a princely bounty of £500. In their No. 1 barathea uniforms, they stood out against the national servicemen in their hairy battledresses, giving them a distinct advantage in any amorous pursuit. Crucially, the NCOs were mainly long-serving regulars who, as one of their officers said, 'were very capable of controlling the novice airmen and supporting the "sprog" officers with skill and patience'.

Manned by the ACB, HQ 5357 Airfield Construction (AC) Wing was based at HQ 2 Group, RAF Sundern, with Wing Commander Bob Creer in command at the start of the Brüggen project, before moving to RAF Rheindahlen, the major new headquarters for British forces in Germany ten miles east of Brüggen. This unit controlled all the 'works and bricks' activity in RAF Germany, Holland and Belgium, with detachments on the stations which drew on direct labour, mostly from the German Services Organisation (GSO), for general maintenance work.

STARTING FROM SCRATCH

Squadron Leader Bill Jennings, an Air Ministry engineer seconded to the RAF and well versed in airfield work, commanded No. 5357 (AC) Detachment at Brüggen in 1952. He was assisted by Flight Lieutenants Barker and Christie, mechanical and engineering officers, and by three pilot officers, Don Hanson, Arthur Porter and Geoff Woolston, graduate engineers with two or three years experience undergoing their national service. In the words of a contemporary at nearby RAF Wildenrath, Bill Hannah, 'this was a formidable team combining the considerable intellect and extensive AMWD experience of their leader with the contractor and municipal expertise of its junior officers.' He went on: 'They undoubtedly gained much from the groundbreaking work at the lead station, RAF Wildenrath, but had to depend much on their own personal initiatives and enthusiasms.' Unlike Wildenrath, where much of the earthwork was undertaken by the RAF using well-worn, ex-Changi (Singapore) plant, the entire Brüggen project was based on a series of contracts with major German contractors, a decision which Bill believes 'speeded up the process even beyond the amazingly quick construction of Wildenrath'.

National Service Pilot Officers (L to R) Arthur Porter, Geoff Woolston and Don Hanson, outside the Brüggen offices of 5357 Airfield Construction Wing Detachment, in 1952.
(*Don Hanson*)

7

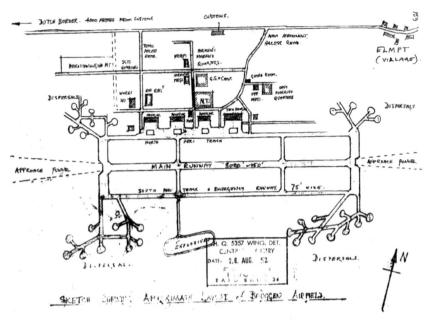

RAF Brüggen – as envisaged in the sketch by 5357 Wing Detachment in August 1952.
(*Arthur Porter*)

The Brüggen team worked from site offices on the embryo station, with the essential support of German typists and translators to help them communicate and understand the many documents and drawings printed in German. Thus established, they were responsible for monitoring progress on the various site projects designed to NATO specifications by the German civilian engineering organisation under the Agent for German Administration (AGA), a very helpful Herr Schlitt. Herr Adolf Hoffman was the German site manager (Bauleiter) and the actual construction work was undertaken by German contractors, among them Sager und Woener for the runway, perimeter track and hardstandings, Kemna Vaassen for the roads and railway, Hochtief and Karsten for buildings and Elsche for landscaping. Overall supervision was exercised by the German Neufinanzbauamt (the equivalent of AMWD).

Don Hanson claims that to make a start they just stuck tall poles at either end of the projected runway 'and took it from there'. The runway and hardstandings were made up of slabs of non-reinforced concrete, 200mm thick with well-designed joints based on a compacted gravel anti-frost layer. Compaction was achieved by one-ton 'Frog' rammers, flat-based cylinders of steel which were 'jumped' forward by diesel-driven pistons operated by one man following behind, or by dropping heavy weights from a mobile crane – both methods simple, effective and still in use. By these means and a 'paving train', which on a good day could lay 220 x 6m of pavement, the runway was completed in three months. The station roads were also to have been built of concrete but, following 'questions in the House' on costs, they were laid with tarmacadam.

State of the art technology. One-ton 'Frog' rammers were used to compact operating surfaces before paving. (*Les Rowe*)

'We just stuck tall poles in at either end of the intended runway and took it from there.' The main runway in 1953 – looking west. (*Don Hanson*)

Don Hanson, Bauleiter Hoffman and the Sager und Woener's agent, carried out an inspection of the partly completed airfield before the first aircraft was due to land there, a Devon carrying the Commander-in-Chief (C-in-C), AM Sir Robert Foster – and found a turnip sprouting through the southern taxiway. How it got there no one knows but there was some suspicion that a Russian military attaché, who had been seen prowling around with a camera, might have been responsible. A Vampire then made an unplanned visit before the runway was finished, Arthur Porter watching it hop over a dump truck to land safely and vanish from sight at the east end of the airfield. He found it there, told the pilot where he was and pointed him towards Wildenrath; he had just met the first of many pilots who would mistake one airfield for the other. With just sufficient fuel and enough runway cleared for his take-off, the embarrassed pilot left to face the music at Wildenrath.

Bauleiter Hoffman (foreground) supervises the harvesting of a turnip on the southern taxiway. (*Don Hanson*)

OC 5357 Wing Detachment, Sqn Ldr Bill Jennings, welcomes the C-in-C,
AM Sir Robert Foster, to Brüggen.

The first (planned) aircraft movement, a VIP Devon brings the C-in-C,
AM Sir Robert Foster, to Brüggen in June 1953. (*Don Hanson*)

Viewed from No. 1 Hangar, re-assembled from its original home at Berchtesgarten, the
rail spur and northern perimeter road heading east. Flying Wing HQ is on the right of the
picture. (*Don Hanson*)

Geoff Woolston was responsible primarily for the first three hangars, which had been dismantled elsewhere in Germany for re-assembly at Brüggen. Typically, No.1 Hangar was believed to have come from Berchtesgarten. Fg Off Alan Arber, who joined the detachment in 1953, was heavily involved with building Hangar 4, the MT Servicing Unit, Dilborn Fuel Storage Farm, additional married quarters, barrack blocks and a railway – a formidable range of tasks for an officer on his first tour.

Arthur Porter was also thrown in at the deep end, with responsibility for the water supply drawn from a well at the south of the site into a reinforced concrete reservoir, and a troublesome semi-underground signals block which 'for unfathomable reasons' continually lagged in progress. He soon learned about deep trench fill and dry-mix concrete foundations for mundane structures such as offices and messes, they being stronger than the UK strip footings with wet concrete and were better able to resist frost heave in the colder continental winters. Many walls were of 'Ytong' lightweight blocks made of sand and aluminium powder compound base and cut to shape when set, giving good insulation but with a tendency to shrinkage cracking.

These were interesting times in the changing landscape of the Elmpt Forest, with all manner of nefarious activities possible on the new base and in the surrounding border hinterland. With fencing incomplete and only sporadic patrols, it was not difficult to cross the German/Dutch frontier away from the main road without being noticed – as Arthur Porter found out when walking back alone through the forest from Roermond. He was accosted by some 'shadowy characters travelling in the same direction carrying sacks over their shoulders', and there was little doubt that they were smuggling. Perhaps they were carrying coffee, which cost three times more in Germany than in Holland, but Arthur did not enquire; his personal safety seemed more important. Fortunately, any potential threat diminished when it became clear to his new companions who and what he was – and they walked on together before parting amicably at the airfield. The story might have had a very different ending had they met up with the Grenzland Polizei.

All the ACB officers at Brüggen had particular praise for Frau Adelburger, their 'Miss Money-penny' or general factotum in the site office, Don Hanson commenting 'she was with us from day one and deserves serious praise for her work with the detachment'. It was she who got to the bottom of some skullduggery concerning the street traders who had set up shop on the opposite side of the main road past the airfield, to cater for the needs of some 1,500 civilians involved in work which went on from dawn to dusk. Useful though their services were, it transpired that they were trading under licences issued illegally by – and to the benefit of – the main detachment interpreter. He was dispatched forthwith, forcing the RAF officers into more self-help with the German language, now inevitably mixed with traces of Dutch.

STARTING FROM SCRATCH

Before the servicemen and their families moved into quarters at Brüggen, an event celebrated at a party in the officers' mess in June 1953, the ACB officers travelled each day from Wildenrath. Initially, with all their expenses reimbursed, they lunched on fillet steak or wild boar at the Burg Brüggen, a luxury hotel then and now, but all this changed when a fixed daily subsistence allowance was introduced. Thereafter they bought 'wonderful cheese and butter on freshly baked rolls, sometimes with ham' from a farmhouse in Brüggen village. They were living a busy but good life with no secondary duties and by day (in Arthur's words) 'almost as civilians', but not quite out of sight and mind. Surprise visits by the inquisitive were not infrequent, one by Wildenrath's station commander, the renowned Group Captain Johnny Johnson, catching them off guard after a rather long lunch and dressed in rather less than orthodox uniform. After working hours hospitality flowed freely between all those working on the airfield, in an enduring pattern. The Germans invited the airmen to their private parties and local functions and the latter reciprocated on the station. Typically, the German staff and contractors were invited to the first film to be shown at the station's Astra Cinema, 'A Queen is Crowned', on the then recent Coronation of Her Majesty Queen Elizabeth, Alan Arber remarking on the great number attending, their appreciation of the gesture and the good that it did for community relations.

There was frantic activity in June 1953 as completion target dates drew near, and to save time a member of the RAF Commissioning Party now attended the handover of each project from the contractor to the 5357 Detachment, Geoff Woolston officiating when the all-important station sewage works was ready on time. Huge quantities of RAF equipment were now beginning to arrive, including two snow ploughs in the first convoy that summer, and to the great credit of all, the station was ready to receive No. 112 Squadron with its Vampires in July 1953. Bill Jennings, a job well done, then returned to the UK and Don Hanson took over the detachment.

Although aircraft could now operate from the station much remained to be done. Alan Arber remembers how quickly the 11km rail spur was completed from the airfield to the Deutches Bundesbahn main line and Petroleum Depot at nearby Arsbeck. He had been a railway engineer in civilian life and this is how he described his first major assignment with the ACB. 'I was given a large-scale map with a line on it representing the route of the railway and a fleet of six ancient RAF bulldozers and scrapers from the ACB Plant Squadron and told to get on with it. Some 100,000 cubic yards of soil had to be excavated and compacted to form the cuttings and embankments that would provide acceptable flat gradients for the railway. This work had to be finished in six weeks, allowing a further two weeks for a civilian contractor to lay the rail track. Fortunately the weather was on our side and by working 12-hours a day, 7 days a week, the objective was narrowly

Working 12 hours a day, seven days a week, with 'six ancient bulldozers', Plt Off Alan Arber and the ACB Plant Squadron took six weeks to prepare the ground for 11km of rail track from RAF Brüggen to the Bundesbahn main line at Arsbeck. (*Don Hanson*)

achieved by mid-June. Completion, with the station now coming up to strength, was celebrated most convivially on 15 July 1953. A locomotive and carriages were borrowed from the Deutches Bundesbahn, loaded with liquid refreshment, and shuttled back and forth between Brüggen and Arsbeck until stocks were exhausted. Navigation was assisted by several newly-arrived pilots perched precariously on the engine's roof. Delivery of operational supplies and equipment started flowing into the station next day.'

No. 5004 (AC) Squadron with its CO, Squadron Leader H.D.M. Seymore, joined No. 5357 Detachment at Brüggen in November 1953. It set up shop in the north-west corner of the airfield with organic MT and plant, the three flights manned largely by national service airmen, many from the building trades, but direct labour was recruited from local German and Dutch nationals. The squadron was established to 'carry out emergency repairs of airfields and installations, for the construction of airfields and buildings in forward areas and to execute approved works services'. In its primary role at Brüggen, the squadron would construct airstrips at Wegberg and Mönchengladbach, and in Exercise Battle Royal lay a temporary runway in open country with perforated steel plates (PSP). Liberal interpretation of its terms of reference also allowed useful initiatives to be taken without too many questions asked. So it was that a pig farm, golf course and other essential lifestyle adjuncts would come to be built on the station.

By the end of 1953, major road surfacing and the station boiler house had been completed, as had the General Equipment Park (GEP) in the north-west corner of the station. Leisure and sport facilities were not forgotten, with the opening of the cinema and gymnasium, and with the seeding of the sports fields having gone well, sports teams were now being raised and trained for football, rugby and hockey. There were mixed feelings among the growing number of children on the station when work was expedited to ensure that their new school would be ready to open in time for the next term. By mid-1954 nine miles of six feet chain linked fence, the first of its type in the Command, circled the airfield.

Open for business. The Main Gate at RAF Brüggen in 1953; a far cry from the activity and security to come. (*Don Hanson*)

Flying Officer Jack Campling joined 5004 Squadron on Good Friday 1954 to become the third flight commander, the other two being Sid Geoghegan and Johnny Everett. Other contemporaries were Flying Officers Les Rowe and Johnny Whitehouse and in their time the squadron would reach its full establishment of men and plant, except for wheelbarrows, which Jack remembers had still not arrived when he departed in 1955. Recently married, he and his wife lived for a few months in a flat in Roermond before, at the age of twenty-five, he was given one of the new married quarters on the station – fortuitously just before the onset of the very harsh winter of 1954-55. He recalled the day in 1955 on which the formal Peace Treaty with Germany was signed, and the re-formation of the Wehrmacht and Luftwaffe was announced, because, in anticipation of trouble, the Orderly Officer was issued with a bullet for his revolver.

There was plenty of excitement for the men of the ACB as they continued their work on the now operational airfield. Jack Campling saw the pilot of a Sabre eject safely over the base, the doomed aircraft just missing the bomb dump. He also saw a Meteor disintegrate at the end of Runway 09, the pilot again escaping unhurt but reputed to have been ignored by the crash crews who couldn't stop because they were 'going to a crash', so he made his own way to the mess and bottle of whisky.

The story of how the RAF Germany Golf Course was authorised, funded and came into being in 1955 remains a little obscure. Squadron Leader Ray Pixley, an ACB officer serving in the HQ at Rheindahlen at the time, believes that a young ACB officer doing his national service as a civil engineer, with a low golf handicap, was tasked with designing the course. Officially, 5004 Squadron would do the work as a training exercise and Flight Lieutenant Trevor Redley, the squadron's training officer, saw this as 'a wonderful opportunity to develop their diverse and advanced skills, and for construction plant to be worked to fine limits'. In the event

The 'reserve hospital' surrounded by 'eighteen aircraft dispersal pens', in 1955. (*Ron Powell*)

16

much of the work may have been carried out by Elsche, the station's maintenance contractor. There were rumours that grass seed was flown out from the UK, with topsoil from there or elsewhere, that funding came largely from money allocated to aircraft dispersal pens (their costs having been 'slightly overestimated') and that the temporary clubhouse was, in fact, a 'reserve hospital'. In any event, work started in August 1954 and in March 1955, the F-540 (RAF Operations Records Book) notes that redundant photographic huts were re-erected as a temporary measure until permanent foundations could be laid for a clubhouse. It may come as no surprise that everything was in place for the formal opening of the course by the Chief of Air Staff (CAS), MRAF Sir William Dickson, on 9 May 1955.

Incidentally, an access road seems to have been drawn inexorably towards the clubhouse rather than to the bomb dump as was originally intended but Ted Willis believes that it was part of an experiment in soil stabilisation. Whatever the truth, one of the most urgent tasks for Flight Lieutenant Frank Hulse, when he joined No. 5357 Detachment, was to arrange, by hook or by crook and with meagre resources, to put a road through to the bomb dump.

Trevor Redley said that for all its efforts 5004 Squadron was treated royally by the club before the unit moved from Brüggen to the UK in September 1956, with a farewell pledge that the squadron's crest would remain in pride of place on the chimney breast 'throughout the life of the club'. However, when he returned to Brüggen in 1976 the crest was nowhere to be seen.

In 1955, as part of the major live flying exercise 'Carte Blanche', 5004 Squadron moved out to the trotting racetrack outside the town of Mönchengladbach to develop the rudimentary runway there into an advanced landing strip to NATO specifications. This was done against the clock in full exercise conditions, with infiltration by 'enemy forces' to test the squadron's ground defences, but work was suspended on the Saturday afternoon to allow races to proceed without the noise and disruption of construction work. During this lull the officers, NCOs and airmen of the squadron were given grandstand views of the races (from a separate viewing area), the latter forming a profitable relationship with the jockeys. At a generous steak supper to show their gratitude for the new runway, the Mönchengladbach Flying Club granted honorary membership to Squadron Leader Joe Chater and Trevor Redley, the squadron CO and his number two, presenting them with buttonhole badges which entitled them to free accommodation, meals and entertainment whenever they returned to the Club. Visiting in 1978, Trevor was treated to a cup of coffee. Ray Pixley, from the Wing HQ at Rheindahlen, who had acted as liaison officer with the town officials, was also presented with an 'Ehren Nadel der Stadt' (symbol of the town). The airstrip was later developed into a municipal airport for Mönchengladbach.

Back at Brüggen the perimeter road and hard standings for fuel bowsers were completed in 1955, as were the sports pavilion and water supplies for the sports fields. Alan Arber remembers that a swimming pool was allowed for in the overall plan but that it had to be funded by the UK and in consequence was limited to 'a very simple design, comprising only a shallow square hole with sloping sides plastered with concrete'. This was clearly inadequate and it was only by means of considerable innovation and self-help, in the guise of another 'training exercise', together with a cleverly negotiated price for reinforced concrete work by contractor Helde Franke, that the men of the ACB eventually produced a conventional pool to international standards, estimated to be worth four times the money originally allocated. Frank Hulse added that concrete diving platforms were included but to the embarrassment of the professionals of the ACB the top stage was later found to be slightly out of alignment with the centreline of the pool – a rare error indeed which can still be seen to this day.

The AGA often arranged excellent parties in Düsseldorf to celebrate the end of each phase of construction and with the speed of progress tracks to favourite hostelries became very well worn. There was also the German ritual of 'Rikfest', a party to mark the roofing of a new house, but with 500 married quarters completed throughout 1954 and 1955, this could have been a daily event so the contractors and AGA agreed on a weekly party. To get the party going, the men would start off with a traditional beer and bowls competition before joining the ladies for more beer, food and dancing to an 'Um-pa, Um-pa band'. It was certainly not all work and no play for the men of the ACB at Brüggen.

This intensive programme of work and play generated excellent relations between the local people and the British newcomers, extending beyond social activities into some mutually beneficial two-way interactions. Ted Willis recalls that, in 1955, when it was discovered that none of the houses around the edge of the airfield had running water, the 5357 Wing Detachment found ways of supplying drinking water to many of them from the airfield's treated water distribution system. The detachment also gave material assistance to local communities during the great floods of that year.

In the summer of 1956, 5004 Squadron built an emergency landing strip on the airfield, for use when the main runway was 'black' with snow or ice, or was otherwise obstructed. Flight Lieutenant Doug Coulson, then 'C' Flight Commander, was involved in this major excavation in which bulldozers and scrapers moved some 100,000 cubic yards of trees and soil necessary to provide operational clearance for the Ground Controlled Approach (GCA) system. The station diarist wrote: 'A fantastic array of heavy equipment descended to destroy the countryside between the runway and southern taxiway, and all this was done close to the main runway, but without interrupting the continuous take-offs and landings of Hunters, an ear-splitting experience for the workers.'

From March to June 1956, Lieutenant Alec Robinshaw RE, a lance corporal and four sappers were attached to No. 5004 Squadron from 41 Army Field Park Squadron RE. Their primary job was to evaluate a mobile soil and materials testing laboratory and a Howard Soil Stabilising Train which blended, spread and compacted soil, cement and water to leave a road pavement which only needed to harden and be surfaced. They also helped with the emergency landing strip and with the design and construction of that length of road of the greatest strategic importance to the Golf Club. Their work was not without risk and the sappers found a new role for their D8 bulldozer as a shelter when a Belgian F-84 overshot the runway, the pilot escaping before the aircraft exploded leaving live ammunition flying in all directions. Alec maintained that: 'The RE had been called in to do the civil engineering because the ACB was too busy cutting the airfield grass and supervising the sheep.' No response can be found from the officers of the ACB, one of whom, Flying Officer David Hattersley, remained his close friend. David, who had joined 5004 Squadron in January 1956, claims that his national service was 'a grand apprenticeship' for what was to follow in his life. Although paid only 13/- a day he became the proud owner of a 1949 Mercedes, putting it to good use, and the custodian of a black labrador handed down by one of the pilots who impressed him with his shooting skills adapted to dart throwing against moths fluttering against the ceiling of their mess.

The ACB men of 5004 Squadron who had given the station so much were recalled to the UK in September 1956; their work has stood the test of time and Brüggen should remember them with great gratitude. This left Brüggen's 5357 Wing Detachment, which had been there from the start and had shown so much ingenuity, industry and determination to create what would become RAF Germany's primary base, and to do so in what must surely be a record time.

Chapter Three

No. 135 Fighter Wing

Royal Air Force Brüggen began life as a fighter station within 83 Group, with its HQ at RAF Wahn responsible directly to HQ 2TAF at Rheindahlen. The station commander, Group Captain Bill Crawford-Compton, together with a nucleus of his operational, administrative and engineering staff, began to assemble at Brüggen in March 1953 while much work remained to be done on the airfield. In June 1953, Nos. 85 and 89 Squadrons of No. 55 Wing, RAF Regiment, arrived with their Bofors L40/60 light anti-aircraft (LAA) guns for the defence of the airfield against air attack. Wing Commander 'Johnny' Johns, Officer Commanding (OC) Flying Wing, moved into Flying Wing Headquarters, the turnip had been harvested from the southern taxiway, and the airfield was ready for full flying in July 1953.

Elements of 85 and 89 Squadrons, 55 Wing RAF Regiment (LAA), the first operational units to arrive at Brüggen in 1953, firing their L40/60 guns at Todendorf Range on the Baltic. (*37 Squadron*)

No. 112 Squadron arrived from RAF Jever, with a swarm of Vampire FB5s, on 6 July, mounting a spectacular attack on the Regiment's gun positions. In Air Traffic Control, Flight Lieutenant Les Hutchinson was ready for them, albeit with rudimentary equipment in four vehicles rather than the control tower. Les had the secondary role of security officer, charged with guarding the as yet unfenced, nine-mile airfield boundary against pilferers, or worse. With few resources at his disposal, but great initiative, he persuaded the riding club, then thriving just inside the main gate, to mount horse-patrols, day and night, around the perimeter, to what effect is not known. These continued until the new C-in-C found that his personal horses, stabled at Brüggen, were being tired out by these unofficial exertions, and had police dogs flown in to take over the role.

No. 112 Squadron, with its motto 'Swift in Destruction', had a distinguished war record and was easily identified by the 'shark's teeth' motif painted on the nose of its aircraft. Having made itself at home, the squadron moved to the Belgian base at Florennes in the Ardennes on 22 July for Exercise Coronet, to operate under canvas and in the mud until the end of the month. Meanwhile, for its role as the exercise spectator centre, Brüggen conjured up extra parking space, accommodation and special communications for 150 key members of the press and a large number of guests from national and NATO headquarters.

No. 96 Squadron was attached to the station for the exercise, Flying Officer David Spink flying one of its sixteen Meteor NF11s from RAF Ahlhorn in 'gorgeous sunshine' and landing 'with some disarray in a complete clamp' at the new airfield. The squadron was then left to fend for itself, dispersed in tents on the far side of the airfield, far away from the VIPs. There they were entertained by strange nocturnal noises and hosts of unfriendly ants, which were said to be responsible for Sergeant Ron Dedman appearing after the first night with 'his eyes barely visible through swollen cheeks'. This jungle survival in Brüggen's deep south, with its insects, wild boar and steamy July bogs, is how operations began at 'Flugplatz Elmpt'.

August was marred by the station's first fatal accident when a visiting Venom crashed on the final approach, but also marked by the reformation at Brüggen of No. 130 (Punjab) Squadron, with Vampire FB5s, its motto: 'Strong to Serve'. The two fighter squadrons were fully mobile and largely self-contained for first line operations in the day fighter/ground attack (DF/GA) role. Put to the test in September, on deployment to the southern side of the airfield for Exercise Monte Carlo, they operated very effectively on the ground and excelled in the air against ground targets defended by F-86 Sabres. Routine air-to-ground weapons training now took place on the local Monschau range. The wing had its first fatal accident on 2 December 1953, when Pilot Officer Eric Kitwood of 112 Squadron was killed on an air test in Vampire WZ261, his aircraft crashing close to Brüggen village.

Gun change at Brüggen for this Vampire FB5. (*RAF Brüggen*)

The two squadrons went to RAF Sylt for an armament practice camp (APC) in December. Appalling weather curtailed flying so a caring hierarchy, ever anxious to shield bodies and souls from the temptations of the Copper Kettle, Witte Haus, Chez Katrinas and the Tower at Hornum, laid on an escape and evasion exercise. The cold and wet of that North Sea Island in December had to be experienced to be believed and half the escapees were captured. Not so one enterprising couple; in a story with several versions Flight Lieutenants Holmes and Mellors, flight commanders from Nos. 112 and 130 Squadrons, 'borrowed' a service Land Rover and drove to rendezvous in comfort.

In those days, every fighter squadron in Germany went to the holiday island of Sylt periodically for air-to-air gunnery training, taking much of their equipment with them on organic transport for additional mobility training. Long convoys, mainly of Magirus three-ton trucks, were often driven by young pilots and airmen with very little driving experience at rather higher speeds than they were briefed. They thundered through Hamburg, led with great panache by German police who threw their motorcycles into the path of any offending vehicle, got lost in the winding ways of Schleswig-Holstein and crossed the causeway by rail from Niebul to Westerland. Other than by air, this was the only legitimate way on to the island; even the most mischievous and courageous were loath to negotiate the slippery, sloping sides of the ramp. There were surprisingly few accidents on these epic journeys, exciting preludes to detachments promising hard work but plenty of fun on the nudist beaches by day and in the many welcoming haunts at night, but some were thankful to return to 'rest' at Brüggen.

Alarm over the potential of the Russian MiG fighters, demonstrated in the Korean war, resulted in the short-term loan to the RAF of 430 Canadair F-86E Sabres, pending re-equipment with the Hawker Hunter. With leading edge slats, a fully-flying tailplane, nose wheel steering, a comfortable cockpit, and a quantum leap in performance, this became a very popular aircraft with the pilots. The RAF now had a proven operational aircraft which manoeuvred well and could reach supersonic speeds in a dive. While this new technology and additional support requirements were not conducive to autonomous or off-base operations many of the design features (such as ease of access) helped to simplify servicing. In its 1953 Christmas card, 112 Squadron pleaded 'All we want for Christmas is our wings swept back' and their prayers were answered early in the new year when both Brüggen squadrons began re-equipping with the Sabre.

A prayer in 112 Squadron's 1953 Christmas card: 'All we want for Christmas is our wings swept back' would be answered, but this Sabre went to 130 Squadron. (L to R): Sqn Ldr Mejor (CO), Flt Lt Jeffreys, Wg Cdr Johns (OC Flying Wing), Flt Lt Fabesch, Gp Capt Crawford-Compton (Stn Cdr), Fg Off Sommerard, Fg Off Dingle, Plt Off Chitty. (*RAF Brüggen*)

Those pilots who had trained on the Sabre in the USA had to become acclimatised to very different weather and operating procedures in 2TAF, while those who converted to the American aircraft in Germany had to became acquainted with unfamiliar systems, including the luxury of a radio compass. In the poor winter conditions this transition took time and later 135 Wing would have to get used to their new 'hard-edge' (fixed leading edge) Sabres, which had slightly different handling characteristics to the 'soft-edge' (slotted wing) variants provided initially at Wildenrath and Brüggen. Despite these bases having the long NATO runways, the Sabre's faster landing speeds and very different braking techniques were largely responsible for a number of burst tyres and other landing incidents, several aircraft ending up in the overshoot (there were no arrester wires or barriers in those days). However, there was also a growing suspicion that the runway surface at Brüggen was unsuitable for these aircraft. North American influence increased further, in the spirit and practice of NATO, when a very dynamic 23 Squadron, Belgian Air Force (BAF), joined 135 Wing for a year's detachment with their F-84 Thunderjets. They too would have difficulty on Brüggen's 2,700-yard runway.

On 23 January, OC 112 Squadron, Squadron Leader Frank Hegarty, was the first of his squadron to get airborne in a Sabre (XB893) and on 23 February he and

New braking techniques and a slippery runway at Brüggen led to some mishaps.
(*RAF Brüggen*)

A truly NATO base, RAF Brüggen hosted No. 23 Squadron, Belgian Air Force, with its
F-84 Thunderjets, throughout 1954. (*RAF Brüggen*)

his two flight commanders established their credentials on the aircraft with a three-
ship fly-by. With nineteen 'soft-edge' and later twenty-two 'hard-edge' variants for
the thirty-one pilots on 112 Squadron (against typical fighter establishments then
of fourteen aircraft and twenty-two pilots) this was big business. Along with the
Sabre came new personal safety equipment: the G-suits, 'bone domes' and 'escape
boots', the latter being so comfortable that pilots wore them everywhere, chancing
the frowns of senior officers; while 'in civvies' they sported the golden Sabre
broach, or much-prized Mach Buster buttonhole badge. The shriek of many new
jet engines and novelty of breaking the sound barrier quickly wore very thin with
those on the ground, particularly in the Joint Headquarters (JHQ) at Rheindahlen,
and as the sonic booms and number of broken windows increased, it soon became
a prohibited sport.

One of the crucial problems facing 112 Squadron was how to scribe their much
coveted 'shark's teeth' trademark on to the Sabre's nose. The preferred solution was
to enclose the teeth around the gaping air intake, but the radar gunsight panel above
could not be painted so the shark's mouth had to appear below, passing underneath
the fuselage. All this was contrary to Air Ministry policy but the squadron got away
with it, perhaps because the C-in-C, Air Marshal Sir Harry Broadhurst, had been
on 112 Squadron during the war. The pilots themselves worked overtime to have

No. 112 (Shark) Squadron airborne. (*RAF Brüggen*)

their aircraft properly dressed for the forthcoming visit by Her Royal Highness, The Princess Margaret.

Flight Lieutenant John Chick knew something about Sabres. He had flown in combat against MiGs while on exchange with a USAF squadron in Korea and then served for a short time on the conversion unit at Wildenrath before taking command of a flight on 130 Squadron. He liked the aircraft's 'superb, sleek airframe and the fully flying tail, which gave it a magnificent air combat capability', but found it hopelessly underpowered and poorly armed: 'I had seen 0.5-inch shells bouncing off MiG wings.'

Everyone involved with the Sabre faced a steep learning curve, particularly the equipment section with the aircraft's spares back-up and the engineers with the Sabre's idiosyncrasies, the F-540 reporting that 'several aircraft undercarriages collapsed due to the cold'. Generally, the groundcrew coped very well with the new aircraft, its American technology and terminology, but there were mishaps. Corporal 'Pop' Miles, an instrument fitter on 130 Squadron, recalls a 17-stone engine fitter (just recovering from a road accident when the wheels of his 'put-put' got trapped in tram rails) leaping from the cockpit of a Sabre when an overcharged oxygen system exploded.

Pop Miles was at the formal opening of the first dedicated Corporals' Club in Germany, managed by NAAFI but run by the members, its collocation with the NAAFI girls' quarters making it an added attraction. Formalities over, the station commander, together with Les Hutchinson (in another of his secondary duties as officer-in-charge), other officers and the NAAFI manageress, Mrs Pitchford, joined the corporals in celebrating this milestone occasion.

Corporal Bob Jones arrived at Brüggen in February 1954, travelling, as most did then, by troopship from Harwich to the Hook of Holland, then by one of the Blue, Red, Yellow or Green colour-coded trains which went to different parts of Germany. At Brüggen he found that muddy paths had yet to be paved through the pine woods and scrub between their billets, places of work and play, but they could wait, whereas the formation of a pipe band, to which Bob would belong, could not. Soon, Dutch and German music lovers in local bars were regaled with sounds such as they had never heard before, but they were still rewarded with great hospitality. The good people of Roermond had to put up with a lot, coming to expect that their bicycles would disappear on a Saturday evening but reappear, as if by magic, during the following morning.

Despite improving aircraft serviceability, poor weather in March limited Sabre flying on 112 and 130 Squadrons to 194 and 156 hours respectively, while 23 Squadron, BAF, flew 540 hours in their well-tried F-84s. Not to be outdone,

The RAF Brüggen Voluntary Pipe Band, outside the Station Armoury circa 1954, including FS McAuley, Cpls Brown, Barltrop, Adams and Critchley, SACs McEwan, Calder and Nicholl. (*RAF Brüggen*)

112 Squadron mustered eleven of their twelve Sabres on 30 April, to wave the flag locally with impressive arrowhead formations, thereafter congratulating themselves on this achievement with a party which went on well into May Day.

No. 11 Signals Unit Detachment provided UHF telephone links with the outside world.
(*RAF Brüggen*)

In May, F-84s of 23 Squadron flew unwittingly into East Germany during the electronic counter-measures (ECM) Exercise Prune 2, all too successful jamming masking their recall from an easterly vector. Not intercepted, they returned safely and without repercussions at Wing level, but no doubt some serious questions were asked elsewhere on both sides of the border.

There were now several lodger units at Brüggen. No. 11 Signals Unit (Det), later known as the Radio Relay Squadron, had been *in situ* from the start to provide ultra high frequency (UHF) telephone links with the outside world via Rheindahlen and Wildenrath. Its three 108-feet masts were situated beside the public telephone exchange (PBX), opposite the two main station churches. The GEP had set up shop in the north-west corner of the station, where it was joined in June 1954 by No. 317 MT Squadron from RAF Ueterson. This self-contained unit, with its motto 'Any load, any time, any place' was responsible, among other duties, for transporting aircraft and heavy freight across Europe in their massive, ten-ton lorries. The drivers, mostly in their early 20s, were given three months' training on the continent before they were allowed to 'go solo', and be rewarded with the nickname 'wommit' (a worm-like creature which appears only occasionally). Finally, a police detachment was now in place to see fair play throughout.

'Any load, any time, any place'; a 'wommit' of 317 MT Squadron negotiates a typical German village in one of the unit's 10-ton lorries. (*Bob Knight*)

The Brüggen Fire Service was also ready for anything from the start. Flying Officer Dennis Cassell, an air signaller on ATC duties at Brüggen in 1954, left himself wide open with an 'incautious question' to OC Flying Wing and picked up the secondary duty of Station Fire Officer. An 'instant expert' after two weeks at the RAF Fire School, Sutton-on-Hull, he was given charge of one sergeant, fifteen airmen (mostly carrying out their national service) and fifteen GSO firemen (some ex-Luftwaffe). He recalled that much of their equipment '300% above establishment' (more than was currently held by the City of Bath), was prudently secreted away from prying eyes. In his own words, 'I became a power in the land, always available to fill swimming pools, hose down fuel spills, take part in local celebrations, and just occasionally to attend fires or aircraft incidents.'

In fact, there was plenty of unsolicited excitement for Brüggen's emergency services. On 16 June, Flying Officer Roger Mansfield had control problems on an air test in Sabre XB884 and had to eject at 1,000 feet on the final approach. He landed safely but the diary records that his ejector seat then hit him on the head 'severely damaging the seat'. As if this was not enough, he was then shot in the hand by a 0.5" bullet 'cooked off' in the fire caused by his own doomed aircraft, which he was helping to extinguish. John Chick also witnessed a potentially tragic

They also serve who sit and wait. Mercedes Fire Tender at Brüggen in 1954, Sgt McSparran (NCO i/c) and Herr Dine (GSO) aboard. (*Dennis Cassell*)

130 Squadron electricians and instrument men with Sabre in 1954
(Cpl 'Pop' Miles on left). (*RAF Brüggen*)

but ultimately rather amusing incident soon after his arrival at Brüggen. A Sabre with engine problems had crashed on landing, shed its wings and come to rest in the woods. A most senior worthy arrived on the scene shouting 'cover up the body', whereupon the pilot emerged from the trees complaining that he had cut his thumb.

The week beginning 12 August was particularly exciting. First, a Vampire of No. 502 Squadron recovered to Brüggen with a broken undercarriage handle and no electrics, then a BAF F-84 went off the end of a wet runway, quickly followed by three others, one colliding with another causing major damage to both. Shortly thereafter another Vampire pilot made an emergency landing with aileron problems and on the 16th, the pilot of a Vampire short of fuel put out a 'PAN' (emergency) call and recovered to Brüggen in an excellent joint effort with Wildenrath and Geilenkirchen. Later the same day, another Vampire was handled equally well after it suffered a hydraulic failure, and on the following day a Dutch Harvard pilot on a 'MAYDAY' diversion to Brüggen, landed at Laarbruch and came to grief on an obstructed runway. To end that dramatic week Brüggen ATC became involved when one of its 23 Squadron pilots had a fire in the air and ejected safely from his F-84 over Dusseldorf.

This may have been an unusually bad week but the incidents themselves were far from uncommon in a rapidly expanding 2TAF, with new aircraft and inexperienced pilots in a largely single-seat force, sometimes inadequate navigation aids and aircraft recovery facilities in the very busy and notoriously poor weather of the Clutch area. To make matters worse at Brüggen, the controllers had to cope for many months with a temperamental VHF homer – allegedly attributed to metal embedded within the aggregate below the runway. With a paucity of aids on board or externally, much depended on self-reliance, cool heads and quick wits in the cockpit, the ability to navigate at low-level and react rapidly to the unexpected. It was a steep learning curve in a hard school, but the accident and incident rate would improve at Brüggen.

Fortunately there were no major dramas when HRH The Princess Margaret visited Brüggen on 15 July 1954, a guard of honour found from the Royal Marines, Scots Guards, Princess Patricia's Canadian Light Infantry and 55 Wing, RAF Regiment. A fly-past by 2TAF Meteor NF11s, Sabres and Venoms went well and the day ended with the Meteors from RAF Ahlhorn overflying in a letter 'M' formation.

In August, 112 Squadron managed an average of only 6.2% on their first APC at Sylt with the Sabre (Flight Lieutenant Dawes coming top of the ladder with an average of 17.2%), but they learned a lot and would do much better. While they were away, work was carried out on Brüggen's runway to improve its retardation qualities in wet weather, and for 'toning down' to render it less conspicuous to an enemy (and some friendly pilots!). However, subsequent braking trials showed little improvement and in November both ends were 'roughened' to good effect. In the meantime, the southern taxiway remained available for use in an emergency and used for some aircraft movements when conditions allowed. In September and October there were two more fatal accidents.

Flying Officers Jenkins and Weir of 130 Squadron were killed in the Station Flight Meteor T7 and Flying Officer Woodruff died when his Sabre exploded in mid-air. Roger Mansfield had another lucky escape when he managed to land at Geilenkirchen after radio failure on a controlled descent through cloud on a runway which was under repair. He stopped in 300 yards, to date the shortest landing by an RAF Sabre. Pilots were now spinning the Sabre, adding to their confidence in the aircraft, and were achieving some very good air-to-ground gunnery scores. The records for 12 October credited Flight Lieutenant McConnell with 44.8%, and Flying Officers Brown and Crumpton with 38.4% and 30.5% respectively. The wing's Sabres could now be fitted with external wing tanks, extending flight times but with handling limitations.

1955 started badly, the wing unable to get airborne on thirteen of a possible twenty-three flying days because of bad weather. It snowed hard on 14 January and the following day budding skiers could be seen on the short slopes of 'Hill 60', at the end of Runway 27, as none-too-fit pilots tried to rid themselves of their Christmas excesses, get in shape and rehearse their stem turns in preparation for the Winter Survival Course at Ehrwald (later Bad Kohlgrub). The return of Flying Officer David from Ehrwald, via RAF Hospital Wegberg, with his right leg in plaster, was a timely reminder of what might lie ahead (without safety bindings in those days). Leading from the front, the station commander showed what was possible by starring in the 2TAF Skiing Championships, while his protégés provided rather more unorthodox entertainment. Thinking it to be less dangerous, the men of 112 Squadron challenged 130 Squadron to a downhill race on a purpose-built, multi-man sledge and applied themselves diligently to its construction, the necessary trials and training (from which the sledge emerged rather better than its riders). It was all to no avail; on the appointed day their adversaries failed to turn up.

The weather in London was also miserable on that night in February when Senior Aircraftsman Michael Hudson and many others set out for Germany after a few last pints in 'Dirty Dick's', the popular rendezvous beside Liverpool Street Station. Suitably fortified, and after more beer on a seemingly endless train journey to Harwich, they boarded the now not-so-good ship *Vienna* from a dreary Parkstone Quay. Leaving home and family, a long, cramped and sleepless night in the company of poor sailors in rough seas and unstabilised boats, made this voyage one to remember, but at least Mike had taken the sensible precaution of bagging the top bunk in a crowded cabin. A cold and cheerless dawn and 'unmentionable breakfast' at the Hook of Holland preceded the long train journey to Wildenrath and a night's sleep there before the final road journey through 'featureless, snow-covered flatlands' to Brüggen, where Mike joined the Mechanical Transport Servicing Unit (MTSU). Having come from RAF Medmenham, which he described as a holiday camp in the UK, he did not take kindly to the food and billets at his new home but enjoyed 'the great culture shock' of German revelry throughout the festival which culminated on Rosenmontag. When this was all over he started work as an equipment accountant in offices manned jointly by RAF and 'very helpful' German personnel. Came the Suez crisis, it was all hands to the pump day and night, to prepare, respray and drive fleets of assorted British vehicles to Antwerp for loading on to an aircraft carrier bound for the Mediterranean. Later, the now Corporal Hudson helped swell the lines of vehicles again when the MU at RAF Bückeburg closed and all its vehicles were transferred to the MTSU at Brüggen.

But it was not all work. Mike admits that some Volkswagen cars which had passed their sell-by dates were driven around the compound, perhaps less than expertly, sometimes to destruction and certainly without authority, before they were given their final rites. He reminisces over a packed Astra Cinema, which sometimes staged live entertainment, paying the princely sum of 2/6 (12½ new pennies) for a flight in a glider and 3p for Public Services Institute (PSI) transport organised by the Womens Voluntary Service (WVS) for 'educational' visits to such mystical places as the Rhine, Luxemburg and Amsterdam, places only dreamed of by those serving in the UK.

As always in the service certain personalities livened up the routine and in Mike's section there were Jack and Ellis. Their first time abroad and far from their Yorkshire home, these two AC1s soon made their presence felt and exploited every opportunity, getting themselves mentioned on Sunday BBC's 'Family Favourites' and generally causing mayhem at work and play. In Mike's words 'they were dynamite – and boy, did they like to party'; it was they and those like them who helped make Brüggen what it was, providing that essential ingredient to service life and camaraderie overseas.

In March 1955 it happened again; a Sabre from Wildenrath landed without R/T, taxied around the airfield and took off again without a word. An apology came later, from another pilot who had mistaken Brüggen for Wildenrath. The two squadrons went to Sylt again in April, during which time the airfield was 'Black' to jet traffic as the grass 'islands' in front of the hangars were filled in with concrete to increase the size of the Aircraft Servicing Platform (ASP).

135 Wing deployed for Exercise Carte Blanche in June 1955, to dispersals at RAF Geilenkirchen. There, on the twenty-third, an atomic explosion was simulated by 'a scarcely audible "pop" and a small mushroom of smoke in the vicinity of 112 Squadron', the umpires declaring all the squadron's aircraft destroyed and most of its personnel dead or injured. The wing's intelligence officer, having inexplicably escaped unscathed, telephoned this catastrophe to ATC at Wildenrath from a local police station. The controller who answered the call asked enviously, 'How do you get these breaks; can we have one?' Meanwhile, 112 Squadron rose from the dead and flew off to Beek, in Holland, where it rejoined the exercise.

The Brüggen squadrons were not the first to get the Canadair Sabres in 2TAF; No. 71 ('First from the Eyries'), one of the famous American-manned RAF Eagle Squadrons, and No. 67 ('No Odds Too Great') had converted to the aircraft at RAF Wildenrath in October 1952 and April 1953 respectively. In July 1955, both squadrons moved to Brüggen, via Cyprus, to join No. 135 Wing, now supported by No. 471 Ground Liaison Section (GLS) and a troop of 21 Signals Regiment.

The two new squadrons had gone to Cyprus to prove a route to the Middle East, for an APC and to show the flag. The APC did not go well: 71 Squadron achieved a final average of only 8.7% (from a mean of only 4.5 shoots/pilot), the low score attributed largely to the frequent failure of the radar-ranging to lock on to the target flag's reflector.

Bob Jones, an armourer on 130 Squadron, worked on the Sabre's six, 0.5-inch machine guns; he was surprised that, with 60% of the groundcrew on national service and not short of complaints, the gun stoppage rate and overall spirit on the squadron was so high. Corporal Bob Copping, also an armourer, said the same of 71 Squadron. He too remembers the high percentage of national servicemen and how well they served, given the right leadership and specialist trade guidance by the corporals of the day. It was up to the pilots to check the harmonisation of the guns but the armourers made any necessary adjustments and if two guns only were used on each training sortie, three sorties could be completed with rapid turnrounds before a complete reload.

While the armourers came into their own during intensive gunnery training at Brüggen and on APCs, they were often under pressure and accidents could happen.

When one of Bob Copping's team tried to join two ammunition belts together with a standard screwdriver instead of the correct tool, a round detonated and became embedded in the airman's thigh. Then there was the armourer who got sucked into a Sabre's engine air intake, only the soles of his boots remaining visible. Quickly on the scene, a doctor crawled up to the boots, found life therein and administered morphine before (one story has it) ropes were attached to ankles for the luckless airman to be extracted. He was rushed to RAF Hospital, Wegberg with a cracked skull but was back on duty in six weeks and as a result of this incident new safety measures were introduced.

Cpl Bob Copping, Cpl Jerry Clugan and LAC Jock Payton, with other 71 Squadron armourers, sunning themselves on an APC in Cyprus before the squadron moved from Wildenrath to Brüggen in July 1955. (*Bob Copping*)

Nos. 71 and 67 Squadrons flew back from Cyprus to Germany in six stages, the night stops in Turkey, Greece, Italy, France and Bavaria going unreported in the records, to land at Brüggen on 5 July 1955. Flying Officer Akin did not return with his squadron. At a time when terrorism was rampant on the island he had failed to stop his motor bike when ordered to do so by an auxiliary policeman whom he did not recognise, and was shot in the leg in the fusillade of shots which followed. He would recover.

Two fatal accidents in ten days spoiled the arrival of the new squadrons. Flying Officer Mike Smith of 112 Squadron died when his aircraft crashed near Heerlen in Holland on 5 July; it was believed that he tried to avoid the town and for this he was thanked posthumously by the Dutch. Then on the 15th, Squadron Leader Cherry, OC 71 Squadron, was killed on the final approach to Brüggen, and Squadron Leader B.N. Byrne took command of the squadron. The Brüggen Sabre squadrons were now facing many engineering problems, including cracks in the fuel cells and a breakdown of insulation around the VHF aerials which led to unacceptable static on the radios. Also, a shortage of engineering manpower was seriously affecting the whole RAF Germany Sabre force, typically with 71 Squadron down to one serviceable aircraft in the third week of July. After what Byrne called 'this disastrous month', hard work and much overtime led to a gradual improvement and the squadron was able to muster twelve out of its fourteen Sabres for an APC at Sylt in September. While the radar-ranging still gave trouble, nine effective shoots at 20,000 feet for each pilot resulted in a much improved final average of 12%, thought to be the best score to date for any Sabre unit in RAF Germany.

The highlight of 67 Squadron's APC at Sylt in September was air-to-air gunnery against glider targets using all six guns, firing out full tanks of ammunition to enable complete reloads to take place as part of operational turn-round (OTR) training. On this occasion the OTR on four aircraft simultaneously took 12 minutes and 10 seconds – a very creditable performance. The fate of the gliders is not recorded. The squadron left Sylt with an average of 9.8% and the belief that they were then getting the better of their radar-ranging.

Resuming normal training at Brüggen in the autumn, 71 Squadron took to the upper airspace to concentrate on the fundamentals of their primary fighter role: battle formation and combat. In the final months of the year the squadron produced an average of 5–6 serviceable aircraft on the line every day but then came the poor weather of winter.

In addition to the fatal accidents, Brüggen had other airborne accidents and incidents worthy of mention. A mid-air collision on 3 May 1954, during the rehearsal for the AOC's fly-past, had involved two Sabres of 130 Squadron as the final box of four hurried to join up with the main formation after take-off. Number four (in the box position) overshot his leader and as he decelerated his aircraft started porpoising (a common feature of the Sabre known as the 'Jesus Christ' manoeuvre), during which his tailplane struck the nose of his leader's aircraft. He lost his starboard aileron, most of his starboard tailplane and in his own words '50% control', the debris entering the leader's engine causing it to lose power. Happily, both pilots managed to land their aircraft safely at Brüggen.

Flying Officer Phillips had a salutary experience when his dinghy began to inflate at a critical time on take-off, but with great presence of mind he was able to puncture the ballooning mass with his knife before it filled the cockpit, allowing him to 'return to his seat from the roof of the canopy'. The author remembers that for such a contingency they were issued initially with a piece of hacksaw blade slotted into a block of wood by station workshops – a far cry from the lavish flying equipment of today.

No. 67 Squadron, commanded by Squadron Leader Hugh Walmsley, was also concentrating on tactical formation training to enhance its target acquisition, cross-cover and tactical manoeuvring skills. Invariably, one aircraft would be used to 'bounce' a formation of four, or two sections each of two aircraft would plan to engage each other without the help of Ground Controlled Interception (GCI) radar.

The nose of Flt Lt John Chick's aircraft, after a mid-air collision in which both Sabres and their pilots survived. (*RAF Brüggen*)

They flew without external tanks, generating less flying hours but more sorties and allowing the aircraft to be flown at higher altitudes and to optimum limits in the combat regime.

For fighter squadrons and AAA, good aircraft recognition was imperative to avoid fratricide, and to ensure that units did not become complacent there were peacetime competitions with trophies to be won. A surprise visit to Brüggen in November 1955, by instructors from the School of Aircraft Recognition, found by inspection and testing that recognition training and knowledge on the station was less than satisfactory. So it was that the daily five minutes 'flash' gave way abruptly to a more formal thirty minute recognition session once or twice a week. Four months later, when it was hoped that this would pay off, three of the wing's pilots represented 83 Group at a competition in London, but it was said that the three were 'fairly quiet on their return'.

Bill Crawford-Compton handed over the station to Group Captain Tony Dudgeon on 17 December, as the bad weather and now acute groundcrew shortages combined to reduce serviceability and the flying rate. After a busy and difficult gestation, Brüggen was now two-and-a-half years old. Four Sabre squadrons and two RAF Regiment LAA squadrons were fully operational and the essential facilities were in place with all the necessary support. For his part in this success story OC Flying Wing, Johnny Johns, received an AFC in the New Year's Honours and Awards List. A new challenge now lay ahead: the conversion of 135 Wing to the Hunter F4 in the first half of 1956, beginning with 67 Squadron in January. The new station commander could not have been comforted by a flight safety prophecy that there would be five fatal accidents in the Hunter on 135 Wing during his two-year tour (in fact he would have only one and that due to a malfunctioning ejector seat).

Mixed feelings greeted the aircraft replacement programme; the Sabre was now well proven and well-liked, whereas the Hunter was still a largely unknown quantity. The latter was more heavily armed and faster in a straight line but it was less manoeuvrable and subject to engine surges pending modification programmes which would largely resolve these problems and give it the edge over the Sabre. Inbred scepticism, American sentiment and vernacular, died hard with emotional farewells to the Sabre, particularly by the RAF fraternity which had enjoyed those heady training days in the States. With his combat experience in the Sabre, John Chick was able to comment objectively on the two aircraft. He judged the Hunter F4, currently with its sluggish follow-up tailplane, to be 'hopeless' compared with the Sabre in air combat, but found the higher powered and more heavily armed Hunter 'much steadier as a ground-attack platform', as well as being more comfortable at high speeds, low-level.

OC Flying Wing, Wg Cdr 'Johnny' Johns, checks out 130 Squadron's 1955 Christmas bar in Block 171. (*RAF Brüggen*)

In January 1956, 112 Squadron was at Sylt again for its final APC with the Sabre and it may have been there that OC 130 Squadron, Squadron Leader Mejor, landed a Sabre with one undercarriage leg retracted to go into the book of famous last words for saying, 'it seems to be holding', just before the wingtip touched the runway in a spectacular shower of sparks. On the last day of January, OC Flying and OC 67 Squadron got airborne in newly arrived Hunter F4s.

Early Hunter flying was treated with caution. A Brüggen Local Flying Order, dated 3 January 1956, required conversion sorties be flown in better than a 3,000 feet cloud base and visibility of 3nm; there was to be no low flying, formation take-offs or landings and gun firing was prohibited. However, 3728 air traffic movements were recorded at Brüggen in February 1956, more than in any month other than June 1954, when an auxiliary squadron was attached to the station for its summer camp. The order also warned: 'Pilots carrying out unauthorised practices will be severely dealt with.'

On 20 February a new pay scheme was announced for the RAF which exceeded all expectations, increasing a flight lieutenant's daily rate, with flying pay before tax, from £1.18 shillings to £2.18 shillings. After recovering from the inevitable and prolonged celebrations, pilots began thinking more seriously about new cars or marriage (hitherto both were very few) and leading, in the author's belief, to a fundamental and irrevocable change in outlook and lifestyles throughout the RAF. By the end of March, 130 and 71 Squadrons had received their first Hunters, and 112 Squadron began re-equipping in April, all four squadrons reaching their full establishment by the end of that month. The manning of ground trades was improving and despite such stringent weather limits on Hunter flying, the conversion programme went well.

In the following month the wing's pilots could not believe their luck when they were vectored on to a Russian TU-104 transport in NATO airspace and brought back 'some dramatic cine film which showed their target to be well within killing range'. The aircraft was on legitimate business; it had been en route to pick up Marshal Bulganin and Mr Khrushchev from London, and would not be given the same attention on its return to Moscow, with the 2TAF fighters prudently held on the ground while it was within their range. On three separate occasions in the same month 71 Squadron pilots landed at RNLAF Volkel short of fuel, causing the Dutch to suggest that the squadron might wish to establish a permanent detachment there.

112 Squadron was chosen for VIP duties in June, providing four pairs of Hunters, resplendent with their shark's teeth, to escort a Comet carrying CAS part of the way from Amsterdam to Moscow. Its CO was also given the dubious privilege of leading four aircraft over the AOC's Parade within three seconds of the 'General Salute', and those of the time will remember the extraordinary effort which was often devoted to such precision tasks. In this case Flight Lieutenant Pete Frame, overlooking the parade ground from offices in the squadron hangar, kept his CO informed of the parade's progress by radio. He then triggered the 'Present Arms' by signalling with coloured flags from the runway caravan or lights from the hangar, depending which way the parade commander (station commander) was facing, as the aircraft reached a critical point in the figure of eight they were flying nearby. This fly-past was overhead within one second, but it was not always so.

Meanwhile, the eighteen pilots of 67 Squadron each flew sixteen effective sorties on their first APC at Sylt with the Hunter, achieving an average of 10.4% at 10,000 feet, 8.7% at 20,000 feet and a stoppage rate of 1084. Hunter serviceability was improving steadily towards 50% and the aircraft was now cleared for operational flying at low-level.

The whole command was now beginning to feel the effects of Germany's refusal to continue to pay occupation costs after 5 May 1956, special rates for British forces travelling on the German railways being one of the concessions which quietly disappeared. Unconnected, and blamed on confusion in the accounts department, Brüggen ran very short of D-Marks at a critical time, just before the Whitsun grant, rescue coming only at the last minute with hastily arranged pay parades. A rare story with the right ending.

Many spoke of the spirit which prevailed on and between the Brüggen fighter squadrons at the time, but without prejudice to proper rivalry. The need to get 'one-up' on the others went well beyond professional achievements and sporting success. Bob Copping remembers great consternation when one of 71's aircraft went missing on the ground during a foggy day, only to turn up on 67 Squadron's flight line, but that was the mildest of many such japes.

On 26 June, a party of twenty-six local dignitaries on one of their now routine visits to Brüggen watched a Swift reconnaissance aircraft overfly a dummy Hunter on the ground, apparently without noticing that the rubber aeroplane was deflating slowly – but confirming the recce men's ability to 'kill-m with fil-m'! Fortunately they were not there to see Lieutenant Mike Maina, 67 Squadron's RN exchange officer, (who would take the limelight more than once) in his most spectacular feat. On 14 August he ejected from a Hunter seconds after take-off at 700 feet when his engine caught fire and stopped, he and his aircraft landing in the overshoot. This was indeed what the F-540 called a 'sensational start to night flying', and the whole programme was cancelled immediately in favour of a reflective wash-up in the bar. Pilot Officer 'Bugs' Bendell, then a junior pilot (JP) on 67 Squadron, remembers that in its death throes Mike's aircraft contributed a great deal of realism to an RAF Regiment exercise being held in the woods just off the end of the runway, which suddenly became a crash site. Quite by chance, Mike had won a ticket for the Farnborough Airshow in September, thus enabling Martin Baker to treat their latest celebrity royally – which they did.

A likely story? Brüggen mythology has it that Hill 60 (in the background) got its name from the pilot of this Hunter, who saw the threshold of Runway 09 from upside down just before he ejected. Perhaps the fact that a 60 metre contour line bisects the hill is purely coincidental? (*RAF Brüggen*)

Some who ejected successfully were known to have eaten the 'goodies' in their survival pack immediately (there was no time for this in Mike's case) and others to submit dubious claims for kit, such as service watches and stopwatches, lost in the emergency. One desperate inventory holder (believed to have been Bugs Bendell), tried to make good an inventory deficit by persuading Mike Maina that he had five galvanised iron buckets aboard his Hunter when he ejected. Sadly, this would be far from the only Hunter incident at Brüggen.

112 Squadron also had a successful first APC with the Hunter at Sylt in August, with the outgoing CO, Frank Hegarty, scoring a 54%, OC 'B' Flight, Lee Jones, a 42% and Pete Frame a 46%, the squadron average rising to 12.8%. Flight Lieutenant Keith Willianson another veteran of the Korean War, survived when the engine of his Hunter failed at 700 feet downwind in the circuit at Sylt and he ejected into a few feet of water between the mainland and the island, giving rise to several dramatic stories. The radio and press reported correctly that he had been rescued within five minutes but erroneously that he was taken from the water unconscious. However, with so little time in the air he had plunged into the sea with his face mask still attached and nearly drowned inhaling water through his oxygen tube. He could have waded ashore but there was a mischievious suspicion at the time that he took to his dinghy in order to qualify for membership of the prestigious Goldfish Club, an allegation denied by Sir Keith forty-four years later. In fact, he was back in the crewroom within half an hour, apparently little the worse for wear.

Flt Lt Robin Brown, 112 Squadron's 'A' Flight Commander, in a Hunter F4.
(*RAF Brüggen*)

On the return to Brüggen one of 112 Squadron's Magirus lorries hit a tree, sending spare Hunter wheels bouncing all over the local countryside. There is no knowing what Squadron Leader A.R. Wilson thought he was getting into when he took command of the squadron during this detachment, with two accidents in two days, but he need not have worried; he was promoted within six months, and able to leave the squadron to Squadron Leader C.J. Holmes. Discussing lifestyles at the time, 'A' Flight Commander Robin Brown opined that, 'following the pay rise the lads are much quieter now when in their cups and rather different from the old days'. Others on APC at the time (including the author) may have thought that things were quite exciting enough then at Sylt, but it may be that they would come to say the same of newcomers in days to come.

That September Brüggen was among many wings in Germany helping to simulate mass bomber raids against the UK in Exercise Stronghold. From dawn to dusk a patchwork of contrails filled an otherwise clear blue sky, more than a hundred aircraft at a time, as squadron after squadron flew repeatedly to and from the UK. As targets, the pilots could climb gently to over 50,000 feet, where they were able to remain safe from contemporary fighters armed only with a gun. Some pilots, unable to resist combat with their peers in Fighter Command, had to divert short of fuel for their pains. Flying Officer 'Tinkle' Bell had arrived on 67 Squadron in June and was soon to take over as scribe of the F-540. He waxed lyrically over the squadron's participation in the exercise, describing how a pair of Hunter pilots taking off on the last sortie at dusk saw the dying day twice: 'The glowing red of the sun seen from the runway through the evening haze changed to a fiery orange as it filtered through the vaporous gauze and then as they burst through the cloud tops the sun re-arose to an evening dawn and burned briefly in a blue sky. This "second evening" came as the fighters engaged the tangle of contrails glowing alternatively dull bronze and smoky grey.' The author, flying on Stronghold from RNLAF Eindhoven, saw it too; it was an evocative sight.

Pilot Officer Bob Honey joined 67 Squadron on 11 October 1956, fresh from the Hunter Operational Conversion Unit (OCU) with the grand total of 15 hours 10 minutes on the aircraft. One of his abiding memories was of an initial 'sector recce' in the Station Flight's Prentice with Flying Officer 'Sharky' Hastings, into the Ruhr's industrial murk of the 1950s to which he must become quickly accustomed. Then came more revelations. Was it really true that the JPs were always allocated the aircraft known to have the poorest performance while their leaders were given the best? It certainly seemed so when full throttle was the norm for JPs from take-off to recovery, with the consequent fuel penalty, while battle formation turns were prayed for – to help catch up.

On the ground, as the newest JP, Bob reigned over the coffee bar until promotion in a few months allowed him to 'swim anonymously in the large pool of flying officers which contained the majority of the pilots on the station'. Even then he remained vulnerable for many of the less popular jobs, including officer i/c the rail party returning from a Sylt detachment with 100 groundcrew in his charge. This started badly when his train was held at Westerland until some 100 beer glasses were returned to the station buffet, and got worse when several airmen were left behind during lengthy stops in Hamburg and Dusseldorf. What Bob did not know then was that this was by no means unusual, and indeed he got off lightly with no repercussions back at Brüggen. It certainly did no harm to his career; he retired as an air marshal. That said, a JP's life in the 1950s was often not a happy one; he was a marked man and could do nothing right. It was worse for those who chanced marriage below the arbitrary age of twenty-five; they were not entitled to marriage allowance or married quarters and had little wherewithal to buy the car necessary to live off-base. Although Walter Hagen was offering Standard Super 10 cars and Ford Zephyrs at tax-free prices of £380 and £602 respectively, even these prices were beyond the means of many and second-hand German cars were more the order of the day. BEA charged £12 for a return flight to London, but many chose to holiday on the continent, all this requiring careful management and conversion of German D-Marks, Dutch Guilders and the British Armed Forces Vouchers (BAFVs). That said, there were few complaints from the young and married men; the local German and Dutch landlords were often kind, life with the local people was good, drinking and driving rules were not prohibitive, vital commodities were relatively cheap on the station and above all the great majority at Brüggen enjoyed their work and its community spirit.

In a classic story, Brüggen was tasked with providing an airborne salute for the visit by HRH The Duchess of Gloucester to Wildenrath in October 1956, but the weather allowed one rehearsal only for the 16 Hunters, on a Sunday afternoon in marginal conditions. Soon after take-off, as the fog rolled in closing Wildenrath and Brüggen, all the aircraft were diverted to Wahn. There, with no time to call in reinforcements, the one air traffic controller on duty leapt from consol to consol, switching from one radio channel to another in a masterpiece of physical and professional skill to recover all the aircraft safely and earn him the MBE. The F-540 records that: 'Good flying discipline together with some excellent controlling by the Duty Air Traffic Controller at Wahn, saw the safe arrival there of all the aircraft.' This official report did not tell the whole tale; at least one Hunter ran out of fuel on the taxiway and another was refuelled with more AVTAG than its tanks were supposed to hold; it was a very close run thing.

Best laid plans to launch the fly-past from Wahn on the following day had not anticipated a 15-minute postponement announced after the aircraft were already airborne, during which deteriorating visibility, loss of radar surveillance, loss of radio contact with Wildenrath and a near miss with an airliner, led to its cancellation and the 'scattering of Hunters all over the sky'. Veterans of that time will be able to sense the tension which must have prevailed as these aircraft milled around without surveillance in the typical Clutch 'gloom' of its confined airspace, soon to

135 Fighter Wing: Nos. 112, 130, 67 and 71 Squadrons airborne. (*Tinkle Bell*)

get short of fuel, with many of the pilots inexperienced in the new single-seat jets and with only Distance Measuring Equipment (DME) as an internal aid. The fact that all the aircraft again recovered safely speaks volumes for the individual and collective airmanship skills of the day. Never daunted, 135 Wing took to the air again when HRH departed in kinder weather on Wednesday, 17 October, to fly an immaculate formation which drew a congratulatory signal from the C-in-C. All's well that ends well.

On the next day, Brüggen's unsung heroes in Station Flight were given a role in Exercise Guest, their Vampire T-11s tasked to simulate attacks on ground targets which turned out to be beyond their sensible range. With discretion the better part of valour, the pilots elected to land in 'enemy territory' where they were treated with the utmost courtesy, fed, refuelled and sent home. There was room for improvement in battle management.

Down to earth with a vengeance in November 1956, aircrew from Brüggen and Laarbruch took part in the escape and evasion exercise 'Wet Feet'. They were dropped off on the road between Goch and Kalkar to make their way to a 'safe area' thirty miles south, in three days. Trying to stop them were the gunners and infantrymen of Nos. 16 and 55 Wings, RAF Regiment, in their element and very keen to get to grips with the fliers. The Coldstream Guards provided cold cellars in Krefeld for a detention centre, where staff officers from HQ 2TAF, acting as interrogators, plied their sadistic trade. Extremely cold weather led to an early curtailment of the exercise but Brüggen had done well; seventy per cent were at large on the second night and of the fifty-five taking part only twenty-one were captured by 'Endex'. Roger Mansfield tells of finding himself between the wire fences separating Holland and Germany and being hunted in earnest by the Grenz Polizei. On a points score, Brüggen was awarded sixty-five per cent against the sixty-one per cent achieved by Laarbruch. Single-seat pilots do it better.

At the end of 1956, with war raging on the Suez Canal and Soviet occupation of Hungary, service wives were warned to be ready to get themselves and their children to the channel ports, as best they could. In this high state of military alert and flurry of domestic activity, Robin Brown remembers teaching his pregnant wife to drive on the airfield over one weekend – but these sensible precautions became unnecessary.

112 Squadron's diary notes that on 5 November someone thought it would be a good idea to start up all the Hunters that had been left standing for a cold, wet week, and in the process 'Yankee' caught fire, causing Tinkle Bell, 67 Squadron, to post the following (sensibly anonymous) verse on the officers' mess notice board:

> Remember, remember the fifth of November
> The 112th did not
> Starting a Hunter in a pool of old AVTAG
> Exploded the whole bloody lot

Proving the old adage that 'pride comes before a fall', a 67 Squadron Hunter exploded on the flight line at Sylt some weeks later, with even greater effects all around; neighbouring aircraft were pushed frantically to safety, while visiting Venom pilots offered to feed their aircraft into the inferno – to hasten their re-equipment with Hunters. One incident report stated that a Flying Officer Foulkes had started up his aircraft to taxi away, but another reported that a Flight Lieutenant Foulkes had emerged from the flames; perhaps supernatural forces were at work to render this rapid promotion?

An embargo on travel to the UK over Christmas 1956 left an unprecedented number of hungry and thirsty people on the station throughout the stand-down, but that in itself made it a time to remember with the catering staff pulling out all the stops to provide a Christmas lunch and an evening buffet which 'would have done credit to the Savoy'. Thereafter there was plenty of time for more celebrations and recovery; as was to be expected at that time of year, the weather put paid to thoughts of flying and moved Tinkle Bell, again in poetic mood, to observe in the F-540:

> So winter with his icy hand
> Brought frozen stillness to the land
> At Brüggen and for miles around
> The aircraft rested on the ground.

It was quite usual for the officers' mess to end its year with a fancy dress ball and Bugs Bendell had good cause to remember New Year's Eve 1956. In his book *Never in Anger* he tells how appropriately clad 'marauding Vikings' from his squadron took the mess by storm and how he added a dramatic touch by bursting into flames. Unbeknown to him, his long, flaxen and very realistic hair was highly flammable and should have been nowhere near the un-Viking-like cigarette he was lighting at the time. He passed out before several pints of beer doused the fire and recovered to find himself in the care of a pimply urchin in short trousers (the station commander) and a very ugly old woman (the senior medical officer). Fortunately, this painful and visible legacy of 1956 had no lasting effects and he was back on flying status within a week.

1957 dawned fresh and bright but it will come as a surprise to many now that, notwithstanding the traditional festivities and their inevitable aftermath, many of the revellers were working and flying on that first day of the year, Tinkle Bell flying two sorties at low-level. The men of 135 Wing were resilient.

In the first months of 1957, Brüggen's Hunters were modified at RAF Bückeburg for air-to-ground operations and training for this additional role at low-level began at once with great enthusiasm. On 15 January alone, 67 Squadron flew twenty-two sorties at low-level and boasted that 'all our pilots found their pinpoint targets'. However, high level air defence training continued as a priority, and it was while he was intercepting a section of Hunters that Flight Lieutenant Bruce Wingate, a flight commander on 67 Squadron, had an engine surge followed by a flame-out at 38,000 feet. He relit the engine but the same happened again and with the weather having already closed Brüggen he decided to divert to Wahn where conditions were deteriorating fast and the GCA was unserviceable, but he had little choice. He was not on his own; with many others heading that way, some already short of fuel, he played down his plight despite the faulty engine sticking first at 4,500 rpm (not enough to stay airborne) and then 6,500 rpm. In the end he completed a difficult QGH, continued his descent to below a 200 feet cloud base, found Wahn and landed safely without disrupting a now very busy traffic pattern. For his exemplary airmanship, Bruce was awarded a Green Endorsement for his Flying Logbook by the AOC 83 Group, Air Vice-Marshal H.A.V. Hogan, who wrote: 'Wingate's behaviour throughout this diversion was most creditable and in accord with the highest traditions of the service.' Bruce later graduated from the Day Fighter Leaders School.

It was the fashion then for RAF fighter wings in Germany to launch Saturday morning 'wing-dings' or 'balbos' (named after the Italian Marshal Balbo who pioneered long-range flights by formations of aircraft in the 1930s). These called for maximum effort by the squadrons to fly in close formation at low-level to show the flag, or carry out pre-arranged combat on a grand scale (many talk of eighty aircraft in the same space of sky). Bob Honey tells of one such sweep into the American Zone, in which the four Brüggen squadrons, with two more from

Geilenkirchen, were led by the redoubtable Flight Lieutenant Lee Jones. As they clawed for height they were engaged by American and Canadian Sabres coming out of the sun and, in the ever-descending combat which followed, any planned cohesion was soon lost in one enormous free-for-all. This was invariably the result, claim and counter-claim made with the utmost confidence at formal debriefings, and in the bar afterwards on long Saturday lunchtimes.

This sort of activity was only possible because of the freedom then from the restrictions and surveillance which exist today. 'See and be seen' was the rule, pilot navigation above and below cloud a personal responsibility, with use of the 2TAF Fixer Service a last resort for the proud. Bob Honey summed it up with: 'For a new JP it was an exciting, stimulating life – all that I had dreamed of.'

In February, flying was restricted to 13 hours/pilot because of the Suez crisis but Mike Maina performed again for all at Brüggen to see when he broke out of the landing pattern to lead his section of Hunters in a spectacular fight against four Meteors attacking the station on a legitimate exercise. This much is documented; there is no verdict on who won the fight but, having flown with Mike, the author is in little doubt as to the outcome.

In deference to German ritual, and to popular acclaim, there was no flying on the 4 March, when Brüggen turned out in numbers to support the carnival and other festivities on that Rosenmontag. Again, there was no suggestion that flying should be curtailed on the morning after the night before. Sabre Mk6s of 434 Squadron, RCAF, arrived at Brüggen on 18 March, with their groundcrew in Dakotas and Bristol Freighters, for a 10-day exchange with 67 Squadron, a contingent from which made the longer, reverse journey to Zweibrucken in three-ton trucks. Operationally and socially the exercise was a great success; the powerful Sabres provided stiff opposition for the Hunter F4s in the air and the Canadians an all-round challenge in the bars thereafter.

No. 112 Squadron was in very good heart; its pilots claimed that they could out-turn the Sabre 6 at 25,000 feet, their aerobatic team 'Sky Sharks', led by Lee Jones, was shaping up well, serviceability was improving and there was now the prospect of re-equipment with the Hunter F6. After a difficult year of transition and turbulence this positive mood prevailed throughout the station and all seemed set fair for the new Hunter FGA Wing at Brüggen – but it was not to be. On 4 April 1957, 'Black Thursday', came the worst news of all; that the four squadrons were to disband immediately, in line with the Sandys dictum that surface-to-air missiles (SAM) could replace fighter aircraft. There was more bad news on Friday when Flying Officer Shucksmith, 71 Squadron, was killed during a very low-level ejection after his Hunter had flamed out on the final approach.

There were of course concerns over immediate postings and career prospects, together with financial worries for the many who had not had their tax-free cars overseas for the required time. Much was done to alleviate these problems, typically with short-term postings to fill vacancies or overbear on other units in the command. That said, a large number of pilots who had looked forward to satisfying flying careers would now be disappointed and many would retire to civilian flying.

No. 71 Squadron became non-operational on 12 April, all its aircraft having to be returned to the UK by the 17th No. 67 Squadron had its final fling on 16 April, when twenty-four sorties were flown, Mike Maina having the honour of leading their farewell formation of eight Hunters over Brüggen.

At such a dire time, there was no better man to salve the spirit than Air Marshal The Earl of Bandon, the C-in-C, who was dined-out at Brüggen on 26 April before leaving for his new appointment in the Far East; his brand of leadership would be sorely missed. The 'abandoned earl' carried a lasting memory of 135 Wing with him, three sharks being painted on the star plates of his staff car by Flight Lieutenant Jimmy Jewell while he was visiting Brüggen; he is said to have had a fourth shark added when promoted to air chief marshal.

On 30 April, the date of the official disbandment of Nos. 67 and 71 Squadrons, Tinkle Bell wrote his last words in the F-540: 'The merciless onslaught on our property today reached the office furniture and it is becoming increasingly difficult to write this diary as the tables and chairs disappear' – a sad end to an illustrious past.

No. 130 Squadron became non-operational on 30 April but 112 Squadron continued to fly until a final, maximum effort was mounted on 16 May, Robin Brown leading eight aircraft over Laarbruch, Volkel, Eindhoven, Kleine Brogel, Geilenkirchen and Rheindahlen, to signal the end of 135 Fighter Wing. The squadron became non-operational on 17 May and would disband officially on 30 May, but not before one final social fling on 18 May, the nineteenth anniversary of its re-formation in the Second World War. This was celebrated with great panache as a wake, with black drapes, subdued lighting and reverent organ music creating the right atmosphere for the consumption of vast quantities of 'Wake's Water', as better days were remembered. Hosts and guests were dressed in mourning clothes, a shark's fin protruded from a mock coffin bearing the legendary shark's teeth, resting on a beribboned catafalque surrounded by black candles. The ribbons carried a fitting epitaph to the last of the ......Brüggen fighter squadrons:

> Ashes to Ashes
> Dust to Dust
> If the drink don't get you
> The big axe must

Attending one of the many farewell parties at this sad time, the station education officer, veteran of tank warfare in North Africa and Normandy, 'Boss Bas', was heard to say: 'same faces – different battlefield'. That was the spirit on 135 Wing.

Marshal of the Royal Air Force Sir Keith Williamson summed up that spirit with: 'I think that we all took the friendly rivalry between squadrons for granted, each one of us convinced that we belonged to the sharpest unit on the station, and we did our best to prove it at every opportunity.' This universally held view stemmed from a clearly happy and harmonious station, perhaps unrivalled anywhere else in the command at that time.

An eerie silence then descended on the huge, new and now well-endowed airfield, below a once crowded sky in which so many jet engines had roared with such optimism. In the space of four years new pilots and old had cut their teeth there on the second generation jet fighters, learning their skills the hard way and always looking for a fight. They found out how to fend for themselves with few aids and not much fuel in the dreary Clutch weather, adrenalin rushes calmed later in the traditional manner. This had been a hard school in the air and on the ground, with camaraderie at its best; it had been a single-seat day fighter wing in the old style, the likes of which would soon be history.

The F-540 reported that, 'all life had departed from the body with only the corpse left, and that was growing cold.' A state of suspended animation pervaded all – but resurrection was nigh.

Chapter Four

Multi-Role Station

By August 1957 Brüggen could give real credence to its motto 'To Seek and Strike', with No. 80 Photographic Reconnaissance (PR) Squadron to 'seek' and No. 213 Squadron to 'strike'. No. 87 Squadron added a fighter element to make Brüggen a truly multi-role station, Group Captain Tony Dudgeon presiding over this rapid and complex transition from the relative simplicity of day fighter operations.

No. 80 Squadron had reformed at RAF Laarbruch in 1955 with Canberra PR7s and on 12 June 1957 the squadron commander, Squadron Leader Eddie Brown, led the squadron to Brüggen with No. 8 Mobile Field Processing Unit (MFPU) in support. Flying Officer John Hare and his pilot Flying Officer 'Murph' Morrison, both first-tourists, were among the first to arrive at Brüggen within a squadron establishment of ten, two-man crews, which included some non-commissioned aircrew.

Sqn Ldr Eddie Brown led the first Canberra PR7s of No. 80 Squadron to Brüggen on 12 June 1957. (*Eddie Brown*)

In its early days the Canberra flew high level reconnaissance, but latterly its primary role became that of day, low-level photography with F.95 oblique cameras, together with visual reconnaissance, primarily for line searches and in support of the nuclear strike programme. The motto of this famous squadron, 'Strike True', might have seemed a little less appropriate in this role but collective effort was the name of the game, a reconnaissance element being an integral part of the strike plan. Despite this realistic appreciation, 80 Squadron was required to retain its high level expertise in vertical photography to meet non-operational, peacetime tasks and in preparation for a forthcoming night reconnaissance commitment.

The squadron was well settled at Brüggen by its 40th anniversary in August having, by hook or by crook, secured most of what it needed for work and play. John Hare recalls that the staff officer who refused them a refrigerator for their crewroom changed his mind after being given a ride in a Canberra with a conveniently defective cooling system; he passed out after 1½ hours at low-level and the fridge arrived next day.

No. 87 Squadron, which had been adopted by the United Provinces of India during the Second World War and boasted the motto 'The Most Powerful Fear Me', arrived at Brüggen from Wahn with its Meteor NF11 night fighters on 2 July 1957, Wing Commander L.W.G. Gill in command. Corporal Bill Rose, an engine fitter on the squadron, saw all twelve aircraft join in immaculate formation, taxi to the ASP in close line astern, stop engines and open canopies as one. Unfortunately, this impressive arrival was spoiled when a refuelling hose fractured on the pan outside No. 2 Hangar, spilling fuel and causing a fire. The official records record that, 'with courage and great presence of mind the groundcrew pushed the blazing aircraft away from the others, where it burned beyond repair before the station's fire tenders could attend to it.' Another story involved ex-Luftwaffe fireman Josef Lang, who 'got quite a kick out of smothering a pilot with foam as he created a fire gap by taxying one aircraft out of the way.'

Squadron Leader Dick Smerdon, commander of No. 187 (Ferry) Squadron, delivered Javelin FAW1 XA623 from Odiham to Brüggen on 2 August 1957, for 87 Squadron to become the first unit in Germany to convert to the aircraft. In a programme conducted by the mobile Javelin Conversion Unit, navigator training was carried out in a Valetta C1 equipped with an AI 17 radar, pilots going along for the ride and the bizarre experience of fighter interceptions in a slow, piston-engined transport aircraft.

Flight Lieutenant Dick Carrey found the transition 'painless', if hampered by poor serviceability and an acute shortage of radar spares, so the Meteors continued to be used as targets and for continuation training. The new aircraft was well-liked, pleasant to fly and a crowd-pleaser with its size and noise at speed,

Javelin FAW1s began to replace the Meteor NF11s of 87 Squadron in August 1957. (*Dick Carrey*)

but 'Pilots' Notes' decreed that G-stalling was not permitted, turns must not be tightened beyond the onset of buffet and that aerobatics in the looping plane were prohibited, constraints hardly welcomed by fighter pilots. Low speed scissoring was ill-advised, particularly against the Hunter, and if the speed was allowed to decay below 150 knots it could very quickly 'fall off the clock', with recovery from the ensuing stall nigh impossible. Despite the limitations, Javelin pilots were always ready for combat and could do well with the aircraft's low wing loading and twin Sapphire engines, particularly in high speed yo-yo manoeuvres, while unwary adversaries attempting to follow its 'last ditch' half roll and pull through, with full airbrake out, could soon find himself overtaking his target. Using this attribute in what may have been a rather unofficial rejoining procedure, sections of Javelins were known to roll inverted over the airfield at 40,000 feet, pull through into the vertical and, with barn-door airbrakes extended, rarely exceed 0.8M before breaking over the runway very shortly thereafter at circuit height.

No. 213 Squadron arrived from Ahlhorn with its B(I)6 Canberras in formation on 22 August; crewed by a pilot and two navigators, it would be the only squadron to operate this much-modified version of the B6. For its day/night interdictor role a Boulton and Paul ventral gun-pack could be fitted at the rear of the bomb bay to accommodate four 20mm Hispano-Suiza cannon, leaving room for three 1,000lb bombs, while two 1,000lb bombs could be carried on the wing pylons; a forward-facing F-95 camera added a limited reconnaissance capability. The aircraft had an Air Position Indicator (API), the original GEE and Rebecca fit being replaced by Decca Doppler. For night operations the pilot, assisted by the navigator/observer lying in the nose, would look ahead for hazards and navigation pinpoints forewarned by the nav/plotter in the rear preserving his night vision for map-reading.

The squadron had reformed in 1955 at Ahlhorn, with an establishment of sixteen B(I)6 aircraft, sixty-one aircrew and 134 groundcrew, to concentrate first on day and night low-level bombing, air-to-ground gunnery and anti-shipping operations. This very demanding role called for great crew co-operation, particularly in dive bombing and gunnery at night when targets, illuminated by flares, could impair night vision. At Brüggen the squadron developed its primary role, the delivery of American tactical nuclear weapons using the Low Altitude Bombing System (LABS). This required the aircraft to be flown from an initial point (IP) on a timed run towards the target at a precise speed and height to a pull-up point. On pull-up, the bomb would be released automatically at a pre-selected angle, thereafter following an upward trajectory to about 5,000 feet before descending to its target at a pre-determined range. The aircraft continued in a three-G loop until inverted at 7,000 feet and 170 knots, when it rolled out and

No. 87 Squadron, with the Javelin FAW1, in 1957. (*Bill Rose*)

No. 213 Squadron arrived at Brüggen from Ahlhorn with its Canberra B(I)6s on 22 August 1957. This aircraft shows the additional bomb racks on the wings but not the centreline gunpack. (*RAF Brüggen*)

descended at full throttle to low-level in the direction from which it had come. With this technique the delivery aircraft could avoid its own nuclear burst but it was vulnerable to radar-laid AAA and SAM. Later, the squadron would be able to deliver nuclear weapons in a less vulnerable, lay-down mode.

Brüggen became a ghost town on Sunday, 6 October, when all servicemen not laid low by a virulent Asian Flu, or required to hold the fort, were moved to a tented camp at Waldniel, eight kilometres away. This unkindly named Exercise 'Picnic' rehearsed plans to minimise casualties in the event of a nuclear strike by bussing those needed to operate the aircraft to and from the airfield. The big test came at 0900 hours on 9 October, when 80 Squadron 'lost' all its aircraft, together with 208 personnel who were close to 'ground zero'. With this being only 10% of the number which might have been on the airfield, the exercise was judged a success and the concept of dispersal proven. Tony Dudgeon was one of the casualties but he enjoyed a proper floral tribute and an obituary (which appeared within an hour of his demise), in a suitable 'swan song' before handing over the station to Group Captain C.D. Tomalin on 30 October 1957. No. 55 Wing, RAF Regiment, made non-operational in September, also left in October.

Cold weather flying jackets and boots were 'de rigueur' – these Canberra crews living 'alfresco' during a 1957 dispersal exercise. (*RAF Brüggen*)

The first of 213 Squadron's three fatal accidents in the B(I)6 occurred on a night low-level sortie in marginal weather on 30 December. At a quiet spot near Gottingen where the aircraft crashed, killing Flight Lieutenants Clarke and McCarthy and Pilot Officer Milne, the Deutsche Rote Kreuz Jugend (German Red Cross Youth) built a monument of Solling stone. A commemoration service was held there on 24 April 1958, in appropriately poor weather, attended by the crew's relatives, RAF and Luftwaffe officers, the German children and 200 local dignitaries. In return for this kind gesture the children were presented with a squadron crest and a guitar.

Flying operations during this first winter for the new wing were severely limited by poor weather, aircraft and GCA unserviceability's, but in December came the good news that 80 Squadron had won the Sassoon Photographic Challenge Trophy for high level photography. Eddie Brown was on leave in the UK at the time but his euphoric officers sent him a telegram telling him that they were celebrating their success at Brüggen on his bar book. He replied, 'You fools – this will mean a parade!'

A monument of Solling stone, built by the German Red Cross Youth where
213 Squadron suffered its first fatal accident, was unveiled at a well-attended ceremony
on 24 April 1958. (*Clive Compton*)

OC 80 Squadron, Wg Cdr Eddie Brown, receives the Sassoon Photographic Trophy, won by
the squadron in 1957, from C-in-C 2TAF, AM Sir Humphrey Edwards-Jones. (*Eddie Brown*)

No. 87 Squadron became operational with the Javelin FAW1 at the end of the year, thereafter holding one aircraft at fifteen minutes readiness, day and night, on Quick Reaction Alert (QRA), with a second 'on call' at forty-five minutes.

On 20 February 1958, Flight Lieutenant Peter Stanning and Master Navigator Rand of 80 Squadron were killed when WT526 broke up in the air over the village of Gesher in Low Flying Area (LFA) 2. A hospital was among many buildings damaged and five people on the ground suffered minor injuries. The accident was attributed to a fault in the tailplane which led to an extensive technical modification.

His Royal Highness Prince Philip, Duke of Edinburgh, visited Brüggen on 11 March, during which a Canberra demonstrated the LABS manoeuvre over the airfield and a formation of four Javelins of 87 Squadron thundered across at 150 feet and 530 knots. With RAF Brüggen fast becoming a showcase for the RAF, the Right Honourable Duncan Sandys, Minister of Defence, followed on 27 March, to be greeted with the proper courtesies despite the swingeing cuts he had recently inflicted on the RAF.

HRH Prince Philip, The Duke of Edinburgh, with officers from HQ 2TAF and RAF Brüggen, outside the Officers' Mess, 11 March 1958. (*Dick Carrey*)

Canberra aircrew reviewed by the Rt Hon Duncan Sandys, Minister of Defence, architect of great change in the RAF, escorted by Wg Cd I.R. Campbell, OC 213 Squadron, 27 March 1958. (*RAF Brüggen*)

The Javelins were now equipped with long-range ventral tanks, offering extended sorties which helped 87 Squadron exceed its self-imposed flying target of 200 hours/month. This should have been a good time for Wing Commander G.C. Lamb (of rugby fame) to take command, but there were problems ahead. Bill Rose, who enjoyed working on the new aircraft, remembers a fire on the ground which destroyed a Javelin after the starter motor on its port engine disintegrated on start-up sending hot metal into its wing tanks and igniting the fuel. A major modification programme was then required to resolve the engine and trim problems and, to ease the engineering burden, it was decided that flying should cease once the monthly target had been achieved.

Tragedy then struck on 5 June, when first one engine of Flight Lieutenant Brakewell's Javelin failed and then the second flamed out on the final approach, allegedly due to fuel flow problems. Reacting to the crash alarm, Eddie Brown was first at the scene of the incident just off the end of the active runway. He found the navigator, who had ejected first, 'shaken but safe, his parachute folded in his arms' but Brakewell was still strapped to his seat on impact, his parachute having failed to deploy fully at such low level, and he died shortly afterwards from his injuries.

In May 1958, HQ 83 Group closed, placing Brüggen under the operational command of HQ 2 Group at RAF Sundern, until that group too disbanded in August. Command responsibilities were then transferred to HQ 2TAF, shortly to become HQ RAF Germany to differentiate it more clearly from NATO's HQ 2nd Allied Tactical Air Force (2ATAF), both being based at Rheindahlen.

During an intensive programme of gun harmonization, air-to-ground gunnery at Nordhorn Range and air-to-air cine training at 25,000 feet – in preparation for 87 Squadron's APC at Sylt in August – another Javelin exploded on start up. The pilot, Dick Carrey, escaped injury but the squadron was now down to ten aircraft. The APC went well; fifteen crews averaged eleven accountable sorties, achieving scores of 19.7%, 11.6% and 8.3% at high, medium and low levels respectively, the stoppage rate rising from 342 to 520. On operational shoots with all four guns firing full loads of ammunition, all the target flags and gliders were destroyed. To the squadron's previous CO must go the credit for persuading the establishment that, if 87 Squadron was to lead the way in developing Javelin night/all-weather operations in Germany, it could ill-afford to miss the long night hours of other seasons and should go to APC at the height of summer. The fact that this would coincide with the legendary Sylt holiday season was purely incidental.

It was also show time for the squadron with its new aircraft. For the Sylt Open Day Flight Lieutenant Peter Woodham led a mixed formation of Belgian and German F-84Fs, together with an RAF Hunter, Swift, Meteor and Vampire. On 19 September, the CO took three Javelins over Sundern to say farewell to the AOC, Air Vice-Marshal Ubee, and in another 'first', Dick Carrey and Peter Woodham demonstrated the Javelin at low-level during the Wildenrath Open Day on 24 September.

In October, the squadron was nearly caught short when the whole of 'A' Flight was airborne and the officers of 'B' Flight were erecting a marquee for the officers' mess ball and 'Exercise General Alert' was called, but it rose to the occasion, with nine crews reporting for duty within seven minutes and the two armed aircraft on state on the Operational Readiness Platform (ORP) in seventeen minutes. The two were scrambled fifteen minutes later, by which time the whole squadron was operating from its on-base dispersal site. With a similarly impressive turnout by the station as a whole, the exercise was called off after two hours, and the men of 87 Squadron returned to the mess to celebrate their laudable performance before resuming work on the marquee, which perhaps predictably fell down overnight.

Periodically, the RAF awoke to the need for more physical exercise to counter the ill-effects of the aircrews' sedentary life and the autumn of 1958 was one of those times. The F-540 for October records that 'the resulting contortions evoked much merriment, but led to painful after-effects when the disused muscles tumbled to the game.' Fortunately, for whatever reason, these bursts of enthusiasm for the body beautiful were usually short-lived and there is no further mention of such exertions in subsequent entries.

The first Javelin FAW5 was delivered to 87 Squadron in October. Hitherto employed mainly in close controlled interceptions, the squadron was now rehearsing a 'broadcast control' system in which information on targets was updated continuously by the Sector Operations Centre (SOC) at Udem. The Javelin crews were then left to plot their own interceptions, which might have been more successful if their AI 17 radars had been more serviceable.

The squadron had more unwanted excitement on 12 December when Flight Lieutenant Ken Pye had a double flameout at 40,000 feet. He jettisoned his ventral tanks, managed to relight one engine at 25,000 feet and the second at 8,000 feet while diverting to Florennes in Belgium, where he landed safely. No fault was found on the ground and the aircraft got airborne again, only for the whole sequence of events to be repeated on the return trip to Brüggen. The story seems to end there.

Eddie Brown was awarded an AFC in the New Year's Honours List and left 80 Squadron, with nine PR7s and a T4, to Wing Commander John Hurry in January 1959. Aircraft modifications in the UK, to replace Rebecca with the Instrument Landing System (ILS) and add an Identification Friend or Foe (IFF) fit, together with spares and manpower shortages, were making it increasingly difficult to maintain four PR7s on the line needed to achieve the required flying task, prepare for the NATO reconnaissance competition Royal Flush III, and train new crews. However, on completion of the modification programme and a reorganization of Technical Wing, aircraft serviceability improved markedly and the flying hours achieved in December, albeit in unseasonably good weather, were the highest since July.

On 18 February 1959, Dick Carrey was ejected inadvertently from Javelin XA569 at 40,000 feet. His seat separated automatically at 10,000 feet and his parachute opened, but so did its quick release box, leaving him suspended upside down by his right thigh strap only. Shortly before reaching the ground Dick managed to right himself but landed with spinal injuries and ended up in Wegberg Hospital. He recovered to fly again, by which time an additional safety measure had been incorporated. His navigator, Flight Lieutenant Cooper, ejected normally but his seat failed to separate and he was killed.

Eight officers of 87 Squadron may also remember that February for a double defeat suffered at the hands of the gentlemen of the Dortmunder Union Brauerei in Cologne. Losing at skittles was bad enough, but being beaten by the Germans at one of the RAF's traditional sports, that of 'schooner racing', was hard to take.

Among the more active sports proliferating at Brüggen, go-karting brought all levels of the community together. Jim Peters, who joined the GEP in April 1959, watched 'a very laid back' Duke of Kent, then serving with the British Army in Germany, speed around the Brüggen circuit. He was unable to remain incognito despite his very informal dress, and a mantelpiece or two may be graced by innocent photographs of a favourite son standing nonchalantly beside the unwitting royal. However, to exploit such an opportunity further entailed risk. One enterprising national service airman did become rich overnight, after a national tabloid featured the Duke go-carting at Brüggen, but his fortune, if not his fame, was short-lived. He was next seen leaving the CO's office between two service policemen and while no charges were laid it is believed that a certain RAF charity benefited from his indiscretion. The man in question went on to be a successful solicitor. The next station commander would also prove to be a regular and formidable competitor on the carting track, a sport which clearly attracted the best class of people.

With new servicing schedules helping to achieve 20 hours/crew and a total of 250 hours for the month, 87 Squadron did well at its APC in June 1959. Dick Carrey headed the cine table with 93% and Peter Woodham had the best gunnery average of 27.6% within an overall squadron average of 15.4%. In July, operational control of the squadron was transferred from SOC Udem to the SOC at Brockzetel, and the long-awaited Javelin T3 arrived to ease pilot conversions and supervisory checks.

No. 213 Squadron, under the command of Wing Commander Ian Campbell since July 1958, was disappointed with its results in the Salmond navigation and bombing competition held in March, but the news was good for 80 Squadron in June, when Flight Lieutenant Brian Stead's crew came top in its class in Royal Flush IV.

Major fatigue problems were now seriously affecting Germany's Javelin and Canberra force. All but two Javelins were grounded, but 87 Squadron managed to fly 170 hours in October, albeit with forty hours in the Meteor. The Canberra restriction of 250 knots below 2,000 feet, at all-up weights above 33,000lb, was particularly punitive for 213 Squadron but 80 Squadron found ways and means of achieving proficiency at night, with flash illuminated photography over the ranges at Nordhorn, Terschelling and Vliehors.

By November 1959, 87 Squadron's engineers had to cope with a mix of 2 x FAW1s, 1 x T3, 1 x FAW4 and 2 x FAW5, but the aircrew had the benefit of the two-seat trainer and a Javelin flight simulator at Geilenkirchen. By the end of the year the squadron had 10 x FAW4s and 5s, and the T3, and began the new year by taking an unexpected and most creditable second place in the Duncan Trophy for air gunnery against the well-established Hunter squadrons.

Group Captain Eddie Crew took command of the station in December 1959 as it prepared for the arrival of the US tactical nuclear bombs with which 213 Squadron would be equipped. Very strict new disciplines and procedures would be enforced for weapon storage and security, employment planning and ultimate release. RAF crews did not fly with the live weapons but a replica in size, shape and weight (known as a 'shape') could be carried. Small practice bombs would be used for training at ranges in Germany, the UK and Libya.

One of the most popular venues for conventional weapons training was RAF Akrotiri in Cyprus, and at every APC there 213 Squadron began its social programme as it meant to go on. On the first evening a rather surly barman was a little too zealous when it came to closing time, whereupon the squadron commander ordered eighty-four brandy sours (it is not known who paid) and the squadron had no trouble with early closing thereafter. Perhaps the same crews had hoped to return to that bar some nights later after the first of its crews had scored direct hits on the bombing target, doing so much damage that the range had to be closed. They were to be disappointed: with an eye to the all-important flying hours target the CO sent the remaining crews off on long-range navigation sorties.

Back at Brüggen, practice alerts in the small hours of a morning, followed by take-offs in clear skies before dawn, often ended in diversions to faraway places when the Clutch airfields become fogged-in. So it was, on one occasion, when Flying Officer Frank Leeson, 213 Squadron, ended up at the USAF base at Fürstenfeldbruck, near Munich. By the time Brüggen opened again the weather at the American base had fallen below USAF limits, and Frank had great difficulty persuading the Americans to allow them to take off again. The Officer of the Day was not convinced that a low-level map sufficed as a legal departure procedure, or that a Green Card Instrument Rating allowed RAF pilots to go anywhere in any weather on their own judgement – but the Brüggen Canberra went anyway. What was it about Brüggen which made the crew forfeit an impeccable excuse and forgo the cultural delights of a night in Munich?

No 80 Squadron and its MFPU was now going from strength to strength, winning the Sassoon Trophy again in March 1960 with 4,726 marks out of a possible 5,000. All its squadron aircraft were modified for night photography by the end of the year and, during his visit to Brüggen in May, HRH The Duke of Gloucester was treated to a demonstration of this capability, which included an impressive photoflash run over the airfield. For these night operations a navigator would lie in the nose with a 'torch box' shining light on his map from below, allowing map-reading without destroying his night vision.

Jim Peters, now promoted to Corporal Technician Supplier (believed to be the only one of his kind in Germany at that time), was given twenty minutes notice that HRH The Duke of Kent would be coming to his unit in the GEP during another Royal Visit, and was tasked with the resurrection, cleaning and laying of long runners of red coir matting for the royal feet. Had the Duke's attention not been redirected as he passed by he might have seen Jim's hurriedly mustered volunteers genuflecting and muttering his praises. It had all been a false alarm.

Throughout RAF stations in Germany, drab green German service vehicles were now being replaced by their British counterparts in attractive air force blue, Bedford for Magirus trucks, Minis for Volkswagen 'Beetles', large stocks of the latter becoming available for a mere £50. It was during the disposal of redundant vehicles that a flatbed became disconnected from the station train, bursting through the GEP gates and narrowly missing a fuel bowser as it spilled men and machines in all directions. This too would not have been a suitable sight for royal eyes.

In 1960 there was a very visible change on the domestic front when airmen were no longer required to bring their own mug and 'irons' (knife, fork and spoon) to their mess. Evolution might have turned to revolution among the kitchen staff at Brüggen had not £298 been authorized for the purchase of a suitable washing machine to clear the inevitable mountains of communal utensils. Quick to trumpet such innovation with pride, this new attraction was immediately included in the station's VIP visit programmes.

The first day of June 1960 was a milestone for Brüggen operationally when 213 Squadron passed all its tests to become 'strike capable' with nuclear weapons. Such a status did, however, have its down side, with an on-going commitment to QRA (Quick Reaction Alert) which meant that the squadron had to keep one aircraft armed with a live weapon, together with its crew, at fifteen minutes readiness at all times, ready to launch against pre-planned targets.

No 80 Squadron, with its pre- and post-strike reconnaissance role, did not escape QRA; it too maintained one aircraft on the fifteen minutes state. Incarcerated in the QRA compound, the crews could study target material, catch up on personal administration or relax a little, but always knowing that their reaction to the point of starting engines could be tested at any time. Complex arrangements, with very specific responsibilities, were now in place for targeting, tasking and execution of the war sorties, ultimately with the station commander given full discretion should all communications fail.

Those not committed to QRA, or other essential duties, could enjoy the festivities in the various messes and clubs throughout the station on New Year's Eve 1960. Entering into the spirit, Javelin pilot Ray Fenning drove from Holland dressed as a 'raddled old charlady, complete with fancy headscarf', without drawing any interest or comment from the Dutch or German border guards – they were used to the RAF by now. The evening had a sad significance for Ray and the rest of 87 Squadron; it was their last ball at Brüggen. The squadron, which had shown the way for the Javelin in Germany, had its share of incidents and accidents as it progressed from the Mk1 to the Mk5, but achieved excellent flying statistics and gunnery results, would disband on 3 January 1961 and pass into history.

There was plenty of interesting flying to be had on the Canberra squadrons. Lone Ranger navigation exercises, which combined business with pleasure, took crews far away from base for as long as seven days, giving responsibility to individual crews and providing endurance tests for them in the air and on the ground. Lone Rangers went north to Denmark and Norway, south to Italy, the Mediterranean, Aden and Africa, terminating at Nairobi for the PR crews and (for whatever logic) in Southern Rhodesia for the bombers. Richard Howard, then a flying officer on 80 Squadron, said: 'If I had to pick the most awe-inspiring trip of my air force career it would be my first, non-stop 2,200 mile flight from El Adem to Nairobi, a navigational challenge in itself.' These exercises allowed some escape from the problems of poor weather in Germany and added very significantly to the flying hours achieved.

There were also the squadron exchange visits, typically taking 80 Squadron to a Norwegian RF-84F squadron based at Sola Stavanger in June 1960, during which many maximum range sorties were mounted against Russian naval vessels. 'Round Robin' sorties were also programmed to rehearse cross-servicing at other bases (the French could not understand why RAF crews would not take wine with their lunch) and squadrons would deploy regularly to their war dispersal bases (No 80 Squadron to Woensdrecht, Holland).

Fg Off Richard Howard, 80 Squadron, photographed Mount Kilimanjaro from his PR7 at 22,000 feet during a Southern Ranger sortie to Kenya. (*Richard Howard*)

The social life was equally active (and demanding), Eddie Crew often leading from the front on Saturday nights in the officers' mess. There were also many attractive local hostelries, one of 80 Squadron's favourites being the Maas Hotel at Arcen, north of Venlo, renowned for its Indonesian 'rijsttafel speciaal', a huge rice dish. It was a varied, interesting and happy life at Brüggen.

Given free driving lessons for service duties, access to cheap cars and an allocation of petrol coupons, servicemen went far and wide when off duty. At that time the coupons tended to be issued *en masse*, queues of impatient airmen waiting their turn as officers wrestled with their needs, and tried to keep the books straight. On one such occasion a weary flight sergeant wailed, 'What did I ever do to get a job like this?' Rewarded at once with, 'Uneasy lies the head that wears the crown', he demanded, 'Who said that?' 'William Shakespeare,' returned the deep baritone voice of a well-read and articulate West Indian SAC (Senior Aircraftsman). 'Well listen here SAC Shakespeare, another crack like that and you'll be on a charge,' threatened the NCO, now almost at the end of his tether. New arrangements for dispensing petrol coupons came too late for him – he had retired.

Jim Peters had a UK licence which entitled him to drive a motor cycle and, on the convenient assumption that he was an experienced 'biker', he was made a convoy escort. This was a mixed blessing; given a free rein on his service motorcycle and the authority of an illuminated 'Polizei Lollipop', he tasted power, but the practicalities proved less appealing. The smart leather jerkin did little to protect its wearer against the elements and the pot-like steel helmet rested as heavily as the responsibility which went with this ensemble. It may have been exhilarating to drive fast on ill-kept country roads, through lines of inexperienced RAF truck drivers who believed they were fleeing from the Russian hordes, but attempting to stop or redirect drivers hell-bent on freedom could be a thrill too far. On the day that the discipline of one convoy broke down, and he was forced to leap into a roadside ditch, Jim realised why other bikers had kept their experience to themselves and volunteered to drive the trucks.

In the summer of 1961 it seemed that Brüggen might become involved in open conflict for the first time when General Kassem of Iraq laid claim to Kuwait. In response, Operation 'Vantage' required eight of 213's Canberras (and four B(I)8s of 88 Squadron from Wildenrath) to detach without delay to the Persian Gulf as a deterrent and to be ready for overt action should this become necessary. The aircraft had to be reconfigured for full conventional operations overnight so it was all hands to the pump at Brüggen, with crews from 80 Squadron helping to compass-swing the aircraft before they departed on 30 June. The mood was tense; *en route* near Egypt one crew reported that it was being shadowed by a hostile fighter – which turned out to be a bright star. The bombers were armed and refueled immediately on arrival at RAF Sharjah while their crews were briefed and allocated possible targets, among which was the airfield at Basra, a former RAF station on which some older members of the squadron had served. Initially, armed Canberras patrolled just outside the border with Iraq as a visible deterrent – but there was a problem. Flt Lt Tony Wells was one of the first to find out, almost to his cost, that the Canberra had great difficulty getting airborne from the oil-sanded runway available, in the heat of the day, with bomb loads and the fuel necessary to complete the round trip. Thereafter, these missions were flown with the gunpack only, but in anticipation of more serious work to come some aircraft were retained at a high state of readiness, fully 'bombed-up', their crews committed to long periods of abstinence.

In a seemingly interminable waiting game, aircrew and groundcrew occupied themselves with diverse activities ranging from a rather too hot and active cricket match against the residents to the more sedentary compilation of a squadron newsletter. One edition of the latter, dated 12 July 1961, contained all manner of political, sporting and extraneous items, including a little ditty offered by 88 Squadron which reported:

> We landed from a four hour flog
> No ruddy aids no ruddy log
> With two miles vis and a chance of fog
> At Sharjah
> We dream of women sweet petite
> They'd be quite safe if we should meet
> We couldn't make it in this heat
> At Sharjah.

Canberra B(I)6s of 213 Squadron, wearing sunhats, in a waiting game at RAF Sharjah during the Kuwait crisis, July 1961. (*Clive Compton*)

213 Squadron bombed up and ready to go at RAF Sharjah, July 1961. (*RAF Brüggen*)

With several long hops and short fuel stops Eddie Crew flew out to visit 213 Squadron at Sharjah in a PR7 with 80 Squadron's navigation leader, Squadron Leader David Edwards, and Brüggen's OC Technical Wing, Wing Commander Ivan Whittaker ('Micky' Martin's flight engineer on the Dambusters' raid). It is said that Dave had such confidence in all the expertise on board that he fell asleep during one hot leg, leaving the pilot and engineer to cope with a hydraulic failure, an undercarriage which had to be pumped down by hand, and a flapless landing. Eddie Crew was then conveyed to the officers' mess on a local donkey, led very professionally by Flying Officer Clive Compton attired convincingly as an Arab. Eddie was sure that: 'This charming creature (the donkey) – a distant relative of Christopher Robin's Eeyore but much more optimistic in outlook – seemed to appreciate the solemnity of the occasion as she carried me with dignity if not with speed to the 213 Squadron Headquarters.' Paying his way, Ivan Whittaker repaired the broken hydraulic pipe with a piece of tube taken from one of the mess refrigerators. It is not known who repaired the refrigerator.

VIP transport for Gp Capt Eddie Crew, Fg Off Clive Compton 'driving' when he visited 213 Squadron at Sharjah in July 1962. (*Clive Compton*)

In the event, deterrence prevailed and no shots were fired in anger, but in Europe tensions were rising in the Cold War and the bomber squadrons were needed back there. Returning at the end of July 1961, 213 Squadron had been away from Brüggen for a mere three weeks; they had shown their ability to deploy very rapidly over long distances in the conventional weapons role and it was time to resume their deterrent posture back in Central Europe.

Life had gone on as usual back at Brüggen with staff, clerks, cooks and bottle-washers continuing to go about their more mundane business, which sometimes revealed a surprise. It was during a routine check of field reserve equipment in the GEP that Jim Peters discovered 6,000 pairs of handcuffs, enough to join the whole RAF Germany police force together in one long daisy chain. This idea did not appeal to the police hierarchy, who having checked the crime figures, ordered the disposal of 90% of this rather excessive holding. How this was done without attracting attention and causing unnecessary embarrassment, and where they went no one seems to know, but in the course of their wider duties RAF policemen are believed to have found some use for them in the hot spots of Hamburg and Amsterdam!

In an amalgamation of units in 1960, the General Equipment Park was renamed 431 Maintenance Unit (MU). Its thirty-eight acre fenced site at the north-west of the airfield contained thirty storage sheds, twenty-five workshops, a high density hangar, specialist MT facilities, many miscellaneous buildings and large open storage areas. In addition, the MU had the use of other facilities throughout the station, including two engine test rigs. Comprising three squadrons and an HQ Flight, 431 MU reported directly to HQ RAF Germany but was administered by Brüggen; it would prove to be an invaluable adjunct to the station. The Aircraft Engineering Squadron carried out the inspection, categorization, modification and repair of all RAF and British Army aircraft in Germany, second line servicing of aircraft engines, ground radio, aerial servicing and battle damage repair. Mechanical Transport and General Engineering Squadron, with a fleet of heavy lorries, was tasked with the servicing, storage and movement of all Command vehicles, while Supply Squadron received, stored and issued assorted equipment requirements, from aircraft, weapons, command war reserves, to contingency pack-ups and mundane domestic items. Twelve miles away, at No. 3 Base Ammunition Depot (3 BAD), Bracht, the MU retained a further fifty acres of army land for storing RAF conventional explosives, weapons and ammunition. This was big business.

431 MU became the proud possessor of a flag presented to one of its core units, the Mobile Repair and Salvage Unit, by King Leopold of Belgium in 1946, in recognition of the assistance given to the civilian population by the unit as the Allies advanced through Europe in the Second World War. It would be cared for by the wives of the unit until its disbandment, when it was laid to rest in St. Nicholas Church.

Always in the forefront with independent or collective effort, 431 MU joined the British Army in helping the host nation maintain the flow of heating fuel when the River Rhine, on which the fuel barges plied, became ice-bound. They were able to keep essential fuel supplies flowing to local hospitals, schools and public buildings by running their road tankers through snow and ice in a 17-hour round trip to and from the main fuel depots, prompting the Oberburgermeister of Mönchengladbach, Herr Wilhelm Maubach to say: 'We are most grateful to the RAF and British Army for coming to our assistance so quickly; without their help we would have suffered greatly.' Another job well done.

Rivalry between the Canberra interdictor squadrons in this message on a nacelle of a 16 Squadron B(I)8 – 213's 'Bumbly' leaving its mark. (*RAF Brüggen*)

The Canberra was now having more than its share of technical and operating difficulties, with spells of poor serviceability, many incidents and accidents. The major concern in its early days, that of a runaway tailplane trim, had been remedied before the squadrons arrived at Brüggen but engine, hydraulic landing gear and random problems persisted. Back in September 1957, Murph Morrison and John Hare were at 40,000 feet when the starboard engine of their Canberra PR7 disintegrated, causing damage to the fuel tanks and hydraulic system which necessitated a wheels-up landing at RAF Gaydon in the UK. For their calm and professional handling of this emergency the two were commended by the AOC.

On 28 August 1961, Flying Officer Tony Pearson took a shortcut back to the hangar when dirt in a sequence valve led to retraction of the starboard undercarriage door before the leg, making a landing with that wheel jammed up unavoidable. Concern that any remaining ammunition would be an added hazard if the gun pack came into contact with the ground, and that the navigator's hatch might strike the tail when jettisoned, proved unfounded. After burning off fuel Tony was able to

Fg Off Tony Pearson taking a short cut back to the hangar when one wheel of his B(I)6 failed to lower at Brüggen, 28 August 1961. (*RAF Brüggen*)

hold the starboard wing off the ground during the landing run down to 40 knots before the Canberra slewed off onto the grass with little damage; indeed, the aircraft is believed to have flown again two days later.

Tony was the deputy conventional weapons leader, and it was in the course of this secondary duty that he tells a story against himself which will lighten the hearts of all navigators. With the primary incumbent absent, he was required to accompany a visiting weapons specialist to Nordhorn Range in a Hunter T7 for a demonstration of the foul line strafing techniques which were shortly to be adopted by the squadron. He had been to Nordhorn many times but now he had to find it without his navigator – and it proved elusive. When the range eventually hove into view there was enough fuel left for only two passes, and the visitor was not impressed.

There were several spectacular hydraulic and brake failures. Flying Officer Naidoo's B(I)6 ran off the end of the runway at RAF Idris, crossed a main road and narrowly missed the Station Warrant Officer's car before ending up with Category 3 damage in an olive grove, while Flying Officer P.J. Maitland, in a PR7, ended another Lone Ranger with a wheels up landing at El Adem. Back at Brüggen, on 30 May 1968, a PR7 entered dispersal out of control with brake failure and struck the canopy of a B(I)6, causing an ejector seat to fire, before coming to rest in the woods – fortunately with no casualties.

This 80 Squadron PR7 (above left) careered across the ASP at Brüggen with brake failure, clipping a B(I)6 of 213 Squadron (above right) and triggering its pilot's ejector seat. No one was hurt. (*RAF Brüggen*)

Some potential disasters were averted by vigilance on the ground. Corporal Greaves, a 213 Squadron armourer, was plugging in the guns on a B(I)6 prior to its take-off on a live weapons sortie when he noticed a pool of hydraulic fluid below a bomb door hydraulic jack. He informed the pilot who returned to dispersal where a major hydraulic leak was confirmed. Greaves was awarded a 'Good Show' for preventing what might have been a serious emergency.

Bird strikes took a heavy toll on airframes which were not built for the Canberra's low-level role. In September 1960, Flying Officer P.H.F. Wright had his canopy and visor shattered by a bird in LFA 5, and in 1962, Squadron Leader 'Thump' Thompson diverted to Leipheim Air Base when his navigator, Flight Lieutenant Laurie Rosefield was slightly injured as a result of a rook colliding with the nose-cone of their PR7. Most seriously, birds caused an engine failure and loss of a 213 Squadron Canberra in July 1965, the three occupants failing to survive ejections at 300 feet. Thereafter, the force was re-equipped with the Mk.2CA seats optimised for use at very low level and 'Birdtams' restricted low flying, in time and space, during migratory periods or whenever unusual bird activity could be predicted, but they were no panacea. On 1 July 1966, while on a bombing run at Nordhorn, Flying Officer Hellyer's aircraft sustained a bird strike which shattered the cockpit canopy, damaging the port engine and intake, tailplane, fin and navigator's hatch, the wind blast exacerbating the pilot's problems. With help from another B(I)6 'shepherd' and a replacement helmet from one of his navigators, Hellyer diverted to nearby Hopsten airfield and landed safely, earning a 'Green Endorsement' for his Flying Logbook and some very laudatory comments on his 'presence of mind and extremely fine handling of a difficult situation'.

Random incidents included the loss of a navigator's hatch in the air, a lightning strike which shattered a nose-cone at night and those attributed to freak weather conditions. In November 1966, two Brüggen Canberras suffered engine flameouts which were put down to intake icing induced by a very cold and unstable airstream, accompanied by heavy and prolonged showers.

Away from work, Brüggen had become justly proud of its sports record, both in individual and collective effort, within and between the stations. Flying Officer B.M. Anderson and Flight Lieutenant Ken Wilson, both from 213 Squadron, were made 'RAF Germany Sportsman of the Year' in 1961 and 1964 respectively, a title taken by Flight Lieutenant Ernest McIntyre, a 42-year-old navigator on 213 Squadron, in 1965. The station's sporting achievements had now become too numerous to list here, suffice it to record that in 1963 it won the Sir Robert Foster Trophy, presented by a former C-in-C RAF Germany and awarded annually to the station with the best overall record in fourteen sports events.

Many will remember hard fought inter-squadron and inter-station matches, often between aircrew only, and the pleasure derived from the annual Station Sports Days. The number of sports catered for at Brüggen would proliferate with ever-increasing scope, going further afield and often connected to a charitable initiative, so much so that only a brief mention of individuals and events can find space here. Every effort was made to encourage sport of all kinds in changing lifestyles and patterns, but Wednesday sports afternoons would soon be a thing of the past, as would working on Saturdays.

For the time being, however, Brüggen still flew on Saturdays, one pilot remembering a particular 'balbo' of Canberras which, for reasons which elude him now (and probably did then), braved an ever-lowering cloud base and deteriorating visibility in the Ruhr and crossed an active Düsseldorf Airport in line astern with each aircraft only just visible to the next. It is not known whether permission was given for this display of British might, but it must have been an impressive sight as each aircraft appeared, stacked down to avoid jet wash, below a cloud base then alleged to have been 500 feet above the ground – or water. From the last aircraft in this long line came a plaintive 'glug-glug-glug', suggesting that had they been any lower they would have been in the Rhine.

Alas, 1962 started very badly for 213 Squadron, with a mid-air collision between two of its aircraft, one taking a photograph of the other with its F.95 camera, south of Nordhorn Range. Attempts were made to minimise the more general risk of collision, typically by establishing standard, unidirectional routes between LFAs, along and within which flying was permitted down to 250 feet. Routes 13 and 17 covered the northern and southern areas respectively, both routing via bombing ranges; there were also bookable, standard night low-level routes, to be flown mostly at 1,000 feet. In training, the Canberras would fly the routes at 240 knots, only accelerating on the run in from IP to the target for their LABS manoeuvre.

Although night photography had priority, 80 Squadron, now commanded by Wing Commander K.R. Richardson, won the long-range day class in Royal Flush VII at Ramstein, in May 1962, by an appropriate eighty points against the USAF's RF-101s of the 66th Tac Recon Wing. Then in July, as if to rub salt into the wounds, the squadron went to its adversaries' home base at Laon, France, on an exchange visit.

Flight Lieutenant Tom Robertson VR(T), the commander of the RAF Section of John Lion School Combined Cadet Force (CCF), expressed his gratitude to everyone who, through hard work on essentially secondary duties, helped make the school's camp at Brüggen in 1962 so worthwhile. The cadets were treated to an intensive and instructive programme, including participation in a realistic station defence exercise (with somewhat less expertise than their RAF Regiment mentors!). All this would be repeated several times a year throughout Brüggen's history, underlining the breadth of responsibilities and sense of duty on the station, while surely whetting the appetite of 'the right stuff' for service in the RAF.

With noise unabated, every effort continued to be made on the station to develop amicable relations with its German and Dutch neighbours, on which the efficient working of the station and its peripheral lifestyles depended so much. To this end the range of activities increased, sponsored top down and generated bottom up, visits by the local great and good being regular events. One such visit, featured in the October 1962 edition of the *RAF News*, recorded that, as guests of the station commander, local German mayors and their councils toured the airfield, watched aircraft operations from the control tower and were wined and dined formally before being presented with signed photographs of their local towns of Erkelenz and Elmpt taken by No 80 Squadron. On this occasion the hosts were rewarded with a comment from their guests that, 'for the first time, we understand the problems faced by the RAF and appreciate the way in which they were being tackled'. Another worthwhile job well done.

Individuals could do much towards this 'togetherness'. In 1962, Squadron Leader 'Tam' Colley became one of the few foreign nationals to be granted the status of a German 'Jaeger'. The great honour of being admitted into such a close fraternity was due to his skill with the gun, his fluency in the hunting language and in the songs they sang. He was an acknowledged expert and dressed properly in his hunting green he made a visible and valuable personal contribution to community relations.

In October 1962, Eddie Crew handed over command to Group Captain Ivor Broom, an experienced Canberra pilot who had helped develop the aircraft's LABS and Decca navigation systems at the Bomber Command Development Unit. Arriving during the Cuba crisis he had to ensure that his squadrons were ready for any operational commitment, with two Canberras on QRA and seventy per cent of the total force ready for operations against pre-planned targets within three hours. For 213 Squadron to be able to achieve this requirement Ivor Broom ordered his armaments officer, Flight Lieutenant Archie Campbell, to train all his weapons teams to load a Canberra with a nuclear bomb within twenty minutes. Fortuitously, Campbell completed this training on the eve of a no-notice Tactical Evaluation (Taceval), enabling Brüggen to become the first RAF Germany unit to be rewarded with the coveted grading of '1' in this area.

Such a performance would not have been possible without many rehearsals and it was not without a little cunning that Ivor Broom convinced many at Brüggen that it was 'the real thing' when he called out the station only hours before a Command Sports Day. Aware that he himself was a keen sportsman, few believed that he would place such an important event at risk, and indeed he himself did not intend to take things too far, so after an excellent response to the call-out the alert was terminated in time for battle to commence on the sports field.

Perpetually high states of readiness remained the order of the day, calling for engine runs and air tests to be carried out well outside normal working hours but Ivor, like all Brüggen COs before and after him, was at pains to explain the need to residents on the station and their neighbours 'outside the wire'. Likewise, he too did all he could to show visitors to the station that Brüggen was professional in all it did, and 80 Squadron was always ready to oblige with photographic evidence. It was now standard practice for them to photograph VIPs from the air as they arrived at Brüggen and present them with the result very shortly thereafter, usually mounted and framed in some twenty minutes, in a demonstration of rapid processing and printing by 8 MFPU, commanded by Flight Lieutenant 'Chick' Evans. Ivor Broom went one better when Lord and Lady Tedder told him during a lunch at Brüggen that they were having a house built on Uist in the Outer Hebrides, by scrambling a PR7 on a good training exercise to produce a photograph by the end of that afternoon showing progress on the house. Needless to say, the squadron did the job well, and the Tedders were impressed.

Notwithstanding all its work at night with the three-man crews, 80 Squadron lost the night phase of Royal Flush in April 1963 to the USAF RB-66s. Then, from May to October, while work was being carried out on the runway at Brüggen and barriers were installed at both ends, the squadron was detached to Laarbruch. 213 Squadron went to Wildenrath but QRA remained at Brüggen, if necessary to be launched from the southern taxiway.

Going from strength to strength, 213 Squadron won the Salmond Trophy in April 1964, Ken Wilson's crew scoring the highest marks, and not to be outdone 80 Squadron regained its laurels in Royal Flush IX in May 1964, when it was named best day reconnaissance squadron in a victorious 2ATAF.

Victory parade at Brüggen in May 1964 when 80 Squadron, named 'best day reconnaissance squadron in 2ATAF', wins Royal Flush IX. (*RAF Brüggen*)

Her Royal Highness The Princess Margaret came to Brüggen on 15 July 1964, a glorious hot summer's day, to present 80 and 213 Squadrons with Standards to honour their twenty-five years of continuous service. 80 Squadron's Standard had the bell as its centrepiece above the motto 'Strike True', while 213's motif was a Hornet (its 'Bumbly') with the message 'Irritatus Lacessit Crabro' (The Hornet Attacks When Roused); both carried eight battle honours. The welcome included a fly-past of Javelins from Nos 5 and 11 Squadrons before the Presentation Parade, commanded by Wing Commander R.C. Simpson, who had taken over 80 Squadron in the previous January. This was a most auspicious occasion for Brüggen, with many former members of both squadrons and a large number of station personnel, accompanied by their ladies, watching the ceremony from specially erected stands. At a formal lunch in the officers' mess the usual protocol was waived, the two squadron commanders being seated either side of the Princess and their

During her visit to Brüggen on 15 July 1964, HRH The Princess Margaret, attended by
the station commander, Gp Capt Ivor Broom, and C-in-C, AM Sir Ronald Lees, watched
a fly-past of Javelins from Geilenkirchen in a letter 'M' formation. (*Sir Ivor Broom*)

flight commanders opposite. For those not invited to the Royal Lunch, Catering
Squadron had laid on a magnificent spread at various places around the station.
The visit ended with a fly-past of eight Canberras from the Brüggen squadrons, in
preparation for which (one F-540 noted) all flying throughout the preceding two
weeks had been devoted. Her Royal Highness had clearly enjoyed the company of
her relatively lowly luncheon companions and asked why they had not been invited
to the Ball at Rheindahlen that evening.

The following day, looking its best with all the Royal Visit displays still in place,
Brüggen opened its gates to the public to give 4,000 German and Dutch civilians an
insight into the work of the station and of the RAF in Germany as a whole.

What they did not see was the voluntary work going on behind the scenes to
enhance life on the base and for those less fortunate elsewhere, through charitable
initiatives. Typically, the wives started a Marks and Spencer Order Shop, acquiring
goods on demand and selling them on to earn a rebate of five per cent for the Station
Commander's Welfare Fund in a successful scheme which was soon copied by others.
Not only the wives but also some busy servicemen and civilians were involved in
myriad charities. In 1964, Sergeant William Clark, RAF Police, his wife and a team

of helpers raised enough money in six weeks from civilian traders, employees and wives, to buy a guide dog for a most deserving case. In the same year the Brüggen Buffaloes hosted twins from a Dr Barnardo's Home on a two week holiday at the station; they were met at Ostend, accommodated with Sergeant Syd Bennett and his wife and treated, among other things, to swimming, glider flights and a visit to a German zoo. Thus, the good people of Brüggen set precedents which would be developed in increasing numbers, scope and reward for all. Again, this history can only touch on a few examples of these most laudable sidelines in the life of the station.

All this was encouraged actively by Ivor Broom, whom Corporal David King of 431 MU remembers above all as a 'people person'. David was busy in his quarters on one Sunday morning in April 1964, when the station commander and OC Technical Wing, Wing Commander Searle, and their wives arrived to enquire after the health of his wife who had just undergone major surgery to her knee. The ladies disappeared upstairs and the men to the kitchen for a beer, where Ivor complimented David on his culinary skills before doffing his jacket to make the gravy. David adds, 'I wager that not many young corporals have had part of their Sunday lunch prepared in their own home by their station commander – but that was the sort of man Sir Ivor was.'

Although not a drinker by contemporary standards, Ivor Broom was ever present on the social scene. He did enjoy the odd glass of wine but this pleasure was denied him at the start of one guest night when a new officer, observing protocol, approached to pay his respects. Ivor, glass in hand, pointed to a more senior person present, but the newcomer misunderstood, accepted the drink and walked off. His overall popularity with all ranks was legion, evident in an unusual presentation of Belgian cut glass wine glasses and a decanter by the airmen when he completed his tour, leaving the station in good heart for Group Captain Ted Sismore to assume command in November 1964.

The new station commander spent many of his early days in HQ 2ATAF helping to review and revise Brüggen's war missions to improve his crews' chances of reaching their targets and returning home; that he had some success must have come as some relief to the crews involved. Later, he would find himself in a Canberra at 250 feet off Wilhelmshaven in the exact spot he had been some twenty years before in a Mosquito at 50 feet, on one engine, doing battle with a German cruiser.

On 25 May 1965, both Canberra squadrons took part in a mass fly-past of all RAF squadrons in RAF Germany, each with a formation of six aircraft over RAF Gütersloh for the visit there by Her Majesty Queen Elizabeth. The author led the 11-mile stream of sixty-six aircraft on all the rehearsals and the fly-past, invariably in less than ideal weather somewhere on route. The weather was acceptable on the day, but with six minutes to go to the overhead, Gütersloh ATC warned that the Queen was going to be late in arriving by road: how late they did not know. While able minds in every cockpit pondered how they would deal with this problem if they had been in the lead, and the seconds ticked by, a voice from somewhere in the formation proclaimed 'God save the Queen'. There was nothing more to be said.

In 1965, 213 Squadron won the Salmond Trophy for the second year running and went on to represent RAF Germany in the six-nation annual NATO Tactical Weapons Meet (TAM). Wing Commander Brian Stansfield took over 80 Squadron in December 1965, as the squadron began its work up for the night phase of Royal Flush X with the new, much improved 1.75" flares. The priority given to crews initially selected for the competition drained resources and left little flying for the others, but it bore fruit. In May 1966, after long periods of poor weather, sickness, a paucity of night ranges and flying restrictions due to the UK lambing season, the four 80 Squadron crews beat their opponents, the USAF's RB-66s of the 19th Tactical Reconnaissance Squadron, by seventy-one per cent to fifty-four per cent. Crucially, 8 MFPU, now commanded by Flight Lieutenant Ken Halfacree, excelled in photographic processing and printing. This was a good start for the new CO, Group Captain C.D.A. Browne, who had taken over the station in April 1966.

In August, 80 Squadron also changed hands, Wing Commander R.E.W. Nettley taking command as euphoria over its success in Royal Flush X gave way to disappointment when a target miss-plotted by an outside agency placed the squadron last in September's Sassoon competition. However, it did well in October's Taceval, all aircraft tasked being airborne within thirteen minutes of 'General Alert'. The end of this year of mixed fortunes was celebrated with a squadron coffee morning on 23 December – an unusual way to begin the Christmas festivities but in keeping with the new campaign against drinking and driving.

By the mid-1960s, grave and growing concern over the structural integrity of those Canberra airframes subjected to high speeds at low level and a 3-'G' LABS manoeuvre, led to severe limitations which would curb operational training in certain conditions and configurations. In 1966 ultrasonic tests then revealed unconnected structural problems arising from the initial casting and machining of certain components. An increasing number of Brüggen aircraft were found to have stress corrosion cracks in their fuselage main spars and undercarriage legs, faults which demanded remedial work expected to take eight months to complete on each aircraft. As an added precaution, those aircraft found to be fault-free were restricted to 250 knots, 2-'G' and a minimum height of 1,000 feet – except on final bombing runs.

At the beginning of 1967, 80 Squadron's night flying task was increased from twenty to thirty per cent, clashing with the requirement to start training for the day phase of the next Royal Flush. This was no time for any of its crews to come to grief on the Winter Survival Course at Bad Kohlgrub, but Flying Officer Wellings suffered severe frostbite, with which he was hospitalised, and Flying Officer Sinker had to take a spell off flying with a twisted knee. This inspired an order to those scheduled for the next course to 'survive' and ski without injuring themselves – but it had little effect.

On 213 Squadron in 1966, the vulnerable and sometimes exciting LABS delivery was giving way to laydown bombing, discarding the popular 25lb training round for the Mk.106 practice bomb. The latter was cheap, crude, tended to hang up, and when it exploded on impact its pathetic little flare and almost inaudible 'pop' made it hard for the range staff to 'spot', so it was far from popular. Conventional weapons training included thirty degree dive bombing with 1,000lb inert bombs which could be seen from the nose of the Canberra entering the sandy range at Nordhorn and burrowing their way underground. Flying Officer Dick Milsom, a pilot on 213 Squadron, remembers that 'the pull-up and tip in was interesting, particularly if you were inclined to rudder the aircraft on to the target, when sideslip and bank could flame out an engine, which certainly exacerbated directional control in the dive.'

Dick was among many who were fulsome in their praise for Brüggen's officers' mess staff in the mid-1960s: 'the food, standard of hygiene and presentation, value for money, superb guest nights and specially selected Dutch waitresses – were all down to Herr "Willy" Seidenthal, a mess manager in the old German style, and his assistant Frau Bull.' By all accounts life for the living-in officers of Brüggen during the 1960s left little to be desired.

QRA duties and frequent practice alerts at any time of the day or night marred an otherwise idyllic life for many, frequently interrupting card games when hands were at their best. The aircrew would then rush to strap into their aircraft and start engines, not knowing until they checked with the duty operations officer, whether it was a practice or the 'real thing'. When Dick Milsom checked in at 0200 hours on one such alert, he was horrified to hear the intercom crackle: 'this is a real, real authentication message', but before he could initiate the Third World War the order was countermanded by a more senior voice.

Had he got airborne he would have protected one eye against a nuclear flash with a black eye-patch, transferring it to the other eye after the explosion and hoping that there would be no more detonations in his area – a forlorn hope indeed. The qualification for a 213 Squadron 'QRA Tie', a Roman 'C' enclosed by barbed wire, was the completion of 100 QRA duties, but few would volunteer for this prestigious award.

Flt Lt Dick Milsom, unwinding on 213 Squadron after a stressful tour as an ADC in HQ RAF Germany. (*Clive Compton*)

A strong bond had developed between 80 and 213 Squadrons. They had come together initially in the Middle East during the Second World War and were now working most amicably at Brüggen. To mark this relationship they now formed, by simple addition, the '293 Club' and produced a joint tie which displayed 80 Squadron's bell and 213 Squadron's hornet. This is not to say that individual squadron pride did not abound, indeed it probably contributed to some very lively social activity, particularly on Friday evenings and at weekends when a certain tree outside the officers' mess filled with officers from both squadrons bent on erudite discussion over liberal quantities of 'black velvet'. The tree, and Brüggen's social reputation generally, drew many a 'bird' from the RAF Hospital at Wegberg, schools and hunting grounds further afield, so it was no surprise that when the Red Arrows had performed at a nearby station, but were barred from that mess for being improperly dressed, they climbed back into their Gnats and headed for Brüggen. On the following day, in return for the now legendary hospitality received, they carried out a full aerobatic display for the station.

On the other hand, this Brüggen of the 1960s was not inclined to enforced socialising and it was only because of their innate discipline in all things that the officers responded to an order to support the officers' club at Rheindahlen. Because of the potentially dangerous drive from their home ground, buses were organised on one Friday evening to take their combined might to Rheindahlen, where they found a sanctity redolent of India and the colonies in bygone days. The three-piece salon group soon succumbed to Brüggen voices rendering 'The Flag flies high from the Masthead we'll drink to the glory of the Reich – Sieg Heil!' and other traditional German songs, given proper emphasis and body language. The visiting revellers continued to spread their special brand of bonhomie liberally among the *habitués* of the club until the German staff walked out, the telephone lines became red hot and the Brüggen contingent was invited to return to base immediately. One-sided interviews continued for several days and there was no further mention of massed forays to the Headquarters Officers' Club.

In February 1967 there were two more fatal accidents to RAF Germany Canberras; one flew into high ground in Scotland and another crashed in LFA 2 after failing to recover from a descending turn at low-level. The latter was hard to explain but it was followed by an apparently similar incident in which Flight Lieutenant Ray Passfield was able to regain control from a turn initiated at low-level only by instant and judicious application of rudder, normal aileron control returning inexplicably some minutes later. Subsequent investigations failed to reveal any fault in the aircraft's systems but there was much speculation that these unaccountable incidents were connected, and the Board of Inquiry observed that the causes might have been discovered had the aircraft been fitted with a flight data recorder.

With thirteen crews and a flying task of 310 hours, 80 Squadron was hard put to meet all its commitments in 1967. New shift patterns generated more flying hours but the squadron did not do well in Royal Flush XI or Sassoon, one crew losing many crucial marks in the latter for flying too low; perhaps they would have survived in war? In August 1967, between the two competitions, the squadron celebrated its 50th anniversary.

Throughout October, while the airfield was closed for runway resurfacing and the Canberras were dispersed to Wildenrath and Laarbruch, 80 Squadron moved from Hangar 4, to share Hangar 2 with 213 Squadron. This rendered greater efficiency within the wing generally, both squadrons now being close to the station's operations, engineering and administration facilities. Expanding its activities, 431 MU moved into Hangar 4.

Unaware of what lay ahead for him, Group Captain Tim Lloyd took command of the station in January 1968. He was thrown in at the deep end with a Taceval in his first month and Exercise 'Quicktrain' in March – but the station was up to it. Indeed, 80 Squadron was on a high, generating nine of its ten aircraft in four hours thirty minutes, against a requirement for seven aircraft in twelve hours and had its best month's flying training for five months. It was a good start.

Even those who had to continue their peacetime routines could not escape some aspects of Taceval. During one evaluation the medical staff had been playing the war game since 0400 hours, but by mid-morning they had returned to the needs of dependants. Suddenly, two firemen and a burly RAF Regiment officer umpire burst into the Medical Centre and declared it 'bombed', with all therein 'dead' except one dental corporal who they categorised as 'badly hurt'. Although complaining loudly that he was no longer taking part in the exercise, the luckless 'casualty' was rushed to the exit in a fireman's lift, his head becoming caught between the double doors, rendering him unconscious and silencing his protests. Medical attendant Mel Smith, who saw it all, was able to report that the victim recovered from concussion but he could not comment on the state of the doors. Mel also remembers that the Senior Dental Officer, Squadron Leader Terry Hanbury, sought to use his handsome black labrador retriever to calm his patients, but that it howled louder than any occupant of his dentist's chair when the high speed drill was brought into use.

When becoming the principal stockholder on 431 MU, Squadron Leader Mike Allisstone was required to take over an inventory from a hurriedly departing predecessor in 1968 relying, as one so often did, on good faith rather than a 100% check. Later, within a cavernous shed, he found 'mountains of hessian bales, some canvas and pieces of unidentifiable hardware', purported to be 'No. 1 Field General Hospital', only ten per cent of which seemed to have been checked in previous years. Here lay the remnants of a 400-bed Field Hospital, the tents probably plundered over twenty years to enhance the decor at officers' mess balls, a few beds rusting beyond use, badly infested mattresses, together with food and drugs which were well past their sell-by dates. To avoid a punitive inquiry

Medical staff at Brüggen waiting to examine Dick Milsom. Wg Cdr Alan Cox, Senior Medical Officer, (centre) Sqn Ldr Hanbury, Senior Dental Officer, (second from right) and SAC Mel Smith (far left). (*Mel Smith*)

and embarrassment up the line, Mike offered to 'put things right' over his next three years – which he did. From the ashes of 'No. 1 Field General Hospital' rose two sparkling new 200-bed Mobile Hospitals, modern and fully equipped with everything that a tactical air force could want in war. It had been a hard lesson, but 431 MU and Mike Allisstone were the better for it – he leaving Brüggen with a promotion to wing commander.

For 80 Squadron, the first half of 1968 was again dominated by Royal Flush training, hampered this year by the non-availability of reinforcement PIs until the final rehearsal in May. RAF Germany's Canberra PR squadrons came last among the 2ATAF teams in this year's competition, prompting the compiler of one F-540 to note that 'the two-crew advantage has yet again been disproved'. Wing Commander Ray Offord took over the squadron in July but its luck in academic competition did not change. In November's Sassoon one pilot had his Mae West inflate as he approached a target, resulting in the loss of photographic cover and ultimately the trophy.

No. 213 Squadron celebrated its 50th Anniversary in July 1968 with a full ceremonial parade followed by guest night attended by former squadron commanders. A flying display included solo aerobatics by 213's Flight Lieutenant Eric Tilsley, RAF Germany's Canberra Display Pilot for 1968, and a formation sequence performed by four B(I)6s led by the squadron commander, Wing

Commander Mike Chandler. Then came tragedy, when, during the Salmond Trophy competition on 19 August 1968, one of the squadron's Canberras (WT325) collided with a Victor in heavy cloud over Norfolk, killing all aboard both aircraft. No one was held to blame.

The first edition of the station magazine *Brüggen Circuit* appeared in October 1968, with a cover photograph of four Canberras, two from each squadron, flying in formation at low-level. Initially, one thousand copies of eight pages were produced by a volunteer staff headed by Pam Lloyd, wife of the station commander. The *Circuit* would make a major, if informal, contribution to the history of the station in its primary and extraneous activities for the remainder of its life.

1969 began well with a very successful station Taceval, but the Canberra was now showing its age. No 80 Squadron was committed to a non-destructive testing programme, a demanding night flying task, Royal Flush training for selected crews and SACEUR's generation requirements, making it very difficult to complete the additional basic training requirements and achieve the monthly targets. Only by sensible management of Southern Ranger and Blue Diamond sorties to overseas bases could respectable levels of training be maintained for all crews. The squadron was now averaging over the target errors of only 137 yards in its night flash work

The cover of the first edition of the *Brüggen Circuit*, October 1968, showed this formation of two Canberras of 80 Squadron and two of 213 Squadron. (*Brüggen Circuit*)

but, although it scored the highest marks recorded to date by the RAF, it failed to beat the USAF RB-66s in 1968's Royal Flush.

The end of the Brüggen Canberra Wing was announced by the C-in-C at the end of 1968, with some hope that both squadrons would be re-equipped with Phantoms and Buccaneers, but this was not to be. Ray Offord wrote the last entry in 80 Squadron's F-540 in August 1969, a month which ended with a farewell formation fly-past. The Standard was paraded for the last time on 5 September, the Deputy Commander (Dep Cdr) RAF Germany, Air Vice-Marshal J.A.C. Aiken, taking the salute. Six of the squadron's Canberras flew to Laarbruch to join 31 Squadron, the remaining four to MUs in the UK. The Standard was laid up in St. Clement Danes on 28 September; much of the squadron silver went to the command mess at Rheindahlen and other memorabilia to the Air Historical Branch in London. The squadron disbanded formally on 30 September 1969. Writing in the *Brüggen Circuit*, 'D.A.R.' reflected: 'We shall take away memories of Brüggen which will sustain us on less happy stations, things like the speed trap in Elmpt and being asked "Are you fit to drive?" at 0930 hours in the morning with a car load of kids on the way to the Rheindahlen NAAFI. We shall remember giving our hangar to 431 MU and moving in with the "Bumblies", then finding out that they weren't hard to live with as long as they got their three o'clock feed.' Then, in a special message and tribute to the station support staff, D.A.R. goes on: 'One phrase in common RAF usage goes "sounds like a personal problem", which is alright as a "funny", but no one in the service should have to suffer a problem alone, and somewhere at Brüggen there was always a helpful specialist who knew the answer. They say "the sharp end" is where the aeroplanes are but that's not entirely true; all ends have to be sharp to cut through the frustration and delay that abound when not everyone is doing his or her best. Remember this when the Phantoms arrive, for only with your help will they be efficient and safe. They will be grateful too – as we have been.'

Brüggen was involved in more ceremony on Sunday, 14 September, when it provided men for an RAF Germany Guard of Honour in Brussels, before the King and Queen of Belgium, to celebrate the 25th Anniversary of the liberation of the city by the British. The detachment marched off from the Grande Place to enthusiastic applause and cries of 'Vive le RAF' from thousands of spectators.

No. 213 Squadron had another few months to go. It had won the Salmond Trophy in 1968 and in a moving gesture the wives and parents of the crews who died in the collision over Norfolk in August presented a new trophy, the 'Henlow Shield', to the crew with the highest score in these competitions, this honour going first to Flight Lieutenant K. Robertshaw, Flying Officers N.J. Wilkinson and J.P. Mullan. The squadron did not go out with a whimper, again winning the Salmond Trophy in 1969, with the squadron commander and his navigators, Flight Lieutenant J.P. (Jim) Anderson and Flying Officer G.G. Grumbridge taking the Henlow Shield.

213 Squadron 'Bumblies' go out on a high, winning the Salmond Trophy again in 1969. (*RAF Brüggen*)

In October 1969, the disbandment of the squadron was brought forward; it came 'off state' in November and disbanded in December, with no expectation now of a future with fast-jet aircraft. The following signal was made to HQ RAF Germany:

> We have liked being Bumblies
> But now we've had our day
> Someone else can have the Salmond
> So farewell to Taceval, target study, joint inspections, staff visits and 'Q'

A very special guest night was held at Brüggen on 5 December to mark the end of another fourteen year episode in 213 Squadron's history. This night of very mixed feelings, a proud wake and a celebration, was attended by the C-in-C, Air Marshal Sir Christopher Foxley-Norris, who paid tribute to the squadron and read a moving epitaph, after which the squadron presented a sundial to the officers' mess – perhaps with some hidden meaning? On the following evening, having had little time to recover from the night before, and being in none too reverend a mood, the officers of 213 Squadron dominated a cabaret in the officers' mess, 'burying' their Hornet figurehead 'Crabro', with proper military ceremony. For their part, the groundcrew of the squadron presented the station with a 'Bumbly' Trophy. A clever photograph of squadron aircrew and groundcrew aboard a B(I)6 overflying the Kremlin marked the end of this unique, innovative, industrious and highly successful squadron.

In his poignant speech at the Farewell Guest Night for 213 Squadron, C-in-C RAF Germany offered a suitable epitaph. (*Clive Compton*)

Perhaps with a message, the officers of 213 Squadron presented their Mess with a sundial – a memento which remained until the Station closed. (*RAF Brüggen*)

It's not all over until the fat lady sings – or in this case four men in mourning (believed to be officers from 213 Squadron), in their final cabaret in the officers' mess on 6 December 1969. (*Unknown*)

Some tricky flying and photography over the Kremlin – for 213 Squadron's farewell card in 1969. (*213 Squadron*)

Gp Capt Tim Lloyd (right) flew the last Brüggen Canberra to Wildenrath in February 1970 – ending another episode in the Station's history. (*Tim Lloyd*)

On their last sortie Mike Chandler and his navigator Jim Anderson flew a 'valuable package' of specially issued first day covers to commemorate the disbandment of the squadron. Most fittingly, the covers were then handed over to Flight Sergeant Hale, the station philatelist and SNCO who had been charged with the sometimes difficult servicing of the squadron's aircraft.

There is a sinister story of 213 Squadron's reluctance to go. It is said that a corporal policeman, on security patrol with his dog one dark night just before the squadron disbanded, found a door open on one of three aircraft lined up in front of the squadron hangar. As he approached the aircraft the dog began to whine and pull on his lead; with hackles raised he would go no further. The corporal left the dog, peered into the cockpit with his torch and found it empty, closed the door and noted the aircraft's number. At the end of his shift he reported the details and went to bed, soon to be awakened, told that there was no aircraft with that tail number and ordered to return to the flight line to explain himself. There he too, now found only two Canberras and needed a great deal of persuasion that there could have been no third aircraft, the one he had reported bearing that number having been involved in a fatal accident some years before. The outcome of the ensuing discussion is not known. The corporal was on duty again at the disbandment ceremony, but once again his dog refused to go near the spot where he had reported the third aircraft.

As if to ensure that the station did not relax, a grand fire interrupted the Christmas festivities for those who were left behind. Believed to have been caused by spontaneous combustion in a carpet of pine needles, it started one evening behind QRA and spread quickly towards the nuclear storage area. With every prospect that it would soon be beyond the resources of the station fire services, help was sought and was soon forthcoming from eight Dutch fire appliances and many members of the sergeants' mess, in full mess kit, who rushed to the rescue from their Christmas Dinner. Who did what to bring the fire under control in three hours is not recorded but, in a masterly piece of understatement, Tim Lloyd commented, 'If it had spread further we could have been in for a fairly noisy evening.'

Tim Lloyd flew the last of Brüggen's Canberras, a T4, to Wildenrath with a select crew, OC Engineering Wing occupying the right-hand seat and the acting OC Flying Wing, navigating from the rear – he was taking no chances.

In February 1970 the airfield was closed for extensive work to be carried out in preparation for the arrival of the Phantom and Bloodhound squadrons. It was the end of another era and the beginning of the next.

Chapter Five

Brüggen Phantoms

It was a relatively peaceful winter of 1969–70 at RAF Brüggen, the noise of Canberras having given way to major works services as the airfield was made ready for the next stage in the station's seek and strike commitment, the coming of the heavier, faster Phantoms. Convoys of lorries loaded with stone from the River Maas, cement from Hanover and steel from Essen lumbered on to the station. Vast quantities of special asphalt were laid along the airfield's taxiways, enough to pave a garden path to and from the town of Roermond. Aircraft arrester gear was installed at both ends of the runway, the approaches to which were strengthened. An imposing building was constructed to house the sophisticated flight simulator and a custom-built laundry sported a two-story drying tower for brake parachutes. To minimise noise nuisance, a giant steel 'saxophone' was built in the woods on the south side of the airfield for ground testing aircraft engines.

The station mascot, Barrel, welcomes Gp Capt John Curtiss to Brüggen. (*RAF Brüggen*)

Group Captain John Curtiss took command of Brüggen from Tim Lloyd on 17 April 1970, with the task of giving a sense of purpose to the 'massive influx of new people to the station' and barely enough time for the collective effort to meet the necessary deadlines. It was a close-run thing; on the last weekend of the close down period 'large numbers of officers, men and civilian clerks, with brooms and shovels, were still engaged in the task of cleaning the runway', to be ready to take aircraft on the following Monday, 1 June 1970.

The aircraft duly arrived on time and in numbers, the first two Phantoms and a full complement of Lightnings from Nos. 19 and 92 Squadrons, detached from Gütersloh while its runway was being resurfaced. The station now resounded to a crescendo of new and unprecedented noises, more powerful engines with reheat and night fighters plying their trade well beyond the late dusks of the coming summer. Hard won public acceptance of the airfield was now at risk again; indeed one edition of the *Daily Mirror* reported that the sex lives of the locals was being affected. True or not, John Curtiss used the talents of his German secretary, Magda, to best effect in helping to pacify the hierarchy of Elmpt which suffered a great deal more noise than the village which bore the station's name: Brüggen. In a job well done these good burgers worked effectively on their people, ultimately asking them whether they would prefer the noise of Russian MiGs to that of the RAF fighters. For her long and loyal service to the station, Magda was awarded the MBE.

Reheat roars, as Lightnings of 19 and 92 Squadrons, detached from Gütersloh, precede the arrival of Brüggen's Phantoms. (*RAF Brüggen*)

The Europa Club, formed at this time, also helped improve local relations, although a toast to 'The Haggis' and a rendition of 'Tam O'Shanter' by a Scottish doctor late into a Burns Night dinner may have left the Germans and Dutch a little puzzled. It was quid pro quo. Many will remember the Dutch priest, Father Grypink ('Grip-niks') not only for his ministrations to catholics on the station but for his involvement in other activities at Brüggen. He loved food, to which his 'sit up and beg' bicycle homed unerringly. So it was that he wobbled his way uninvited to the rehearsal for one Royal Visit, where lunch was already well underway, demanded a place at the table in front of the Dep Cdr, RAF Germany – and got his way! The children knew him well; he once asked a poorly-attended Sunday School: 'Why am I a very, very unhappy man?' to be rewarded with the answer, 'Because you are not married, Father.' Out of the mouths of children.

A prototype of the American MacDonnell F-4 Phantom II, destined initially for the US Navy, but later accepted for general purposes by the USAF, first flew in 1958. The F-4K was chosen for the Royal Navy and in 1965 the F-4M variant, to be known as the FGR2, was ordered for the RAF. In Germany, the RAF Phantoms would be committed primarily to nuclear strike, conventional attack and reconnaissance roles, until replaced by Jaguars, after which they would be transferred to air defence duties. The FGR2 incorporated British avionics and other components, was powered by reheated Rolls-Royce Spey engines and equipped with a long range, pulse doppler (PD) AWG 12 radar to give it a head-on, look down/shoot down capability with its AIM-7 Sparrow air-to-air missiles (AAM), well beyond the parameters of its short range AIM-9 Sidewinders. For offensive operations it could carry a nuclear store, 1,000lb free-fall or retarded bombs, BL755 cluster bombs, SNEB rockets, and a podded GAU-4/A 20mm Vulcan rotary cannon on the centreline pylon.

John Curtiss remembers the complication of having to manage a mix of American and British spares, the extensive range of electronic equipment and the consequent paucity of storage space. Initially, stocks overflowed from the Equipment Section into tents but a station initiative to expedite the provision of the additional accommodation necessary, using a local contractor at half the price quoted by the Public Services Agency (PSA), fell on deaf ears.

In June 1970, No. 14 Squadron became the first of the Phantom fighter-bomber, strike/attack (FBSA) squadrons to form at Brüggen. The squadron had begun life in 1915 and spent most of the First World War in the Middle East and North Africa, this long association being reflected in its motto, suggested by Jordan's Emir Abdullah and translated from the Koran into: 'I spread my wings and keep my promise'. With its aircraft bearing the insignia of a red St. George Cross on a white disc under a knight's helmet and flanked by wings, the squadron would be known as the 'Winged Crusaders'. No. 14 Squadron returned to England in 1944 to operate over the North Atlantic with Wellington bombers before moving to Germany in 1945 with Mosquitos and remaining there, subsequently with Vampires, Venoms, Hunters, Canberras, and now Phantoms.

Wing Commander John Sutton, the squadron commander designate, and a core of the new 14 Squadron trained together on the FGR2 at RAF Coningsby in Lincolnshire before proceeding to Brüggen. There was much to do on their arrival, setting up optimised facilities and in the protocol of taking over the nameplate from No. 14 (Canberra) Squadron which was still in business at RAF Wildenrath. Squadron Leader Bob Honey, one of the flight commanders, knew Brüggen from the 1950s as a first-tour Hunter pilot; it was he and Squadron Leader Tony Gregory, the much-respected Phantom staff officer at HQ RAF Germany, who established the initial operating procedures for the new wing.

The station started its new life as it would go on, taking every new task in its stride and meeting deadlines. In the first month of its reincarnation, Beverley aircraft brought men of Nos. 15 and 51 Squadrons, RAF Regiment, to the south-west corner of the airfield on a UK reinforcement exercise, and on 30 June, SACEUR called an aircraft generation exercise 'Quicktrain', in which the Lightning squadrons excelled by having a total of nineteen aircraft at five minutes readiness before 'Endex'. By that time, 14 Squadron, although not required to participate in the exercise, also had all four of its Phantoms ready to task. The new squadron continued its build-up and took over the 14 Squadron Standard on 7 July. Both Lightning squadrons had an excellent month's flying with 92 Squadron achieving more hours than in any month since its arrival in Germany. It had all started well, and in August the Lightning squadrons departed for Wildenrath (the runway at Gütersloh not yet ready for them to return), while the station prepared for a Royal Visit in September and No. 17 Squadron began to re-form at Brüggen with the Phantom.

No. 17(F) Squadron (motto: 'Strive to Excel') formed at Gosport in 1915 and spent the First World War in Egypt, Greece and Turkey before disbanding in 1919. It re-formed in 1924 and began the Second World War in the UK before going to India, Burma, Malaya and finally Japan, where it disbanded again in 1948. Re-activated, the squadron served at Wildenrath with Canberra PR7s from 1956 to 1969. Having been the Phantom desk officer in the MOD, Wing Commander Paddy Hine was an ideal choice to be 17 Squadron's first Phantom squadron commander, he and the first half of the squadron converting to the aircraft at Coningsby's Operational Conversion Unit (OCU). The remainder of the crews, coming direct from the OCU or transferred from the two UK Phantom squadrons, would arrive in September, together with their tenth and last FGR2. The squadron aircraft would be identified by black and white chevrons in an arrowhead and (on the port side only) a red and white segmented shield bearing the unit's gauntlet and giving the squadron the name 'Black Knights'. Experienced pilots were crewed with inexperienced navigators, and vice versa.

Squadron Leader Bill Wratten, who would be one of the flight commanders, brought 17 Squadron's first Phantom (XT 901) to Brüggen in August 1970. He had the benefit of a short instructional tour on the aircraft at Coningsby behind him but as an 'air defender' on previous tours he was new to 'mud-moving'. First, however, all hands were needed for much menial work to be done on the ground and the station commander, strolling by the squadron hangar one Sunday morning that summer might have been forgiven for mistaking Flying Officer Ian Travers-Smith, who was mixing concrete outside the hangar, for a German worker. To his kind enquiry in broken German, Ian volunteered that it was all part of the job and that he was on the first sortie next morning. Ian was the cause of much merry-making when the squadron celebrated his final night as a bachelor in London and his peers persuaded him to relieve the doorman of the Dorchester Hotel of his elegant top hat. This he did, escaping from his pursuers with all speed bearing a memento of an eventful evening which would thereafter reside in the crewroom as a trophy for the squadron's monthly bombing competition.

As always with busy people there was time for relaxation in the traditional manner, but that in itself could be hard work, tiring and confusing. Late one night, Squadron Leader Leon Roseveare, 17 Squadron's 'A' Flight Commander, had difficulty negotiating his way through the vehicle barrier on the path from the officers' mess to his married quarter and was found on his way back to the mess by kindly pilots who, after some discussion, were allowed to point him back in the right direction. Bob Honey remembers the relative luxury of his married quarter at Brüggen, with central heating from a temperamental coke boiler in the

Sqn Ldr Leon Roseveare, 17(F) Squadron's 'A' Flight Commander, welcomes Sqn Ldr Bill Wratten and the Squadron's first Phantom FGR2. (*RAF Brüggen*)

cellar being infinitely preferable to the poor heating in UK quarters. Few, however, could master the X/Y factor, a complicated equation which adjusted the actual cost of coke used by applying various obscure inputs to arrive at the final bill. The ubiquitous cellars themselves provided a fascinating insight into their occupiers' ways, with some converted into children's playrooms, workshops or hobby centres, others into offices, 'dens' or exotic bars. The variations seemed limitless.

The increasing demand for married quarters in the area was eased by the building of a multiple hiring estate for 400 RAF and army families at Wickrath, fifteen miles south-east of Brüggen. At the beginning of the 1970s this was being developed with education, medical, NAAFI and social facilities, as a prototype for nineteen similar centres to cater for the basic needs of the service community in Germany.

On the station, Mavis Newstead, assisted part time by a very willing and able Dulcie Puddick, presided first over the refurbishment of the Malcolm Club and later its move to larger premises in the old Corporals' Club. The 'Mally Bar Flies' went too (albeit with much nostalgia for the 'old place') and instituted a system of fines for anyone mentioning 'Good old Coningsby' and the 'wonderful Phantom'. By this means they soon had enough money to fund a Christmas party in the club for the Brüggen Orphanage, this laudable initiative motivating local traders to similar generosity in what became a truly joint Anglo-German-Dutch effort, with another boost to community relations. The club's mobile canteen van was also a welcome sight around the station, Mavis herself nearly bringing one Taceval to a halt when weary warriors left their posts and crossed into a non-exercise area for much needed tea and sticky buns. Fortunately, this brief lapse went unnoticed by the evaluators, but John Curtiss was not amused. For Mavis Newstead the Brüggen Malcolm Club was not so much a job as a way of life and Sir John Curtiss remembers very little trouble there during her tenure.

'Flexible Response' was now the name of the game, with a period of conventional warfare envisaged before any nuclear exchange with the Warsaw Pact (WP). The FGR2s were therefore likely to be used initially in counter-air and interdiction operations, or if really necessary in close air support, but by day only. Nuclear operations could be carried on at night, down to 200 feet in clear weather with some moonlight.

The new concept also called for greater airfield survivability and to that end No. 25 Squadron deployed to Germany with Bloodhound Mk.2 surface-to-air missiles (SAM) in the latter half of 1970. Hitherto a distinguished fighter squadron, 25 Squadron would now provide long-range SAM defence in a sector which covered the important RAF stations of Brüggen, Wildenrath and Laarbruch and other vital military assets. Flights were located at each of the three stations, with 'A' Flight and Squadron Headquarters setting up in the north-east corner of the airfield at Brüggen. 'A' Flight was declared 'ready for action' by the end of the year and the whole squadron became operational on 31 January 1971.

In the semi-active Bloodhound system, targets were handed on from acquisition to target-illuminating radars for terminal guidance; launched by two ramjets, the missile was then accelerated to Mach 2 by four rocket boost motors. Compared with Bloodhound Mk.1 the Mk.2 was air transportable, was more resistant to electronic counter-measures (ECM) and had a range of fifty miles; it could engage targets below 1,000 feet and up to 60,000 feet, with a proximity fuse which had a lethal miss distance of 120 feet. At Brüggen, 'A' Flight would always maintain a number of fire units at immediate readiness.

On 16 September 1970, Her Royal Highness The Princess Anne came to Brüggen to present the Queen's Colour to RAF Germany and to tour the station. Heavy rain at the start did little to dampen spirits during the moving ceremonies, informal meetings with all sections of the service community and immaculate ground displays. Sir William Wratten remembers that as he and Paddy Hine were waiting to show HRH the FGR2's cockpit the C-in-C, Air Marshal Sir Christopher Foxley-Norris, sauntered up to them and 'with an absolutely straight face', told Paddy: 'the Princess would like to see someone eject from an aeroplane and would he please arrange it.' For once, Paddy was lost for words. Finally, the Princess

HQ and 'A' Flight, 25 Squadron, were now on guard at Brüggen, with their Bloodhound missiles, watching and waiting. (*RAF Brüggen*)

initiated a 'scramble' from ATC and watched airborne displays by the resident Phantoms, visiting Harriers and Lightnings. In his farewell, Group Captain Curtiss echoed hopes throughout the station that Her Royal Highness would return one day to Brüggen.

No. 17 Squadron re-formed officially at a ceremony on 16 October attended by Sir Christopher and Lady Foxley-Norris. The parade, fly-past (led by Bill Wratten) and lunch went well, after which there were less formal celebrations. It is said that, when the C-in-C went about other business (at the golf course?), some gentlemen of 17 Squadron, who were perhaps not well versed in social protocol (Flight Lieutenant Jock Cairns was mentioned in this number) all but persuaded Lady Foxley-Norris to join them in a visit to the Rio Bar, a strip club in downtown Elmpt. Fortuitously (or otherwise) the station commander counselled against it and prevailed. The month ended with a memorable farewell to the C-in-C and Lady Foxley-Norris, who departed on the 'Brüggen Belle', to the whistles of the train and cheering of well-wishers along the line.

With good weather in November the Phantom squadrons both achieved their flying targets for the first time and their operational training was well advanced. Others on the station were also making their mark. In December, the men of Brüggen's crash, fire and rescue services, who spent so much of their time waiting for the worst, earned the unofficial title of RAF Germany's fire-fighting champions in the command's first inter-station crash services competition. While previous exercises had simply tested fire precautions and administration, this one demonstrated practical efficiency in dousing an intense aircraft fire and rescuing a dummy body from the inferno.

The re-equipment of No. II (AC) Squadron with Phantoms, Wing Commander Brian Stead in command, began at Brüggen in December with the arrival of seven crews and five FGR2s modified to carry a reconnaissance pod containing optical cameras, infra-red linescan (IRLS) and sideways looking radar (SLAR). The squadron would stay at Brüggen until completion of construction work at Laarbruch in the following April. 'Shiny Two', the first RFC squadron to fly aeroplanes, had unbroken service in army co-operation and reconnaissance roles, serving in Germany since the end of the Second World War. Their Phantoms, which would take over the tactical reconnaissance duties of the squadron's Hunter FR10s still operating at RAF Gütersloh, displayed the Wake Knot on a white disc flanked by white triangles within a black panel.

Squadron Leader Sandy Wilson, who had flown these Hunters with II Squadron, was in at the start of the transition to Phantoms. He arrived at Brüggen to find the first five aircraft and twenty groundcrew in an otherwise empty Hangar 4, but with generous help from the station and both resident Phantom squadrons the bare essentials were soon installed.

No. II (AC) Squadron carried out conversion and initial operational training on the
Phantom at Brüggen, before deploying to Laarbruch in April 1971. (*Sandy Wilson*)

On 7 December Sandy completed his own statutory local checks on the Phantom
and, as more aircraft became available, began checking out the other squadron
pilots. They were soon into an intensive programme of basic reconnaissance
training and night flying. The first sortie with a reconnaissance pod was flown
on 8 January 1971, with Sandy Wilson and his navigator Flight Lieutenant Derek
Andrews aboard, the IRLS giving 'very high quality results'.

1971 also started well for the other two FGR2 squadrons at Brüggen, which
forged ahead despite a demanding modification programme and very poor weather;
much snow and ice calling for hard work by all to keep the airfield open. At 0600
hours on 20 January, John Curtiss called the first of his many new-style Minevals,
in which all aircraft had to be dispersed on base and full NBC kit worn during
the strike phase. This was followed a week later by NATO's Exercise Wintex, for
which Rapier SAM missiles and elements of No. 33 Wing RAF Regiment were
deployed to Brüggen for additional short range air defence of the airfield – in
keeping with the concept of flexible response.

The Brüggen based Phantoms would be equipped with American nuclear weapons, under USAF custodianship. The detachment attached to Brüggen created a 'little America' beside the sports field, complete with a small base exchange (BX store) for national essentials, a very popular barbecue and a seemingly endless supply of canned beer. The operational team consisted of the commander, Major Kipness, commissioned warrant officers (CWOs), NCOs and airmen of assorted specialisations, all of whom appeared as if by magic whenever exercises involved the 'special weapons' within their care. These men played by the rules but, contrary to popular belief, they did not go overboard. Dutchman Willie Luys, who began working as a painter for PSA in 1969 and would rise to supervisor before seeing the station through to the end, remembers that when they had to work in the USAF Special Storage Area (SSA) the Americans allowed them to stand on the dreaded bombs to do their painting, whereas they were not permitted to look at the British equivalents which came later and had to face the wall or lie on the ground with eyes averted whenever they passed by.

Nos. 14 and 17 Squadrons and the supporting units on the station were now well advanced in their preparations to become strike-qualified. In January a pre-

OC II Squadron, Wg Cdr Brian Stead, congratulates Sqn Ldr Sandy Wilson and Flt Lt Derek Andrews after their first sortie with the reconnaissance pod. (*RAF Brüggen*)

operational study group evaluated the rigid procedures prescribed for the carriage, handling, storage, targeting, release and delivery of the American weapons and reported that Brüggen could meet the necessary criteria. As for the actual delivery of these bombs in the air, Bob Honey viewed the Low Angle Drogue Delivery (LADD) with mixed feelings. The requirement was for a pull-up from low-level at 500 knots, followed by a roll through 120° after the bomb had departed, to pull below the horizon before rolling the wings level and diving back below radar cover. This was relatively easy by day and in clear weather, but far more exciting at night and in cloud. Getting around at low-level in the notoriously poor visibilities of some parts of Germany could also get the heart racing, but here the Phantom had the advantage of the pulse doppler automatic acquisition function in its radar, by which navigators (some better than others) could foresee collision risks. When visibility or cloud base fell below regulation minima, which was subject to individual and sometimes less than accurate assessment, the low fliers were required to climb into the middle or upper airspace and come under area radar control. This was not as easy as it sounds; initial contact with the appropriate agency was rarely simple and violations of the complex airspace structure were common. Then there was the problem of descending again safely, if better conditions were expected below in the target area, all of which added to a general reluctance to climb in the first place.

By February, II Squadron was getting the measure of the IRLS and SLAR and was close to assuming a full night capability. To simulate night, the 'back-seaters' navigated on the Phantom's mapping radar 'under the hood', down to 250 feet by day, while their pilots acted as safety monitors. Sandy Wilson did not ask this of Station Commander John Curtiss when he led a section of II Squadron Phantoms in an airfield attack against Laarbruch (the squadron had a secondary attack role, albeit without the gun). He does remember that visibility was very marginal when the Group Captain found Laarbruch on the mapping radar, with very few clues from the surrounding terrain, and talked him successfully onto his assigned target.

While at Brüggen II Squadron had very few setbacks, but one of its Phantoms did suffer a serious bird strike. The pilot had a close shave, with minor injuries to his eyes and what would have been crucial damage to his ejector seat had he had to use it, when a bird shattered the left-hand quarter panel of his canopy as he departed from Brüggen at low-level.

In March, with a full establishment of ten aircraft and twelve crews, II Squadron was ready to take over from the Hunters at Gütersloh and this was formalised with the transfer of the Standard in a parade at Gütersloh reviewed by the new C-in-C, Air Marshal Sir Harold Martin. The Phantoms then moved from Brüggen to their permanent home at Laarbruch in April, after a memorable pyjama party in the officers' mess. No. II Squadron aircrew had been without their wives throughout the detachment to Brüggen and the mess was noticeably quieter after their departure.

Perhaps Sandy Wilson was a little too confident or failed to clarify the ground rules when he bet Flight Lieutenant Tim Thorn, one of the pilots on the squadron's residual Hunter element, a bottle of champagne that he would not catch him and his navigator unawares in their Phantom. This was grist to the mill for Tim, who lay in wait on the approach to Gütersloh when he recognised Sandy's voice calling for joining instructions; he then manoeuvred to get the Phantom in his gunsight and proved it with a perfect photograph taken from his Hunter's nose-facing F.95 camera during the ensuing GCA. A little unfair perhaps, but the champagne did taste good.

March also featured weapons old and new. Two Second World War 88mm shells were found in different parts of the station, one being pronounced 'safe', the other definitely not so. The latter, found at a crash gate and guarded all night, was detonated with great drama and noise by a bomb disposal party the following morning. Perhaps there were – and are – more relics of the past hiding with the wild boar in the deep forest 'within the wire'.

Flt Lt Tim Thorn, in a II Squadron Hunter FR10, caught Sandy Wilson unawares on the nose-facing, F.95 camera – and won champagne. (*Tim Thorn*)

Later in the month 17 Squadron followed 14 Squadron to Decimomannu ('Deci') for its first APC with the Phantom. There, one practice bomb went wildly astray when Paddy Hine himself got it wrong with his Lead Computing Optical Sight Set (LCOSS), bombing with 35 mils set instead of some 140 mils and prompting the rest of his squadron to conclude that it could therefore happen to anyone. At the same APC, Flight Lieutenant Roy Booth scored direct hits with his first five SNEB rockets and his normally placid navigator Flight Lieutenant Gay Horning suggested that he should relax to achieve the much vaunted 100% with his sixth rocket. If Roy did relax it didn't help; his last shot was almost off the plot and he declined any further advice of the sort from the rear seat. Back at Brüggen, Bill Wratten blamed himself for not ensuring on his 'walk-around' inspection, that a practice bomb carrier had been attached securely to his aircraft, with the result that it broke off on take-off and come to rest unseen just inside the airfield. Unaware of this, Bill had continued to Nordhorn Range and carried out bombing runs for half an hour wondering why no bomb left his aircraft. For the record, he was credited with a score of '21 miles at 6 o'clock'. It could happen to anyone.

The USAF Capability Inspection Team gave Brüggen its official seal of approval to handle and deliver nuclear weapons in June, and the great effort which had gone into achieving full operational status in strike and attack roles was rewarded in July after a very demanding but 'highly satisfactory' NATO Taceval, with ratings of '1' or '2' across the board. Immediately after this gruelling exercise Paddy Hine invited the Taceval team to watch a fly-past of 'the remnants of 17 Squadron'; every one of its established aircraft overflying in a 'diamond nine' formation! This had been a very impressive first evaluation of the new Phantom Wing.

It might have been a different story when Paddy Hine put the USAF nuclear custodians to the test, albeit unintentionally. While touring dispersals to encourage his weapons teams during the strike phase of the exercise he fell from his bicycle into a 'no-lone' (no-go) zone around an armed aircraft; he is in no doubt that had he not pleaded accident most convincingly, the American guard would have shot him. That would have made and changed RAF history.

Such was the state of the station when No. 31 Squadron, the third Phantom squadron, began to form there in August 1971. No. 31 Squadron had started its operational life in India in 1915, giving rise to its motto 'First in the Indian Skies'; it remained in that region for the next thirty-one years on army co-operation duties and then in the transport role, latterly flying Dakotas. In its next incarnation, it became a communications squadron at RAF Hendon until re-equipping with Canberra PR7s at Laarbruch in 1955, before standing down again in March 1971 pending its resurrection with the Phantom. The squadron's new aircraft would bear a gold, five-point star on a white disc, flanked by yellow and green checks, to reflect the squadron's eastern connections and their nickname, the 'Goldstars'. The new CO would be Wing Commander Chris Sprent.

The first of 31 Squadron's officers to arrive at Hangar 4, while II Squadron was still in residence, and two months ahead of the main body of aircrew, were Squadron Leader Graham Gibb and his pilot Flight Lieutenant David Pollington. Their first task, as with all newcomers, was to build a bar in the crewroom.

Debate over the inherent efficiency of centralised servicing against the advantages of a semi-autonomous system for tactical squadrons which could be re-deployed at any time, for operations elsewhere, or survival, resulted in a victory for the Brüggen squadron commanders who favoured the latter. However, a high price was exacted for this concession, the squadrons being required to work with the same manning levels established for centralisation. The penalty was accepted; flexibility, mobility of manpower and help from 431 MU all contributing to semi-autonomy at Brüggen. With manpower now sorely stretched, leadership and management had to be at its best and 31 Squadron's Senior Engineering Officer (SEngO) was only too well aware that those on his night shift often worked all night to have the required number of aircraft available next day. His airmen certainly did, to their credit they frequently achieved far more than one had the right to expect, but they rarely complained.

No 31 Squadron had the added problem of being located furthest from the station's operational facilities and the engineering wing hangar in which minor servicing and deep rectification took place, and in the north-west corner there was room for only five Phantoms on the hardstanding outside their hangar. The remainder of its aircraft had to be dispersed singly in nearby revetments, each needing its own Houchin starter, whereas for routine, peacetime operations, the other squadrons operated from lines of adjacent aircraft on the ASP, where one starter could be positioned to serve two aircraft. For dispersed operations, the normal requirement in exercises, and particularly when a minimum delay/mass launch was called for, all squadrons had Houchin management problems, and with reputations at stake, competition between engineers vying for limited resources was very natural and sometimes acrimonious. This could, of course, be very detrimental to the overall good if an aircraft of one squadron remained on the ground for want of a spare Houchin secreted away by another.

After a brief post-Taceval pause, station Minevals resumed with a vengeance, usually terminating with a mass launch of all available aircraft, simulated by a 'taxi-through' if the weather was not fit for flying. It was definitely not fit on one particular morning and several crews did not worry to strap in properly when the launch order specified a 'taxi-through'. However, the first aircraft to reach the runway threshold had not got the message and took off into the gloom, prompting

A 17 Squadron Phantom FGR2 over the Mohne Dam. (*Brüggen Circuit*)

other crews to strap in hurriedly as they wondered whether it was they who had got it wrong. Confusion reigned and who did what at this point remains unclear but lessons were learned – and re-learned. In 1959, the pilot of a Hunter had to stagger over the author's Swift, still on the runway, in a 'taxi-through' on a similarly foggy day at Gütersloh, but again no one came to grief.

From August 1971 Brüggen resumed its QRA role, No. 14 Squadron being the first to commit RAF Phantoms to this duty. At full strength, the wing would hold two aircraft at maximum readiness at all times, with crews sleeping in their flying kit ready for the inevitable practice scramble during their 24-hour tour of duty. The all-important inertial navigation system was pre-set for a three-minute heading and bearing alignment only, rather than the full alignment which would have taken an unacceptable ten minutes. These aircraft were of course armed with live weapons and when a practice was ordered (and very carefully monitored by the USAF custodians) the crews were stood down after they had started engines and checked in with wing operations. It is believed that at no time in its history did Brüggen launch an aircraft carrying a live nuclear weapon.

Nuclear brotherhood. A UK Vulcan welcomes 14 Squadron back to QRA. (*RAF Brüggen*)

The station was now settling into a routine at full strength. Operational imperatives had the highest priority but behind the scenes much was being done to improve the support services and lifestyles of the families. There was a chronic shortage of married quarters but July brought the news that 300 flats were to be built for officers' and airmen's families in Elmpt, a complex which would become known as 'Legoland'. Community relations were on the agenda again in September, when Brüggen opened its gates for 360 selected guests from the local area to see, as far as was allowed, how the station went about its professional business.

At 31 Squadron's official re-formation ceremony on 7 October 1971, the C-in-C warned that the versatility of the Phantom would demand ever higher levels of professional knowledge and expertise. How right he was, and indeed this would be increasingly the case with future generations of aircraft at Brüggen.

On the flight line, 31 Squadron was responding well and said to be 'racing towards its strike qualification', but autumn birdtams, poor serviceability, and above all, serious Spey engine problems, were beginning to affect all three squadrons. With engine/intake matching, reheat problems and limited repair capacity at Rolls-Royce, the wing could now expect to be short of serviceable engines for the foreseeable future.

Local military commanders, including Gp Capt John Curtiss (right), attend the German ritual of 'Schutzenfest', at Brüggen in 1971. (*RAF Brüggen*)

However, expertise generally was building up fast, 31 Squadron's Flight Lieutenant Trevor Nattrass, a Qualified Weapons Instructor (QWI) and ex-USAF Phantom exchange officer, being the first pilot at Brüggen to notch up 1,000 hours in the Phantom. This was celebrated in the usual fashion with champagne for the crew (and the hierarchy) on landing. Winter at Brüggen was largely a time for consolidation, but in February 1972, 14 Squadron went to RAF Valley for its first Missile Practice Camp (MPC) and 31 Squadron became 'strike qualified' with a score of 98.5% in the required examination, and joined Brüggen's QRA force on 1 March. The wing's operational capability was thus increasing on schedule and unseasonably good weather in February enabled all three squadrons to achieve more than 200 flying hours, with an emphasis on night flying.

A typical night strike training sortie would be flown on an established route around the North German Plain, initially at heights of 1,000 feet but with some concessions down to 500 feet and reducing to 250 feet on the final run into Nordhorn Range at 500 knots, the aim being to release the bomb within five seconds of a given time. With good flight planning, the Phantom's INAS and radar prediction, VMC conditions and some moonlight, safe and accurate navigation was possible down to 200 feet above the ground.

The cause of a memo from the Station Commander to OC 17 Squadron, Wg Cdr Paddy Hine, on where wings should be worn and which hand to shake. (*RAF Brüggen*)

Strike Target, Nordhorn Range. (*Jerry Gegg*)

Night or day, even with the best laid plans and the most capable crews, things did not always go smoothly. One pilot was halfway round a delaying orbit at the beginning of the bomb run when the navigator changed his advice from 'one minute early' to 'one minute late', but an immediate acceleration to 600 knots resulted in an error of only three and a half seconds over the target. Former single-seat pilots were reluctant to leave low-level navigation wholly to their navigators or the INAS, which was unreliable in the early days. On the argument that two heads were better than one and that many of the pilots were already good at low-level map-reading, a joint effort was the order of the day and (unlike elsewhere) Brüggen's Phantom pilots carried maps.

Despite the potentially hazardous nature of its operational role, the wing had an almost accident-free first eighteen months with the Phantom, the one exception being the unavoidable bird strike on the II Squadron aircraft, and for this outstanding flight safety record in 1971 the station was awarded the Sir Ronald Lees Trophy. Brüggen also won the Command Engineering Efficiency Trophy, awarded each year to the station in RAF Germany which demonstrated the greatest gain in engineering efficiency over the year. Brüggen was doing well.

It might not have been so but for a vigilant groundcrew. No. 31 Squadron's David Pollington had good reason to be grateful to his starter crew, Senior Aircraftsmen McDade and Stubbins, who noticed that a small piece of metal had been ejected through the starter door during start-up and called for the engines to be shut down. The subsequent inspection revealed this to be part of an anti-icing valve and the damage it caused could have led to the loss of the aircraft. Both airmen were awarded a 'Good Show' for their prompt action. No. 31 Squadron's CO, Chris Sprent, also had a near miss while on APC at Deci when, after start-up, Senior Aircraftsman Baxter noticed 'what appeared to be a slight misalignment of the Phantom's outer wing leading edge flap'; in fact the flap had become detached from its hydraulic jack. Again, this could have had disastrous consequences.

Demarcation had no place at Brüggen and flight safety was everybody's business. So the station dentist, Flight Lieutenant Pete Morgan, who had been known to fit a gold tooth to an RAF police dog, showed his versatility again, this time in aircraft engineering. It took place after a Phantom swallowed a bird and Peter volunteered to crawl into the engine air intake to take a dental impression of the dent it had caused. With a type of plaster of Paris normally used for building models of patients' mouths, he then made a cast of the problem which allowed the engineers to take precise measurements without stripping the aircraft down. Afterwards, he commented: 'I'm always happy to help with any teething troubles.'

The pleasure and pain of the Winter Survival Course at Bad Kohlgrub continued to generate good stories. Paddy Hine got it wrong when he chose to join the last course of the season, with the expectation that the weather would be at its best, but justice prevailed and he was faced with the coldest spell of the winter. With temperatures down to –26°C, 'survivors' were ordered to remain in pairs, but when his group was illuminated by a starshell it was every man for himself and Paddy was the only one to escape capture. Deciding to proceed alone in the dead of night he made for the nearest village, where, dishevelled and in halting German, he threw himself on the mercy of a baker on his night shift. This good man warmed to the occasion, warded off inquisitive searchers and sent Paddy on to the rendezvous with his wife on her early morning delivery round. Bearing whisky, Paddy returned to Bavaria in the following summer to thank his nocturnal friends.

June 1972 saw the culmination of two years' hard work to bring Brüggen's dual role FGR2s to full operational status. This was certified by a Taceval which awarded all three squadrons the highest possible ratings of '1' in all areas and the station a '1' for strike but a '2' for attack operations, the latter downgraded because of spares problems which were beyond the control of the station. The Phantom fliers were quick to praise OC Ops Wg, Dennis Allison, OC Admin Wg, 'Sammy' Samouelle and OC Tech Wg, 'Wally' Ormrod and their staffs for their contribution to this success. Two of the three squadron commanders had particular reason to be grateful to Wally who, in his last week at Brüggen, helped to extricate the Phantoms they had been flying from the mud beside the runway.

Also in 1972, Her Majesty The Queen approved a badge for 431 MU, with an outer cog wheel depicting the engineering element, an inner wheel motor transport, and a plumed pen for stores, accounting and supply. The three colours of black, yellow and red symbolised the unit's association with the host nation of Germany.

When he handed over command to Group Captain David Harcourt-Smith, John Curtiss looked back on his tour with pride and pleasure. He had reared a happy and highly professional strike/attack wing equipped with the complex, hybrid Phantom, and despite the extra noise he had consolidated relationships with the local community. He had also found plenty of time for extraneous activities. No mean squash player, he was able to overcome most of the opposition on the station (given that it might have been imprudent to beat him), and was frequently found on the golf course, even tobogganing on the fairway to the sixth hole during the harsh winter of 1970/71 – but perhaps with an ulterior motive. It so happened that his high-priced help was needed in an on-going battle against the powerful Forstmeister. Perhaps there was little to be done about the rabbits which plagued the course, but the wild boars were a different matter; they tore up the sixteenth fairway looking for the little white bugs which lived four inches below the surface and they needed to be culled. It had been hoped that the main culprit at that time had perished on the station railway line (perhaps too full of bugs) but other boars were ready and willing to take his place and problems with the golf course would continue to engage the attention of future station commanders. For them it was a full and varied life at Brüggen.

BRÜGGEN PHANTOMS

In September 1972, the three Brüggen Phantom squadrons returned the highest average score of the six national air forces taking part in what was described as 'Europe's most important military air contest' – the NATO Tactical Weapons Meet (TAM), this year held at Florennes Air Base, Belgium. The aim of the fortnight-long meet was to test the participants in the planning and execution of bombing, rocket and strafing missions. Flight Lieutenants 'Raz' Ball and his navigator Bob Woodward, of 17 Squadron, came top in the RAF order of merit.

On the national front, 14 Squadron, now commanded by Wing Commander Derek Bryant, won the Salmond Trophy for navigation and bombing, the crews being required to fly 300-mile sorties, passing between umpires spaced 100m apart, within fifteen seconds of their assigned times, carry out timed, simulated attacks on field targets and deliver bombs or rockets at a weapons range. A Buccaneer squadron took second place in the competition and 31 Squadron came third.

As with all flying competitions, the aircrew were fiercely competitive, and may have been tempted into a little skullduggery, with more 'gamesmanship' than was healthy for the overall good, as they attempted to put one over their peers. It could be 'dog-eat-dog'. Acrimonious accusations abounded over the interpretation of competition rules, adherence to regulations, restrictions and operational practices generally, culminating, after one Salmond competition, in a bar brawl between two squadron commanders, who had to be separated physically by a burly engineering officer before real harm was done. One-sided interviews with the station commander were said to have followed.

The April 1973 edition of the *RAF News* confirmed that Brüggen would soon undergo major changes in infrastructure and *modus operandi* to become a unique, dual-role Jaguar base and to develop further the concept of flexible response. A Rapier squadron would be posted in to increase active airfield defences, hardened facilities built for aircraft and aircrews, the latter with air filtration, and passive defence would be enhanced with more camouflage, concealment and deception measures. Brüggen was to be reinvented but, despite the magnitude of this work, Phantom operations were to proceed as normal.

None of this would worry two of the most venerable fast-jet pilots of the time, Squadron Leaders Arthur Vine and Taff Freeman, who were to meet once more at Brüggen. Taff, on 31 Squadron, had a mere 4,400 flying hours in thirty years when he was assisted from his Phantom to a wheelchair by his 23-year-old navigator, Flying Officer Jim Stutard, in March 1973, but Arthur, on a visit with the Central Flying School's examining team, could do better. He had been in the RAF for thirty-three years and had amassed 6,000 flying hours when the two flew a Phantom together to celebrate, with an appropriate fanfare, the achievement between them of more than 10,000 flying hours. No. 31 Squadron also had something to celebrate, winning the Salmond Trophy in 1973. It was a good time for Wing Commander Tom Stonor to take over the squadron.

Sqn Ldrs Arthur Vine (left) and 'Taff' Freeman, veteran pilots with 10,000 flying hours between them, fly together in a 31 Squadron Phantom. (*Brüggen Circuit*)

While the old and bold, young and brave were breaking records and winning accolades in the air, not everything was as rosy on the domestic front. Many incumbents will remember that the euphoria among those taking over forty-seven OMQs and forty-eight AMQs in Elmpt, completed in 1973, faded rapidly as delays in carpeting the dining and lounge floors extended into months. The fault was alleged to lie with the Army depot at Viersen, but this was no comfort to the deprived, any more than the news appearing on the same page of the *Brüggen Circuit*, that approval had been given for the swimming pool to be tiled, a second squash court to be built, and improvements made to the athletics track; to them carpets had a higher priority.

OC 31 Squadron, Wg Cdr Chris Sprent, holding the Salmond Trophy won by the squadron in 1973. (*RAF Brüggen*)

David Harcourt-Smith added his views on the Phantom in the *RAF News*. He claimed it was 'one of the finest weapons systems in the world', that its crews 'had the benefit of regular and realistic training' and that the groundcrew, in full NBC clothing, could refuel and rearm a Phantom in fifteen minutes. Everyone had a war role, cooks and clerks likely to find themselves guarding aircraft and vulnerable points against saboteurs and paratroops. The station was doing all it could to be ready for anything.

Those who had the time, inclination and intellect to plough through the erudite commentaries from individual units in the monthly *Circuit* magazines could be richly rewarded, but the uninitiated would sometimes find the vernacular too intimidating. However, in January 1974's edition, a New Year's resolution by 17 Squadron, written in plain English, promised to be nice to the 'Met Men' of the weather forecasting office. This tall order did nothing to cheer the embattled team of nine incumbents, working twenty-four hours a day for five days a week, in their lonely green hut on the airfield; they had heard it all before. In their 'no win' situation they were still mumbling their nights away with 'when I am right no one remembers but when I am wrong no one forgets'. When the author left Brüggen several years later, they presented him with a plaque showing Brüggen 'green' (full flying), but all possible diversions 'red' (a flight supervisor's nightmare). It did pay to be kind to 'Met Men' and, as with everyone else at Brüggen, they were better than most.

The station's collective effort was recognised with the award in 1974 of the Wilkinson Battle of Britain Memorial Sword for the most valuable contribution in the previous year to the development of operational tactics for conventionally armed RAF aircraft. The Brüggen entry had taken six months to prepare in a combined effort involving the aircrew and operational support staffs, with every supporting adjunct and facility brought into play. Prominent was the RAF's only radar prediction centre, a navigator's training aid based on photographs taken as high-powered light was played on small plaster models depicting a typical navigation route, the resulting shadows giving the expected radar returns. By moving the light along the aircraft's planned track the radar route could be predicted and a facsimile produced to the same scale of the map used in low-level navigation. Likewise the Brüggen flight simulator, usually associated with practising emergencies on the ground, was also used in operational training. This simulator incorporated a terrain model representing a typical operating area of 135 x 38 miles and a smaller area containing different target arrays, over which a crew could 'fly' operationally and practise weapons deliveries. Veteran Phantom pilot Arthur Vine would become an instructor on this simulator. The Wilkinson Sword was presented to the station by Air Chief Marshal Sir Denis Spotswood on his final visit to Brüggen as CAS, on 14 March 1974.

In May, a Brüggen team led by the OC 17 Squadron, Wing Commander George Ord, competed in the 11th TAM at RCAF Baden-Soellingen in southern Germany. They repeated the success of the Brüggen Phantoms at the previous meeting in 1972, by achieving the highest national scores against USAF Phantoms, German, Belgian and Canadian F-104s and Dutch NF-5s. Flushed with success, 17 Squadron went on to represent the station at the Strike Command Fighter Meet at RAF Leuchars in Scotland in July. The three squadrons were still flying more than 200 hours a month and had been given excellent ratings by the USAF Nuclear Safety Team, but there was now a shortage of training bombs and fuel economies loomed.

When David Harcourt-Smith handed over command of the station to Group Captain Peter Harding in July 1974 he wrote in the *Circuit*: 'I have been greatly impressed by the feeling of community spirit that exists at Brüggen and by the work of such organizations as the Wives' Club, the many adult and youth clubs which cover such a wide span of activities, and the wonderful support both on the field and the touch line that has been given to a whole host of sporting activities.' Such initiatives had flourished in the early 1970s, many enhancing further the already good relations with friends and neighbours on and off the station. Brüggen churches continued to contribute much to this togetherness, in their turn hosting

OC 17 Squadron, Wg Cdr George Ord (with trophy) led a Brüggen FGR2 team to victory in the 1974 NATO Tactical Weapons Meet. (*Brüggen Circuit*)

members of the Roermond, Elmpt and Waldniel congregations at international services in St. Andrew's Church. These acts of fellowship, with their special Orders of Service conducted in three languages and followed by refreshments, had been rotating between each location four times a year since 1969, and they would continue. The Wives' Club was indeed thriving, popular and constructive in its pursuits, developing to give a more international dimension to national interests. The programme for the first quarter of 1974 included shopping and health hints, station activities, holiday opportunities and social events.

One of the most prominent contributions to the international social and charity scene was the formation at Brüggen in 1974 of the Der Adler Karnival Group (The Eagle Carnival Club), an initiative which would mirror a German tradition. This brief overview of the club comes from one of its original long-standing members and one-time President, Mick Phipps. An airman at Brüggen in the 1960s, Mick married a German girl and returned to work again as a civilian in the station carpenter's shop in the 1970s, and it was there that the author found him in 2000.

During that time Der Adler KG held spectacular, all-ranks social events throughout the karnival season, from the 11th minute of the 11th hour of the 11th day of the 11th month until the start of Lent, the German ritual stretching back to Napoleon's rule of the Rhineland by means of regional councils or 'elferats'. These unpopular puppet bodies, protected by élite French guards, were replicated with much buffoonery by the local people who held 'sitzungs' (sittings) during the karnival period, with their own versions of the elferats and guards. With no chance of overthrowing the governing regimes the purpose of this mimicry was to poke fun at the establishment – and fun remained the name of the game.

Der Adler KG at Brüggen was the only British club of its kind, in bringing this unique entertainment to the servicemen and their families in Germany, to raise money for charity and to promote friendly relations with the local communities. Their sitzungs grew in magnificence as more and more local clubs attended with their own elferat, tanz guards and tanz madchens (dance maidens), the club expanding into a huge hangar provided by 431 MU. Many clubs, from such local towns as Alsdorf, Mönchengladbach, Letterich, Brunssum and Dulken, attended with their own band and often a cabaret. Brüggen added its own unique themes with a male guard portraying British 'bobbies', city gents, highlanders, or morris men. More serious dance routines, reflecting traditional culture, were performed by the tanz madchens and tanz guard, an altogether more glamorous and an impressively dressed group of Brüggen ladies.

The winter of 1974-75 was the first season for Der Adler KG and it ended with two major 'Sitzungs' in the Chicken Club, the first featuring Dutch carnival clubs and a visit by their 'Grote Vorst' (the 'AOC' of carnival in the area), and the second a number of German groups. Then came 'Alte Nacht Fraus', when the station was invaded by weirdly dressed revellers who cut the end off the station commander's tie and demanded food and drink (duly supplied) for his safe return. In the penultimate event on Rosenmontag, Brüggen provided one of the 169 floats in the huge Roermond Carnival Parade, perhaps rather incongruously depicting a composite RAF Germany aircraft, all bombed up and ready to go. The end of this first season was celebrated with a domestic night in the clubroom which included the 'de-frocking' of the outgoing president, Denis Wolstenholm, and the swearing-in of the new incumbent. Denis and his wife Pat were not to know then that the club they had helped to found would grow to such strength, but the March edition of the *Circuit* was fulsome in its plaudits: 'With them will go the knowledge that they created at Brüggen a club which is entirely new in concept and which has not only contributed a total of DM3,530 to the Station Charities Fund during the season but has also made many new friends among the international community.' Ten years later the club was still going strong with many larger contributions to charity (DM10,000 in one year). One of many letters on the file, to Mick Phipps from a station commander, said it all: 'Brüggen is very proud of the good work "Der Adler" does for charity and recognises the tremendous dedication of the club members.' Unhappily, as the operational commitments and detachments for the Brüggen units increased in the 1990s, regular membership of Der Adler declined rapidly and the club ceased to exist.

In 1974/75, with contributions big and small, the many Brüggen charities were able to provide the Bridgend and District Handicapped Club with a £3,000 Commer Personnel and Wheelchair Carrier, a gift most gratefully received via the station's padre, Graham Corderoy. On a smaller scale and closer to home, but no less appreciated, sufficient funds were raised by station units, typically the newly created Brüggen Cabaret Club which toured messes and clubs with one-hour sketches, to buy a fish tank and TV for the hospital at Wegberg and football kit for the Brüggen Youth Club.

Thrift Shops on RAF stations were meccas for many as well as lucrative sources of funds for charity and the green hut off Harris Road at Brüggen was no exception. 'Attica', in the August 1974 edition of the *Circuit*, put it very well: 'One of the best things about living on an RAF station is the Thrift Shop. Before I was

Der Adler KG's first 'Sitzung', the Chicken Inn, 30 November 1974. (*Mick Phipps*)

married I had so many old clothes it wasn't true (no new clothes you understand, just old ones), so when we moved into quarters I vowed that the Thrift Shop would change my life. No more suitcases crammed with things I never wore but someone else might, I would have a regular sort out, and so I marched down there virtuously loaded with the contents of tidied-out wardrobes. You cannot imagine, unless you are a hoarder yourself, how noble it feels to dispose of something, and to actually get some money for it is even better. The only snag is, I see such bargains there that I always end up bringing back more than I took.' The Brüggen Thrift Shop was a great success.

Not to be left out, the Brüggen police were quite rightly very visible, not only on their professional rounds of QRA, SSA and station generally, but in support of charities at their annual Police Dog Trials. The *Brüggen Circuit* recorded that in September 1974 this event opened at lunchtime with 'the rhythmical beating of drums' heralding the magnificent sight of the Mönchengladbach Schlopp-Op band marching down Harris Road, resplendent in their nineteenth century uniforms 'reminiscent of King Geordie's men of old in their wigs, tricorn hats, red coats and white breeches'. The rain came down as the first competitors entered the arena but the band played on until it all became too much and the station's first lady, Sheila Harding, was forced to take cover until the rain abated and she was able to award the prizes. But it's an ill wind that blows nobody any good and Miss Bridges' team from the NAAFI did a roaring trade in hot snacks and drinks, while the Brüggen dogs did themselves proud in conditions with which they were well acquainted.

Having contributed to Brüggen's success in the 1972 and 1974 TWMs, in which 2ATAF was victorious over 4ATAF, 14 Squadron, with Squadron Leader Pete Goodman and Flight Lieutenant Nick Brown, won the United States Air Force Europe (USAFE) Radar Bombing and Electronic Warfare (EW) Competition 'Creek Scope III'. This night exercise was flown out of Ramstein Air Base against F-4Ds and F-4Es of 'the best radar bombers in USAFE', at heights of 3,000-4,000 feet – foreign territory to the low level men of RAF Germany. However, Brüggen's Radar Prediction Centre provided an invaluable service, groundcrew patience and perseverance with some very temperamental equipment paid off, and the 'Scope Wizards of the 14th Tactical Fighter Squadron' finished the job in style.

Not all went right for 31 Squadron. On 11 October 1974 the pilot and navigator of Phantom XV431 had to eject at 50 feet after take-off when its wings, which had not been properly locked down, folded in the air. Serious repercussions and soul-searching were inevitable but the crew survived their injuries, faults were freely admitted and hard lessons were learnt. No.31 Squadron's SEngO, Del Williams, admired the behaviour of the aircrew throughout but felt that the engineers should have shouldered more of the blame. He believed, however, that in the end the squadron emerged 'stronger and more cohesive'.

The spirit of the station in sport, extolled by David Harcourt-Smith in his farewell message, was alive and well in the Brüggen Bears Rugby Football Club's

This Brüggen Phantom failed to get airborne when its wings folded on take-off.
The crew ejected safely. (*RAF Brüggen*)

tour of Berlin in 1973. The initial problem for the visitors was that the 12-hour train journey and then the attractions offered by that great city did not mix well with rugby. It was just as well that winning was not as important as playing the game because in their first match the Bears lost to RAF Gatow 37–3. Their next opponents, the Royal Military Police, had problems of their own when some of their number were withdrawn to deal with a suspected terrorist bomb and had to be replaced by a creditable number of Bears who had survived the night before. A rash of minor injuries and other distractions finally led to the abandonment of this match after thirty-five minutes when Brüggen was leading 3-0. All this smacked of the 'art of coarse rugby' and was not unusual for a Berlin tour, typically when one Bear lost his crucial travel documents and had to fly out over the heads of the Russian guards in East Germany a day after his team mates returned by train. They had all learned, inter alia, that twenty-five beers in the Berlin Hofbrauhaus cost DM150, that the sauna in Heerstrasse was the place to go, glass ashtrays should not be carried in the back pocket if you are likely to fall down and that an East German officer wearing something like a flying helmet was not the 'Red Baron'!

Sport continued to help bring the local communities together; in 1974, station tennis players reached out to clubs in Belgium while the motor sport fraternity shared its interests with the German Erkelenz Club. The Brüggen skiers took their sport very seriously; they were out to win and did just that at the RAF Germany ski championships for three years running in the mid-1970s. Peter Harding had taken over what he described as a 'mature Wing', with many of its aircrew in their late twenties or early thirties, but he had his share of innocents and miscreants on the station. On Old Fraus' Night, before Rosenmontag, a young airman was picked up by two ladies of many seasons from the Main Gate, entertained and deposited back there three days later, rather the worse for wear, but quite happy. He accepted Peter's fine for being absent without leave with alacrity, confiding afterwards that 'it had been worth every pfennig'. Another German lady, of ample proportions, brought a very small corporal to the guardroom with an accusation of rape, which at best was very hard to believe. Among the more outrageous requests from local people, one worker asked Peter to have a sonic boom aimed at the brewery from which he had been sacked, with the objective of shattering all the windows therein. There is no record of a reply.

The excellent relationships between the Phantom Wing at Brüggen under Peter Harding and the Harrier Wing at Wildenrath, now commanded by Group Captain Paddy Hine, were epitomised in a joint beer call attended also by a visiting Canadian fighter squadron, all of which featured in one of the great piano-burning stories of the time. Paddy had persuaded the NAAFI manager to lend the officers' mess a much-valued piano for the night so that Peter, an accomplished pianist, might lead the inevitable sing-song. Late that night a very sheepish Canadian presented the two station commanders with a single piano key, all that remained from the ashes of the much cherished instrument. After difficult negotiations, Paddy persuaded the NAAFI manager to accept compensation of £100, then called Peter to tell him the good news that a figure of £200 had been agreed, Brüggen's share being £100. With equal cunning, Peter told the Canadian commander the good news that the bill was £200 and that their share was £100. Then they all went back to work.

Solidarity between station commanders in RAF Germany was manifest in the 'Colonels' Dinner', held periodically at each other's houses and from which many a plot might have been hatched. The author can vouch for the fact that there was some trepidation in the headquarters at Rheindahlen whenever one of these events took place.

A major aircraft accident on 21 November 1974 had a happy ending and did nothing but enhance public relations. Flight Lieutenant Mike Keane, 14 Squadron, could have ejected with his navigator as soon as fire took hold in their Phantom and loss of control seemed imminent, but he remained with his aircraft until clear of a built-up area in Holland, ejecting later than was recommended. This 'act of unselfish courage' earned him a Queen's Commendation for Valuable Service in the Air and the gratitude of the local people.

Wing Commander Mike Stear, an experienced Phantom pilot who had flown the aircraft before on exchange duties with the USAF, took command of 17 Squadron from George Ord in December 1974. He began as he meant to go on, the squadron achieving 330 flying hours in January 1975, more than any RAF Germany Phantom squadron to date, despite a reduction in monthly targets, fuel conservation measures and Spey engine problems. The wing was now prioritizing the development of counter-air operations with the Phantom, Peter Harding leading a powerful team to HQ AAFCE in December to offer solutions which optimised the FGR2's weapons' delivery modes and particular capabilities to penetrate and egress at low level. Meanwhile, OC 4 Wing, RAF Regiment, Wing Commander George Stockdale, now firmly established at Brüggen with full responsibility for

Rapier operations, was leading in the development of procedures for the area's Short Range Air Defence (SHORAD).

On 15 April 1975, each of the three RAFG Phantom squadrons and two Buccaneer squadrons were joined by a Harrier and a Lightning, in a fly-past led by OC 14 Squadron, to celebrate their respective squadrons' sixtieth birthdays. Although fatigue constraints were now adding to their problems, the three Phantom squadrons exceeded 300 hours flying in February and March, as if to show Wing Commander Anthony Mumford, OC 14 Squadron (designate), who arrived at Brüggen with the first Jaguar for the squadron, that they were still very much in business. No. 17 Squadron received its first Jaguar in April but both squadrons were initially very short of aircraft spares and ground equipment for their twelve GR1s and one T2 aircraft.

The Crossbow Club, scene of many good times in the past and to come, with cabarets, discos, folk concerts and private parties, and a few less admirable events when spirits became a little too high, opened to all ranks and their adult families in April 1975. Trade would be brisk.

By this time work to 'harden' and disperse the station's operational facilities in the Airfield Survival Measures (ASM) programme was well advanced. Ten Hardened Aircraft Shelters (HAS) and a hardened Pilot Briefing Facility (PBF)

In April 1975, OC 14 Squadron, Wg Cdr Derek Hine, led this fly-past of three RAF Germany Phantoms, two Buccaneers, a Lightning and Harrier, to celebrate the 60th anniversaries of their respective squadrons. (*RAF Brüggen*)

would be dispersed tactically in each of the four corners of the airfield, using natural cover and sowing suitable vegetation in an attempt to destroy the contours and add camouflage to soil-covered roofs. The network of taxiways was designed to give some redundancy, in an attempt to avoid a HAS becoming isolated. One Phantom or two Jaguars could be accommodated in, started up and taxied out from each HAS, and be winched in backwards on return for refueling and re-arming under cover. A custom-built Command Operations Centre (COC) located on the edge of the domestic area, would occupy an extensively modified HAS, the COC and all four PBFs being equipped with auxiliary power units and air filtration plants, enabled the incumbents to continue to operate without gas masks during periods of tension, but masks were always worn as an added precaution when a local air attack seemed imminent.

That spring of 1975 was unusually dry, good in most ways but not all. OC Ops Wing, Wing Commander Tinkle Bell (then on his second tour at Brüggen) observed, 'It is ironic that the record for low rainfall coincides with the urgent need to grow grass in the south-east dispersal as the contractor completes his construction work. Without grass we face a FOD problem as the jet blast of taxying aircraft moves the loose soil on to the complex of taxiways and the pans, and the accompanying erosion jeopardises the seeds' chance of survival.' The site was not yet ready for the Jaguars of 14 Squadron. This was one of the few comments in official records on the momentous work which went into this ASM programme, the biggest airfield construction programme at any RAF station since the Second World War. Moreover, it continued without detriment to operational commitments, with little interruption to normal airfield operations and an overlapping aircraft replacement programme. The station's strike/attack role would remain unchanged but the modus operandi would be very different, the many problems arising from the simultaneous activities in this transition finding Brüggen at its best.

Wing Commander Gordon Massie took over 25 Squadron in March 1975. Often in the shadow of the flying squadrons, it was making the best of a difficult job with obsolescent Bloodhound equipment and drew unsolicited praise from Peter Harding for its sense of duty, surprisingly high levels of serviceability, and commitment to the station generally. This was the year when Squadron Leader Neil Pollock led his 25 Squadron shooting team to victory in the Champion's Cup at Bisley.

Albeit also in the shadows, the contribution made to the station's professional and domestic life by Major Kipness and his USAF detachment did not go unnoticed; the doors of 'Little America' were always open to the RAF and its personnel mingled freely. Mrs Kipness was said to have had the best of British hats for one of the Royal Visits, and it became a ritual for the USAF commander to have a good cigar ready for the station commander to light up as soon as the last aircraft got airborne in the mass strike launch which invariably brought live flying/evaluation exercises to an end.

The station commander presents Sqn Ldr Neil Pollock, and his team from 25 Squadron, with the Champion's Cup for shooting, won at Bisley in 1975. (*Peter Harding*)

New domestic facilities were also being completed on the northern side of the runway and June was a busy month for all. On the sixth, Group Captain Leonard Cheshire formally opened the Cheshire Middle School, to cater for a mix of 9 to 13-year-old RAF and Army children from Brüggen and Bracht. Then on the seventeenth, Group Captain Douglas Bader opened the Bader First School, to supplement the Barnes Wallis First School for 5 to 9-year-old children. Both distinguished gentlemen and their ladies stayed with Peter Harding in Brüggen House, each leaving lasting, if very different, memories with those who dined with them there. Finally, there was the annual AOC's Inspection on 24 of June.

Serious problems with the Phantom's fuel system, 'oil-canning' with leaks and the risk of fire, threatened the traditional mass fly-past for the Queen's Birthday in June. However, 431 MU pulled out all the stops to recover the nine Brüggen and nine Laarbruch Phantoms grounded as a consequence, and on the day Mike Stear led a formation of sixteen aircraft over Rheindahlen.

In July, their last month together, all three Phantom squadrons achieved their flying tasks before 14 (Phantom) Squadron began its run-down and 14 (Jaguar) Squadron moved in to the south-east corner of the airfield, pioneering hardened and permanently dispersed, single-seat strike/attack operations in the RAF. Jaguar serviceability was improving slowly, but spares were still in short supply; the aircraft had been cleared to operate in temperatures up to 40° Centigrade, but not below specified dew points.

Gp Capt and Mrs Douglas Bader, at Brüggen in June 1975 to open the Bader First
School, hosted by the station commander and OC 14 Squadron, Wg Cdr Derek Hine.
(*Peter Harding*)

Brüggen Phantoms get together for a fly-past over HQ RAF Germany, (below) led by OC 17 Squadron, Wg Cdr Mike Stear, to help celebrate the Queen's Birthday, 1975. (*RAF Brüggen*)

No. 17 (Jaguar) Squadron formed officially on 1 September, with eight pilots and seven aircraft and, when HRH The Princess Margaret visited Brüggen on 24 September, she was treated to a display of Phantoms and Jaguars to reflect the overlapping re-equipment programme. One of the highlights was a Phantom aerobatic display by Flight Lieutenant Jock Watson and his navigator, Flight Lieutenant John Cosgrove, who went on to impress many other audiences throughout 1975.

All this meant considerable domestic turbulence, with an enlarged Families Flight working at full stretch and married quarters at a premium. There were now 1,322 quarters on the station, while the families of 206 other ranks lived in private accommodation in Germany and another sixty-two in Holland, where there were also 114 individual hirings in the Donderberg area.

'Over here – or is it over there?' Wg Cdr Anthony Mumford leads HRH The Princess Margaret, Gp Capt Peter Harding the Lady in Waiting, on a tour of 14 Squadron in September 1975. (*Peter Harding*)

In the Control Tower, Brüggen's OC Ops Wg, Wg Cdr 'Tinkle' Bell, briefs Princess Margaret on the flying display. (*Tinkle Bell*)

Royal Visit, September 1975. Princess Margaret is flanked by the C-in-C AM Sir Nigel Maynard and the Station Commander Gp Capt Peter Harding. (*Tinkle Bell*)

While these changes were taking place there were sinister stirrings on the domestic front, with the ladies on the station beginning to flex their muscles, using the *Brüggen Circuit* to jump on the bandwagon driven by the Rt Hon Mrs Thatcher in this International Women's Year of 1975. The Sex Discrimination Act and Equal Opportunities Commission encouraged the stand-in editor to float a 'Wives' Page', which called on the women of the station to 'take the initiative' at all levels. Nothing seemed likely to be the same again but subsequent copies showed the movement to be more benign than was first feared by the menfolk. By fair means and foul, move and countermove, the crusade progressed before the status quo prevailed, the latter helped by a story which appeared later in the *Circuit* (with apologies to 'MCP'). It seems that a dynamic lady official, not known to take 'no' for an answer, picked up a 'Herr Ludwig' from the guardroom and took him to St. Andrew's Church Hall to deliver a presentation to the Wives' Club on glass-blowing. The man spoke very little English but, subdued by charm, he did what he was told. On finding the hall locked, the worthy lady left her guest and took a lift back to the guardroom for the key. There she met a second Herr Ludwig, who seemed to know a thing or two about glass-blowing, and back they went together to the hall, where the first Herr Ludwig was nowhere to be seen. He, in fact, was a works contractor who spoke no English, and he had seized his chance to escape from this mad English woman

127

who had kidnapped him and driven him to some dark and secluded place before changing cars and driving off. Where he went no one knows but questions were raised on the prudence of devolving power to new aspirants who had yet to learn that most important of service advices: 'never assume – check'.

Adding to the airfield's defences, No. 66 Squadron, RAF Regiment, arrived at Brüggen with their Rapier missiles in September 1975, to join No. 4 Wing RAF Regiment, under George Stockdale's command. The squadron took three months to become operational and was declared to SACEUR on 1 January 1976.

No. 66 Squadron (soon to become 37 Squadron), RAF Regiment, arrived at Brüggen in 1975, with Rapier missiles for airfield defence. (*RAF News*)

November was a significant month for 14 Squadron; the Phantoms departed with their flight safety record intact and the Jaguars won the Salmond Trophy only eight months after their first aircraft had arrived at Brüggen. Raz Ball was back at Brüggen after converting from the Phantom to the Jaguar, and continued his winning streak by scoring 100% on his competition sortie.

November 1975. A 14 Squadron Phantom, crewed by Wg Cdr Derek Hine and Flt Lt 'Bertie' Southcombe, peals off in farewell from a Jaguar GR1 flown by the new CO, Wg Cdr Anthony Mumford. (*Brüggen Circuit*)

Many innovative ways were found to sustain acceptable lifestyles without prejudice to the new ASM measures, but some were ill-conceived. Works supervisor Willie Luys queried one Form 2110 (new works request), raised by an overzealous young officer, for a window to be installed in the toilet of the squadron's airtight, blast proof PBF. The request was withdrawn.

The last of 17 Squadron's Phantoms departed in February 1976, the diarist reporting that in the last five and a half years its aircraft had flown 16,500 hours and consumed 20 million gallons of fuel, enough to run every car at Brüggen for thirty years; 1,118,800 man hours had gone into generating these hours and three lives had been lost. The squadron got through five 'bosses' and ten flight commanders, the aircrew climbed a quarter of a million rungs to board their aircraft and the groundcrew opened or closed the HAS doors 3,000 times. Pre-empting the question 'Was it all worth it?' he added a reminder that the aim had been to help deter war and that there had been no war. Although it had flown some 8 million miles in the Phantom, 17 Squadron had got no further abroad than Deci. How life would change.

Last in and last out with the Phantom at Brüggen, No. 31 Squadron, reinforced from the disbanding squadrons, bore the brunt of QRA during the transition, got plenty of flying and weapons training, and saw the Phantom out with style. It celebrated its Diamond Jubilee in October and excelled when representing RAF Germany at the 1976 TWM at Twenthe Air Base in Holland. The squadron's last APC at Deci also went well in the air but was not without incident on the ground. As one of his 'swan-songs', OC 31 Squadron, Wing Commander Tom Stonor, blazed a trail from Sardinia to Turkey, sensibly taking his SEngO with him. Perhaps he had a premonition that mischief might be afoot and counselled his men to behave themselves in his absence, but he got back to Deci too late to see a well-known tree outside the 'Pig and Whistle' watering hole for pilots, catch fire mysteriously – apparently of its own accord.

Looking back in their retirement, Air Chief Marshals Sir Sandy Wilson and Sir Patrick Hine, both of whom would go on to command RAF Germany and beyond, shared views on the impact of the multi-role Phantom. Sandy Wilson saw it as a watershed in the post-war development of RAF air power and Paddy Hine believed that the first RAF Phantom squadrons in Germany, manned by experienced crews with a mix of Canberra, Hunter and Lightning backgrounds, heralded a new era in operational capability. While the aircraft was not difficult to fly it could 'bite' if mishandled and its great potential, with an inherently complicated radar and INAS, depended on a great deal of support on the ground and maximum crew co-operation in the air. These prerequisites were clearly in place at Brüggen, leading Paddy Hine to reflect that 'we really had a very sharp capability'. TWMs and above all the AAFCE run, multinational Taceval system, which spawned a competitive spirit, pride of achievement and cross fertilisation of ideas, proved that the RAF Germany Phantoms had set new standards in their field which would be hard to match. Brüggen was leading the way.

At this mid-point in the station's history it is worth looking at the threats it faced and how its offensive and defensive measures were put to the test in the much talked of Taceval. Notwithstanding the Cold War of political and military words and actions, NATO could not be sure if, when, or how, the Warsaw Pact (WP) would take the next step and quite rightly prepared for the worst in a collective endeavour. Brüggen made a significant contribution to this effort, albeit with changing roles, primarily with an increasing commitment to nuclear deterrence. As such it was an obvious target for the Pact and revelations since the Cold War have shown the wisdom of being prepared for anything.

When West German officers gained access to the East German military headquarters at Strausberg, on the eastern outskirts of Berlin, they found exercise plans which confirmed the aggressive intentions of the WP. One scenario, rehearsed in 1983, postulated an advance to the Dutch border in three days, thereby overrunning Brüggen, but this was based on the use of tactical nuclear weapons from the start and the associated maps indicated the weapons which might have been used against key targets in the West. Such a proposition came as a surprise to many in NATO, and is still thought to have been an unlikely strategy; indeed it may have been no more than an academic exercise hypothesis. The more comforting wisdom envisaged a large scale conventional offensive by air and ground forces with a progressive escalation into nuclear warfare if there was no political solution. Brüggen was well prepared for any eventuality; it had formidable 'teeth' and diverse defensive means to survive and operate and, given the necessary command, control, communications and intelligence (C3I), there was every expectation that it would acquit itself well.

Crucial to Brüggen's reinvention was the establishment of fully-integrated, survivable C3I facilities in the COC, linked firmly into the NATO network to run operations at station level as required by the overall theatre plan. It also made sense to bring flying and logistic activities together in peacetime as they would operate in war, thus ensuring that permanent and co-opted staffs were familiar with the necessary systems and procedures, that they functioned correctly and remained in constant use.

To this end the COC was organised on two levels. Below, OC Eng Wg presided over engineering and supply staffs, their consoles and displays in full view of the 'bridge' above, where all operations were orchestrated by the Force Commander (the station commander). Immediately to hand were the Ground Defence Commander (OC Admin Wg), the Airfield Damage Repair Commander (OC 52 Sqn, RE) and the SHORAD Commander (OC 4 Wg). The bridge itself, manned by dedicated operations officers 24 hours a day every day throughout the year, up-dated a display of alert and flying states, aircraft, SAM and airfield status, weather information and incidents as they occurred on the station. Out of sight, but again immediately available within the COC, were the navigation, plans and intelligence support staffs.

This much can now be revealed to the many who worked elsewhere at Brüggen but were not normally allowed access to this co-ordinating hub of all station activities. Not for them the memories of benign peacetime day-to-day routines, of impressive action when the COC geared up for war, or when the much-vaunted calm and good humour on the bridge and within the command cells may have lapsed as tensions mounted – but the incumbents would not be found wanting.

Despite every practical measure, there could be no guarantees of survival in war, and at Brüggen an alternate COC was set up in a semi-underground bunker, equipped with fully duplicated displays and communications. Here, the Deputy Force Commander (OC Ops Wg) would preside over full manning, ever ready to take command and control. Should both primary and secondary COCs be rendered unusable, executive authority would be transferred again to a pre-selected PBF. All this was rehearsed regularly, culminating in the annual Tacevals which demonstrated to NATO the flexibility and redundancy inherent in Brüggen's readiness for war. OC Ops Wg, Tinkle Bell, was a prime mover in the development of the necessary systems and procedures to bring the whole wing together and get the best out of the facilities provided; he would be rewarded with an OBE and

In January 1976, Air Cdre Peter Harding handed over the key to the station and symbol of the time, a well-worn gas mask, to Gp Capt John Walker. (*RAF Brüggen*)

The USAF Detachment, custodians of the American nuclear bombs with which the Canberras and Phantoms had been equipped, left Brüggen in 1975. Jaguars would carry British nuclear weapons. (*RAF Brüggen*)

promotion at the end of his tour. The next chapter includes a description of how a typical NATO Taceval simulated, as far as was possible, war in the Central Region of Europe and how the station would have reacted. This was a whole new 'ball game' and in its reincarnation Brüggen was ready for it as Peter Harding handed over the station to Group Captain John Walker in January 1976.

Chapter Six

Jaguar Strike Wing

The Phantom men welcomed Jaguars to Brüggen with saucers of milk but the laugh was soon on them as the newcomers started to prove themselves, winning national and international accolades against the best in NATO. With a sophisticated Navigation and Weapons Aiming Sub-System (NAVWASS), one man was now doing the work of two and doing it well; the Jaguar was much-liked, cheaper to operate and perhaps no more troublesome than should have been expected from a joint venture and an aircraft originally designed for advanced training. Few would have foreseen then that it would still be operating, with a new NAVWASS, electronic countermeasures (ECM), air-to-air missiles (AAMs) and precision guided munitions (PGMs), with a limited night capability, well into the new millennium.

Some said that, with a full load of 1,000lb bombs, the Jaguar could not get airborne without the curvature of the earth, somewhat of an exaggeration, but the early variants would have benefitted from more power. However, despite this limitation the two small Adour engines (up-rated later) were comfortably reliable, there were plenty of jobs for the Jaguar in the Central Region. Without external stores the aircraft was every pilot's dream. In its early days, the 286-chip NAVWASS computer tended to 'freeze' or 'dump' with monotonous regularity in the hands of computer illiterates and the older 'map and stopwatch brigade' sometimes had some difficulty making the system work well for them, and would continue quite happily using the rudimentary C2J compass. The younger men, brought up on calculators and computers, took more readily to this newfangled technology, but they too learned to operate effectively without it. There is no doubt that the NAVWASS and its moving map display added significantly to overall capability when it was working and became invaluable as it developed in capability and reliability over the years.

No. 14 Squadron won the Salmond Trophy in each of its first three years with the Jaguar. This was attributed in large part to Anthony Mumford's dedication to the NAVWASS: he and his flight commanders, Duncan Griffiths and Mick Hindley, and their SEngO, Mike Broadbent, doing all they could to get 'the kit' right and the pilots fully capable in its operation. Sad then that at one trophy presentation the C-in-C should refer to him as Wing Commander 'Mugford' (who can say whether

Anthony's subsequent mispronunciation of the C-in-C's name in his acceptance speech was deliberate?). Acrimony was never far away in these competitions, two Jaguar executives being the next to come to blows during one of the post-exercise celebrations. OC 14 Squadron is said to have remonstrated with one of the two combatants in his office on the following morning over a glass of sherry – vintage Anthony! In 1976, the squadron would be the first in the RAF to qualify in the single-seat nuclear role.

Anthony was typically reticent over his contribution to this success story and humble over his personal skills in the air; indeed, he needed some persuasion to include himself in one Salmond team when a place became vacant. He was given 'Echo', the aircraft with the best bombing reputation on the squadron, and overflew the field target precisely on time and on track, to score a direct hit with his first bomb in a laydown attack within an acceptable four seconds of his assigned time over target. However, his next bomb, from a dive attack, was not seen to explode, denying him what might otherwise have been a perfect score. With tongue in cheek, he explained to his squadron warrant officer, Mr Menzies, that he had aimed the bomb at the open window of the lorry target and that the bomb probably ended up on the driver's seat. Dismayed that his squadron's reputation might be at stake, Mr Menzies set off at once in a Land Rover, with his armourers, to search for the errant bomb. They were stopped in time at the guardroom; 14 Squadron had done enough already to win the competition.

A 14 Squadron Jaguar delivers a standard load of 4 x 1000lb 'dumb' bombs.
(*RAF Brüggen*)

Warrant Officer Menzies was a strong and loyal leader in the old style, both at work and play. Rarely was his legendary stamina found wanting, but it did lapse during one gruelling detachment to the French base of St. Dizier. To ensure that he would not forget the occasion, his minions fitted piano wheels to the heels of one of his pairs of shoes, to facilitate his easier removal from any future marathons of the social kind, and to his credit he was seen proudly wearing them many years later. Mr Menzies was properly honoured at the end of his tour with an MBE. Anthony was made an OBE and in typical Mumford style offset disappointment on the squadron that it was not allowed to keep the Salmond Trophy, after winning it three times running, by presenting a suitable memento from the Silver Vaults.

Heritage and community relations were served well again in 1975 when an offer by Brüggen's Mechanical Transport Officer, Flight Lieutenant Len Woodgate, to oversee the refurbishment of the Dutch Overloon Museum's Spitfire by the station workshops was accepted gratefully. At Brüggen, thirty men completed the job in five months – but not without mishap. Ron Bretherton, an MT NCO, had devised an ingenious way of moving the aircraft without a towing arm, but he was not to hand when the veteran aircraft came adrift from a towing vehicle on the taxiway. The Spitfire was damaged and amazingly remained where it was, unnoticed until a visiting Canberra pilot, perhaps believing he was in a time warp, reported that there appeared to be a pilotless, battle-damaged Spitfire blocking his path. Recovery and repairs were effected in time for a ceremonial handover on 8 April, but on the aircraft's return to Overloon the accompanying heavy crane had a puncture, closing a busy Dutch road. Again, the men from MT rose to the occasion and finished the job.

Achtung Spitfire! In 1975, Brüggen's MT Flight moves the Dutch Overloon Museum Spitfire to the station for refurbishment. (*Brüggen Circuit*)

Neither did things go smoothly for the Jaguar simulator. With undue optimism, Flight Sergeant 'Geordie' Carlyle had led fifteen men to Brüggen in October 1974 to make ready for the containerised system. In fact, it arrived eighteen months later on five articulated 'rubber ducks' which lumbered through the main gates at 0230 hours one morning, having got lost in Holland, and in the middle of a station exercise. This warlike environment frightened the life out of the truck drivers from peaceful England and it was some hours before they could be persuaded to take their vehicles round the airfield to the simulator's concrete platforms adjacent to the QRA site. The facility was up and running within five days, the Jaguar pilots greeting this with mixed emotions as the instructors, Flight Lieutenants Clive Osborne and Sam Mason, started putting them through their paces.

Its re-equipment with Jaguars complete, Wing Commander Roy Humphreyson took command of 17 Squadron in early 1976, and followed the training pattern established by 14 Squadron.

When the squadron commander designate of No. 31 (Jaguar) Squadron, Wing Commander Terry Nash, arrived at Brüggen in January 1976 he found that the other two squadrons were already using the aircraft destined for his squadron, but in his usual deceivingly diplomatic way he soon had them where they belonged, in the north-west corner. Beginning with a dual sortie in a Jaguar T2 at Brüggen on 28 January, he collected the first of the squadron's single-seat GR1s on 2 February and started checking out his pilots with Flight Lieutenant Norman Beasant on

One of 17 Squadron's first 'Blackhand' Jaguar GR1s, fully loaded with Cluster Bomb Units (CBUs) – an armed, NBC-equipped guard in the background. (*RAF Brüggen*)

16 February. On 24 March, he flew with Flight Lieutenant Nigel Day, the first pilot to convert to the aircraft on the squadron without undergoing a formal course. Those pilots available at the start were soon amassing forty flying hours a month.

With paint still wet on the walls of its operations room, evidence of a busy weekend for all on 31 Squadron (including some of the wives!), the NATO Taceval team came and went, awarding the highest marks possible for extraordinary achievement. The squadron was declared fully operational, immediately offered to SACEUR, and welcomed to QRA duties. The squadron then took to the road, detached first to Laarbruch in July, while works services were carried out at Brüggen, then to Leuchars to represent RAF Germany at the Strike Command Fighter Meet and Tactical Bombing Competition (TBC), before their first APC at Deci in September.

Spiritual life on the station, in all its diversity, was not neglected. After ten weeks of major refurbishment, St. Andrew's Church was rededicated on 20 June 1976 rendering it, in the words of the Principal Chaplain, Reverend L.K. Darbyshire, 'One of the loveliest Church of Scotland and Free Churches (CSFC) in the RAF'. With industry and ingenuity, Messrs Jeffs and Hanks of Brüggen PSA, with Major Darrel and his Mobile Civilian Artisans Group (MCAG), had interpreted the aspirations of the station's CSFC Chaplain, the Reverend R. Raymond Brown, to excellent effect and the large congregation had added many attractive artefacts.

The padres were equally practical. They had designs on funds known to be building up at 431 MU but Wing Commander Peter Arthur, who took command in 1976, was quick to disabuse them; that money was for a commemorative tile in the RAF Church, St. Clement Danes.

Expanding its empire, the MU now owned the greater part of Hangar 4 for second-line servicing of Spey and Adour engines, 31 Squadron retaining only limited office space for its aircrew when it went over to dispersed operations. In the woods nearby, the MU was now testing, calibrating and diagnosing faults in the Jaguar's Adour Uninstalled Test Facility, testing 172 engines in the first fifteen months, with a dramatic reduction in ground runs and overall costs.

Peter Arthur also rationalised the MU's contribution to Brüggen's exercises, bearing in mind its independent responsibilities, diverse and widespread commitments in war. He ensured that all his personnel were fully-equipped and trained in the use of their personal weapons for basic defence duties and was then able to offer the station a defence flight of one officer and sixty men from whoever was available at the time.

No. 66 Squadron, RAF Regiment, was redesignated No. 37 Squadron on 1 April 1976, the year in which the squadron was granted its Standard for twenty-five years of unbroken service. No. 37 Squadron, with a badge depicting the head of a typical English fighting Bill (a formidable and versatile weapon in the hands of the foot soldier and hence the squadron's motto 'Versatilis') was soon in the headlines with Senior Aircraftsman Cosbie-Ross firing the 1000th Rapier missile at the squadron's MPC in the Outer Hebrides in June 1976.

Not to be ignored, their big brothers on 25 Squadron remained ever watchful, with their impressive array of Bloodhounds pointing eastwards and their contribution admirably summed up in the poem by D.R. Conran-Smith 'Bloodhound' which finishes thus:

> Our SAM's a semi-active bird, his homing is quite true:
> Unlike his small foil counterpart he stoppeth one in two.
> And that is at the very worst for, when all things are right,
> He'll hit each single aeroplane that cometh in his sight.
> It matters little how much noise the foe he may deploy –
> For noise to Bloodhound missiles is the thing they most enjoy.
> And other countermeasures too he'll handle in his stride
> This noble, versatile old bird that sits his perch with pride
> So when you gauge our air defence we hope that you'll take heart
> And rest more easy knowing that once more our SAM's a part.

As for day-to-day ground defence against intruders, be they self-styled peacemakers simply bent on mischief or clandestine forces on intelligence-gathering missions, this was primarily the responsibility of Brüggen's security squadron, at this time developing under the command of Squadron Leader Bill Floydd. A large part of this service police force, already more than 200 strong, was on duty at all times, with dogs, static guards, foot and mobile patrols all armed when required, the squadron's role including the security of nuclear weapons and their ultimate release to the aircrew in war.

In exercise and war, the squadron would become part of the overall defence force, with RAF Regiment, army, organic and specialist ground defence units all responsible to the defence commander.

No. 14 Squadron lost its first Jaguar on the North German Plain one Friday afternoon in the summer of 1976. The officers of the squadron repaired at once to the 'Scruffs Bar' at Brüggen, to remember their friend in the traditional manner – Anthony Mumford delivering a poignant eulogy.

No. 20 Squadron, the 'Double Crossers', became the fourth Jaguar squadron at Brüggen. Formed in the UK in August 1915, the squadron was in France by the end of that year, where it served with distinction until the end of the First World War. Moving to India in 1919, it was given various roles until disbanding at the end of the 1940s. Resurrected in 1951 with Vampires at Jever, the squadron then served at Oldenburg, Ahlhorn and Gütersloh, with Sabres and Hunters, before moving to Singapore in 1961, remaining in the Far East with Hunters until it disbanded again in 1977. Later that year it returned to Germany as a Harrier squadron at Wildenrath, where it continued to serve until the new squadron reformed with Jaguars at Brüggen on 1 March 1977. Many of the new 20 Squadron's pilots came from the now defunct 45/58 (Hunter) Squadron or had been instructors at the Tactical Weapons Unit (TWU). They knew each other and were well-tried fighter/ground attack men – but not on the Jaguar. One of them, Flight Lieutenant Ian Hall, had the added challenge of 'strike training officer', and he remembers that their combined ignorance of the aircraft and its new role made it hard work but that many already close friendships gave the squadron a running start.

OC 20 Squadron, Wing Commander Mike Gibson, retains vivid first impressions of his new workplace: 'I was immediately struck by the grim purposefulness of the place; it looked as though it meant business. The toned-down HASs on the heavily forested site were gaunt and desolate-looking and, being built alongside dispersal pans with high revetment walls which were retained, it was impossible to see more than a small fraction of the complex at any one time. The site itself had a major peacetime operational drawback in that, unlike the other squadron areas, it did not have separate entry and exit taxiways. It being impossible, because of the trees, to see what was coming, careful organisation of aircraft movements was imperative to avoid head-on conflicts on the single narrow taxiway. An alternative access, through the QRA site, was for use in war only; in peacetime this was 'sealed off like Fort Knox'.

Being the last squadron to form at the station had at least one advantage. Noise levels from air conditioning pumps in the other three squadrons having been found unacceptable, 20 Squadron's PBF was carpeted before the building was occupied. However, there were also disadvantages, everything needed to make life more comfortable, and not authorised officially, having been purloined already by the other squadrons.

First things first, the squadron turned out with all hands to build perimeter defences, a difficult task with heavy afforestation denying line of sight between ideal piquet posts and a reluctance of the German Forstmeister to allow the removal of offending trees. As if this was not enough, one HAS was in the way of errant golf balls from that holy-of-holies, the RAF Germany Golf Course, and some had already found lodgings in the HAS exhaust vent doors. Defence imperatives demanded a barbed wire fence across the offending fairway but priorities were clear and the rules were 'adjusted'; golf was allowed to proceed unhindered and aircraft were parked, however inconveniently, out of range. Realities, perseverance and compromise prevailed, allowing seemingly intractable problems to be overcome in time for the squadron to achieve its all-important operational declaration date.

The Brüggen squadrons shared the problem of how to operate effectively from dispersed and hardened accommodation, under threat from air attack and from ground intruders in a conventional, nuclear, biological and chemical environment. Realism was the name of the game and exercises would now simulate everything which could be expected in war. Typically, groundcrew and pilots emerging from their shelters after a raid were likely to find actual fires or very realistic-looking unexploded bombs between them and their aircraft and they soon learned to react accordingly. Every conceivable contingency was rehearsed. On 20 Squadron a Junior Technician, revered by his peers if not by his masters, was briefed by the exercise directing staff ('distaff') to tear off his respirator in front of his SNCOs and to say to his shift boss 'I've had this, I'm going home' – and walk off. This he did, but his leadership was such that others followed suit, shouting, 'We're with you mate!'

Otherwise normal people, distaff belonged to a generally unloved breed, as this ode (by a sensibly anonymous writer) suggests:

> He is a very humble man, all meek and mild and calm,
> He wanders slowly round the camp with smoke and gas and bomb,
> Occasionally throws a thunderflash or sets off an alarm
> To simply test efficiency, he doesn't mean no harm,
> So next time that you see him, don't be mean and spiteful
> Remember that he's just like you – then belt him with your rifle.

There were some very serious lessons to be learned. On one occasion, when an evacuation of the PBF was ordered through an emergency exit, its air lock was filled with CS gas to teach those who were not wearing their gas masks a hard lesson. However, before the evacuation could take place the gas blew back into the PBF revealing an underpressure therein, rather than the necessary overpressure, and giving those inmates not fully protected a very nasty experience. As a result, a fault found in the pumps led to the introduction of a more rigid servicing schedule and installation of an overpressure meter.

By now, almost all trades were open to the girls and Mike Gibson was quick to pay tribute to his female workers. He recalled that in this 'progressive experiment, the girls were excellent trades-persons, they had to be in order to survive in the aggressively masculine training system of the time, and the men had to raise their game if they were to compete. Having women on the squadron also proved to be a particularly civilising influence and I could have taken my mother into the airmen's crewroom at any time without fear of her being embarrassed by the decor or language.'

At that time, the girls were not allowed to bear arms or, therefore, take their share of the guard duties. On a visit to 20 Squadron, Director WRAF met a diminutive girl, barely five feet tall, an airframe fitter who was repairing the nose of a Jaguar following a bird strike, and asked her if there was anything she needed. 'Yes ma'am, there is,' she replied. 'They won't give me a gun!' Shortly thereafter, the girls were allowed to bear arms and play a full part in all the station's military activities.

The now Air Vice-Marshal, Mike Gibson also remembers the extraordinary complexities of getting the right pilot to the right aircraft with the right weapons load, in the right HAS and with the correct release procedures, perhaps with many distractions in the simulated war, but it became a matter of routine. He points with pride to the motivation and competence of relatively very junior and inexperienced men and women, whose enterprise and initiatives so often prevented errors and emergencies – thus saving the day. This was just as well because things did not always go right. The abundance of information piped into the PBF was no substitute for sight of the real world outside. OC 20 Squadron remembers briefing a section for an exercise mission and sending them out to their HASs, only to have them return within seconds pleading, 'Boss, do you really want us to go – it's pitch black outside and snowing heavily?'

The same went for the groundcrew and Brüggen welcomed the reinvention of the corporal, a breed which enjoyed responsibility and scorned the need for close supervision; they rose to the challenge, enjoyed their status and discharged their duties reliably and effectively.

This spirit flowed through all levels on the station, epitomised by the conduct of one of 20 Squadron's most junior airmen during a very successful Taceval. This young man, not usually noted for his reliability, had missed the transport from the domestic site to the squadron and was on the three mile trek by foot at a deserted spot on the perimeter track when an air raid warning sounded. He donned his respirator and protective clothing immediately, took all the prescribed actions and sought cover in a far ditch. Unknown to him, the Taceval chief was watching him through his binoculars and later gave great credit for this unsolicited demonstration of professionalism at the lowest level.

Ian Hall reminisced over another daunting challenge at Brüggen, that of surviving the social whirl. With 'Saturday Night Fever' all the rage, the whole station mixed together regardless of unit loyalties 'as the Heineken and Carlsberg flowed'. This was also 'Muppet' time, certain Brüggen characters soon finding themselves branded with names such as 'Animal' and 'Gonzo', for their remarkable similarity in looks or behaviour. It was work hard and play hard.

In May 1977, Jaguars swept the board in the Salmond competition, with 14 Squadron winning again, followed by 17, II and 31 Squadrons. Eight Jaguar pilots achieved maximum possible scores, leading CAS, Air Chief Marshal Sir Neil Cameron to observe: 'Jaguar is twenty times as effective as the Venom of twenty-five years ago; we are now in the "bomb in the bucket" era'. The competition having become so one-sided, a line search was included subsequently – to give the Buccaneer squadrons a chance.

With inputs from industry and the MU at St. Athan, Peter Arthur was now presiding over major advances in battle damage repair (BDR), offering advice on what could be achieved speedily and in adverse conditions, improvising with whatever resources were available to enable at least one safe flight. In 1977, in order to make this training more realistic, the MU asked the station's bomb disposal men to blow the wings off a shark-nosed B(I)8 Canberra decoy which had long graced the eastern end of the airfield, a task completed with great glee and a large bang. Brüggen benefited directly from this local expertise but 431 MU was also called on to spread the word throughout NATO and in 1978 was the key player at a major seminar on BDR for senior staff and specialists at HQ AAFCE, Ramstein. Ramstein's '*Ramjet*' newspaper reported 'Britain's RAF is by far the furthest along', and that the USAF in Europe intended to begin initial training using RAF BDR facilities. Credit indeed.

Another hallmark of the Jaguar years was the give and take between the squadrons and the support they enjoyed from the station's logistic organisation. This was introduced in the COC by Squadron Leader Dick Coutts and his team of specialist SNCOs; they reported directly to OC Eng Wg, Wing Commander David Pugh and later Wing Commander David Birch, but always in liaison with operational staffs in the gallery above. It was a most amicable relationship.

Meanwhile, Flight Lieutenant Bill Taylor ran station flight and the NATO 'Ample Gain' cross-servicing facility in Hangar 2, earning an enviable reputation for the efficient and expeditious turnround and rearming facility for a wide variety of visiting NATO combat aircraft.

Brüggen now went beyond its normal charitable boundaries in gifting £3,000 to the British Limbless Ex-Servicemens' Association Homes (BLESMA), in recognition of the British Army's work in Northern Ireland, bringing 'warm and sincere thanks' from the Army Benevolent Fund. In the forefront of fund-raising, the wives' club now had a full page to themselves in the *Brüggen Circuit* and boasted

Long a decoy in the south-east corner of the airfield, this Canberra B(I)8 was 'dismantled' by Brüggen's bomb disposal men. (*Brüggen Circuit*)

an average attendance twice that of any other such club in Germany. Through their regular visits to units on the station, the wives became better acquainted with what their men were up to at work – with mixed consequences. Social facilities were also improving all the time, typically with the old American Club in Building 59 being converted for use by the corporals' and married families' clubs with generous donations and enterprising self-help. The station's first lady was not beyond a little cunning to improve welfare by any means, provoking Bridget Arthur with the comment that 431 MU was too big a unit to have a successful wives' coffee morning. Using the MU's *Vier Drei Ein* ('Fear Dry Inn') as a venue, Bridget soon proved her wrong, *inter alia* bringing her 'mother hens' together with many lonely wives and putting them in touch with professionals and friends who might help them with any problems.

Every station has its characters, to keep executives on their toes and many others apprehensive or amused; they are a mixed blessing, but RAF bar talk, reunions and history would be the worse without them. So it was with Brüggen Strike Wing of the late 1970s, no story of the time being complete without mention of a young, first tour pilot who earned a reputation for being different. Since he has not been found to give his side of the many versions of the many stories credited to him, he shall be called Flying Officer 'X'. Perhaps a reincarnation from the 1950s or before, when he might have melded more into the background, 'X' had not grasped the changes in culture since then or the disciplines required by contemporary times. After being asked to leave the nurses mess at Wegberg Hospital during a party for the Lancashire County Cricket Club, and having to return there with an apology to the Matron, banned from the Wildenrath Mess for anti-navigator activity and committing similar offences against a Canberra crew visiting Brüggen, OC 14 Squadron finally lost patience and offered him back into the system. The C-in-C himself then persuaded OC 31 Squadron to lead 'X' into better ways with firm guidance to all, but things then went from bad to worse. The end is said to have come during a detachment to Fassberg Air Base, where several allied air forces were pitting their wits against each other in the air and on the ground. It was on one riotous evening there that squadron commander number two dispatched 'X' to bed after fireworks, specifically forbidden, had exploded close to his master, and he was on his way out of his second squadron – and shortly thereafter Brüggen itself.

It remains unclear who left the message 'X is innocent', imprinted with weed killer in the officers' mess lawn after he left, but executives later reported on him with such memorable words as: 'I don't know what he would do to the Russians but he puts the fear of God into me.' Another wrote: 'He seems somewhat out of place in a peacetime environment and what he really needs is a good war. Should he ever find one then there is little doubt that he would end up with a chest full of medals, and if he became a prisoner of war he would make the camp commandant's life hell. Meanwhile he practices on me.'

After deliberations which went beyond the Air Force Board to ministerial level, Flying Officer 'X' was sent to RAF Finningley to fly trainee navigators for the fast-jet force. There, to the surprise of many, he acquitted himself well, was highly thought of and said to have been an excellent example to the young students! He then took early retirement, but appeared later on television in the 'Krypton Factor' and was last seen by the author at a Jaguar reunion when he burst through double doors into the bar, immaculately dressed and with a beautiful girl on each arm. 'X' did not go unnoticed and will not be forgotten.

On 14 June 1977, Flying Officer Tim Penn, 31 Squadron, was killed when his Jaguar crashed inexplicably in North Germany. A New Zealander, able pilot and popular officer, Tim had recently become engaged to Flight Lieutenant Jenny Cowper, a dental officer at Brüggen. From her very brief service training before

Fg Off Tim Penn, 31 Squadron, photographed from a Belgian Air Force Mirage.
(*Jenny Wilmshurst-Smith*)

Reward or retribution? Flt Lt Al Hudson flew Flt Lt Jenny Cowper, Station Dentist, in a 31 Squadron Jaguar T2. (*Jenny Wilmshurst-Smith*)

starting her RAF career at Brüggen, Jenny knew that she had to do something when she saw the flag waving from the station commander's car as it sped by, so she waved too – and the normally fearsome Group Captain John Walker waved back. Jenny's story had a happy ending; on 23 September 1978, she wed Flying Officer Simon Wilmshurst-Smith, No 31 Squadron's intelligence officer, and at the time of writing, they were running a private dental practice, where the author is one of the lucky ones still able to make good use of Jenny's expertise.

Under Terry Nash, who was always seeking a new challenge, 31 Squadron took over the tripartite Berlin Corridor commitment from a hard-pressed Harrier force and, in September 1977, pioneered Jaguar operations from German autobahns. Flying Officer Gary Rogers, first tourist, station rugby player and squadron standard bearer, was the first to fly a GR1 from a specially prepared autobahn strip at Hagen, north of Bremen, where the Luftwaffe had provided communications and logistics support for their Fiat G91s in Exercise 'Halt Fair'.

With synergies of thought and deed, in the air and on the ground, exchanges of all sorts with RCAF Starfighter men in the Black Forest were hot favourites with the Brüggen squadrons, not least 31 Squadron, but they were not without incident. During one visit, flight commander Jeff Morgan led from the front into one of the famous Baden Baden Spa pools, to find out too late that it was only inches deep; he bore the scars of leadership for some time but otherwise came to no lasting harm.

Fg Off Gary Rogers, 31 Squadron, was the first to land a Jaguar GR1 on an autobahn strip in North Germany, in September 1977. (*Brüggen Circuit*)

The Canadians did not always understand RAF social habits or humour. A call of 'dead ants', which demanded that everyone present fall to the ground and wave all four limbs skywards, often took them by surprise (particularly on a pedestrian crossing in downtown Roermond), costing them yet another round of drinks. They got their own back by 'bearnapping' 31 Squadron's mascot, 'Arris (a stuffed Panda named after a former CO, the legendary 'Bomber' Harris), but there was no shortage of volunteers to take the required ransom of wine to Baden Baden.

The fact that Jaguar had no on-board electronic countermeasures to help it survive in war, and could not, therefore, achieve top marks in Taceval, was unacceptable to John Walker, who would never countenance less than best. It was to John's bathtub musings that the *Guardian* newspaper, of 21 January 1978, attributed the concept of an interim chaff dispenser in the aircraft's brake parachute container welcoming, inter alia, this circumvention of bureaucratic processes and

147

the 'minute bill' incurred. The principle was simplicity itself. When triggered by the pilot, chaff was shot from spring-loaded tubes in a modified 4lb practice bomb casing, in a revolver-style action through holes in a rotating disc, the *Guardian* reporter witnessing 'lengths of broom handle rattling across the hangar floor' in a successful demonstration.

Engineering and Supply Wing was involved but 431 MU did the lion's share of the work, with various degrees of scepticism and support from higher levels. The job was done properly, with detailed drawings, the Jaguar Engineering Authority, an MOD approved Command Modification and flight clearances. After trials over Nordhorn Range, in which the chaff did succeed in breaking radar lock as required, all hands to the pump over the Christmas period ensured that every aircraft at Brüggen would be equipped with the facility before the Taceval early in 1978. When it came, the Taceval Team was convinced of the operational viability of the system, and gave high marks for this local enterprise.

John Walker, while he encouraged aggressive spirit where it belonged, was ruthless where it was misplaced and laid down guidelines on what alleged crimes his unit commanders could deal with. In time-honoured fashion, his executives

Wg Cdr Peter Arthur, OC 431 MU, shows AVM John Sutton, Deputy Commander RAF Germany, the station-inspired chaff dispenser installed in the Jaguar's brake parachute compartment. (*RAF Brüggen*)

sought to keep jurisdiction 'in house' and protect their best from the worst excesses of his punitive action. One squadron commander remembers exchanging erudite letters on definitions, typically on what constituted 'fisticuffs' as opposed to 'open-handed combat'. The reader is left to guess who won this war of words but, for whatever reason, 14 Squadron boasted a particularly low crime rate.

This theme of sensible discipline, spiced by interesting brands of leadership, continued to percolate throughout the station. Security Squadron enjoyed the full support of its immediate master, OC Admin Wg, Wing Commander Ben Nicol, and successive station commanders, with the present incumbent having a particular liking for the police dogs. Before he left, John Walker was dined out by the Police Club and made an 'Honorary Provost Marshal of RAF Brüggen', Bill Floydd presenting him with a suitable armband, notebook and white cover for his service cap. The next morning, a young pilot was stopped for speeding in his sports car, by a very senior officer wearing a white-capped hat.

No. 37 Squadron was also making its mark. In September 1977, it selected a team of four to take part in Exercise Parashot 77 at the Joint Services Parachute Centre, Bad Lippspringe. After parachuting with full equipment on to a precise position, the teams competed in specific tasks on a gruelling 20km patrol to test map-reading and radio procedures, ambush, shooting, helicopter and first aid drills, raft-building and vehicle maintenance. 3 Para were overall winners but

Gp Capt and Mrs John Walker introduced to the winners of the 1977 Brüggen Dog Show, by Sqn Ldr Bill Floydd, OC Security Squadron. (*Bill Floydd*)

37 Squadron did very well in this first test for the RAF Regiment against the cream of the British Army – and promised to return.

At 25 Squadron in the north-east corner of the station, Squadron Leader Neil Pollock remembers the very different life for the missile men, mainly aircrew officers on ground tours who were used to a more active life, and highly specialised tradesmen. Once the equipment had been set up it was merely a matter of keeping it serviceable, rehearsing procedures – and waiting. A shift system necessary to maintain instant readiness at all times meant that the whole squadron could not get together socially at one time, and a combination of these circumstances, so foreign to its many incumbents, placed morale at risk. There was no evidence of this; 25 Squadron was never found wanting in its operational role and excelled in station exercises and Tacevals, never losing sight of its priorities. During a mass exodus from its site after one hard, four-day exercise, an immaculately dressed wing commander arrived from Rheindahlen, identified himself and was waved through without more ado by a rather busy corporal on gate guard. However, the visitor stopped and announced, 'I'm here to do a pre-AOC's inspection and you should put on a better show than that.' 'Sorry sir,' said the weary corporal, pulling out his whistle, swinging it at the end of its chain, doffing his white hat and launching into 'Gimme the moonlight.......'. It is to be hoped that the wing commander remembered then what it was like to be on a static SAM site in Germany.

HQ, 'A' Flight and Bloodhound missiles of 25 Squadron in 1977. (*25 Squadron*)

The squadron was always very visible, playing an active role in many station activities. The CO, Wing Commander Ed Durham, who replaced Gordon Massie, was President of the Mess Committee, Neil Pollock ran his very successful shooting team and Flight Lieutenant John Wood was a highly enthusiastic chairman of the Bears Rugby Club. In more compensation for their routine life every advantage was taken of the many opportunities offered by service in Germany, particularly caravanning. No. 25 Squadron was indeed alive and well at Brüggen.

In his farewell message to the station in January 1978, John Walker spoke of Brüggen past, present and future, saying, 'The Canberra Wing was good, the Phantom Wing left us with a great act to follow but the Jaguar Wing has already proved itself as good as, if not better than both, and being on top of the first division feels good. It will get progressively more difficult to stay there as others try to emulate us but I am confident that Brüggen, in its present heart, will take some shifting.' He would soon be proved right.

Every effort was made to 'guesstimate' exactly when Taceval would come. Likely members of the distaff were interrogated by means of spurious invitations and enquiries as to suitable dates for staff visits, their diaries checked covertly; local hotel bookings were scrutinised and questions asked of an attendant at the local Aral garage, who was reputed to be the first to know everything about to happen on the base. The Taceval team was of course aware of all these efforts and resorted to equal subterfuge to keep the all-important date secret, and in one particular case they succeeded. The surprise was sprung at lunchtime one Sunday in February 1978, with the 'hooter' sounding while many of the executives were enjoying drinks in the officers' mess. One hundred Taceval team members, each a specialist in his field, were already dispersing to assigned locations to observe initial actions, as bars throughout the station emptied. Leaving their wives to walk home, officers, NCOs, airmen, and civilians with war appointments, commandeered cars to get to their place of work, taking care to leave them some way away from key points and if possible under some sort of camouflage. Apart from those away skiing, this was not a popular leave period so in very short order all units were at, if not above, initial manning requirements and shift patterns were introduced to allow those not needed then and there to find 'safer' locations and rest. The new station commander, Group Captain Graham Williams, as Force Commander, was in the always warm and active COC within minutes, his permanent staff therein already well into the checklist of immediate actions. At the same time the author, as his deputy, arrived at the alternate COC to find the doors open and his team monitoring every action. At the squadrons, aircraft and SAM states were already at the minimum levels decreed before work ceased on Friday nights and these aircraft were being armed with prescribed war loads. Elsewhere on the airfield there was similar, feverish activity. Taceval was underway.

The NATO team leader, a Canadian colonel, announced that on this exercise there would be no interval between the alert and readiness and remaining three phases of the evaluation; Brüggen was, therefore, in for four or five days and nights of intensive activity.

Throughout Sunday night and Monday the exercise scenario was one of escalating political tension with a commensurate increase in alert states. Pilots updated their preplanned exercise missions and prepared in every way to fly, going from thirty minutes down to ten minutes and then to cockpit readiness. The exercise scenario postulated Warsaw Pact (WP) troops advancing into the 2ATAF area of responsibility, with its air forces threatening the foremost Allied bases, so the whole wing was 'launched' as tasked or for survival. However, the weather being too bad for peacetime flying, the Jaguar pilots were required to taxi down the runway only, and hold in a designated area throughout their planned sortie time before returning to their dispersals. RAF Brüggen 'flew' more than 100 missions in the first twenty-four hours of the exercise.

By now NBC suits were de rigueur throughout the station, with gas masks to be donned within nine seconds of the call 'Gas-Gas-Gas' and each individual's protective measures checked by another in accordance with 'buddy/buddy' procedures. Failure to adhere strictly to these imperatives in station exercises risked a visit to the gas chamber for a whiff of unpleasant, if innocuous gas; failure to do so in a Taceval could incur some very black marks and exclusion from the exercise, while in war the consequences could be fatal. Wearing this equipment was inconvenient and uncomfortable, often hot and noxious at the best of times, but in some working circumstances it could be a major encumbrance. Brüggen had got used to this new modus operandi very quickly and the Taceval distaff were reported to be very impressed by the way that specialist tasks, such as operational turn-rounds and rearming of aircraft, were carried out in full protective clothing. Those in the fully air-conditioned COC and PBFs did not escape; there being no guarantees that hostile action would not cause leaks in these shelters or damage to their filtration plants, NBC kit was worn at all times and masks donned whenever an air raid was forewarned.

In the exercise scenario for the third day, the military situation on the ground and in the air was deteriorating rapidly and the wing became heavily engaged in ad hoc tasking with conventional weapons by the Allied Tactical Operations Centre (ATOC) in 'The Caves' (2ATAF's War HQ at Maastricht). On the 'bridge' in the COC these tasks were scrutinised initially by executives and Brüggen's Standardisation and Evaluation (Staneval) team. This was an unpopular role for the two squadron leader pilots involved, who would have preferred to be flying, but it was essential that all incoming tasks were checked for viability, in terms of range and target/weapons matching, before they were allotted to the squadrons.

By now, Brüggen was deemed to be under continuous attack from conventional air weapons, missiles and gas. Some ground intruders managed to avoid RAF Regiment patrols around the airfield perimeter but they were not able to penetrate the organic defences surrounding vital areas. These were always closely guarded, on this occasion in appalling weather, often by cooks, clerks, or highly qualified SNCO technicians, but all trained and well tested in defence procedures and the use of their weapons. They, the Explosive Ordnance Demolition (EOD), fire and emergency services, were brought together within an integrated defence organisation run from the COC by OC Admin Wing, in his war role as Ground Defence Commander. Where live intruders failed, distaff created synthetic incidents with written injects. Typically, these simulated the contamination of fuel, a defector landing or a bomb in the telephone exchange, while special patrols were sent out on wild goose chases to deplete resources and add to the confusion. The system withstood the test, the men and women on the ground getting a special mention in the Taceval Report for their alertness and response despite long periods of duty, boredom and discomfort.

It was not always so. On one station Mineval, the daughter of a flight lieutenant on 431 MU, known for her ample proportions and beauty, was persuaded (some say by the station commander) to attempt to infiltrate the closely-guarded COC without the necessary clearances. Apparently she had no difficulty doing so, wandering around therein, to everybody's pleasure, and leaving without being apprehended. Such is human fallibility.

Ben Nicol also had the responsibility for feeding and watering all players and recalls that 'exercise stew' from the airmen's mess proved very popular in the prevailing weather, 'such additives as sherry and bay leaves doing wonders for morale'. He could also authorise a rum ration, a job he took very seriously from the warmth of the COC, relying on others to tell him when this was justified by conditions outside, and there were plenty ready to do so during the fierce weather of this Taceval.

Exercise air attacks were often timed to coincide with the launch or recovery of aircraft, adding to management problems, and the raiders were credited with great skill in hitting crucial points on the runway, taxiway junctions and squadron dispersals. All these incidents required prioritisation to keep up the momentum of operations so, as soon as EOD and rapid runway repair (RRR) teams had carried out their initial reconnaissance, an assessment was made of the time and resources needed to put things right. Based on these judgements, Staneval would then work out what take-off and landing strips remained available and how these could best be used by Jaguars at various all-up weights. By capitalising on the aircraft's short take-off and landing capabilities to the full and the redundancy of paved surfaces at Brüggen (with the possible use of an adjacent road as a last resort), the station remained operational.

For real, the weather was getting worse; there was still no flying and snow was forecast. Now Brüggen had another, unscripted problem: how to keep the runway, taxiways and dispersals open so that a flying programme, or more likely a 'taxi-through' simulation, could be maintained. If it could not, for whatever unfortunate reason, there would be no chance of obtaining the four coveted '1s' at the end of the evaluation. In fact, the weather became worse than forecast and manpower had to be diverted from primary or guard duties to snow and ice clearance, making full use of the hot-sanders and jet-engined runway de-icers. Again, the station rose to the occasion and the airfield was kept open for taxying traffic until 'Endex'.

The end came with the expected (but simulated) mass launch of all serviceable Jaguars on pre-assigned missions or to survive, as 'Armageddon' approached. Some forty Jaguars 'taxied through' to pack tightly into a none-too-adequate area of hardstanding which had been cleared of snow and ice, where they remained for the planned duration of their sorties. These mass launches could be very exciting and open to errors of all kinds. Flight Lieutenant Frank Turner, on 14 Squadron at the time, remembers earlier exercises during which one pilot tried to taxi out with a Houchin starter attached, while another nearly took his ladder with him and a third took off on the wrong runway (narrowly avoiding a head-on collision) – but there were no mistakes on this crucial evaluation.

Drama on that ice-bound airfield was matched by that in the COC, wherein all executives and staff were fully stretched in this final, highly complicated act. A single mistake now, in a call sign, code, release procedure, precise timing, mission cancellation or withhold, could undo in seconds all that had been achieved in days, and drop the station from top to bottom grading. No mistakes were made in this exercise, which ended shortly thereafter.

Bars throughout the airfield reopened on that Wednesday evening but there was little euphoria among the weary participants of that Taceval. Many wondered if they had done their best or let the side down. Others anguished over whether the little mistakes they knew they had made had been noticed, whether they had dealt with that intruder correctly or let one pass through the net, whether they had been spoofed or whether they had given the right answer during the many professional quizzes which had been part of the evaluation. Others were just happy that it was all over, but everyone went to bed wondering what the debriefing would bring.

It took the Taceval team all of Thursday to deliberate on their findings, while some of its members were at last able to get airborne in Jaguar T2s to test selected pilots in weapons deliveries at Nordhorn Range, adding to evidence drawn from individual flight records, weapons scores and supervisors' assessments.

At 1000hrs on the Friday morning, the Taceval team leader debriefed the station executives and key specialists in the Astra Cinema. Despite the appalling weather, which had added very real problems to the script and which allowed only very limited flying, the evaluation was deemed to have been valid. The wash-up went into great detail on each of the four areas evaluated, at the end of which the station was awarded the highest possible ratings for Alert and Readiness, Operations and Support functions, and the author will never forget the overwhelming feeling of elation when the fourth '1' was added for Ability to Survive. Thus Brüggen set a precedent by achieving the ultimate accolade in the eyes of NATO, the nation and perhaps the Warsaw Pact, for single seat strike/attack operations. Who can say that the sign at the gate: 'The Task of this Station in Peace is to Train For War – Don't You Forget it!' (later taken down by a more conservative station commander) did not have the desired effect?

After his success as force commander during this historic Taceval, Graham Williams would star again in 1978 with the station documentary *Watchdogs*. He had to share this honour with thirty-two police dogs, especially Airdog Bruno and his handler Corporal Paul Andrews. Appearing in the opening shots, throughout the film and in the closing frames, the dogs symbolised the 2,500 servicemen and women of Brüggen as *'Watchdogs of Peace in the West'*.

The film opens with Bruno and Paul Andrews on dawn patrol as the station awakes to a routine day. Then the cameras follow quiet domestic scenes in the NAAFI, education and medical centres, supply squadron and sports fields, switching to the flight line as hangar doors lumber open, Jaguars leave their shelters to take off and disappear from sight. Missiles point skywards adding a surreal sense of

Cpl Paul Andrews and Bruno, RAF Police – stars of the Brüggen film epic *'Watchdogs'* – epitomises the station's warcry of the 1970s. (*RAF Brüggen*)

155

calm – but something is afoot. Then a siren wails; an officer leaps from his desk, grabs his NBC kit and hurries out; pilots don flying equipment and HAS doors slam closed to protect their charges; clerks, computer technicians and bandsmen move quickly to their battle stations. This could be war. In an evocative sequence, the cameras pan to a dentist's empty chair, a squash ball rolling slowly across the court, a lone golf ball left inches from the pin and a cup of coffee growing cold. There follow scenes of war play, to a concert of noise and movement, of aircraft taking off, carrying out their missions at low-level and landing for more, of air attacks, intruders, unexploded bombs, fire and casualties, before the station returns to normality, with Bruno and Paul Andrews resuming their comforting patrols.

The film's liaison officer, Flight Lieutenant Tim Gerrard, was easy prey as an extra and reappeared in several shots; he was credited with being 'best supporting actor' and for some unaccountable reason was tagged 'Omar Sharif without legs'. Squadron Leader Duggie Tew, acting as one of the distaff, is shown taking obvious delight in handing the station commander a particularly difficult unexploded bomb inject. Two takes were necessary for the author to get his five words right but the station commander needed five attempts to 'mask up' properly during an air raid alert – after which he became known as 'take five'. More than two million cinema-goers would see the twenty-three minutes of *Watchdogs*, which certainly said it all and put Brüggen on the map.

There was real drama in the air in March 1978, when Flight Lieutenant Pete New, 31 Squadron, claimed the dubious privilege of being the first to eject successfully from a single-seat Jaguar. In full view of his peers and superiors airborne with him, at the RCAF base of Lahr in Southern Germany, he left the aircraft at an estimated seventy-five feet above the ground with his aircraft pointing vertically upwards, after fire in one engine and loss of control. Safely on the ground, Pete plodded over to the airfield boundary and waited for a fireman to crop the bolt of the nearest crash gate to let him in. Found to be fully fit at the base hospital, he made for the bar.

Squadron Leader Mike Gray, Staneval Weapons, also featured in the 1978 incident reviews when the controls of his Jaguar jammed while he was flying at 500 feet above the ground. Using the rudder he managed to gain height, carry out a handling check and land safely at the excessive speed of 200 knots. For his 'fortitude, coolness and presence of mind' he was awarded a Queen's Commendation for Valuable Services in the Air.

By now Graham Williams had achieved operational status in the Jaguar; he celebrated in the usual manner in the bar and in a surely unprecedented gesture, joined all four flying squadron commanders on QRA (for one night only!).

No. 431 MU always had a few stars among its German and Dutch civilian workers. In 1978, Herr Matthias, who looked after barrack furniture, was crowned Schützenkonig (Shooting King) at the Schützenfest in the local German town of

Gp Capt Graham Williams, station commander, about to drink from the 14 Squadron 'Op Pot', on becoming fully operational in the Jaguar at Brüggen in 1978. (Front, L to R): Author (OC Ops Wg), Wg Cdrs Howard and Gibson (OCs 31 and 20 Sqns), Station Commander, Wg Cdrs Houghton and Sim (Ocs 17 and 14 Sqns). (*RAF Brüggen*)

Oberkruchten. Then there was the charismatic Mijnheer Frans Meuwissen, from the MU's MT staff, the 1978 World Formula 1 Stock Car Racing Champion; he died tragically in a race on 10 June 1978, aged thirty-one.

For his 'swan-song' in July 1978 (after what he called an 'all too brief' two-and-a-half-year tour), Terry Nash took 31 Squadron to RAF Lossiemouth, where they represented RAF Germany for a second time at the Strike Command Fighter Meet and Tactical Bombing Competition (TBC); he then handed over the reins to Wing Commander Richard Howard. Richard accompanied the squadron to Deci for an APC in October 1978 and was flying number three in a formation led by Flight Lieutenant Steve Griggs when the latter had the first of his three major emergencies in the Jaguar. Steve handled a serious fire in his port engine very professionally and had a Green Endorsement written into his Flying Logbook.

Wing Commander John Houghton, who took over 17 Squadron from Roy Humphreyson in July 1978, led the squadron to Nellis AFB, Nevada, in November, on the first Exercise 'Red Flag' for RAF single-seat aircraft. The requirement for and concept of Red Flag was based on evidence from the war in South East Asia, that aircrew expertise and survivability increased markedly after ten combat missions and this exercise was designed to give this experience without the ultimate risk. F-5Es of the USAF's Aggressor Squadron emulated Warsaw Pact fighters using tactics and procedures known to be part of its integrated radar, AAA, SAM and ECM defence system simulated very closely the environment in which NATO crews might have to fly. Realistic targets, including dummy airfields lined with representative aircraft, replicated those operating in East Germany, and many of these could be attacked with live weapons.

No. 17 Squadron had prepared well, making good use of card-four/six formations, counter-fighter weaves, 'push-pull' anti-AAA manoeuvres (sadly causing battery spillage in the Jaguars which was hard to put right), within their intensive operational low flying (OLF) training down to 100 feet over Scotland. The six aircraft deployed had uprated Dash-26 engines, a NAVWASS 'tie-down' facility which improved performance and reliability, a low height audio warning and other modifications. After a theatre orientation sortie at Nellis, each Jaguar pilot flew eight missions within fully integrated force packages. Transponders on the aircraft fed solar-powered receivers on the ground, enabling exercise staff to monitor individual aircraft and the entire battle as it developed, and to use in playback facilities at debriefings. A twenty per cent improvement in overall performance was expected – and achieved – at the end of a Red Flag exercise.

John Walker, fresh from Brüggen and now Gp Capt Offensive Ops at HQ RAF Germany, was the overall commander of the detachment, which included Buccaneers fitted with Pavespike designators for Paveway Laser Guided Bombs (LGBs) carried by the Jaguars. With further evidence from this exercise, John took the opportunity to stress the need for offensive aircraft to carry air-to-air missiles (AAMs) and streamlined bombs to replace the high-drag, Second World War bombs once carried internally. The Under Secretary of State for the RAF, James Wellbeloved, who was there to observe the exercise, agreed that the RAF was 'receiving immense value from participation', but was more cautious over the AAMs. The Jaguars eventually got their missiles but Tornados were still carrying high-drag bombs to war many years later. The aircrew on this first detachment were accommodated on base but they found time to yield to selected temptations in Las Vegas. The *RAF News* carried photographs of three 'mascots' recruited for 17 Squadron by three of its pilots (reputed to be Buckland, Bremner and Brookes) from the Tropicana Club on the 'Strip'. The sight of these ladies, dressed only in baubles, bangles and beads, did not go down well with everyone back at Brüggen, within the hierarchy in HQ RAF Germany or London. The groundcrew were better off from the start, being bussed daily between the base and hotels downtown. 'Circus Circus' became one of their most popular venues for an evening's entertainment, although they were banished from one of its stalls for making too much money with their natural abilities on the darts board.

Back at Brüggen, the ladies continued to occupy their time with many charitable projects, some taking to the catwalk in station fashion shows for good causes. One such event, in the Chicken Inn just before Christmas 1978, attracted

Officers' Mess Summer Ball 1978. (L to R): Wg Cdr Peter Arthur, Bridget Arthur, Meg Pexton, Margreet Walpole, Wg Cdr Brian Pexton, Author, Wg Cdr Ben Nicol, Ann Nicol. (*RAF Brüggen*)

Octoberfest 1978. The officers' mess staff – ready for the onslaught. (*RAF Brüggen*)

an audience of 350 and generated DM1,170 towards a kidney machine for RAF Hospital Halton. The children were not forgotten, Judy Williams, Dorothy Gibson and Margreet Walpole taking toys worth DM500, money earned in their Thrift and Wool Shops, to the servicemen's nursery school at Donderberg, and SSAFA benefited from the sale of home-made cakes et al, in the Wool Shop's Tea Bar.

Money also poured in from social events and other sources such as Der Adler KG, the Crossbow Club and Darts League, smaller but no less welcome sums coming from the dressmaker, P2, scrap car merchant and 'Zap' sticker initiative. One lesser known charity, with the rather intriguing name of 'The Alcoholics', sprung up in the Community Centre at Wickrath; it is not clear how they raised their contributions. Again, it is regretted that not all charities, big or small, can be given credit here.

With over-indulgence not unknown at this time of year, Brüggen's Senior Medical Officer (SMO), Wing Commander Jim Greig, used the *Brüggen Circuit* to espouse the wisdom of moderation and the truism that 'there is only one way to lose weight and that is to eat less'. Not everyone heard his message, the station medical centre and hospital at Wegberg having their usual Christmas trade. Always vulnerable and favourite whipping boys when things did not go quite right the station medical services came in for proper praise in another edition of the *Circuit*,

The station commander's wife, Judy Williams (centre), Margreet Walpole (left) and Dorothy Gibson (right), take toys bought from the proceeds of station charities to the children of Donderberg Nursery School. (*Brüggen Circuit*)

for their tireless care and rapid response to emergencies in an endless range of pro-active and remedial actions.

Likewise the dentists, also all too often maligned, deserved tribute. With peaks and troughs in capacity it was the *Brüggen Circuit* again which kept the station up-to-date on what was available and how it could be accessed. The Christmas 1978 edition noted that the refurbished dental section was then able to offer a daily clinic for inspections and emergency treatment with waiting time for routine work down to one week. Sadly, this healthy state of affairs did not last when the number of dental officers was reduced, increasing waiting times to six weeks. Notwithstanding, when back in the UK many would have cause to remember the advantages of these on-base facilities.

No. 17 Squadron had its share of drama and sadness. Shortly after John Houghton arrived one of its Jaguars crashed on a beach in Sardinia, killing its pilot, but Flight Lieutenants Willie Kirkpatrick and Mike Brookes survived their ejections from a Jaguar T2 in the Spring of 1979, after a bird strike had caused a double engine failure. Months later, Willie was presented with his ejection seat handle, beautifully mounted, and it may have been the emotion of this ceremony which led him to drive his brand new car off the perimeter track and on to the brink of a twenty-five feet deep static water tank. A concrete lip and chain link fence prevented a greater disaster but the car doors had jammed and keys had to be passed through a window to an interested bystander for the escape to be made, this gave rise to a question frequently asked in the bar thereafter: 'How does an Irishman dip his headlights....?'. Unscathed, Willie was then driven home by his squadron commander to face a greater ordeal with Mrs Kirkpatrick, hard words soon to be heard ringing through the married quarters. Willie lived dangerously.

The 21 May 1979 generated one of those legendary flying stories which has improved with the telling. The version which follows comes largely from the pen of the station commander, Graham Williams, who took the lead in exercise 'Strangled Sonata'.

It all began when Wildenrath challenged the Brüggen wing to deliver a direct hit with a bomb on a piano on Nordhorn Range, within a thirty minute slot, the losers to host a beer call. This required the use of 28lb practice bombs in fifteen degree dive attacks, a mode with which the wing was not familiar and would have no time to rehearse, but the station commander had another problem. Just before take-off, in marginal visibility, the Inspector of Flight Safety (IFS), Air Commodore Ken Hayr, a most reputable fast-jet pilot but one who now had very clear flight supervision responsibilities, arrived at Brüggen on one of his statutory 'no-notice' visits. Needing little persuasion, IFS was soon aboard a T2 flown by OC 14 Squadron, Wing Commander Joe Sim, flying No. 6 in the stream of twenty-five Jaguars each armed with four bombs, which would occupy Nordhorn Range for the whole thirty minutes allotted.

Seen from above the bombing looked good but the piano appeared to remain intact until the last pass by the penultimate aircraft, flown by Mike Gray, when it succumbed. In fact, the piano had already taken several direct hits but from bombs which did not explode. So Brüggen carried the day; IFS (who also dropped a bomb) seemed happy and Wildenrath paid up. The successful officer is always ready for the worst and the now Air Vice-Marshal Graham Williams admits that he was also carrying a full load of 30mm high-explosive ammunition in his guns, in case it became necessary to destroy the piano by cannon fire.

On the ground below, to see fair play, was Wildenrath's Padre Ray Hubble who had, in another place, played many a good note on the now defunct piano. Despite the faith he had had in the predictions of his own flock, he had resisted the temptation to play on while the bombs fell and lived to serve the last rites on his inanimate friend.

Father Hubble plays the prelude to
'Exercise Strangled Sonata', on the
Strike Target at Nordhorn Range.
(*Keith Reyner Collection*)

'Strangled Sonata' – The End.
(*Keith Reyner Collection*)

It is time to spare a thought for the padres on these hyperactive stations, the men who did so much, so often behind the scenes, for spiritual welfare, and developed valuable relationships within neighbouring communities. These men had, perforce, to be very down-to-earth in contemporary society, and with good humour they made it look so easy. Visiting Brüggen, the Reverend William Gowland commented in awe from the cockpit of a Jaguar that all chaplains should learn to fly, for the fear of God that this must instill – or perhaps to just get them a little closer to their maker?

Intensive flying of a different kind took place every weekend at Brüggen, when the very active Phoenix Gliding Club took to the air. The club boasted Ka 7, Blanik, Ka 8, Ka 6, ASK 18 and Libelle gliders, with twenty fully qualified British Gliding Association instructors to take ab initio students up to Bronze C certificate standards, in flights up to 10,000 feet over distances of 300km. In addition, the Phoenix Club ran a thriving social side, adding much to a balanced life at Brüggen.

Lining up for take-off. The RAF's Red Arrows (background) give Brüggen's Phoenix Gliding Club's ASK gliders a head start. (*Jochen Ewald*)

Phoenix landing. A glider pilot's view of Brüggen airfield – looking east. (*Hans-Jürgen Fischer*)

The gliders flew on rest days for the air traffic controllers whose vigilance at work was so important to flight safety. In July 1979, runway caravan controller Corporal Mike Wilson reported an excessive amount of liquid spilling from a Jaguar on take-off and was not satisfied with the explanation that this was normal. After the aircraft had taken off he found hydraulic fluid on the runway; the pilot was recalled and was back in the relative safety of the local area when the inevitable hydraulic failure occurred. The station commander was only too happy to present Mike with a 'Good Show' certificate, he having been in the aircraft.

Among the many men who had done so much to establish the Jaguar Strike Wing at Brüggen and contribute to its success, and who departed in 1979, was Squadron Leader Bill Floydd. He had pioneered a new dimension in security operations at a major strike/attack base, ending his tour with a squadron strength of more than 300, fifty dogs and fifty vehicles, in a job well done.

Before Peter Arthur handed over command of 431 MU to Wing Commander Keith Gordon in May 1979, he presented the Arthur Cup, to be offered every six months to whoever it was considered had contributed most to the life and well-being of the unit. An early recipient was Sergeant R. Beamish, of Supply Squadron, for the work he and his wife had put into the renovation of the Fear Dry Inn, the MU's ever popular social venue for the whole station. The now Air Chief Marshal, Sir Michael Armitage, then Deputy Commander RAF Germany, recalled the MU's innovation and industry at the time, and that year's AOC's Inspection when he presented Peter with RAF Germany's Safe Driving Trophy, for logging 948,894 miles with only one 'driver to blame' accident. Little did he know then that, as he was doing so, his wife Gretl was taking instruction on a 40-foot lorry and trailer elsewhere on the station – perhaps with a view to a second career?

When Wing Commander Frank Mitchell took over 20 Squadron from Mike Gibson in September 1979 he found much had changed on his return to single-seat operations in Germany after flying Phantoms from the relatively benign environment of a UK station. He was immediately impressed by the great professionalism evident in the warlike

On his AOC's Inspection in 1979, AVM Michael Armitage presented Wg Cdr Peter Arthur with RAF Germany's Safe Driving Trophy, little knowing that, while he was doing so, his wife was being taught to drive a 40-foot lorry and trailer elsewhere on the Station.
(*RAF Brüggen*)

south-west corner of the airfield, exemplified by his flight commanders, Andy Griffin and Ed Jones, and SEngO, Derek Powell, who enforced the all-pervading consciousness that nuclear operations had to run perfectly. Everything had to be thought of; a single error by a confused man, perhaps too long out in the cold or fed on nothing but a greasy bacon butty around dawn, could have crucial consequences.

Frank was one of the map and stopwatch brigade, determined that his men would be ready to return to first principles, develop a 'seaman's eye' and use the 'kit's' reversionary modes effectively for weapons' deliveries, and he ensured that APCs included this training. At the same time he readily accepted the opportunities at Deci: 'to get one's head round the nether regions of the versatile NAVWASS system', and practise 'the more esoteric means of weapons delivery'. This balanced approach was now the norm.

Professionalism of another kind was equally evident when the 'Sappers' of 52 Field Squadron (Construction) returned to Brüggen in the autumn of 1979 for Exercise Hallmark II, to blow holes in Brüggen's taxiways and fill them in again in its Rapid Runway Repair (RRR) role. Soon, the station would have its own resident sapper squadron for this task, and to maintain essential services such as electricity, water and fuel supplies.

There were now more aircraft on QRA than at any time before in Brüggen's history, operational pilots spending three days behind the wire every month and groundcrew one full week every six months. It remained very unpopular but did offer a chance to catch up on paperwork, provide a refuge for the mischievous and escape from domestic chores or affairs of the heart. Good use was made of the collocated Jaguar simulator and there was plenty of time for reflecting on life, but the real reason for QRA didn't bear thinking about, and perhaps very few did.

Those on QRA on one very dank and dreary morning, in December 1979, may not have regretted missing a mass launch during a Mineval which did not go well. John Houghton and his wingman entered cloud at 150 feet and flew most of their equivalent war mission in cloud with only one 'cast iron' diversion available in the far north at Jever. Contrary to the forecast, the weather did not improve and only a few brave souls got back into Brüggen; most ended up at Jever, where it was then snowing. Ever optimistic, the force commander launched what was left of his Wing again during a brief clearance at Brüggen, only to have all these aircraft join the rest at Jever, where impending snow, ice and fog now looked like keeping them on the ground indefinitely. Dressed only in flying suits, they had to be resupplied by road, the luggage in John Houghton's case including his dinner jacket 'in case he needed it over Christmas'. At Jever, the transients were entertained lavishly by the resident Luftwaffe officers, but with much of its strike force out of reach, HQ RAF Germany was not amused.

In fact, the DJ was not needed; the bleary-eyed travellers flew home during one brief interlude in the bad weather and the normal Christmas festivities at Brüggen began early. This year featured the incongruous sight of 17 Squadron pilots, led by Tex Jones, cavorting very professionally as Morris Men dressed in all the finery of ribbons and bells, waving hankies and batons to tunes from an accordion. It is said that when invited to join them, Graham Williams showed an unexpected and uncanny talent for the dance. He then donned a split skirt and net stockings to thrill the crowds with a display of go-go dancing. In the free-for-all, Tiny Tim Gerrard and Long Tom Parkinson danced the *pas de deux*, buxom Bill Rimmer and Ken Carvosso performed an unmentionable act and Tex Jones joined Sid Vincent in a version of the 'Two Ronnies'. Later, and not to be outdone, squadron commanders Joe Sim, John Houghton, Richard Howard, Frank Mitchell and John Ault, playing drums, trombone, string bass, piano and maracas respectively, and supported by the other wing commanders, formed the 'Execs Stompers Jazz Band'. Brüggen thus became a hive of thespian and musical talent, perhaps vaguely reminiscent of Priestley's *Good Companions,* ready and willing to spread their bonhomie far and wide, but sober judgement suggested that these ad hoc entertainers should not give up their day jobs.

Graham Williams handed over the station to Group Captain Peter Taylor in December 1979, on the eve of another decade of change for Brüggen as the squadrons became increasingly mobile. NATO air forces on APC at Deci were now taking advantage of a USAF Air Combat Manoeuvring Installation (ACMI), over the sea off Sardinia. This enabled air combat to be monitored (and replayed on the ground) from signals received through moored electronic buoys fed by transponders in pods carried by the aircraft involved. A giant display showed the relative positions of participating aircraft and the theoretical paths of the missiles simulated, against a background of radio transmissions from the players. Frank Mitchell spoke for most when he extolled the virtues of ACMI, which identified mistakes and helped improve tactics, while ridding the noble art of air combat of hitherto outrageous versions of events which inevitably favoured the teller.

However, bombing was Brüggen's *raison d'être* and most of this training, other than 1000lb and toss bombing, which was carried out at UK or overseas ranges, continued at Nordhorn. Without radar, the bombs had to be delivered visually, against targets which could be very difficult to find at the best of times, let alone in marginal visibilities and at night, although the night target was ringed by two concentric circles of flashing lights. After cruising round a familiar night route at a safe and comfortable height, the bomb run at low level and 500 knots, in a black void over unlighted fields and peatbogs, could be very exciting, and mistakes could happen. One of the wing's most revered weapons instructors (QWIs), Flight Lieutenant John 'Animal' Barrow, spotted the expected lights as he roared towards Nordhorn, on time if slightly to the right of track. In fact he was looking at an almost identical array which had been mounted without warning on the roof of a brick factory, for a local celebration, and it was on these lights that he scored a direct hit at precisely the right time. Brick production was not affected, good relations were quickly restored with a little help from the bar, and John still insists that he should have been awarded the money in the 'pot' for the best bomb of the night.

At Brüggen, the initiation of new pilots coming from the very different training atmosphere of RAF Lossiemouth could be unkind. One flight lieutenant, well known for inflicting excessive misery on the newcomers, decided to take two such innocents directly from the charter flight at Dusseldorf Airport into a carefully staged, fully operational scenario at 20 Squadron. An alert (real or exercise?) sounded on their arrival; NBC kit (with which the new boys were wholly unacquainted) was supplied on the spot and donned at once by all, as incomprehensible orders were shouted between people scurrying in all directions. A suitably harassed operations officer then declared that the squadron was short of pilots and that the newcomers would have to take part.

Accordingly, they were kitted out, given call signs, assigned aircraft and taken to a HAS facility, again totally new to them, wherein their Jaguars, fully loaded as they had never seen them before, waited to be taken to war within a concept of operations with which the new boys were entirely unfamiliar. As they were being helped into their cockpits the order came to scramble and an adjacent Jaguar immediately roared into life and taxied out into the dark. Now came the ultimate test, what would these young braves do? One had had enough and climbed out to seek advice but the other got the bit between his teeth and attempted to start his aircraft. Sensible supervisors had anticipated that the spirit of adventure might not be dead and had removed fuses to ensure that the joke stopped there, and this it did as Frank Mitchell appeared with the customary champagne and two much relieved pilots were welcomed into the fold. It was indeed a steep learning curve at Brüggen.

With such threats to new boys quick to get around, other initiation plots were always being devised. One unsuspecting soul was met quite properly at the air terminal by a young lady officer who, instead of driving him directly to his new squadron, stopped the Land Rover at a secluded spot in the forest, where it seemed that he might first be welcomed in a very special way. However, before things could go too far, two of the squadron pilots, dressed convincingly as RAF policemen, 'arrested' the pair for 'conduct unbecoming' and the new boy was taken alone to a darkened room for appropriate interrogation before being put out of his misery. Frank Mitchell believes that such tests had a 'curiously beneficial effect on the rate at which the new arrivals bonded into the bunch', but others were not so sure.

The author first met Flying Officer Elbert Du Crosses of 20 Squadron, when the latter was being helped from a Sabre at RAF Oldenburg in 1955, after the two had been involved in a combat training sortie. Elbert went on to amass some 200 hours in fast-jets, but being a tortoise he had been a little slow on the uptake and was promoted to flight lieutenant only shortly before he went to meet his maker. To the joy of all Double Crossers, son of Elbert joined the squadron in 1980. His mentor, flight commander Ed Jones, found him suitable housing in a special-to-type Hardened Tortoise Shelter (HTS), but his life was not easy. Being of limited stature, he found it difficult to gain the attention of barmen at beer calls, soon ate the mess out of lettuce, was placed in an oven when mistaken for a meat pie, and went absent without leave shortly thereafter. The trail ends there.

It was at about this time that the station commander ordered the Station Warrant Officer (SWO) to rid his garden of moles. To cut a long story short, the

SWO co-opted the help of the head green keeper of the Golf Club, Mijnheer Kaalk, who managed to shoot himself in the hand while proudly demonstrating his mole-catcher. The hierarchy in HQ RAF Germany, hearing that this most important person had been shot assisting the station commander and would not be able to care for their cherished greens for two months, ordered an inquiry, the results of which are not for these pages!

Throughout 1979–80, underlining the threats facing NATO as tensions increased in the Cold War, 17 Squadron was tasked with evaluating the new AR5 NBC protective ensemble for aircrew under development at RAE Farnborough and Porton Down. This involved a detailed examination of the procedures to be adopted in the air and on the ground, while assessing any degradation in operational effectiveness in war. Pilots selected for the trials flew a number of demanding operational sorties in the front seat of the Jaguar T2, in full AR5 equipment, monitored by a safety pilot in the rear seat. The author, flying one of these sorties, became less conscious of the initial discomfort from the equipment as time progressed and the airborne workload increased. Visor misting and other problems were eventually overcome in a viable if inhibiting modus operandi, which gave the RAF the only protective capability of its kind then in NATO. For his work as the project officer, 17 Squadron's Martin Sinclair was awarded a C-in-C's commendation.

Rarely in the limelight but always ready, willing and able to provide support in many forms, Engineering and Supply Wing was now run by Wing Commander David Birch. In 1980, he presented 'Good Show' awards to Junior Technicians M.R. Yaffie (a prominent member of the Bears Rugby team) and M.A. Morrison, both of Aircraft Servicing Flight, and to Senior Aircraftsman A. Griffin of 17 Squadron – all for vigilance which might have prevented serious accidents.

Emphasising the increasing co-operation between NATO air forces in the Central Region, the Tactical Leadership Programme (TLP) had got underway in 1979 with ground seminars at the Luftwaffe base of Fürstenfeldbruck, Bavaria, Brüggen being fully involved from the start. Joint flying exercises involving offensive and defensive aircraft from all participating nations began when TLP moved to Jever in 1980, one of its staff, Dutch Lieutenant Colonel Frans Hartl, observing correctly that in a crisis there would be no time for the luxury of comparing tactics and aircraft capabilities. TLP graduates would expect to be their nations' leaders in the air and as battle managers to use the corporate experience in optimising the employment of combined resources in the force packaging which was fast developing.

A perennial highlight of the officers' social calendar was the Burns Night, arranged and run meticulously at this time by the SMO, Wing Commander Jim Greig (who in his day job was reputed to be able to inflict pain for weeks with a simple injection). Jim was a very proud honorary member of 14 Squadron, and repaid the tribute handsomely in every squadron activity; he would not allow any other doctor to carry out medical examinations on his fellow squadron members.

The Brüggen team in the Tactical Leadership Programme at GAF Fürstenfeldbruck, debriefing in Munich's Hofbrauhaus in February 1979. (Front, L to R): Author, and Flt Lt 'Animal' Barrow; GAF Lt Col 'K-B' (Staff), Flt Lt Nigel Elsdon. (*Author*)

Nothing was left to chance in his dedication to Burns, although the issue of a full bottle of whisky to each guest at the table was surely tempting providence? It was during one of these celebrations that Frank Mitchell excelled, or at least captured the attention of the fellow diners, as the 'musical director' and pianist. At the beginning of the evening, his reasonably accurate Victor Borge-style rendition of Grieg's *Butterfly* went down well, but much later, very much later, his accompaniment of a very talented ex-opera singer, the wife of an American general from Rheindahlen, in three Burns songs, had a very different effect. Frank's problems started with the elation of his first success, which justified a few swigs of whisky, and was then compounded by his generous offer to help the lady by his side finish her bottle when his ran dry. When it came to his all-important support of 'My Love is Like a Red Red Rose', Frank was feeling no pain and he had some difficulty finding the piano, let alone reading the music. In his own words his 'thoroughly unmusical crashings and bashings on the piano did no justice to the charming lady's beautiful voice'. Perhaps it was not one of Frank's most professional performances but from all reports this unique double act turned out to be one of the most memorable events of a very long evening. The author recalls that, at a previous Burns Night, when his wife was replying for the ladies at 0200hrs in the morning, and many were close to sleep, Frank's predecessor was similarly affected by the emotion of the occasion, or was it an urge to finish his bottle. Perhaps it was a 20 Squadron tradition?

Post-exercise parties were less well structured, based more on impulse and opportunity. So it was that an old piano appeared as if by magic in front of the officers' mess after another very successful Taceval, as an offering for ceremonial sacrifice by the axe; a 20 Squadron flight commander, Joe Whitfield, was allegedly behind what followed. He was said to have persuaded Frank Mitchell, who was in good shape after three days of exercise sobriety, to play the last rites, and Joe, who accidentally spilt a full can of petrol into the venerable instrument, sealing its fate as Frank rendered 'Roll out the Barrel'. Denied his primary target, now in flames, a mad axeman took a swipe at a nearby tree, shaking two innocent spectators from 14 Squadron out of its branches and almost into the inferno, while sending the axe head into orbit. No one was hurt, the fire brigade had a field day in their full protective clothing and in time-honoured fashion the officers cleared up the rubbish and paid for the damage, leaving a hole in the road for the rapid runway repair team to ply its trade.

A mark of its credibility, the *Brüggen Circuit* fooled many on 1 April 1980 with a black-edged announcement that Brüggen would close in 1981 (as it once did with an article on the Royal Navy's Mohne See detachment). This spoof caused such a flurry of activity and concern, with telephones red hot, that an official denial had to be circulated.

No. 17 Squadron's Willie Kirkpatrick ejected for a second time after two Jaguars collided on the break overhead the airfield on 28 May 1980. Tragically, Flight Lieutenant John Cathie was killed instantly, but Willie was able to extricate himself from his parachute (which had snagged on the fence surrounding the bomb dump) and thumb a lift back to the squadron. Convinced that the Lord was trying to tell him something, and with Mrs Kirkpatrick adding some rather forceful views of her own, Willie decided to take a rest from flying for a while.

In another fortunate escape Flight Lieutenant Jerry Whittingham, also of 17 Squadron, abandoned his Jaguar on 17 July 1980 after a fuel leak led to a double engine fire on the final approach to Brüggen. His aircraft landed in the local adventure park, where forty children had been playing shortly before, with little damage and no injuries caused, while he parachuted into the car park of a bank in Elmpt, narrowly missing a 150-foot church steeple. Various stories circulated over his subsequent treatment by the ladies of the bank; suffice it to say that he was found to be in very good order when rescued from his hosts.

It seemed time for 17 Squadron to get away from it all and its exchange visit to the RNoAF at Bodo, north Norway, in July, was just what was needed – being rather out of the ordinary. A continuous diet of fish and boiled potatoes might not have appealed but flying in perfect weather over magical scenery, watching the midnight sun and climbing the Okstindan glacier on foot certainly did. Arrangements for the return visit to Brüggen also set precedents; Norwegian egalitarianism demanding that all its air and groundcrew should (with few exceptions) be officers.

Wing Commander David Baron took over 14 Squadron from Joe Sim in June 1980, and was thrown straight in at the deep end. After a brief handover he was on his own and failed to recognise the station 'hooter' for what it was when it signalled a Mineval a couple of days later. For a man with a background in the UK, Aden and the USA, what followed was a great culture shock and he left his senior flight commander, Peter Day, to 'run the desk' throughout the exercise. Interestingly, Brüggen's single-seat Jaguar strike/attack squadrons were established initially with two squadron leaders only, a far cry from the five or six who would serve on the two-seat Tornado squadrons in the same role, and be supported by dedicated operations assistants to help run their desks. Later, the Jaguar squadrons would get a third squadron leader and David remembers that the first of these on 14 Squadron, Nick Rusling, had an exciting time. First, a 'near miss' with a German F-104 turned out to be a hit when much of the tailplane of his Jaguar (which continued to fly well) was found to be missing when he landed. Next, scrapes and scratches around a gun-port of another of his mounts were eventually attributed to a German model aircraft (which came off worst) and finally, his car went missing while the family was on holiday in Sardinia, committing them to a long, slow train back to Brüggen. After a year of this, Nick sensibly went off to the staff college.

No. 31 Squadron did well in 1980, winning the Broadhurst Bombing Trophy and, with a team of four pilots led by the CO, Richard Howard, the strafe event at the Tactical Air Meet (TAM) at Ramstein AB. Flight Lieutenant Ian Kenvyn scoring maximum points and the squadron's groundcrew producing the fastest operational turn round. Flight Lieutenant Jeff Morgan was awarded a Queen's Commendation for his work with the squadron on the Jaguar's laser-ranging and Paveway LGB and, to end a good year, a senior USAF officer at Red Flag was heard to say, 'We've flown against the best, and for my money you Jaguar boys are as good as any of them, and better than most.' So the squadron was on a high when Wing Commander Ted Edwards took command in 1981, its sixty-fifth year, twenty-five years with a Standard and sixteen years at Brüggen all celebrated by a reunion at which thirty-four ex-members were flown from the UK in a Dakota, one of the squadron's wartime aircraft.

Perhaps not on the primary operational agenda but now an essential extra, a spectacular hijack exercise took place at Brüggen in November 1980. Planned by the Security Squadron, now under the command of Squadron Leader Rob Murray, the station joined forces with the German police, counter-terrorist and national crime teams, in a truly joint effort. An incident room was set up, with comprehensive communications established and the area secured before the arrival of an RAF Hercules simulating a BAC Trident containing sixty-five hostages and four hijackers. After fruitless negotiations the incident was brought to a satisfactory conclusion amid a cloud of smoke and to a crescendo of shots and stun grenades. A joint wash-up concluded that the exercise had been of great value to all, and this was celebrated with equal success in the station's Portcullis Club.

No. 20 Squadron was also doing its bit, winning the best Jaguar team and best RAF team prizes in the 1981 TBC at Lossiemouth, ceding only to the USAF F-16s for

Exercise 'Hijack' at Brüggen. Two 'terrorists', with 'hostage', make a break.
(*Brüggen Circuit*)

best team overall. Any suggestion that this had something to do with the fact that the competition rules were written by an ex-Brüggen Jaguar pilot would be a calumny.

1981 was another year of mixed fortunes for 17 Squadron. Flight Lieutenant David Plumbe lost his life in a Jaguar at Red Flag, but Flight Lieutenant David Needham recovered a Jaguar with severe control problems, earning a Green Endorsement for 'professionalism and skill'. The squadron had 'twinned' very successfully with the Luftwaffe's 34/2 (F-104) Squadron, at Memmingham, leading to many useful and enjoyable professional and social exchanges, and had forged a very strong relationship with its ex-members.

Throughout his tour Peter Taylor presided over many successes in Brüggen's extraneous activities. The Sir Robert Foster Trophy for sport was retrieved in January 1980, the year in which the station also won the RAF Germany Marching Competition for the third time running and, in 1981, the Lady Foxley-Norris Trophy for ladies' sports was added to the silver collection. Charitable activities continued to increase, typically with the RC Chaplain, Father Cassidy, making two monthly runs with clothes and food to the Little Sisters of the Poor in Liege, and Peter himself went to London's Royal Festival Hall to receive the Diamond Jubilee Sword from HRH The Princess Anne, for the station's outstanding services to the RAF Benevolent Fund. Domestic welfare was enhanced with the opening of a Families Information Centre, and a major project was initiated to turn the Astra Cinema into a Bowling Centre.

Before he handed over command to Group Captain John Thomson in December 1981, Peter Taylor drove his officers from Brüggen to a beer call at Wildenrath in the station train. Despite the short distance involved, delays in clearance on to the Bundesbahn main line extended the journey to three hours. 20 Squadron was well-prepared, the antique carriages assigned to them stocked with champagne, beer and canapes, which were dispensed by junior pilot Dave Froggatt, suitably dressed in a waiter's white jacket and gloves. This was the stuff of the 'Orient Express'. Other squadrons aboard had no such forethought and 20 Squadron were forced to lock their carriage doors against marauders; they could not, however, conceal either their sufficiency or their glee at seeing the less prudent suffer. Tensions increased, and when one of the fortunate responded to a call of nature beside the tracks, during one of many stops, he was captured by a jealous mob and tortured in full view of

Gp Capt Peter Taylor's last train ride to Wildenrath, December 1982. In the 20 Squadron carriage of plenty, squadron commander Frank Mitchell (centre) is attended by Fg Off Dave Froggatt. (*Frank Mitchell*)

his peers. Frank Mitchell was all for leaving him to his fate, it being his own fault for exposing himself, but the scene was too horrible for the more squeamish who paid a suitable ransom in kind for his release. A less than harmonious party carried on to Wildenrath, where they quenched their thirst among friends and returned rather late – but in thirty minutes by road.

In his 1982 New Year's Message, John Thomson outlined his three goals: to maintain and improve the station's operational capability, to provide every opportunity to develop individual potential and to encourage recreation, sport and travel. In so doing he accepted that he was merely endorsing and reinforcing what had gone before but forewarned of times of considerable change and disruption.

In keeping with his primary objective, the Station was again awarded four '1s' in the April 1982 Taceval – but there was more to be done. Like John Walker before him, who had driven the initiative to provide the Jaguar with a makeshift chaff dispenser, the new station commander became impatient with delays in equipping the aircraft with Sidewinder missiles for self-defence. Wing Commander Del Williams, then OC Eng and Supply Wg, remembers that circumventing the system with this covert and wholly unauthorised enterprise did not go down well in some high places – but it did achieve its aim of attracting attention. The missile's underwing installation was designed and proved at Brüggen, using some Phantom instruments and electrical equipment borrowed from Wildenrath, and

Station Commander Gp Capt John Thomson goes operational with 14 Squadron.
(*Jan Thomson*)

174

Flt Lt Nigel Demery, 14 Squadron, flying with Brüggen's own Sidewinder fit. (*RAF News*)

the launcher adapter for the outboard mainplane pylons was manufactured from material available from the stores catalogue. A dummy modification pack was prepared, giving installation details, part numbers and sources for all materials. Based on the well-proven Phantom system, all the necessary safety interlocks were in place – but there was no flight clearance. Dummy missiles were, however, flown on a 14 Squadron aircraft by Flight Lieutenant Nigel Demery and photographs circulated in the hope of speeding officialdom into providing this much-needed capability. In the event, the Jaguars at Brüggen were replaced by Tornados before over wing Sidewinder launchers became a standard fit on the residual Jaguar force at Coltishall, fortuitously in time for the Gulf War.

Wing Commander J.M.H. Sabben took over 431 MU in 1982. Now with a manning strength of 500, including 100 UK dependent, Dutch and German employees, it had become highly efficient in the deep, second line servicing and testing, fault diagnosis and defect rectification of Spey and Adour aircraft engines. The Adour, stripped down to fourteen modules, could be turned round in six weeks, whereas the Spey might take six months. Always innovative, the MU was then producing Jaguar engine bay doors and ammunition boxes and was already thinking ahead to the introduction of the RB199 engine for the Tornado, prompting Sabben to comment in the *RAF News*: 'Our job is to produce high quality and long term permanent work.' Always more visible to the outsider, MT Flight moved Spartan armoured vehicles for No. 1 Squadron, RAF Regiment, from Catterick in Yorkshire to Laarbruch and a Spitfire from Cracow in Poland to the RAF Museum in Hendon. The MU's drivers were always on the road, often engaged in diverse and difficult tasks, and it was a great credit to them that they had now retained the RAF Germany Safe Driving Trophy for four years running.

There was no afternoon nap for the flight safety, offensive, defensive or engineering staffs at HQ RAF Germany, or at Wildenrath and Brüggen, on 25 May 1982, when the news broke that a Sidewinder fired by a Wildenrath Phantom had shot down a Jaguar. Disbelief quickly gave way to the fact that Flight Lieutenant Steve Griggs, number two in a pair of Jaguars, had ejected successfully from 14 Squadron's 'AL' (XX963) after the Phantom crew, on an otherwise legitimate interception exercise under Clutch Radar control, had committed the *coup de grâce*. Seeing the whole tail section break away and the remainder enter a flat spin, his leader, Flight Lieutenant Paddy Mullen, called Steve to eject, which he did at about 700 feet. On the ground, with only minor injuries, he was greeted by farmer Gerd Molleken and his young daughter, who wished him 'happy birthday' (a Harrier pilot had ejected in the same place ten years earlier) before taking him off for a brandy or two. The incident occurred as the Jaguars, making a visual recovery to Brüggen, neared the huge POL (petrol, oil and lubricants) site near Wesel on the River Rhine, so familiar to all Brüggen pilots, a greater catastrophe being avoided when the aircraft crashed a short distance away. When the Phantom crew told Clutch Radar that they had shot down the Jaguar on to which they had been vectored, the controller congratulated them and offered them another target. Watching all this while waiting his turn for a target, a Luftwaffe pilot in an F-104 confided in the controller that this was all too realistic for him and asked, 'If a Brit could do this to one of his own, what would he do to me?' Without waiting for an answer he selected afterburner and went home. Much soul-searching, rule-reading and revision followed, the outcome of which is beyond the scope of this book; suffice it to say that the Sidewinder proved its worth, this one giving the Phantom crew and others a difficult time thereafter. This had not been a fair fight; Steve Griggs was one of Brüggen's elite Staneval team and would have known what to do had he thought he was truly threatened.

Three months later Steve ejected, again safely, from a Jaguar with an engine fire over Scotland; this time he was flying OC 14 Squadron's 'AA' and the epic was filmed by Flight Lieutenant Norman Brown with a Buccaneer's Pavespike infra-red LGB designator. Paddy Mullen was there again, and on both occasions Steve's parachute was packed by Senior Aircraftsman Cusak. David Baron became the only RAF CO to have an aircraft shot down over Germany since 1945 and he had lost two of his squadron's aircraft – including his own. The beer flowed freely.

Brüggen squadron commanders now became a little reluctant to let Ops Wg staff fly their aircraft. Not only had Steve Griggs disposed of two of their aircraft

Flt Lt Steve Griggs, shot down by an RAF Phantom, walked away from Jaguar XX963 just short of the huge POL site near Wesel. (*Steve Griggs*)

177

but OC Ops Wg, Wing Commander Malcolm Lovett, added another. Malcolm was one of a pair of GR1s leading two Luftwaffe F-104s on a low-level sortie during an exchange visit to Brüggen, when his starboard engine gave an alarming 'pop', and he decided to return home. After dumping fuel to expedite landing, the same engine had a catastrophic failure, caused by the ingestion of a compressor stator blade. The emergency panel 'lit up like a Christmas Tree', vibration rendered the instruments unreadable and the engine wound down. The main fuel pipe had fractured and when reheat was checked for landing the port engine also gave up; the controls then seized up and it was clearly time to go. Malcolm was able to point the aircraft towards a clear area before ejecting successfully at 800 feet into a turnip field, returning to Brüggen uninjured, courtesy of a Luftwaffe rescue helicopter.

In September 1982, 31 Squadron was back at Fassberg for the annual tripartite exercise. Under the heading 'Pandemonium Strikes Fassberg', the *Brüggen Circuit* reported that the 'Fassberg Liberation Army' (FLO) had attempted to upset international relations by bearnapping 'Arris. Although 'Arris was said to have gone bearserk, he was bundled successfully into a Panda Car and driven to an unknown destination from whence came a ransom note, accompanied by a bear ear and pornographic photographs, purported to be 'Arris, with Swedish bears of dubious sexuality in compromising positions. Although beareaved and bereft, the squadron could not pander to the demands made and counter-kidnapped a lady by the name of Mary Lee, said to be a key member of the FLO, an exchange of hostages thereafter bringing the matter to a satisfactory conclusion and the exercise was then allowed to proceed.

Brüggen was in good order for two very important occasions in November 1982. On the 26th, Nos. 14 and 20 Squadrons were presented with new Standards by CAS, Air Chief Marshal Sir Keith Williamson, and on the 30th, HRH The Prince Philip, Duke of Edinburgh, visited Brüggen. The Prince met a cross-section of people, including local German VIPs, and saw demonstrations of equipment in his wide-ranging tour of the station's main facilities. Later, a Brüggen schoolgirl, Vanessa Leigh, wrote thus to him, 'Thank you very much for coming to visit Germany. I hope you liked Brüggen and the Jaguar Fly-past, my daddy was in one of the aeroplanes. It was a very exciting day for me because I had never seen a Prince in real life before. Have a happy Christmas.' Not everything went well when the Jaguar Strike Wing showed its muscle. However well planned, the vagaries of weather and vicissitudes of the human performance could upset the applecart. So it was on the occasion of a much-rehearsed visit by the then Secretary General of NATO, Dr Luns, when both cloud base and visibility were just below limits. A formation of Jaguars was airborne for an airfield attack, to be repelled by the combined might of Brüggen's Bloodhound and Rapier missiles. Air raid sirens announced the incoming raid but the Bloodhounds were pointing in one direction and the Rapiers another as the fighter-bombers roared in, heard but not seen, their leader (who had just rejected an offer of assistance from air traffic) failing to find the airfield. Nothing daunted, the ground party set off the explosives to signify a successful attack from the never seen and now departing Jaguars. Diplomacy came to the rescue with Dr Luns congratulating the station commander on this splendid display of all-weather, stand-off bombing. There is no record of John Thomson's post-visit debriefing, nor of Mrs Thatcher's visit that month.

It is sad that embarrassment, harm and even disaster can accompany over-zealous dedication to duty. Such was the case when an EOD officer at Brüggen did all that he should and finally blew up a suspect package addressed to him but from a sender he could not identify. It transpired that the parcel had come indirectly from his wife, containing something very special. Again, misfortune so often seems to strike the more diligent, loyal workers, as it did to a most worthy corporal on 14 Squadron, who began to tow a Jaguar with a Houchin trolley still attached. The damage done called for extensive remedial work at 431 MU and a heavy statutory punishment for the perpetrator, but the squadron rallied round and the job was done at that level, with much overtime but to complete satisfaction, saving the career of an excellent tradesman and it showed again that the Brüggen spirit remained alive and well.

On a dreary Sunday in the winter of 1982, '31's All Stars' and '17's Softees' did battle in a rugby match of sorts, declared (by one side only) to have been a draw. To be sure, the game was played with determination and vigour, for the

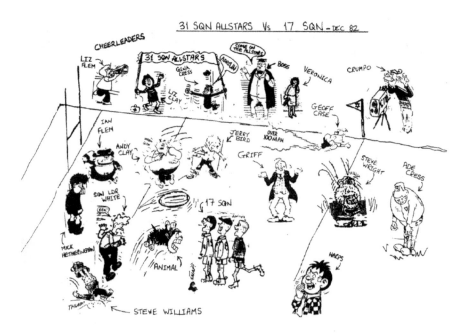

The best of 31 Squadron's rugby 'All Stars'. (*31 Squadron*)

first two minutes, after which the Brüggen Bears talent scouts departed – sorely disappointed. There were curses, grunts and puffs aplenty, largely from Squadron Leaders Griffiths and Barrow leading from the rear, but not much blood to salve between essential admin breaks for alcohol and cigarettes. Whatever happened to that aircrew fitness campaign?

By April 1983, all three flights of 25 Squadron, then commanded by Wing Commander Tony Collins, had returned to the UK, 'A' Flight to RAF Barkston Heath. Largely unsung, the squadron had played a full part in the business of deterrence, and in every aspect of Brüggen's life.

Deputy Commander RAF Germany, AVM Alan White, and Plt Off Dingle, lower the last of 25 Squadron's Bloodhounds at Brüggen. (*Brüggen Circuit*)

Another Brüggen innovation in the Jaguar era during Del Williams' tenure of Eng and Supply Wg, one which did eventually enjoy official recognition and was adopted for general use, was a communications system which enabled the PBF to brief pilots at cockpit readiness in the HAS. This robust and ultimately reliable system took two years to perfect but led to a major improvement in reaction times. Also at this time, Eng Wg and 431 MU joined forces to retrofit defensive countermeasures to the Brüggen Jaguars for the 1983/84 Red Flag exercises – where these measures proved very effective.

Meanwhile, the four Jaguar squadrons went about their routine business, working to standard procedures so that the pilots could fly with any squadron on the wing and carry out joint, precisely timed and coordinated attacks safely and effectively. Wing Commander David Henderson, who had taken over 14 Squadron from David Baron in June 1983, described Jaguar attack missions for the *RAF News* in September 1983. He spoke of the meticulous preparation for every sortie, albeit often against the clock, which enabled them to be flown without radio communication (except in emergency), essentially at low level. Personally prepared, hand-held 1:500,000 scale maps and traditional low-level navigation practices were used to provide a back-up to the Jaguar's ever-improving NAVWASS. A potential conflict between the need to look down into the cockpit and outside for navigation pinpoints and to avoid hazards was alleviated to some extent by use of the Head-Up Display (HUD). All this was part of John Thomson's relentless determination, as with predecessors and successors, to enhance the wing's operational capability, showing the way himself by flying regularly with each of the squadrons in turn.

Helped by a willing staff and the ladies of RAF Brüggen, John could also claim continuing improvements in the station's domestic facilities and activities. With Wyn Williams, wife of Del Williams, the moving force and first headmistress, a nursery school was set up in a redundant but custom-built facility in Elmpt, ideally located for the service flats there and with buses provided to take children to and from the station. On the base, older children from Cheshire Middle School won a BFBS Drama Competition and appeared on German television with their entry. Del Williams himself, as Chairman of a Joint Parents' Committee, masterminded the removal and reconstruction of wooden huts from 431 MU to Shepherd's Fields by Major Hawkins and his 217 MCAG(RE) unit, for use by the station's hitherto nomadic scouts, guides, cubs and brownies. The new, joint centre was opened by the wife of the C-in-C, Jill Hine, on 9 June 1983 and, in another major project, the Malcolm Club was completely refurbished. Brüggen had all that a small town could wish for.

However, not everyone wanted to play an active part in station life and it was sometimes difficult to find leaders and helpers for the less popular charities. Persuasion, bribery and coercion had their place and it was not unknown for certain sponsors to lock doors until sufficient 'volunteers' were forthcoming. A little subterfuge worked well when much-wanted but reticent contributors to a charity cook book were threatened with attribution for less than best recipes, a headmaster's wife succumbing when it was mooted that she might be associated with an unacceptable entry for 'Mushy Peas'.

Old stories are the best, especially when they feature the station's hierarchy. Take the one about the first lady who returned to Brüggen House after an evening of bridge, without a key and with two young daughters wrapped in blankets. The now Lady Thomson recalls that her man, back early from a dining-in night and already in a deep sleep, remained oblivious to her efforts to wake him. Fortunately, he had left a window to the master bedroom ajar, and late night revellers from the officers' mess were treated to the sight and sound of this resourceful lady using a borrowed ladder to climb up to the window and exchange a few words with her rather befuddled husband. He, after confirming that his daughters were alive and well, invited her in, presumably through the window because he didn't open any doors, and promptly moved into the spare bedroom. To cheers from the spectators below, Jan Thomson climbed through the window, retrieved her daughters by a more orthodox route, and the crowd melted away into the night.

Other stories tell of wives seeking solace when their men were away on detachment, in refurnishing their houses by means of clever, seductive deals with local furniture agents, usually without the need for cheque books. Delivery was often very early in the morning, the first some husbands would know of these 'must have' acquisitions. Then came the vocal drama of getting traditionally large German and Dutch schranks into the small married quarters.

While the lot of a serviceman's wife was not always a happy one, and some resented being 'wife of....', there were those who redressed the balance by looking on the bright side. In a long diatribe in the May 1983 issue of the *Brüggen Circuit* 'Eileen G' saw both sides.

> Years of shift work, detachments by the score
> Exercises, burnt dinners – who could want for more?
> Meeting people, strange customs, different foods to eat,
> Superb holidays, taken for granted – what a treat!
> When I go back home and meet old friends
> Semi, telly – their life begins and ends
> Would I swap my nomadic existence for their stable life?
> No way – I love being a 'serviceman's wife'!

In 1983, 37 Squadron won the Barnard Trophy with top marks in Rapier Categorisation, Senior Aircraftsman Dempsey scoring an unprecedented 100% as an operator and Sergeant Harfield the highest marks ever as a tactical operator. Then, at a Missile Practice Camp (MPC) in the Hebrides in October, Senior Aircraftsman Andy Freeman had the honour of firing the range's 6,000th missile, while Senior Aircraftsman 'Chang' Mayer won a crate of beer for shooting down a Skeet target. While travelling at only 130 knots, success against the £8,000, nine feet long Skeet with its eleven feet wingspan, under radio control to evade the Mach 2 Rapier missile was no mean feat. Also unusual at this MPC, a missile fell mysteriously from its launcher, adding 'Missile on Floor' (MOF) to the gunners' vocabulary. Squadron Leader Michael Valentine, the squadron's CO, asked what made it fall and was rewarded with a technical explanation from Senior Aircraftsman Sid Backhouse: 'gravity, Sir'.

The squadron went on to win the Premier Regiment Trophy for Rapier Squadrons and many RAF Germany sporting accolades. Now twinned with the local town of Niederkrüchten, sport at a rather lower level was at the core of a final get-together with this local community before the squadron departed for its second detachment to the Falklands in February 1984. On its first tour there in 1982, it had depended much on legendary Regiment improvisation at its remote sites, often living under canvas in continuous rain and mud with no creature comforts and resupplied only by air. This four month detachment would be very different;

The Commandant General RAF Regiment, AVM Reed-Purvis, presents OC 37 Squadron, Sqn Ldr Mike Valentine, with the Barnard Trophy for gaining the highest marks in Rapier Categorisation in 1983. (*Brüggen Circuit*)

Black Eagle Camp, Stanley Airfield, in 1984, home for Rapier squadrons during their four-month Falkland Islands detachments. (*37 Squadron*)

they would live on permanent sites or in floating 'hotels' ('coastels') with greatly improved leisure and sporting facilities, but still with plenty of scope for Regiment ingenuity at work and play.

The other operational squadrons were also twinned with local towns in partnership arrangements which had been ratified at Brüggen on 23 February 1983; 14 Squadron with Schwalmtal, 17 Squadron with Stadt Viersen, 20 Squadron with Nettetal and 31 Squadron with Brüggen. All this added to the bonds already well established between the station and the local communities.

Important to these bonds were the civilians who worked so loyally for the RAF at Brüggen. Among them, Herr Jan Gutjahr had a particularly interesting past; he had trained as a pilot on the Fiesler Storch in the Luftwaffe and went on to fly the Me 109 and Fw190 before transferring to the elite Parachute Corps, dropping with special forces behind Allied lines. He saw service in Norway, Belgium, Crete, Russia, Africa and Italy, was taken prisoner, escaped three times and stole a Spitfire with too little fuel aboard to take him anywhere. He had been at Brüggen from the start, progressing through a number of jobs to become the all-important Barrack Warden.

Herr Herbert Gisbertz had also completed thirty years' service on the station by 1983, to become head cook in the airmen's mess. He remembers feeding 1,300 predominantly single men there in the early days of National Service, this number dropping progressively over the years to a level of 800 men and women. The menus had also changed dramatically, from hot pot, Irish stew and meat pies, to choice turkey, chicken, steak and pork, with a cold table, continental bar and barbecue now often available in much enhanced facilities overall. Vive la change! Herr Gisbertz would almost certainly have been involved in the great 'Banjo controversy'. Banjo was a slice of cooked ham with fried egg between slices of bread, much-loved in the hot-box breakfasts provided during exercises. When a new catering officer proclaimed that banjos did not comply with health and safety requirements there was general outrage, accompanied by a campaign demanding 'Bring back the Banjo', 'Banjos are good for you', 'A Banjo a day...' etc, until the station commander became personally involved. He asked two questions: firstly, 'How many Banjos have been served over the years?' Answer: 'Hundreds of thousands'; and secondly, 'How many cases of food poisoning have resulted?' Answer: 'Nil'. Banjos were back.

Among the honours and awards for Brüggen in 1983 was a Queen's Commendation for Valuable Services in the Air for the very popular OC 20 Squadron, Wing Commander Dick Wharmby, who had taken over from Frank Mitchell in May 1982. When Dick died of cancer in 1999, ex-Jaguar pilot John Pym wrote a moving tribute to him, this one verse saying it all:

JAGUAR STRIKE WING

You touched each one of us who passed
With gentle honour, strength and charm
And in your lea was peace and calm
A rock to stem life's winter blast.

An invaluable asset to the management of the front line tactical squadrons in Germany was the establishment of operations assistants, SACs of the Air Traffic Control branch, tasked with caring for myriad routine matters in the PBF (squadron operations room). In that role, Senior Aircraftsman Steve Hill was one of three ops assistants assigned to 17 (Jaguar) Squadron between 1983 and 1985, and as such he was responsible for updating the weather and air traffic information, preparing briefing material and submitting flight plans, liaising with the COC, ATC and the squadron engineers. He accompanied the aircrew on detachments to 439 Squadron RCAF at Baden Soelingen, RAF Machrihanish, Decimomannu and Akrotiri. From senior flight supervisors down to junior pilots, the squadrons came to depend heavily on these operations room clerks, and Steve was rewarded for his efforts with a flight in the two-seat Jaguar T2, flown by Squadron Leader Chris Lorraine, on a typical operational training sortie, led by Flight Lieutenant Al Hoy in a GR1. In a busy flight, they dropped practice bombs and fired the Aden cannon on Vliehors range in Holland, inter alia 'taking a close look' at a Luftwaffe Phantom, an F-104 Starfighter and one of their own Jaguars, all flying low and fast in the Low Flying Areas (LFAs). There could be no greater payback for a man who made such a contribution to the squadron's operations.

On 9 December 1983, John Thomson handed over command to another Jaguar pilot and one-time CO of 14 Squadron, Group Captain Joe Sim. With the demise of RAF Germany's Jaguar force now on the horizon, John left having done all that was reasonable to achieve the objectives he had outlined at the start of his tour; the station was now more effective in its role and its people were in good heart. The new commander was taking over a going concern.

In his 1984 New Year's message, Joe Sim spoke of the name Brüggen as synonymous with the word excellence and announced his determination to continue seeking operational goals while maintaining the quality of life. He too would be as good as his word during a most demanding transition from Jaguar to Tornado in the two years ahead.

The Jaguar men were leaving Brüggen with their heads held high, working and playing hard up to the end as the resident squadrons overlapped with their Tornado successors without detriment to operational commitments. Looking back at the previous eight years, they had much to be proud of. In 1978, Brüggen had become the first NATO air force strike/attack wing to be awarded the highest possible gradings in all aspects of its Taceval and went on to repeat this outstanding achievement in 1980 and 1982. They did it again in 1984, in what the NATO

Taceval team called 'the hardest test they had ever seen', a very fitting end. So it was right that the farewells were not wakes but celebrations within a highly professional and historically happy band.

On 30 June 1984, 20 Squadron redeployed to Laarbruch to become the first RAF Germany squadron to be re-equipped with Tornados, and Germany's Jaguar bombers began taking their leave.

Chapter Seven

Tornado – Change and Continuity

At 1230 hours on Wednesday, 13 June 1984, Group Captain Joe Sim and Wing Commander Dave Phillips (OC Ops Wg), flew the station's first Tornado GR1 into Brüggen. The aircraft, ZD712, a training variant, was destined for 31 Squadron.

Tornado was a joint product of the British, German and Italian aircraft industries, with British Aerospace and Rolls-Royce heading the UK team. Originating as the Multi-Role Combat Aircraft (MRCA) it was spawned of the ill-fated TSR2 and the Anglo-French Variable Geometry project but it would prove to be very much more than the 'Much Refurbished Canberra Again' MRCA predicted by the sceptics. The

The first Tornado GR1 arrived at Brüggen on 13 June 1984. (R to L, front): AVM Alan White, Dep Cdr RAF Germany; Wg Cdr Dave Phillips, OC Ops Wg (navigator); Gp Capt Joe Sim, Stn Cdr (pilot). (*Brüggen Circuit*)

Out with the old and in with the new; 31 Squadron Jaguar and Tornado. (*Brüggen Circuit*)

aircraft was superior to the Jaguar in range, payload and top speed, and above all it had a more sophisticated navigation and weapons system, with a Terrain Following Radar (TFR), which would enable it to operate at very low levels at night and in all weather. It handled well over the full speed range, had a roomy cockpit, gave a quiet, comfortable ride, and thus become very popular with its crews.

The Brüggen Tornados would carry the new JP233, with its runway cratering and airfield denial munitions, in addition to the full range of contemporary nuclear and conventional weapons. It was equipped with a 27mm Mauser gun and Sidewinder missiles for self-protection, a radar homing and warning receiver, Boz chaff and flare dispenser and a Skyshadow ECM pod.

Brüggen's Jaguars had not gone yet; for them it was business as usual, but 14 Squadron's scribe might have been feeling a little cynical when he offered the *Brüggen Circuit* some random thoughts on how they spent their time during the APC at Deci in the summer of 1984. He wrote of long, hot working days which were often far from routine, with Capo Frasca Range opening and closing most unpredictably, for reasons which were often hard to understand, then back to hot rooms, all-American radio and attempts to talk to civilisation over telephones which took 'ridiculous-shaped coins', before repairing to the bars to practise NATO 'togetherness'. There were memories of junior ranks celebrating D-Day in a German bar, of NCOs taking sherry with 'some rather dubious' naval types and of pilots in the 'Pig and Tape' pondering from which tree to hang their JEngO. Sorties to Gibraltar provided some respite and at weekends there was a twenty-five minute, nerve-wracking van journey to Cagliari 'to watch the "sooties and fairies" collecting shells (?) on Poeto Beach', or the shorter trip to Assemini for pizza, pasta or gelati (ice cream). To be fair, the July 1985 edition of the *Circuit* carried another account of Deci days by a 14 Squadron winged crusader which, perhaps because it was the last APC there for a single-seat strike/attack squadron, was rather more benevolent.

When work on Brüggen's runway began in May 1984, the Jaguar squadrons dispersed to Wildenrath, Cyprus, Gibraltar and Deci, returning in August for the transition from Jaguar to Tornado to begin in earnest, with overlaps to avoid a gap in the RAF's commitment to NATO.

Wing Commander Dick Bogg, a navigator, had arrived in July to command the first of four Tornado squadrons at Brüggen, his squadron initially being known as 31 Squadron (Designate), and he as 'Des'. Among those there to meet him and his wife Peg were his squadron warrant officer, Jeff Field and his German wife Erika, who would play a crucial role in bringing together a squadron which would comprise thirteen aircraft, eighteen crews (some thirty per cent 'first tourists') and 185 groundcrew. Joe Sim left them in no doubt as to their first mission: 'Pass Taceval!'

Beginning as he intended to go on, Dick demanded that his embryo squadron take part in a station Mineval as soon as it received its first Tornado and, to the admiration of all, the aircraft flew three successful sorties in one day. Then, on 31 October, John Bolton relinquished command of 31 (Jaguar) Squadron, and the Standard was transferred in a parade and fly-past, as the band played 'Will ye no come back again?' Speeches and presentations followed at lunch in the officers' mess, champagne flowed in the Crossbow Club and the less formal celebrations began in earnest. Back at the squadron, last rites were read over the Jaguar, and an unconventional parade of aircrew-manned, aircraft-like bicycles came to a sticky end at the hands of unruly spectators. Flight Lieutenant 'Arris' Arriatis presided over an all-ranks HAS party in the evening, resplendent in his No. 1 uniform and accompanied fleetingly by his venerable Dad, who was dressed in flying suit and clearly bent on some clandestine mission. This cherished 'Arris family of well-stuffed, much-travelled and all-knowing pandas, symbolised the best of 31 Squadron past, and reminded their successors that they had much to live up to. So ended the first of three ceremonies at Brüggen to mark the changeover to Tornado. 'Des' was dead and buried with due ceremony in the south-west corner, and in the busy weekend which followed, the squadron moved into its rightful place in the north-west.

A healthy rivalry soon developed between the new crews and the outgoing 'single-seaters', with plenty of banter and no opportunity lost to score at the other's expense. When bad weather precluded a mass launch at dawn to complete a station exercise, and a 'taxi-through' was ordered, 31 Squadron Tornados taxied out apparently without their navigators. The duty Jaguar pilot and Mineval monitor in the control tower were incensed that the newcomers did not seem to be taking 'the war' seriously, preferring breakfast to duty, and they made their views known in no uncertain manner. In fact, the navigators were on board, head-down and with seats fully lowered as they passed the victims of this ruse.

Then, through no fault of his own, Dick Bogg deposited millions of pieces of chaff all over his squadron's dispersal while taxying out for the first 'live' sortie in Germany with the recently cleared Boz chaff and flare dispenser. There were of course many at Brüggen and elsewhere who saw the funny side as the story spread, but it was no joke for the inimitable Mr Field and his team who had to clear it all up. In another evaluation, Dick, flying with Squadron Leader Mike Dineen, the wing's very capable QFI, was wont to extol the virtues of the Tornado's SPILS (Spin, Incident Limiting System), and in a sometimes lively debate he remained firmly convinced that the system saved lives and aircraft.

While the 'Goldstars' of 31 Squadron were hard at work with their new aircraft, 'Arris went missing. It was thought at first that he had absconded willingly to Wegberg, to be among the girls, but it transpired that he had been abducted forcibly and transported there in the boot of a car (was this the action of caring nurses?). A ransom note threatening 'pay up or the Bear dies' called on the officers of the squadron to attend a dinner at the nurses' mess, properly attired in black tie – but without trousers. The demand was accepted without hesitation. The keeper of the bear, Flying Officer Kim Dove-Dixon, was 'court-martialled' by his peers and found guilty of 'gross dereliction of duty in failing to prevent a bearnap', and there was more distressing news to come. Following a routine medical inspection during his incarceration at the hospital it was alleged that 'Arris was in fact 'Arrista', a female of the species, and this was confirmed by the appearance shortly afterwards of two baby pandas, clad in nappies, bearing the names 'Arris Tweed and 'Arris Junior.

In September, the whole station was involved in Exercise 'Lionheart', the largest exercise mounted by British forces since the Second World War, with 130,000 troops, both regular and reservists, deploying to Germany 'to demonstrate NATO's ability to fight a war in the Central Region'. Brüggen was a major airhead in the Rear Combat Zone, for the reception and dispatch of troops and equipment, and its aircraft flew in support of ground operations.

31 Squadron's 'Arris (or Arrista?), incarcerated in the Intensive Bear Treatment Unit at Wegberg – allegedly with offspring. (*Brüggen Circuit*)

That invaluable adjunct to training, the Tornado flight simulator, was late. Flight Lieutenant Martin Wistow, who would command the unit, remembered that the commercial convoy bringing the containerised unit to the station got lost in Belgium (as did the Phantom simulator years before), on one cold December night in 1984 while the reception committee waited for it at Brüggen. When it did arrive, difficulties with the mounting platform and drainage arrangements, then initial teething troubles, delayed its handover to the operators until June 1985.

At the end of 1984, Joe Sim congratulated the station on having initiated a smooth transition from Jaguar to Tornado and, according to the AAFCE Taceval team, on completing 'the best Taceval ever witnessed (to date!) on a strike/attack base.'

As always, there had also been time for charity and welfare. General Engineering Flight raised DM2,000 for MENCAP from a 24-hour sponsored run; Brüggen's wives collected DM2,000 for the Muscular Dystrophy Fund and Security Squadron contributed much of the DM111,500 collected by the RAF Police in Germany for the Westminster Hospital's bone marrow unit. In September, Lady Hine, wife of the C-in-C, opened the Medical and SSAFA Clinic at the Elmpt Community Welfare Centre, obviating the need for families living there to travel to the station for these facilities.

Gripped by the 'big freeze' in that winter of 1984/85, the usually hyperactive Brüggen seemed to go into hibernation. Cars outside Air Traffic Control were replaced by moon boots as the 'air traffickers' (and others) dug endlessly at the snow covering the runway lights and tried to keep the airfield open. They thought that their pleas for an arduous duty rum ration had fallen on deaf ears, until one of their number was heard giggling inanely behind a locked door in the gentlemen's toilet, where he was purported to be taking good care of their precious allocation. Among those who missed this just dessert on the eve of his retirement was Warrant Officer Vic Cooper, a much-respected controller who, in the latter days of his thirty-eight years of service, is reputed to have reduced '161 pilot officers (at least) to tears and generally terrorised air traffic assistants'. Many will also remember Mrs 'Goody' Cooper who ran Brüggen House so efficiently for several station commanders.

Brüggen Air Traffic Control Tower – in bleak mid-winter, 1985. (*Brüggen Circuit*)

191

Wing Commander Grant McLeod, late of 31 (Jaguar) Squadron, returned to Brüggen in December to take command of the 'Black Knights' of 17 Squadron from Wing Commander Andy Griffin, as the squadron transferred its allegiance to Tornado. A former squadron commander and now C-in-C RAF Germany, Air Marshal Sir Patrick Hine also returned to Brüggen, on 8 February 1985, to present the squadron with a new Standard on the occasion of its 70th Anniversary. The squadron's re-formation with Tornados took place formally at 1700 hours on 1 March, presided over by the Dep Cdr, Air Vice-Marshal Derek Bryant, the Jaguars flying their farewell salute in a figure '17'.

Farewell to Brüggen. 17 Squadron Jaguars – in numbers. (*RAF Brüggen*)

The 'Winged Crusaders' of 14 Squadron were making sure that the Jaguar Strike Wing remained in the news to the end. In January, World Land Speed Record holder, Richard Noble, well versed with speeds of 600 mph in 'Thrust Two', was invited to get airborne with Squadron Leader Jerry Parr, to go a little faster. The squadron celebrated its 70th anniversary with great style in February, and one of its pilots survived the loss of a Jaguar in April, the month in which its first Tornado arrived with its new CO, Wing Commander Joe Whitfield.

February had brought great tragedy when many members of the RAF Germany Band were killed or injured in a coach accident, while travelling to Bavaria for an anniversary of the Winter Survival School in Bad Kohlgrub. The author was among many servicemen and local Germans who were clearly moved by the loss and by a most poignant commemoration service in the beautiful village church. It was with great pleasure that Brüggen welcomed the re-formed band back in business for the first time on 23 April, at the station's Annual Formal Inspection carried out by the Dep Cdr.

For the first two Tornado squadrons, the gruelling work up to operational status was rewarded by a highly successful Taceval in June. The much vaunted '1' was awarded for Operations, but Support and Survival to Operate activities missed this ultimate accolade 'by a whisker'. The NATO team reported: 'The enthusiasm and evident commitment of all ranks was most noticeable and the level of skills and general professional standards was exemplary.'

No. 37 Squadron flew to the new Mount Pleasant Airport in the Falklands at the end of June for another four-month detachment, while the flying squadrons began showing off their new Tornados in the squadron exchange programme. They were also flying frequent sorties to the tactical Electronic Warning (EW) range at Spadeadam, to prove the Marconi Radar Homing and Warning Receiver (RWR). It was a demanding, fast learning curve for the new force, during routine operational training and at their APCs, ACMI exercises and MPCs. Sidewinder AAM firings did not always go to plan; on two separate detachments at Valley, the missiles launched by 31 Squadron fused on the Jindivik drones rather than on the flare they towed, destroying them at a cost of a quarter of a million pounds apiece.

Low-level tactics had been Brüggen's modus operandi for many years and would remain so, but the avionics and weapons available to Tornado would greatly enhance the effectiveness of Brüggen's contribution to NATO, as the squadrons progressed towards proficiency in large tactical formations, flying very low by day and night and in all weather to achieve ever greater weapons accuracies. This began with day-only training in Germany and the UK, then night flying in Scotland, in fair weather, before the squadrons went further afield to Nellis AFB in Nevada, and the Canadian Air Force Base at Goose Bay in Labrador, for the Flag and Western Vortex exercises respectively. Nevada had almost everything the men from Brüggen desired, from demanding and exhilarating flying against realistic targets in the most operational environment possible in peacetime, plenty of light refreshment in the clubs on base and unparalleled entertainment of all kinds in downtown Las Vegas. Here the weather was almost always excellent, if rather too hot in summer, although sandstorms could be a problem. There was time for golf, skiing on nearby lakes and on snow in the local mountains. A less likely sport was rugby, but the records show that on one occasion an all-ranks team played the Las Vegas Rugby Club, and to their shame 'were robbed' of their expected victory. Flying discipline was necessarily strict, even by US standards, and all those who went to Red Flag around this time will remember the sanctity of the airspace (known as 'Dreamland') around the F-117's home base. Flight Lieutenants Dick Downs and Wally Grout of 31 Squadron found out about it the hard way when they had to land there short of fuel, were arrested, interrogated, and had their fortunes told before being released.

Goose Bay had less of the extraneous attractions but it was there, over frozen lakes and snowfields in Exercise Western Vortex, that many crews had their first taste of Automatic Terrain Following (ATF) at very low-level in formation, at night and in bad weather. Dick Bogg, who led the first of these detachments with 31 Squadron, recalls: 'This was the ultimate peacetime test of both man and machine and, by the end of three weeks, all crews had participated in tactical formations which involved taking off at twenty second intervals, entering cloud almost immediately, flying parallel tracks 1.5 NM apart, making closely-spaced attacks on simulated targets while still in cloud and not seeing adjacent aircraft until on the final approach to land, with about a minute to go to touchdown. A hair-raising experience and it made no difference whether a sortie was a crew's first or thousandth trip; the work demanded the highest possible concentration by both pilot and navigator for the full two hours, and an absolute trust in machine and fellow aircrew.'

In his book *Tornado Times* Wing Commander Ian Hall, who commanded 31 Squadron later in its life, remembers preparing for Western Vortex in the Scottish Highlands in a typical trip on a 'dark and dirty winter night, with the terrain following radar and auto-pilot pitching the aircraft up hill and down dale as the system followed the rugged contours. Every now and then as the route broke out of cloud there would be reassuring glimpses of the three other aircraft in the formation, each a couple of miles away on its own track and time, but the whole perfectly co-ordinated.' Thrilling stuff.

No. 52 Field Squadron (Construction) returned to Brüggen in the spring of 1985 for Exercise Flying Eagle, to continue their task of making the station more survivable and operationally effective in war, when it would take over repair and maintenance tasks from the PSA. Manpower and equipment were deployed from its base in the UK to supplement a small cadre of resident artisans and pool of heavy plant now held permanently in a compound beyond 431 MU in the north-west corner of the airfield. Despite an absence of eighteen months the squadron had clearly not lost its expertise in making and filling holes in the airfield's paved surfaces, firefighting and maintaining essential services. In the tactical phase, 25kg of explosives in a Runway Cratering Kit went up with a bang leaving a hole in the taxiway seven metres in diameter and two metres deep. Well-rehearsed runway repair, which in war would make use of the aggregate and matting stockpiled

Summer in the Falklands for Brüggen's 37 Squadron, RAF Regiment. (*Brüggen Circuit*)

around the base, involved six machines filling the crater at one time before a 7 x 5 metre, 13 tonne mat was laid and bolted in place, all in some twenty minutes. All this was thirsty work and the *Circuit* recorded that 'in the limited free time available 52 Squadron made full use of Brüggen's excellent facilities, with enthusiastic investment in the Crossbow Club'.

The station commander and his wife had cause to remember this particular detachment when they were woken in the dead of night by noises below, and found a newly-arrived sapper, suffering from fatigue and an excess of Grolsch, recumbent on their sofa. The ensuing conversation is not on record but it seems that the unwanted guest believed he had been shown to his room by new 'friends' on the resident 37 Squadron, RAF Regiment; he had wondered at the luxury of other ranks' quarters in the RAF, but then fell asleep. Thereafter, the legitimate incumbents kept their doors locked at night!

This was not the only story of unexpected visitors to married quarters. One officer's lady heard the key in the lock, guessed that her husband had returned early from a detachment and rushed down to greet him, perhaps ready for an amorous reunion. Then she remembered, just in time, that the burglar alarm had been switched off and that she had lent PSA's Willie Luys a key to let himself in to finish a works service in the house. It could have been embarrassing.

Things were changing on the domestic front too. Old timers will remember the Public Services Institute (PSI), but in 1985 all its activities were centralised in the renamed Services Institute Fund (SIF), located in new premises built by 217 MCAG between the Families' Office and the Scout Hut. These included a central SIF office with the cashier, sports and gift shops, haircraft salon, travel and information bureau; it was a veritable shopping centre with many concessions and extraneous facilities available specifically for servicemen and their families. Life was improving all the time at Brüggen.

52 Squadron, RE, invaluable for rapid runway repair, airfield survival and enhancement, on Brüggen's Exercise 'Flying Eagle' in 1985. (*Brüggen Circuit*)

First in last out, 14 Squadron had introduced the single-seat nuclear role into the RAF with the Jaguar and was the first to operate the aircraft from the newly 'hardened' facilities at Brüggen; it now had the distinction of mounting the last single-seat nuclear QRA on 14 October 1985. At the end of the month, after a final review by a former CO, Air Marshal Sir Christopher Foxley-Norris, David Henderson and his Jaguar men began their farewells to Brüggen. The Squadron Standard was handed over on 1 November, in a ceremony reviewed by another ex-CO, Air Vice-Marshal Derek Bryant, and Joe Whitfield took command of the squadron. The boss's Jaguar 'AA' had returned to the UK with the rest but a ghost remained. Being from 14 Squadron himself, station commander Joe Sim ensured that the Jaguar, and particularly 'AA', would not be forgotten. By devious means and a lot of help from the engineers, he had a hybrid constructed, mounted in front of Station HQ and unveiled in December 1985 by Derek Bryant. This was one of the last events in Joe Sims' busy tour, covering two years of transition from the Jaguar to Tornado, a further hardening programme and many associated changes in the infrastructure, operating procedures and engineering support. In December he handed over command to Group Captain John Houghton, a former 17 Squadron Commander.

The last of the wing's Tornados (ZD895) arrived from RAF St. Athan on 16 March 1986 and in April the C-in-C, now Air Marshal Sir David Parry-

First in – last out. 14 Squadron's Jaguars in a final photo-call, October 1985.
(*RAF Brüggen*)

Evans, presented OC Eng Wg, Wing Commander Ian Brackenbury, with the 1985 Engineering Efficiency Trophy. A turbulent and difficult year of re-equipping and reorganising had been rewarded.

Brüggen's generosity over Christmas 1985 knew no bounds, so much so that one charity, the Helen House hospice for children in Oxford, took the unprecedented step of asking the station to stop sending them money. With enough funds now to meet their running costs for the foreseeable future, these grateful recipients pleaded that the money which continued to roll in be diverted to the Martin House hospice.

April 1986 was another good month for leisure and sport at Brüggen. The Astra Cinema had been converted by 217 MCAG into what would become one of the most successful leisure facilities on the station: the Brüggen Bowl. Opened by the station commander, John Houghton, and run by Derek Charles, this 6-lane, 10-pin alley was financed initially from non-public funds at a cost of DM250K, the conversion and installation of equipment taking eight months. Had this work been carried out commercially the cost might have been as high as DM2.5M. The supplementary loans necessary at the start were soon paid off and several charitable events were thereafter sponsored by, or held at the Brüggen Bowl, typically a 24-hour non-stop bowl which generated DM17K for station and German charities. At one such event the Armament Engineering Squadron presented an inert 28lb practice bomb, to go on show in the glass cabinet in the bar along with many other trophies, including a splendid miniature silver dog, presented by a grateful British Guide Dogs for the Blind.

The Officers' Mess Annual Reception for military and civilian guests, held on the beautiful evening of 7 May was particularly memorable, with the RAF Germany Band, now reformed, playing on the lawn in front of the famous Brüggen tree, and four Tornados flying overhead in salute.

It was a rude awakening for all as a station Mineval got underway at 0230 hours on 9 June. After the aircraft generation phase the wing's battle management staff and operational squadrons underwent three days of intensive interoperability training, to develop procedures for co-ordinating large formations, day and night. The exercise concluded with a mass launch, during which the 'Top Dog' (bomb on time) competition was resurrected, with presentations to the winners (names not recorded) at the first ever Tornado Wing lunch.

In October 1986 Brüggen became the largest Tornado base in the RAF when No. IX Squadron deployed from RAF Honington to the south-west corner of the airfield, to a site rebuilt and optimised for the new aircraft following the departure of No. 20 (Jaguar) Squadron. No. IX Squadron's badge, carrying the motto 'Per Noctem Volamus' ('We fly at night') configured a bat rampant; it had been a distinguished bomber squadron since its formation in 1914, notably equipped with the Vimy, Wellington, Lancaster, Canberra and Vulcan. A IX Squadron Vulcan took part in the Falklands campaign, the only Brüggen squadron able to make that claim, and in 1982 it became the first operational Tornado squadron. Justly proud of

217 MCAG completed the conversion of the Astra Cinema into the Brüggen Bowl in April 1986. (*Derek Charles*)

17 (F) Squadron, 1986.

its heritage, its prized possession was a piece of bulkhead from the German pocket battleship *Tirpitz*, made of heavy steel plate measuring 4 x 3 feet and awarded to IX and 617 (Dambuster) Squadrons for sinking the ship on 12 November 1944. Since the presentation, the two squadrons have waged a veritable war to possess the memento, it changing hands several times, so the first priority at Brüggen was to secure it to the wall of the squadron crewroom. Five years later the 'Dambusters' entered 'Gotham City' while IX Squadron was away on detachment, removed the plate (destroying half the wall in the process), and mounted it even more securely in their PBF at Lossiemouth. It was there at the time of writing, when it was rumoured that an accommodation had been reached between the two incumbent squadron commanders that the real thing be committed to posterity in the RAF Museum at Hendon and a single replica be produced to allow the competition of wits to continue.

No. IX Squadron arrived at Brüggen under the command of Wing Commander 'Alfy' Ferguson, the third navigator among the five wing commanders on flying duties in Operations Wing, and immediately proclaimed 'The Year of the Bat'. The *Circuit* called for bats migrating from the UK 'not to be left in the dark', but dedicated drinkers turned a blind eye to the apparitions which hurtled none too silently through the officers' mess at a welcoming beer call, clad in what looked like black bin bags, before hanging upside down from the awning outside. On the other hand, the station certainly took notice when, within weeks of their arrival, the 'batmen' relieved the older residents of their Salmond Trophy.

To underline Brüggen 'togetherness', a photograph was to be taken of four Tornados in formation, each aircraft resplendent in its own individual squadron markings. The first attempt to record this unique quartet failed when it was found, after they had taken off, that the 14 Squadron Tornado carried no such markings. The gleeful telling of this unusual 'Crusader' reticence was matched only by another tale, told with equal relish, of a neighbouring squadron which managed to dispatch an aircraft on a major air-to-air refuelling (AAR) exercise without a refuelling probe. Even Brüggen men could sometimes get it wrong. By now the station had made a habit of picking up most of the best sporting awards, so it was no surprise when they won the Sir Robert Foster Sports Trophy for the eighth consecutive year in October 1986. In presenting the trophy to the station yet again, Air Marshal Sir David Parry-Evans commented: 'RAF Brüggen seems to have hit the right balance between operational tasks and sporting commitment.' This happy combination of business and pleasure came naturally to the hot shots of 37 Squadron RAF Regiment who, in 1986, did particularly well in shooting competitions, firstly against their rivals in RAF Germany and then within the annual RAF Small Arms Association meeting at Bisley.

In October 1986, QRA was relaxed from fifteen minutes to twelve hours. No one regretted the passing of this onerous commitment, with its long hours of standby for air and groundcrews in confined quarters or the tedium of extra guard duties for the RAF policemen. True, living conditions had continued to improve, but any opportunity for personal administration or relaxation was always threatened by an exercise alert. NATO and the nation had demanded that every cockpit, HAS and release procedure be deeply ingrained in the mind, adhered to strictly and rehearsed religiously, every target and route known by heart. Myriad checks were carried out to ensure that this was so, imposing additional stress and strain on all involved, but the author is not aware that Brüggen was ever found wanting. It is said that in one final, irreverent act, Brüggen aircrew on QRA duty over the previous Christmas had managed to telephone their opposite numbers on a base in

Properly dressed this time; Tornados from Brüggen's four flying squadrons get airborne together. (*RAF Brüggen*)

East Germany, to exchange the season's greetings. The devil makes work for light hands and the unwary could fall foul of mischief-making boredom in QRA, as one guard found to his cost. He had dozed off in the quiet hours while on duty, to be awoken by an alarm initiated for his benefit. Attempting to redress his crime by springing into action he found the door to his sentry box jammed closed and a large audience outside witnessing his strenuous exertions to free himself.

No. 31 Squadron changed hands officially on 14 November 1986, when Dick Bogg, promoted to Group Captain in July, handed over to Wing Commander Pete Dunlop during an evocative parade, at which a new Standard was presented and Dick was heard to say: 'They're all yours – you lucky man!' Getting his priorities right, Pete Dunlop very prudently made friends with the 'works and bricks' man, Willie Luys, clearly with an eye to expediting those works services he felt the squadron needed. Wasting no time, he showed Willie what he wanted by taking a hammer to the wall between an office and adjacent crewroom, with the object of enlarging the latter. Willie took the hint and had the job completed professionally. In their gratitude, the squadron made Willie an honorary member, perhaps with other jobs in mind.

Within his mid-term message, John Houghton reiterated the policy of alternating the station's charitable donations one year to good causes off-base and the next to domestic needs. In 1986/87 the station presented the RAF Benevolent Fund with £15,000 from its collective efforts, then turned to support the community and welfare centres at Donderberg and Elmpt, facilities for the clubs and societies made homeless by barrack block modernization. He also intended to improve the many sporting facilities on the base which had deteriorated naturally in the thirty-four years of its life, well beyond their sell-by dates, and make improvements to its swimming pool.

The station commander got 1987 off to a business-like start with a Mineval on 6 January. Additional security measures were put in place, to protect the Tornado force on the ground, with the arrival of No. 51 Light Armoured Squadron, RAF Regiment, to patrol the base in their Spartan armoured vehicles and No. 52 Regiment, RE, to help keep the station operational. Brüggen now had a new potency. The *Brüggen Circuit* recorded the scene graphically, pictorially and for posterity, emphasising the team effort and giving proper credit to the support forces. The airfield was shown to be under attack, with the Ground Defence Operations Centre directing the evacuation of 14 Squadron when their PBF was threatened by an unexploded bomb, while the EOD teams dealt with anti-personnel mines on the site. Dispersed medical specialists tended life-like casualties, quietly and efficiently as the caterers, with splendid improvisation, delivered hot meals and drinks to all the 'players' around the clock. The strain and tension on men, women and machines as these exercises stretched non-stop into several days and nights cannot be described adequately here; this was a whole station virtually at war and these memories will be familiar to all those who served there at the time.

As was so often the case at Brüggen, the weather put paid to best laid plans, and that spring of 1987 was no exception. It had been intended to taxi the whole Tornado wing on to the runway, for a unique press photograph on return from a Mineval mass launch, but an unexpected snow squall so reduced the visibility that aircraft taxying out had to stop and close down their engines. They were eventually towed into position, in eight 'Vics' of five line astern for a massive show of force which the *Sunday Express* called 'the £784M Mean Machine'. The *Circuit* also told the story of an ejection from 14 Squadron's Tornado ZD894, near Wesel on 30 March, in which Flight Lieutenant Moloney escaped largely unhurt but his navigator Flight Lieutenant Jon Hill was not quite so lucky. Jon was left suspended 60 feet up a tree, still attached to his parachute and with a clearly broken arm, 'looking far from happy'. Although delighted that he was otherwise in one piece, Jon received little sympathy from his pilot, who likened his appearance to that of Pooh Bear stuck in his tree looking for honey. He recalls that, with a lot of yelling, the local fire brigade seemed to be 'practising Benny Hill sketches or an old Bavarian dance number', and that the one with the ladder fell over twice before being relieved of the job. A recitation from A.A. Milne seemed to do little for Jon's morale but it earned a generous round of applause from the firemen who had now finished their dance. Then, to cheers from a second fire brigade, three ambulance men and two helicopter crews, many sightseers and a man from the press, they managed to get half way up to the unfortunate Pooh, before running out of ladders. Plan B, to cut down the tree and catch Pooh as he fell, was roundly condemned by the local Forstmeister and Pooh, who was no more impressed by Plan C, in which he would be blown down to earth in the downwash from a helicopter. Plan C (as modified) did eventually work, when, on a third swing into the tree, the chopper's winchman caught his prey and returned with him into the helicopter for onward dispatch to the Intensive Bear

THE BIGGEST AND THE BEST

The Brüggen Tornado Wing of 1987 disappears into the distance – an awesome show of force which the *Sunday Express* described as a '£784M Mean Machine'. (*Brüggen Circuit*)

Unit at a hospital in Duisburg. Here, priority was given to the determination of who would pay the bill for the forthcoming, very adequate bear-care. The original author of this epic would have it known that, in reality, the response and efficiency of all the German emergency services involved was excellent.

That the ejection seat helped so many to safety can in part be attributed to the men of the Arm Eng Sqn, who were responsible for aspects of their maintenance and servicing, but their job was done when the incumbents reached tree-level. Most armourers beavered away, largely unseen in that prohibited part of the airfield south of the runway, putting together their instruments of mass destruction while others had more immediate tasks.

Since the 1970s EOD teams, with their robots, were committed ever more frequently throughout the station to deal with 'suspect packages' or hoax bomb calls. The disruption caused by these incidents, particularly when unmarked personal possessions were blown up as a precaution, became an all too regular feature of life at Brüggen. Then there were relics of the Second World War to deal with, such as in May 1987 when the PSA found something very sinister by Crash Gate 16 on the airfield's perimeter; they showed it to the EOD team and left the area. What was believed to be a 105mm shell was placed in a big hole and (at the second time of asking) detonated; it certainly did contain 1½kg of TNT. The EOD team was able to open up a second shell, found shortly afterwards, using the 'charge linear cutting' technique, and found the booster to be in remarkably good condition, with the date of manufacture clearly visible on its paper wrapper. It was wise to be cautious.

In July 1987, Brüggen lost another Tornado, ZD738 from 31 Squadron, this time in the UK, when Squadron Leader Ivor Walker and navigator Flight Lieutenant Steve Lloyd had so many failures that the Central Warning Panel (CWP) was showing 'more captions on than off'. The crew ejected at 800 feet in a 30° nose-down attitude; Lloyd suffered minor injuries and the aircraft crashed in Sedmoor, ten miles north-west of Pickering. Otherwise, July was a good month for flying at Brüggen, 14 Squadron achieving more hours (524) than any squadron in RAF Germany since the introduction of Tornado.

An oft-forgotten legacy from the early 1970s, the Phantom simulator at Brüggen continued to serve the Wildenrath Phantom squadrons throughout Jaguar times and well into the Tornado era. Not so easily forgotten, and well known to so many within the fighter business, was one of its most erstwhile instructors, the aforementioned Squadron Leader Arthur Vine, who joined the RAF in 1941 and retired at Brüggen just after his sixty-fifth birthday in 1987.

Cries of 'It's a goat!', which once boomed throughout 17 Squadron's site whenever its CO, Wing Commander Grant McLeod, was less than pleased, became mere echoes in the mind when he handed over to Wing Commander Nial Irving in October 1987. However, the memories would be kept alive, with McGinty the goat, a gift from Flight Lieutenant Tim Anderson, departing 17 Squadron from his first of four Tornado tours at Brüggen in July 1988.

'It's a Goat!' Wg Cdr Grant McLeod's familiar cry earned him a real goat, McGinty, which he passed on to Wg Cdr Nial Irving (right), with the command of 17 Squadron, in October 1987. (*Brüggen Circuit*)

Was there a synergy between the character of the squadrons and their choice of mascots, they being McGinty; 20 Squadron's Elbert Du Crosses, the tortoise; 'Arris the bear on 31 Squadron and Eric Androvani, a 7-foot Rock Python on 14 Squadron? Pet owners should have been a little wary of 14 Squadron's advertisement in the October 1987 edition of the *Brüggen Circuit*:

GOING ON HOLIDAY? WORRIED ABOUT YOUR PETS? WORRY NO MORE!
No. 14 (Snake) Squadron offers a unique pet-sitting service. We will pick up your pet and sit it in a warm, friendly environment for the duration of your holiday. Regrettably, only hamsters and rabbits this year, however, if business continues to grow, we hope to accommodate cats and dogs next year!

John Houghton, recently promoted to air commodore, was also preparing to leave, but with panache. There is something anomalous about aircrew jumping out of fully serviceable aircraft but charity at Brüggen was a powerful incentive. Leading from the front, if perhaps a little 'boat-happy', John 'invited' Wing Commanders Joe Whitfield, Frank Short and Tony Levitt, Squadron Leaders Dick Turner, Rick

Woodroffe and Derek Jones to parachute with him from an Islander aircraft onto the airfield. For some unreported reason, perhaps causing some consternation on the ground and in the air, the aircraft circled the drop zone three times before the dispatcher considered it safe enough for Joe Whitfield to jump, but in the end the event raised DM5,000 for station charities.

John Houghton's 'volunteers' – about to jump for charity. (L to R): WO Brian McGill (Chief Instructor), Sqn Ldr Nick Woodroffe, Wg Cdr Frank Short, Sqn Ldr Derek Jones, Wg Cdr Tony Levitt, Sqn Ldr Dick Turner, Wg Cdr Joe Whitfield, Air Cdre Houghton (Stn Cdr). (*Frank Short*)

In a final, reflective mood, John led a mixed party of servicemen, wives and children from Brüggen to an Anglo-Dutch Remembrance Ceremony at the Roermond Old Cemetery on 1 November 1987, to commemorate RAF and RCAF aircrew and members of the Dutch Resistance who died during the Second World War. As always, the Dutch contingent was headed by Mevrouw Anja van Leyssen, who had joined the Dutch Resistance during the war at the age of nineteen, and risked her life helping twenty-nine Allied airmen escape capture. Winston Churchill called her that 'Little Tiger from Holland' and after the war she was honoured by several nations with some fourteen decorations, including the British George Cross. Brüggen had become part of this annual and most moving tribute of prayers, the playing of the Last Post, speeches and the laying of wreaths in 1983, all helping to bring the two communities closer.

A contingent from RAF Brüggen, led by the station commander, now Air Cdre John Houghton, joins Anja van Leyssen and citizens of Roermond in remembering Allied aircrew and members of the Dutch Resistance who died locally in the Second World War. (*RAF Brüggen*)

Back at Brüggen things were still going well. In October the squadrons had taken the first three places in the Salmond competition, beating their rivals at Laarbruch for the second year running with 31 Squadron coming first, IX Squadron second and 17 Squadron third. No. 37 Squadron had an excellent MPC, twenty-seven operators firing thirty-one Rapier missiles to achieve twenty-three successful engagements and the station took the Sir Robert Foster Sports Trophy for the ninth year in a row. The clubhouse on the golf course also took on a new look; 232 MCAG RE, propped up its roof while it replaced the wooden walls with brick, and carried out a great deal of refurbishment before a grand reopening by ex-RAF Regiment squadron leader and golf professional Peter Alliss, in April 1988. It was on this high that John Houghton handed Brüggen to Group Captain 'Rocky' Goodall in November 1987, and Wing Commander Rob Wright took over IX Squadron from Alfy Ferguson in December.

The golf club 'reserve hospital' being re-walled and enhanced by 232 MCAG in 1987.
(*RAF Germany Golf Club*)

In his first message to the station after Christmas, Rocky Goodall chalked up what may have been another 'first' for Brüggen, when he reported that 'not a single person was charged with drunken driving over the festive season'.

In 1988 the Brüggen squadrons began air-to-air refuelling (AAR) training, hitherto the preserve of the UK squadrons. A core of expertise in AAR was to be built up in RAF Germany, primarily to supplement the UK force in deployments to North America, and as a contingency for possible operational tasks to come. After the initial indoctrination most crews found AAR a relatively simple task in benign weather, but it could be very different in other conditions, when pilots had to 'joust' the Tornado's probe into a tanker's basket. Flight Lieutenant Frank Neil remembered that it was not easy on a black, bumpy night when 'the more you miss the more tense you get, then the worse you fly and, unless you make a positive effort to relax, the less chance you have of making a successful contact'. How right he was.

Spring 1988 was a particularly busy and traumatic time for the station. IX Squadron was in Denmark, 14 Squadron in Goose Bay for Western Vortex, 17 Squadron on APC in Deci and 31 Squadron in Nevada for Green Flag. The station's AOC's Inspection in May preceded visits by HRH The Princess Margaret (her third time at Brüggen), General Eimler (Dep SACEUR), the C-in-C, Air Officer Engineering and Supply and the Roermond Winter Circus (which took particular interest in the Dog Section!). However, the month was marred by the deaths of Flight Lieutenants Steve Wright and John O'Shea, killed in the first fatal accident

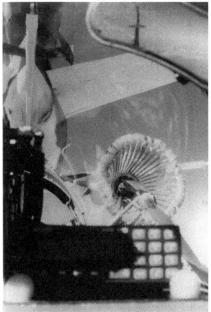
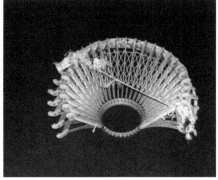

Jousting the Tornado's air refuelling probe into the VC10 tanker's 'basket' did not always go as planned – and there were only so many baskets! (*RAF Brüggen*)

involving a Brüggen Tornado when their aircraft, ZD808, crashed eighteen miles north-east of Hopsten, near Ankum.

Navigator executives continued in the ascendancy at Brüggen when Joe Whitfield handed over No. 14 Squadron (and its Rock Python) to Wing Commander Vaughan Morris in May. Little did Vaughan or Wing Commander John Chandler, who took command of Engineering and Supply Wing in September, know how much they would come to depend on each other in very unexpected circumstances before their tours were over.

The *Brüggen Circuit* was twenty years old in October 1988. An initial print run of 500 copies had been produced in 1968 by servicemen as a secondary duty, simply for internal consumption, but now a full-time paid staff produced 2,300 copies for both on-base and external distribution. Continuous mention of the *Circuit* throughout this book underlines the great value of the magazine in recording the human history of the station for posterity. The story of its growth in a 1988 edition ended with: 'Here's to the next twenty years!' Little did the writer know!

Also in October, 431 MU completed fourteen years of work on Jaguar Adour engines, having serviced their 2,823rd unit. With the Jaguars of II Squadron at Laarbruch now replaced by Tornados, the Jaguar simulator at Brüggen was retired on 15 December, Rocky Goodall switching off the power as Wing Commander Phil Sturley, OC II Squadron, 'ejected' from 'the box' after a catastrophic bird strike. To remember this milestone, Phil was presented with a rubber duck.

Then came a veritable disaster when Brüggen had to cede the Salmond Trophy to Laarbruch. However, Brüggen's engineers salvaged the station's pride by winning

In October 1988, 431 MU completed the last of 2,823 servicings on the Jaguar's Adour engines. (*Brüggen Circuit*)

RAF Germany's Engineering Efficiency Trophy again, while its sportsmen held on to the Sir Robert Foster Trophy for the tenth year running. There were no prizes for 37 Squadron during that bleak November, as they fulfilled one of their lesser known commitments, that of patrolling the Inner German Border (without their Rapiers).

The year ended sadly when a USAF A-10 crashed at Remscheid, causing civilian casualties and impacting heavily on RAF Germany's flying and social programme. Most military flying in the Federal Republic of Germany was suspended from 13 December to the New Year and HMG complied with a plea from Bonn to curtail all social events involving music from 10 to 15 December. Tragedy struck again during a Mineval on 13 January when Flight Lieutenants Alan Grieve and 'Smudge' Smith of 14 Squadron were killed in a mid-air collision between their Tornado (ZD891) and a German Alpha Jet. On the ground, Flight Lieutenant Alleyn Corbitt, acting as Mineval distaff, had a painful but lucky escape while observing the departure of a Tornado from its HAS, when a slab of concrete broke loose from the revetment and hit him on the head, causing serious injury. Nearby, Corporal Hewitt sprung into action; after calling for help, he rendered vital first aid which certainly saved Alleyn's life, for which he earned a C-in-Cs Commendation.

Life went on as usual for 37 Squadron on their MPC at Benbecula before Christmas, firing thirty-seven missiles successfully and indulging freely in the traditional festivities there. In the New Year the squadron moved to Florennes

In 1988, for the tenth year running, Brüggen won the Sir Robert Foster Trophy for sport, this year presented to the Station Commander, Gp Capt 'Rocky' Goodall, by the C-in-C, AM Sir Anthony Skingsley. (*Brüggen Circuit*)

in a very wintry Ardennes, to pit their wits against the Belgians in their F-16s and Mirages, and later in the local bars. To demonstrate its versatility again, 37 Squadron then joined British army units in March for Exercise 'Rorkes Drift', training to attack and defend built-up areas. They gained high praise for their approach, determination and proficiency in basic military skills from the CO of 32 Armoured Engineer Regiment RE, the organisers of the exercise.

As if to celebrate another highly successful Taceval in March 1989, it is said that a Tornado was set to join Jaguar 'AA' outside Station Headquarters, in a first gate guard duo of its kind in the RAF. Unlike its hybrid partner this was to be a 'whole' aircraft, ZD809, initially a prototype but which had an operational life on IX Squadron – but was a picture of the pair in the *Brüggen Circuit* fact or fiction?

Fact or fiction? Jaguar and Tornado, gate guards together? (*Brüggen Circuit*)

While all this was going on the ladies of Brüggen were working on their own unique project, the production of a giant-size patchwork quilt, covering some nine square yards and consisting of sixteen panels in peach, green and pink pinwheel and American lantern designs. A team of sixteen produced this work of art in 'thousands of hours' of hard work, and of course all this effort was for charity; the finished product was raffled at the forthcoming Summer Fête, all proceeds going to the North of England Children's Cancer Research Fund.

Labour of love. Brüggen wives worked for 'thousands of hours' to produce this giant patchwork quilt for charity. (*Brüggen Circuit*)

Out at Cold Lake, 14 Squadron was impressing its peers in Exercise 'Maple Flag', the Canadian version of 'Red Flag', again set against a Central European scenario. They flew 121 sorties in ten days, their tactics and the Tornado's camouflage providing such excellent self-protection against ground-based defences that no 'hits' were recorded against them. In August Nos. 14 and 31 Squadrons were tested again, during a particularly profitable Exercise Mallet Blow in the UK. Opposed by Tornado F3, Phantom and F-16 fighters, they attacked targets on Otterburn Range before running through the electronic warfare (EW) range at Spadeadam. Later in the month both squadrons fired Sidewinders in a very successful MPC at Valley.

In June 1989 the *Brüggen Circuit* indulged in a little nostalgia when it took a look at one of the local landmarks which must be deeply ingrained in the memories of all who served at Brüggen, the Hotel Cox on the German/Dutch border. The present owner, Wim Cox, remembers that his family began there in 1923, with a simple pub on a sandy track in farmland and forest. They were evacuated during the fighting between German and Allied troops on the Maas in 1944, but returned in 1958 to rebuild and extend the premises on an increasingly busy arterial road, ideally positioned for the rapidly growing community at Brüggen. Landhotel Cox is now a thriving modern facility, its visitors book bearing testimony to its continuous, excellent service to Brüggen throughout the station's life.

Rather less formal and conveniently only 100 yards from the station's main gate, a Gaststatte which started life in the 1950s became more anglicized in the 1980s when Martina and Paul Paredis, both from the staff of the Brüggen officers'

Hotel Cox, on the German/Dutch border in 1959, familiar to all who served at Brüggen.
(*Brüggen Circuit*)

mess, took over the premises. The 'Fluggies' was a boon to drinkers and drivers turned walkers.

No. 52 Field Squadron (Construction) RE, hitherto attached to Brüggen in a war role, became residents in April 1989, their arrival formalised by a parade of 128 officers and men in four troops, with plant and vehicles, reviewed by the C-in-C RAF Germany, now Air Marshal Sir Roger Palin. The squadron soon became fully integrated within the station's community, working from their compound beyond 431 MU. Here, new sheds with access roads were constructed for each of the three operational troops, much of this work being done by the squadron itself. The soldiers immediately became the star attraction at VIP visits, with their realistic display of explosive ordnance reconnaissance and disposal, followed by Airfield Damage Repair (ADR) to render the airfield operational again with minimum delay. The sight of Saracen armoured personnel carriers, excavators, bulldozers and tractors with buckets became commonplace on Hill 60. The squadron had timed its arrival well, setting up just before the social highlights of the year, the formal balls in the officers' and sergeants' messes, and of course they were heartily welcomed for the expertise they could offer in the final preparations for these impressive events. The 1989 sergeants' mess ball, on 23 June, was attended by 350 members and their guests, most of whom would not have been aware of the tribulations facing the staff during the run-up. The weather was kind to everyone but them, as they produced with loving care – then tried to conserve – margarine models of Neptune, Bears and Dragons, together with a chess set crafted entirely from chocolate, all for decoration and all wilting as temperatures soared into the eighties. One end of the

213

huge marquee was transformed into a rock pool complete with goldfish, offering a very tempting invitation to the more dynamic revellers seized by the heat of the moment. Suffice it to say that all went well, and for the station as a whole, Der Adler KG continued to provide entertainment in the German style.

McGinty the goat, 17 Squadron's mascot, had passed away early in 1989, allegedly from over-eating, but it seemed that fate might bring a replacement in the form of a pedigree cocker spaniel of Italian descent, in an extraordinary story of rescue at sea. While on APC at Deci, ten airmen from the squadron turned sailors, and were four miles out of Cagliari bound for Forte Villaggio in a hired yacht

1989 Sergeants' Mess Summer Ball. SAC Wakeman puts the finishing touches to one of the many margarine models to be threatened by the heat. (*Brüggen Circuit*)

Der Adler KG. A clown, believed to be the station commander Rocky Goodall, gets into the spirit of things. (*Brüggen Circuit*)

'Bob' – a guest of 17 Squadron after his ordeal at sea. (*Brüggen Circuit*)

when they came across a dog, bobbing around in the water with nowhere to go. Hoisted aboard and given the name 'Bob' (from the initial sighting) the grateful hound immediately made friends with his rescuers, and in the absence of any identification or any success in finding the owner he seemed destined for a new home at Brüggen. However, fate intervened again when, back at Cagliari, Bob was recognised and restored to a grateful owner; he had apparently 'jumped ship' from a local trawler some two hours before the rescue.

In August, Pete Dunlop handed over 31 Squadron to Wing Commander Jerry Witts. Jerry was no newcomer to Germany, having flown Buccaneers at Laarbruch, so it was no surprise to him to be greeted on his first day by a 'no notice' AAFCE Taceval. Whether it was because Pete had left the squadron in such good order that the flight commanders were able to do without a 'boss', or because Jerry was very quick on the uptake, 31 Squadron performed with its usual excellence – as did the station as a whole.

It was turning out to be a good year all round, with Brüggen winning the Sir Robert Foster Trophy for the eleventh year running, if only by half a point from Laarbruch, and IX Squadron retrieving the Salmond Trophy. Fresh from the ensuing celebrations, the squadron commander, Rob Wright, went to London for an interview with CAS, a PSO appointment in the offing. Had his VC10 not been delayed he would have been en route to Goose Bay when this summons arrived, and the story might have been different. In fact, with all his serviceable Tornados in Labrador he flew to England in a Tornado borrowed from 14 Squadron. The interview seemed to have gone well but the return flight from Abingdon at night did not: Rob and his navigator, Squadron Leader Mike Lawton, had to eject on take-off when a flock of birds deprived them of both engines. Recovering in hospital at Halton he was told that this attempt to avoid being short-toured had failed and that he was to report for duty with CAS in December. OC 14 Squadron then added insult to injury by presenting him with an IOU for one of his Tornados. Incidentally, Rob's successor, Wing Commander Andy White, followed a similar route two years later, but he decided to travel to his interview with CAS by car. In one of his final acts at Brüggen, Rob Wright led the parade to celebrate his squadron's seventy-fifth birthday in October, after which a squadron open day generated DM2,000 for the RAF Benevolent Fund's Fiftieth Anniversary of the Battle of Britain Appeal.

Help to service families closer at hand had continued to increase with the years and in that autumn of 1989 one more gap was filled. In October, an MOD-sponsored 'Homestart' scheme, a confidential befriending service run by volunteers, was launched officially at the Elmpt Community Centre; its purpose was to listen to problems and provide practical assistance of all sorts. No one at Brüggen should have gone without the help he or she needed.

On the operational front there was an outstanding need to give Tornado crews more experience of flying with typical heavyweight war loads, and Exercise Gopher Dram, one of which was run from RAF Macrihanish in November for IX,

14 and 31 Squadrons, went some way towards satisfying this requirement. In this, each Tornado carried four live 1,000lb bombs, for delivery in laydown or mini-loft modes at Garvie Island. Fresh fish (not bomb-damaged) was on many a menu at Brüggen when the aircraft returned.

Sqn Ldr Ian Milne briefs a IX Squadron training mission, in which his squadron commander, Wg Cdr Rob Wright (right) would fly 'bounce'. (*Brüggen Circuit*)

Group Captain Tony Harrison took over the station in December 1989, hardly expecting the drama which lay ahead during his tenure. He knew Brüggen and its environs well, having served there in the 1960s as a first tour Canberra pilot with 213 Squadron, when he lived with his wife in Holland, then in the early 1970s when he flew Phantoms with 31 Squadron and lived in a flat in Elmpt. Brüggen House would be more convenient!

The Berlin Wall was now down ('*Die Mauer ist weg*'), and in a proper regard for this momentous event in history the pupils of Cheshire School wrote their thoughts on the matter for the *Brüggen Circuit*. This extract was taken from a contribution by Liam Peter Fairlie, age nine:

> Before I was born they put up a wall.
> Now I am nine and I'm watching it fall.
> Big walls stretched around East Berlin
> East Berlin the sight of death
> Never again will they put up a wall – I hope

Nos. 14 and 17 Squadrons celebrated their seventy-fifth anniversary in February 1990, the latter having signalled the event for some months by flying one of its

Tornados with a black hand stamped on a white fin. No. 14 Squadron then went off to Deci in March, for ACMI and dissimilar air combat training (DACT) with Italian F-104s, then to the Spanish base of Gando, Gran Canaria, for DACT using chaff and flares against Mirage F-1s, all very good experience.

Their boss having used and lost a 14 Squadron aircraft in September 1989, IX Squadron then borrowed a 15 Squadron Tornado (XA454) in April 1990, to further their live ejection seat training during a Western Vortex exercise, the crew again surviving. At the same time 37 Squadron were having more success in the Hebrides on their latest MPC, launching twenty-seven missiles visually in appalling weather, again destroying one Rushton target and damaging two Falconets.

On 26 May terrorists shot dead two Australian tourists, mistaking them for British servicemen, as they returned to their car in Roermond's Market Square. There but for the grace of God... Needless to say the telephone lines were red hot with this tragic news and in the same month the *Circuit* reminded its readers of an all too often maligned, underground and rarely seen but wholly essential adjunct to all life at Brüggen, the Private Branch Exchange (PBX). This small (often too small) group of men and women from the Ground Radio Section, handled several thousand domestic, social, operational and emergency calls a day, 365 days a year, to England and throughout the Continent. The main qualification for the job must surely have been tolerance, not solely of the impatient but of those who might

The unseen voices of Cpl Gary Morgan, SACs Kev Marson and Norris McWalter, in the Station PBX. (*Brüggen Circuit*)

217

want to know, 'When do the clocks go back?' or 'What time is the last train from Roermond to Amsterdam?' Spare a thought for the telephone operator.

The long awaited outcome of the 'Options for Change' review came in July 1990, when it was announced that the British forces in Germany would be cut by half; it had yet to be decided which of the four major RAF stations would be closed by 1995.

Willie Luys, restorer of married quarters and squadron crewrooms, was presented with his station sports colours by Tony Harrison in 1990 for his outstanding contribution to sport. An able runner himself, he was the power behind the ever-growing 'Brüggen 10' road race but he also played football and walked for the station. This was indeed a well-deserved award – and it would be one of several for him before the station closed.

Inconspicuous in the background but all part of Brüggen's dynamic tapestry and most worthy of mention again, were the many organisations which provided services for the station and profits for charity. Among them were the Malcolm Club, Thrift Shop, Wool Shop, Material Shop, Flower Shop, the SSAFA Tea Bar and Book Barn of the Amenities Centre. Some had paid employees but many were run or staffed voluntarily by wives and other family members, who sometimes devoted many hours and much heartache to bookkeeping and similar laborious but essential supporting tasks. Ultimately they all contributed to community well-being and morale, while in 1990 donating a total of DM27,000 to charity.

Dutchman Willie Luys, of PSA and PROM, all-round sportsman and leading light in the 'Brüggen 10' road race, receives his station sports colours from the station commander, Gp Capt Tony Harrison. (*RAF Brüggen*)

The Wool Shop – typical of the myriad station amenities run largely by Brüggen's ladies. (*Brüggen Circuit*)

In keeping with the new 'Perestroika' it was all smiles when the Russians came to Brüggen in May 1990 bearing gifts. Lieutenant General Fursin, Major General Urmanov and Major General Konovalenko, from the Western Group of Forces (WGF), were welcomed by Chief of Staff BAOR, Major General Sugden and Dep Cdr RAF Germany, Air Vice-Marshal Peter Harding. No holds were barred in this first visit at that level to an operational RAF station, with Tornado and its weapons displayed openly and 52 Field Squadron RE showing how the airfield could have recovered had the visit been at a different time and for a different purpose.

Perestroika. Lt Rob Pullman tells Russian generals how 52 Squadron, RE, would have responded had their visit been of a different sort at another time. (*Brüggen Circuit*)

The Cossor Trophy, awarded annually to the Air Traffic Control Squadron which demonstrated the most outstanding professionalism and contribution to life in the RAF, went to Brüggen in 1989. To present the trophy, Controller National Air Traffic Services, Air Marshal Sir Thomas Stonor, brought two air vice-marshals and seven executives of Cossor to the station on 12 July 1990 where they visited the ATC Tower and watched a mock airfield attack before seeing what Dusseldorf had to offer on the social side. There, at a ceremony in the Ramada Hotel, OC ATC Squadron, Squadron Leader Tony Perfect, with twenty-two of his staff in attendance, accepted the trophy and enjoyed generous hospitality.

AM Sir Thomas Stonor, Controller NATS, presents Sqn Ldr Tony Perfect, SATCO at Brüggen, with the 1989 Cossor Trophy 'for outstanding professionalism and contribution to RAF life'. (*Brüggen Circuit*)

Times were indeed changing; as one threat receded another emerged and towards the end of 1990 war clouds were looming in another part of the world. There was relief at Brüggen in November when the station was named as one of the two RAF bases to remain open after 1995, but events in the Persian Gulf were now of most immediate concern.

Chapter Eight

The Gulf War

It is a sad irony that, having worked so hard to help avoid Armageddon during the Cold War, some NATO countries should then have to do battle in areas and ways which had not been anticipated and for which they were not best prepared. Brüggen had not been involved directly in the Falklands, but its turn came when Saddam Hussein invaded Kuwait on 2 August 1990 and Tornados were required to deploy in short order for Operation Granby, the UK's contribution to a Coalition Force mustering for Operation Desert Shield. Against the conventional wisdom of committing whole squadrons as formed fighting units, but for good practical reasons, the Tornado GR1 detachments would comprise an amalgam of crews and aircraft from squadrons in RAF Germany and the UK, and Wing Commander Vaughan Morris, OC 14 Squadron, would command the first of these hybrid units in Bahrain. No. 31 Squadron, on exercise and then stranded in Goose Bay for lack of air transport to bring them home, missed the initial deployment, although the squadron's weapons leader, Squadron Leader Doug Carter, soon found himself in Riyadh, Saudi Arabia, and four of 31's groundcrew, who had not gone to Goose Bay, were sent to Bahrain in this first tranche.

Wing Commander John Chandler, OC Engineering and Supply Wing at Brüggen, was in the thick of it from the start, overseeing the generation of twelve GR1s with weapons and full support within twenty-four hours, after which they were stood down at Brüggen. A fortnight later, the station was given only seventy-two hours to complete several hundred manhours of work on each of fourteen aircraft to produce twelve for early deployment. This work included the incorporation of Havequick secure communications and activation of the high frequency (HF) system, hot weather modifications to oil and fuel sensors, the equipment cooling system and canopy locking mechanism, the uprating of engines and auxiliary power unit, reprogramming of ECM equipment and respraying the aircraft in desert pink. Not until twenty-four hours before departure did they know that their destination was Bahrain International Airport, once RAF Muharraq.

Beginning on 27 August, twenty-eight VC10 and Hercules sorties carried some 300 men and women into the 45°, 100% humidity of high summer in the Gulf, where John Chandler would head the detachment's base support unit. The twelve Tornados, not far behind, were refuelled and armed as soon as they arrived,

Off to War. 14 Squadron Tornados refuelling from VC10 tankers en route to Muharraq
airfield in Bahrain. (*John Chandler*)

ready for what might lie ahead. The initial loading of BL755 reflected a concern
at the time that Iraqi armour might continue south from Kuwait. However, how
could the Tornados become an effective combat unit overnight, operating from a
civilian airport, which had no understanding of military procedures or imperatives;
no suitable communications, on-base weapons or fuel storage, and no effective
defences against terrorist, explosives, chemical or biological attack? Apart from
the Bahrainis, civilian and military, there were Kuwaiti and Saudi elements, RAF,
Canadian and Italian detachments, plus contingents from the USAF, US Army
and US Navy covering every inch of usable ground. The Bahrainis, although very
helpful, had no war plan for this exigency and no experience of how to integrate
the multi-nation assets now available on the airfield so, if only to avoid fracticide,
they agreed to a British offer to table a concept of operations. This was easier said
than done but in the end all parties involved acquiesced in a plan which would, in
effect, give the RAF control of the airfield. There was much to do.

An early priority was to get everyone out of tents lining the taxiways on
this continuously active airfield, where sleep was impossible, and into off-base
accommodation, however makeshift. The ballroom floor of the Sheraton Hotel
provided a better alternative for 120 groundcrew, albeit with the disturbance
inevitable in the programme of shift changes. The aircrew enjoyed the relative
luxury of proper hotel rooms and (unlike those deployed later in Saudi Arabia)
could quench their thirst in the traditional RAF manner.

What was your name again? Wg Cdr Vaughan Morris, OC 14 Squadron, arrives in Bahrain with his Tornado GR1 detachment. (*RAF News*)

The Sheraton Hotel. Wartime home for the Brüggen detachment in Bahrain. (*John Chandler*)

223

The base support team worked ceaselessly, begging, borrowing (or otherwise) what they could to provide rudimentary protection for the detachment's personnel, aircraft and equipment. Weapon storage was a major problem. The airfield consisted of little more than a single runway and parallel taxiways, with crowded commercial ramps on the south side and barracks on the north; villages crowded against the perimeter in any open ground. The arrival of a VC10 or Tristar full of 1,000lb bombs, JP233 or BL755, every three hours, posed a serious safety risk, and with weapons piling up in all corners of the airfield, the airlift had to be suspended temporarily until the Bahraini authorities were able to grant access to a storage site out in the desert. This then required a fleet of massive Mac articulated trucks, hired locally, and several dozen MT drivers, which Strike Command supplied within forty-eight hours of request. Despite their lack of experience in theatre, or of the trucks they were to handle, these men did a superb job, transporting hundreds of tons of high explosives through the busy streets of Manama, safely and without incident. At the same time, the RAF's Tactical Support Wing and the Royal Engineers were providing bulk fuel storage, the airfield having only one above-ground pipeline to feed the civilian ramp. A complete hotel and housing compound was being turned into barracks, as everyone built air raid shelters and took the RAF Regiment's advice on survival to operate. Very soon, as the detachment grew, a recognizable and effective support organisation was emerging.

This was big business, with every facility and space on the airfield bargained for and guarded jealously. The US Navy arrived bearing an agreement signed by Bahrain some months before, which leased a major part of this real estate to them for their exclusive use, but when they saw the ramp (ASP), so full of aircraft that traffic jams were a regular occurrence, they had to accept that occupation was nine-tenths of the law.

Immediately after their arrival in theatre, the Tornado aircrew began an intensive training programme which included air-to-air refuelling, the carriage of operational weapons (JP 233 and 1,000lb bombs), automatic terrain following (ATF), parallel track night and IMC formation, level and dive bombing from medium level, electronic, chaff and flare countermeasures. Although the Tornado's 'fly-by-wire' system eased the problem of flying with full war loads of 8 x 1,000lb bombs or 2 x JP233s, the aircraft's flying characteristics were noticeably different and all the crews completed some sorties to become accustomed to the difference.

JP233 was not designed for routine training sorties, so much use was made of a dummy set of weapons (originally made for trials), until one crew made a rather too realistic dummy attack at night and released them. Training airspace in Saudi Arabia was at a premium and rigidly controlled, so much of this flying was carried out, with AAR support, in Oman. Very soon, these basic requirements would all be incorporated in a standard Operation Granby Tornado training syllabus, for training reinforcements back in Europe.

Then there was the major problem of co-ordinating all the widely dispersed and disparate force components from the various contributing nations into an integrated command and control system centred on the Coalition Forces' Air HQ (AHQ) in Riyadh. The RAF's Tactical Communications Wing was able to deliver the necessary high-tech communications, with secure electronic mail and voice communications but regular, direct face-to-face liaison, so desirable in targeting, tasking and force packaging, was rarely possible, and secure communications with the Americans remained a problem throughout, 'battle management', a euphemism to cover all these activities, suffering as a result.

By the end of October, the core of the Brüggen detachment, with its twelve Tornados, had expanded to over 2,000 personnel, supporting a further six GR1s to enable the Marham Wing to build up in-theatre before moving to Tabuk in north-west Saudi Arabia, the Jaguar force which had moved up from Thumrait, a steadily increasing VC10 detachment and a complete Field Hospital. The REs gave invaluable help in creating this vast military complex from almost nothing and were ready, if needed, to carry out repairs to the airfield. With the British in the lead, much had been achieved, but Saddam Hussein showed no sign of withdrawing from Kuwait and, with the additional threats he posed to Saudi Arabia and the Coalition forces, there was no time to relax. John Chandler returned to Brüggen in December 1990 and was later awarded an OBE for a job well done.

Back at Brüggen, all other exercises and most of the extraneous commitments had been cancelled indefinitely, but 17 Squadron remained committed to a fly-past over London for the Battle of Britain 50th Anniversary. For this they were detached to Honington with eleven GR1s, of which nine and a spare were launched for the 168-aircraft formation, led by a Spitfire flown by Air Vice-Marshal Bill Wratten (an ex-Brüggen man himself and soon to be Gulf-bound). Also, in September's Operation Buxton, Brüggen opened its doors again to a party of Russian VIPs.

On 17 September, Germany and Belgium imposed a blanket ban on all fast-jet flying below 1,000 feet, although flying down to 250 feet in certain areas was negotiated for those crews earmarked for Operation Granby, with a limit of forty-two sorties a day only until 6 October. The need to keep in good low-flying practice was underlined again when a 17 Squadron Tornado had a wire strike while on operational low flying (OLF) training.

No. 31 Squadron had eventually returned to Brüggen from Goose Bay in early September and, although he was not officially required to do so, the squadron commander, Wing Commander Jerry Witts, immediately set about preparing all his crews for possible employment in the Gulf. Typically, but without prejudice to other users with a higher priority, every opportunity was taken to 'bootleg' AAR by routing normal training sorties close to tanker towlines. Night AAR would surely be required so the prerequisite of night tactical formation was practised within a sensible interpretation of the peacetime rules. Such foresight was justified first when 31 Squadron was called upon in mid-September to nominate four of its crews to supplement the GR1 force in Bahrain, to bring the aircrew-to-aircraft ratio there up to 2:1. Jerry Witts was able to capitalise on such ad hoc AAR training when he was tasked, with two days' notice, to deliver four replacement Tornados to Bahrain on 19 September. Inter alia, this provided him with an excellent opportunity to find out at firsthand what was going on out there and how best to continue the preparations for his squadron to join the fray. The tanker 'trail' they took was instructive, the flight meeting Victor tankers over Central France and a Tristar over Sicily, which took them all the way to Bahrain. They were left in no doubt that the situation was serious when issued with personal arms and ammunition and instructions to be ready to don NBC kit and gas masks (the latter essentially within nine seconds) against the real possibility that Saddam Hussein would resort to a chemical or biological attack while they were in the Gulf. They were met by the RAF Commander at Muharraq, Group Captain Rocky Goodall, and departed two days later in four rather tired Tornados with a better understanding of all aspects of the operation, which would stand them in good stead for what was to come.

When he returned to Brüggen, Jerry Witts was able to pass on, with due caution, what he had seen and heard to placate the ever-increasing need to keep everyone in the picture, not least the families of those men in Bahrain. Machinery was already in place for this purpose but there was nothing so good as a face-to-face exchange. The age-old service ethic of mutual self-help, material and spiritual, was much in evidence, with commanders, administrators, community services and padres in the lead, assisting those less formal but essential 'family' links within squadrons and units at all levels, the wives rallying well with little fuss.

The four 31 Squadron crews earmarked to reinforce the Bahrain detachment departed on 1 October when plans for 'roulement' (changeover of personnel) were predicated on three-month detachments. There was

Gulf warriors. Flt Lts Wilbur Wilson and Mike Allton, 31 Squadron, at Muharraq.

Gp Capt 'Rocky' Goodall, ex-Brüggen and now Tornado detachment commander, Muharraq.
(*RAF News*)

226

much speculation that, over Christmas, 31 Squadron would take over from Marham's 617 Squadron which, with 20 Squadron from Laarbruch, had formed the second GR1 unit at Tabuk in north-west Saudi Arabia, but this was not to be. In November, Jerry Witts was ordered to prepare twelve of his crews and one from each of the other three squadrons at Brüggen for a further Granby detachment, destination unspecified; the supplementary crews would be led by Wing Commander Ivor Evans of IX Squadron, Squadron Leader Douglas Moule of 14 Squadron and Squadron Leader Bill Hartree of 17 Squadron. Having been short of supervisors and training opportunities, the latter had much to do to catch up with their peers on 31 Squadron, but catch up they did with an intensive training programme orchestrated by their host squadron. Ivor Evans knew that he would be under Jerry's command when they deployed, an unenviable position for any squadron commander, but time would show that he would accept this with constructive good sense. Some of the twenty-four crews had the benefit of flying against the MiG 29 fighter of the new Luftwaffe in simulated air combat training while others had the opportunity to fly with two dummy JP233 rounds allocated to RAF Germany. With no clearance to fly over Germany with the real weapon, this experience was welcome and comforting, most pilots finding that, although the aircraft was a little more sluggish with the extra four tonnes aboard, it remained easy to handle and was 'still perfectly capable of carrying out manoeuvres such as barrel rolls'.

This was a time when greatness could be thrust upon one in abundance and with consummate speed. It is claimed that before he could complete his arrival procedures Flying Officer Richard Cheseldene-Culley became OLF, night ATF and AAR qualified (day and night), combat ready and therefore eligible for Granby. On the ground in Bahrain, Corporal Charlie Brown, of 31 Squadron but attached to 14 Squadron, was adamant that he should remain in the Gulf when his squadron arrived in theatre. This was the spirit of Brüggen.

It was during a Friday beer-call in December that this mixed squadron got its marching orders, to start up a third Tornado GR1 detachment from scratch at Dhahran, in eastern Saudi Arabia, and to begin to move out at the end of the month. At least they would have Christmas at home but the bad news was that they should be prepared for a six-month detachment. The squadron made the best of it, the heavy workload for all interspersed by a very lively social programme; three officers even found time to get married, albeit without time for proper honeymoons.

During all this hustle and bustle, Jerry Witts heard that his detachment was likely to be enlarged to include a reconnaissance element of Tornado GR1As from No. II (AC) Squadron, equipped with new Infra-Red (IR) video imagery, which had still to be fully proven. This unit would be led by its CO, Wing Commander Alan Threadgould, giving Jerry two wing commanders under his command, and he was not to know then that a third would be added when a second Tornado recce flight, from No. 13 Squadron, deployed to Dhahran with its CO, Wing Commander Glenn Torpy. Everyone wondered then how these four strong characters could work effectively together, under one of their number, in the very trying conditions to come – but they need not have worried.

Deployments to prepared bases by well-established units on exercise were one thing, but, unlike the UK Tornado stations, Brüggen was not used to major moves to predominantly civilian bases with minimal military facilities and for which they had no contingency plans or operational 'fly-away packs'. It says much, therefore, for the immediate, constructive and enterprising response to this order. The twenty-four crews completed their prescribed Granby training, administrative and medical requirements on time, while squadron and station engineers, given all the ground support they needed, worked over Christmas to generate the necessary aircraft by the required deadline. They were ready.

Getting ready to go. 'DA' soon to be in the pink. (*Brüggen Circuit*)

Getting ready to go. The Jerry Witts' supporters club going through the drills.
(*Brüggen Circuit*)

Three hundred Brüggen men and women began to move out to the Gulf in the first of twenty-eight Hercules sorties at 0300 hours on 28 December, to begin an unforgettably long and noisy trip to war which gave them time to contemplate what might lie ahead and what they had left behind. Then they were brought down to earth at Dhahran, often with the greeting, 'Who are you?' before having to unload their own and unaccompanied baggage, the latter being much the heavier.

The advance party, headed by 31 Squadron's SEngO, Squadron Leader Les Hendry, made the best of the operational facilities allocated, which comprised two primitive and very vulnerable Portakabins, recently stripped bare and vacated by RAF Tornado F3 squadrons. With great ingenuity, much local purchase and a refreshing attitude from the RAF suppliers that 'if you want it you can have it', all was made ready in time for the Tornados. For the men and women, domestic accommodation was arranged in the Al Nimran Hotel, twenty minutes away in Al Khobar.

Jerry Witts led the first of this detachment's pink Tornados out on 2 January 1991, the rest following two days later. Each was fitted with two 1,500 litre underwing tanks, fully loaded Mauser 27mm cannons, a Boz chaff and flare dispenser, Skyshadow ECM pod and two Sidewinder AIM9Ls; the aircrew carried fully-loaded side arms. They were seen off into the dark, after a very early breakfast of bacon sandwiches in the crewroom, by C-in-C RAF Germany, the station commander and a group of well-wishers braving the cold at the runway caravan, a scene very reminiscent of airfields in the Second World War. On this cheerless, overcast German night the Tornado crews' hastily acquired night formation and AAR skills were tested to the full as they sped over France and across Sardinia into a welcome dawn, their boredom on the eight-hour trip lightened by music from cassette tapes played on the cockpit voice recorder ('one can tell a lot about a navigator from the music he plays!').

Waiting for the 'off' – pensive families. (*Brüggen Circuit*)

The new RAF commander at Dhahran was Group Captain John Rooum, and the new force came under the command of Air Vice-Marshal Bill Wratten, the UK Air Commander at AHQ, Riyadh, who reported directly to the Granby Joint Headquarters (JHQ) in High Wycombe, headed by Air Chief Marshal Sir Patrick Hine. To the aircrew, Dhahran was an eye-opener; the size of London Airport, with an external perimeter of 69km; it was already crammed with military aircraft of every kind, from a multitude of nations, to add to its regular civilian traffic.

On arrival, the GR1s were loaded at once with JP233, there being little time to prepare for war in this very unfamiliar environment. The in-theatre training prescribed by AHQ called for four sorties for each crew in ten days, a total of 132 and a tall order indeed, and in the event some of the recce crews who arrived

Wg Cdr Ivor Evans, with his IX Squadron aircrew at Dhahran. (*Brüggen Circuit*)

on the eve of the war had to make do with less. With no time to spare, planners and aircrew had to become fully versed in the Coalition system for command, control, communications and intelligence (C3I), the use of airborne early warning and control, and arrangements for the mixed force packages in the Combined Air Operations (COMAO) plans in which they would be included. They worked hard with their on-board countermeasures (electronic, chaff and flare), were briefed on the fighter cover available (F-14s and F-15s) and the ECM offered by EF-111 Raven, EA-6BS Prowlers, C-130 Compass Call aircraft and Wild Weasels. There were many unforeseen problems which demanded immediate attention, typically when it was found that the ATF equipment did not always respond correctly to certain desert features. The larger 2,250 litre under-wing tanks, borrowed from the Tornado F3 squadrons, were welcomed, not only to give increased range but also because they had a higher speed clearance. Formation leaders and their deputies were given some very limited experience of flying with Night Vision Goggles (NVG) on the few flying helmets available which had the required attachments, but the benefits they gave outweighed the discomfort in the wearing. At the best of times, but especially in the daytime heat, NBC equipment was also a very uncomfortable adjunct to survival, but again there were few complaints, while lectures on survival and rescue procedures from the US Delta Force became very popular. Much work remained to be done on the aircraft: its ancillary and weapons equipment, with a shortage of spares, particularly avionic units, already starting to become serious and there was a limit to what the hard-pressed groundcrew could achieve.

In their familiarisation sorties some aircrew waxed lyrical over the diverse tapestry of the desert, great tracts of sand of different colours, textures and hues, countless tracks; but otherwise few signs of life other than the odd Bedouin camp or a lonely camel before suddenly coming across an oasis of green vegetation. It should have been a wonderful new experience but with the seriousness of what might be ahead there was little time or inclination to enjoy it and very soon they would be concentrating on night flying.

On 4 January the GR1 force commanders in the Gulf were called to Riyadh to be updated on the use of JP233 against selected targets in the area of likely operations. An overall, highly co-ordinated and complex plan was made known to only a few, but it was clear that with JP233 the Tornados would be expected to reduce operations at specific Iraqi airfields to levels with which the Coalition

31 Squadron groundcrew treat their allies in Dhahran to RAF vernacular. (*RAF News*)

air defence forces could then cope. The number and size of these targets, their runway redundancy and formidable organic defences, rendered this a daunting and hazardous task but the force was called upon to do its best without placing aircraft or crews at unnecessary risk. A challenge indeed!

By now, the media was assembling in strength, ready for anything. Kate Adie, Peter Snow and especially Christopher Morris of Sky television, were soon mingling with the Brüggen boys at Dhahran, who were quick to learn new skills in front of the cameras and microphones. An easy, pleasant and mutually beneficial relationship developed between both sides, enabling invaluable feedback to the families and friends of those preparing to go to war.

Every possible precaution was taken against air attack, the greatest threat being from Scud missiles armed with high explosive, chemical or biological warheads. 'Porton Liners', inflatable tents with air locks, were housed in standard, lorry-borne containers covered with steel sheeting and sand bags to provide Collective NBC Protection (COLPRO) for all. Should the need arise, arrangements were in place, and were practised in Exercise Safe Haven to accommodate the whole detachment on base at Dhahran. Albeit slowly, more operational accommodation and space for additional aircraft became available, which was just as well as the recce aircraft and their crews began to arrive at Dhahran during the second week of January, the whole British contingent now coming under the command of Group Captain Cliff Spink.

Tornado shelter – Dhahran-style. (*Jerry Gegg*)

The media were there in force for a visit by Prime Minister John Major on 8 January. One gentleman from the press, representing a well-known Sunday tabloid, rather exceeded his mandate by enquiring of the warriors: 'Got any dirt for me then, you know what I mean, sons of the rich and famous – any queers?' Mounted on a bomb-trolley, Mr Major drew much applause from the several hundred British personnel assembled as he expressed his gratitude to them in an honest and forthright speech. Morale at Dhahran was high.

Every effort was also being made to keep up spirits at Brüggen, with continuous briefings and a proliferation of welfare activities. The residue of Nos. 14 and 31 Squadrons was placed under the command of OC 14 Squadron, Vaughan Morris, operating from the south-east corner of the airfield; what remained of 17 and IX Squadrons came under OC 17 Squadron, Wing Commander Dusty Miller in the south-west. Morale improved further with a most successful visit to Brüggen by HRH The Princess of Wales on 13 January.

However, the 13 January was not a good day in the Gulf, Brüggen suffering its first casualties there when 14 Squadron's Flight Lieutenants Kieren Duffy and Norman Dent were killed flying into the desert in Oman. As if any reminder were needed, this tragedy underlined for the aircrew the seriousness of the challenges that lay ahead. More prosaically, that night, the bathroom ceiling in Jerry Witts' and Ivor Evans' apartment, weakened by torrential rain, collapsed into their bathtub.

Meanwhile, back at the ranch, life was anything but normal – a visit by Diana, Princess of Wales helping to keep up morale. (*Brüggen Circuit*)

For administrative efficiency, all the aircrew were moved into the British Aerospace owned Rezyat Apartments, two-man rooms akin to 1960s Butlins' Chalets, on 14 January. This necessary but unpopular move kept the fliers occupied with domestic chores until their new accommodation became habitable, one pilot remembering that he rewired two vacuum cleaners and kicked two more 'very hard' before he got one to work. In true British fashion they made the best of it.

Notwithstanding all the problems, the Tornado 'mud-movers' of Dhahran were all combat-ready by 15 January; the last recce aircraft from 13 Squadron had arrived and Jerry Witts now commanded eighteen aircraft, thirty-three crews and over 300 ground support personnel. A request to train with the GR1's engine extended to 'war only' limits was overtaken by a ban on all further training flying so the new performance available could not be put to the test.

With one day to go to the UN deadline for Iraq to vacate Kuwait, and no sign that it intended to do so, the aircrew were issued with eighteen gold sovereigns (on signature!) and a £5,000 'goolie chit' (later increased to £10,000) which might facilitate their safe return should they have to eject. They were also given location devices, silk maps and 'go-packs' which, among other things, contained condoms and a sanitary tampon. Tension was rising, exacerbated in mid-afternoon by a full air alarm while Tom Carver of the BBC World Service was interviewing Jerry Witts. Jerry dived for his gas mask before dragging Carver bodily into the nearby COLPRO; they were now playing for real. On the evening of 16 January it began. Cliff Spink summoned Witts to confirm that offensive operations were about to start and authorised him to lead the first attack against Mudaysis airfield in central Iraq, with a formation of four Tornados each carrying 2 x JP233, taking off at 0130 hours for a time over target (TOT) of 0300 on 17 January, 'H' hour for Operation Desert Storm.

The mood of the aircrew during their preparations for this first mission can only be imagined. Brutally honest, some told the author of various, personal manifestations of their apprehension, Jerry Witts recalling that 'We were of course apprehensive but there was no time to brood about it.' It was a dark, humid night as they walked out to their aircraft, dressed in cold weather jackets (against the possibility of having to survive in the desert), laden with NBC hoods and gas masks, NVGs, helmets, personal weapons, maps and charts, goolie chits and go-packs. They were about to fly into an airspace protected by an estimated 7,000 SAM, 10,000 pieces of AAA and a fusillade of small arms.

These initial war sorties, flown at night and in close formation to the tankers, could last for four hours or more and involve three or four air-to-air refuellings, all of which were made more difficult by the heavy war loads, bad turbulence and the unseasonal presence of medium level cloud. Several pilots inadvertently 'spoked' their refueling baskets, rendering them unusable, but the mission was not affected. After his second refueling of the night, one flight leader confided: 'I was exhausted and we hadn't really started yet.'

The tension increased as the descent began towards a darker desert, the inertial navigation system was updated from the radar and the radar warning receiver (RWR) scanned continuously for hostile fighters. Now, there was nothing visible outside the cockpit while the autopilot held them at 160 feet above the ground and the fluorescent time circle on the HUD unwound rapidly as they hurtled towards the target at 540 knots. Finally, the pilot selected the Master Armament Safety Switch 'on' and Late Arming Switch, flipped up a safety cover on the control column and held the commit button down to trigger automatic weapons release.

On time and on target, the aircraft vibrated as the two JP233s dispensed their bomblets for what seemed an eternity until two massive thumps confirmed that the canisters had jettisoned. In at least one case, this de-activated the autopilot and caused unforeseen 'unnecessary excitement' as the aircraft automatically climbed rapidly, setting off several alarms in the cockpit and distracting the pilot as he sought again the relative security of the desert 'floor' – without hitting it. The barrage of AAA and SAMs fired at this aircraft also missed, but it could so easily have been fatal.

The JP233s did what they were supposed to do, making holes and leaving many bomblets to be disposed of before that part of the runway could be repaired and used again. Delivered along or diagonally across these targets, the required accuracies could only be achieved at night by flying 'hands-off' on autopilot, a procedure which would certainly not appeal to most uninitiated ground attack pilots.

Many threats remained during the long journey home, with more SAM and AAA sites en route, Allied fixed wing and helicopter aircraft to avoid, tankers to be found in the unkind weather and aircraft unserviceabilities with which to contend. However, the first Brüggen waves returned safely, a monument to skill, training and courage, with more than a little luck thrown in – every crew remembering the most beautiful dawn they had ever seen!

Exhausted and emotionally drained, no words can describe adequately the reception the crews were given by their peers, groundcrew and the media, and while they were being welcomed home, single palm trees were already being stencilled below the cockpit rail of each aircraft. Many more would be added.

It had also been a sleepless night at Dhahran, with many Scud alerts keeping everyone awake – but the first night was over.

The *Brüggen Circuit* would carry this account of the return of the first of the GR1s on the second night of the war, by Flight Lieutenant Ian Stockton of 17 Squadron: 'I was amazed what emotion could be put into the simple handshake and a few words. Our reticence as a nation is sometimes not enough to express our feelings but I'm glad of our understatement; it seems dignified and very British.' Ian went on: 'The war then splits into several parts, some more personal than others. There is your individual war with your own feelings both there and with your family. There is your crew war and then your formation war as you fly with your friends, and there is the squadron's war when you fight as a unit. You feel all these parts simultaneously, working and living as best you can.'

More of the same followed with five Tornados having been lost in battle by the fifth day of the war (none as yet from Brüggen). With no evidence that the Iraqi airfields were being repaired, or that their fighters were going to come out to play, the cost-effectiveness of these very hazardous JP233 missions was being questioned in some quarters – as was the wisdom of lofting 1,000lb bombs ahead in attempts to clear a path for them through the wall of AAA fire. This required aircraft to pull up from low level to release their bombs within range of the Iraqi guns, thereby exposing them to intense, if unaimed fire.

Of these early flights, a crew remembers, 'A sky full of aeroplanes, with radio channels jammed as mission after mission checked in; this was history in the making and there we were right in the middle of it.' Another spoke of, 'The intense blackness of the night; if it hadn't been for the occasional Bedouin camp fire, you couldn't have told which way was up.' An intelligence update just before take-off warned of 'vastly increased' air defences, adding to the stress on another crew which had to change hurriedly to a serviceable aircraft. Then came the defining moment when the aircraft lights were switched off on entering hostile airspace and 'Good Luck' was exchanged between front and rear cockpits. It was 'absolutely, utterly pitch black' with no sensation of movement flying on auto terrain following radar at 200 feet and 450 knots when the RWR signalled an Iraqi Fulcrum ahead, the 'spoke' staying too long before vanishing as quickly as it had appeared. In the target area, faster and lower, 'all hell broke loose' when the first bombs went off and the sky lit up with myriad lines of red tracer. Once the weapons were gone the bombers sought what relative security there was as they made for home, the tanker most welcome as that dawn broke and 'life seemed very sweet'. It had been a 22-hour day and four of the five aircraft in this particular play had been damaged by flak. The author spoke to many of these crews on their return to Brüggen and was struck by their extraordinary honesty, humility and universal fear of letting the side down.

Given the hazards of low-level operations AHQ decided, on 21 January, to give medium level 'dumb' bombing a try. Thus, the RAF joined the USAF above the 15,000 feet 'hard floor' limit of the most effective AAA. The threat from SAMs remained, necessitating external EW support (USAF Wild Weasels and EF-111 Ravens) to supplement the GR1's limited self-defence suite. However, the first target to be allocated for medium level attack, Shaibah (once an RAF station), was so heavily defended by SAM that these EW assets refused the task, as did the Tornados. Jalibah and Tallil airfields were attacked effectively on the nights of 21 and 22 January from medium level; ample Wild Weasel support dealt with the guided SAM, unguided SAM posing little real threat. This new game-plan began with level deliveries of free-fall 1,000lb bombs by night, but the GR1's radar was not optimised for this purpose and results were generally very poor (the ratio of sand to concrete not in the attackers' favour). Level-bombing and subsequent dive-to-level deliveries by day produced marginally better results, but the full-blooded,

45-degree dive attack, right into the throats of the Iraqi guns, and within their range, commended by some in the UK, was rejected in theatre as being unnecessarily hazardous for the results which might be achieved.

The GR1 force had now settled into a routine in which the day of a mission was followed by twenty-four hours of rest, with a further twenty-four hours spent supporting another crew in their planning and preparation – after which the three-day cycle was repeated. The Iraqi fighters still refused to take part in the war and indeed many had fled to safety in Iran. The offensive counter air (OCA) campaign was having the desired effect of achieving air superiority and indeed air supremacy, allowing some diversion of effort to interdiction tasks against power stations, oil refineries and ammunition dumps.

Shortage of spares was now making it difficult enough for the GR1 detachments to guarantee eight aircraft every night but, on 23 January, they were required by AHQ to double their efforts to sixteen sorties. At Dhahran the first eight got airborne but there were two ground aborts and an air abort on the second wave before their trouble really began. GR1 ZA403 was lost in the target area; it was seen descending on fire, presumed then to have been hit by AAA or SAM. Parachutes were thought to have been seen but it was not until the end of the war that it was known that the crew, Flying Officer 'Budgie' Burgess and navigator Squadron Leader Bob Ankerson had ejected safely and been taken prisoner. After the same attack, Flight Lieutenant Stuart Gillies nursed his Tornado 'DH' back to Dhahran after it had been damaged badly by two large explosions immediately below the fuselage after weapons release. There were signs that this had resulted from premature detonation of its own bombs rendering the aircraft unserviceable for some days. A long and tortuous investigation followed, focused on a new bomb fuse used in both cases.

The order to double the number of sorties was withdrawn but pressure to do so remained, or at least to raise the number of aircraft per wave from eight to ten, based on some unfortunate comparisons between the performance of each detachment in their different circumstances. More working hours would not do the trick at Dhahran, which now had only eleven bombers, a critical spares situation and problems with its Skyshadow ECM pods. Suggestions from some quarters that the aircrew should be prepared to brave the Iraqi defences without their full self-protection equipment did not go down well with the fliers any more than a frustrating tendency for staffs to carry out a detailed post-mortem every time an aircraft failed to get airborne as tasked. None of this did much for morale at Dhahran, where sleep was being constantly disturbed by endless Scud attacks and the sudden boom of the Patriot missile defences. Thoughts should have been turning to rest and recuperation but with the current task and establishment there was no hope of that. In fact, the Dhahran GR1 force was very proud of its achievements; by the end of January it had flown 740 hours, more than twice the peacetime flying rate and in these far from ideal conditions. This was recognised by General Sir Peter de la

Billiere, the overall British commander in the Gulf, during his visit to Dhahran on 29 January, where he lifted spirits and made a 'very positive impression' with his realism, knowledge and understanding of air matters.

The *Daily Star* was also impressed, granting the detachment one of its 'Gold Star Awards' for bravery; the paper may have been attracted by 31 Squadron's Star of India badge but it readily acknowledged the presence of all six squadrons. Spin-offs from this 'adoption' came in regular supplies of papers, magazines and videos and more bonuses to come. A photocall of Brüggen men in warlike posture appeared in many UK newspapers and was syndicated around the world; their effort was appreciated.

No. 20 Squadron, operating Tornados from Tabuk, brought another new weapon to the Gulf, the Air Launched Anti-Radar Missile (ALARM), with the help of British Aerospace, but without the usual comprehensive evaluation by the service. They were able to contribute to the overall suppression of enemy air defences (SEAD) by destroying hostile radar emitters or encouraging their operators to switch off and survive, in either case enhancing the survivability of the Coalition forces as a whole.

Stocks of 1,000lb bombs were running down fast, but for several reasons, including the political sensitivity of increasing the total force size with another aircraft type, paucity of space and vulnerability of aircraft in the open, the RAF's 'smart' precision guided munitions (PGMs) were not in theatre. Back in the mid-1970s the RAF had developed very successful tactics for the employment at low-level of the American Paveway Laser Guided Bomb (LGB) on Buccaneer and Jaguar aircraft using Pavespike designators either pre-positioned on the ground or airborne on the Buccaneer. This was a rudimentary system for use by day and in clear weather only but, with simple procedures and joint training, it could be a very cost-effective alternative to dumb bombing. Jerry Witts had been much involved with this innovation as a Buccaneer pilot in the early 1980s; he knew that it could provide 'that important missing ingredient of our current (Gulf) operations – accuracy'. The author also flew in both bomber and designator roles and was equally convinced of its potential; he had led a successful Buccaneer/ Pavespike, Jaguar/Paveway detachment to Nevada in 1983, proving both accuracy and survivability against realistic targets and defences in a demanding Red Flag exercise. Tornado was even better equipped for the LGB role, especially coupled with the new British Thermal Imaging and Laser Designator (TIALD) pod which was then being rushed into service (at Tabuk) to provide improved designation and a night capability. In the UK, Pavespike and TIALD procedures were being developed for delivery of Paveway at the relatively safer medium levels, offering economy of effort with a reduced risk of collateral damage (now an accepted euphemism for civilian casualties). Their time would come.

On 2 February the Tornado detachment commanders were at AHQ for a 'howgozit' and to discuss the way ahead. Again, more sorties were required and they agreed to try doubling their effort to eight missions by day and eight by night, a tall order but more acceptable to them than two consecutive waves. However, JHQ then ordered all night missions to cease in favour of two successive waves of eight aircraft/detachment/day, these to include four LGB sorties every other day when the Pavespike Buccaneers became available at Muharraq. The front line commanders argued against any general return to low-level and received an assurance from the Air Commander that, once a task had been accepted, they should be left to decide how best to do the job.

The arrival in theatre of Pavespike equipped Buccaneers was very welcome, and on 5 February, the bombers from Dhahran met up with their designators from Bahrain to attack a bridge over the Euphrates, only to find that the target had already been destroyed. A second LGB sortie on 6 February also failed, this time apparently because of a breakdown in essential co-ordination between the two bases. The next mission was successful, the necessary details having been hand-carried the forty miles from Dhahran to Bahrain to avoid the delays inherent in secure fax traffic routed via London. Such is progress.

To illustrate the poignancy of the time, the March 1991 edition of the *Brüggen Circuit* published a number of letters to the station, some with gifts for children with fathers in the Gulf. From Tara Woodward aged eight came: 'I thought you might like this little duck to cuddle at night in bed. He is very new so you can

VC10 tanker, Paveway LGB equipped 31 Squadron Tornado (Flt Lts 'Shifty' Young and Adam Robinson aboard), with their Buccaneer Pavespike designator, en route to Iraq.
(*Jerry Gegg*)

Sgts Phil Clarke and Andy Wiles, 31 Squadron electricians, with Paveway LGB – suitably inscribed. (*Colin Gower*)

choose a name for him and love him.' Another present arrived from 'Kirsty', with the message: 'I thought you might be sad because your daddy is in the Gulf so I got you this present to cuddle in bed.' In a letter to Chris Ankerson, whose husband Bob was missing in action, Marion Wakener said: 'As a civilian it is difficult to know what one can do and I feel so helpless but I can pray – and I do.' Another lady wrote of a small village church where 'you are all in our thoughts and prayers'. From Roermond, Jean Roubroeks felt the urgent need to wish the people of Brüggen every luck. He spoke for many.

The same *Circuit* contained copies of some very personal notes to the Gulf unashamedly displaying deep felt emotions for all to see: 'Daddy, hurry home and play snakes and ladders with me'; 'the kids love and miss you'; 'I'm keeping the suspenders warm'(?); 'got the leather and lace ready'(?). Perhaps a little more constructively, Mary Myles, the SSAFA Group Nursing Officer, wrote an open letter giving plenty of news from Brüggen, offering help and giving the comforting assurance on 'the wonderful way your wives or husbands and children are managing to hack this "living without you" bit'! Meanwhile, back in the desert, valentines were not forgotten. It all helped.

A message home, from the heart and heat of Dhahran, courtesy the British media pool.
(*Colin Gower*)

The Prime Minister did not forget those who also served the war at home. He included Brüggen in his first visit to British Forces in Germany in February, where he was welcomed by the C-in-C and Tony Harrison before meeting wives, aircrew and ground support personnel, including representatives from 431 MU. The MU, under Wing Commander Al Smith, had pulled out all the stops to produce and maintain the equipment so essential to the success of the operation. Tornado engines were all uprated and their normal throughput more than doubled; painters had worked ceaselessly to give aircraft and vehicles their new desert camouflage, while fabric workers turned out heat and dust covers for canopies, ECM pods and TV tabulators. Day and night, MT conveyed some 800 Granby loads over 107,000 miles.

The Prime Minister, John Major, at Brüggen in February 1991. (*Brüggen Circuit*)

On 13 February came the politically explosive news that the USAF had killed 'several hundred' civilians (later revised to sixty-four), put down to collateral damage during an attack on a bunker in Baghdad. Collateral damage was now to be avoided at almost any cost; the RAF's answer was to stop 'dumb' bombing and to limit all future offensive action to LGB operations. Fortuitously, from 14 February the addition of two TIALD-equipped Tornados at Tabuk increased the designation capacity and gave the RAF a night LGB capability. For a number of reasons LGBs could nevertheless go astray and cause collateral damage but the risk could be minimised by meticulous planning and co-ordination. At the same time, there was pressure to keep up if not increase the sortie rates but, with the few Buccaneer and Tornado designators available, this could only be done by increasing the number of bombers per designator, but therein lay a danger. When, for a particular mission, one Buccaneer (plus a spare) was allocated to provide designation for each of twelve GR1s in turn, against the same target, the bombers were tasked to run in on the same track at regular intervals. A Brüggen contingent refused to provide the last four aircraft in this stream of twelve on the argument that while the Iraqi gunners, even firing manually, might not hit the early aircraft in this highly predictable 'daisy chain', they were very likely to home in on those at the end of the queue.

And so it was that in the reduced stream of eight aircraft the last in line (with a Laarbruch crew) was shot down by a SAM, the navigator killed and the pilot taken prisoner after ejecting. It was dangerous out there.

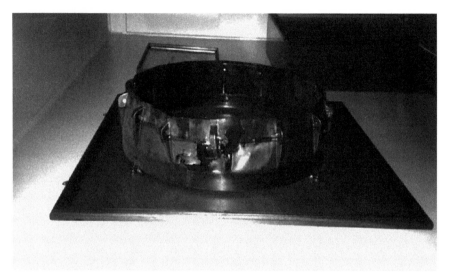

The ring of truth. IX Squadron mounted this battle-damaged engine afterburner ring in its crewroom – as a reminder that it was dangerous out there. (*Author*)

In mid-February, a prolonged period of cloud cover precluded LGB attacks and there were renewed calls in some quarters for low-level JP233 attacks to be resumed. Fortunately the weather improved and a potentially acrimonious debate was avoided.

On 22 February, Iraq rejected another ultimatum to quit Kuwait and began burning everything of value there, particularly the oil fields, and the dense smoke rising to 9,000 feet now added to the flying hazards. A ground war was now imminent.

Coalition ground forces crossed into Kuwait and Iraq at 0400 hours on 24 February and Tornados took off from Dhahran at 1000 hours to attack Jalibah airfield. Not for the first time, a major change of plan was called for, and rejected minutes before the final briefing was to take place, there being insufficient time to ensure effective co-ordination with supporting EW and fighter assets. A warning that the Iraqis would now 'go for broke' proved prophetic and the properly co-ordinated Wild Weasel force was kept well occupied protecting the bombers. The lightning progress of the Allied troops on the ground was clearly visible as endless columns of tanks and trucks headed north, and the mission tallies in the Tornados' nose art bore testimony to their part in the campaign. However, it was not all over and that evening a Scud missile killed twenty-seven Americans in a warehouse some 500 yards from the British quarters.

'Luscious Lizzie', believed to have been based on a schoolteacher at Brüggen, adorns 'Delta Bravo', forty missions to its credit. (*RAF News*)

SAC 'Daz' Whiting puts his 'A' Level art talents to good use. (*RAF News*)

Euphoria at the thought of an early end to the conflict now took hold, prompting questions about plans for going home; this worried commanders who foresaw the possibility of carelessness leading to unnecessary losses. In the event, at 0500 hours on 27 February, the Allies suspended offensive action against Iraq. All missions for the day were cancelled but a force of four fully loaded GR1s were retained on QRA. It was all over bar the shouting.

In what was described as a haze of relief and a carnival atmosphere, with everyone congratulating everyone else, there was still much to do. Among myriad administrative tasks there were demands for reports (including yet another on the loss of Tornado ZA403), citations and inputs for 'lessons learned'; equipment had to be collected, catalogued and made ready for dispatch or disposal, and, of course, there were arrangements to be made for the return home. Bill Wratten visited Dhahran on 2 March to congratulate everyone for their contribution to what was being described as the 'most effective air war in history'; there was plenty of evidence of that and plans were already in hand for him to lead a team in a high level Gulf War Presentation. There was now speculation that the Brüggen warriors would start for home in some ten days' time, during the second week of March 1991.

AVM Bill Wratten, UK Air Commander, Riyadh, congratulates the Tornado detachment at Dhahran on a job well done. (*Bill Wratten*)

The job had been done well. This Iraqi HAS was grist to the mill for Tornado with LGBs.
(*RAF News*)

On 5 March, the Iraqis listed Budgie Burgess and Bob Ankerson among their prisoners of war. The only Brüggen crew hitherto unaccounted for, they were released to the International Red Cross and on their way from Baghdad to Riyadh on 6 March. Kieran Duffy and Norman Dent had died tragically in pre-war training but Brüggen had come through the war itself without any fatalities – a magnificent effort indeed.

The post-war tasks were completed with such zest that time began to hang heavy. The aircrew had hoped to revisit the airfields in Iraq which they had only recently found so inhospitable, but it was their very efforts then that now rendered the ground unsafe for them to do so. There were plenty of rewards for these efforts: generous tributes from John Major and Sir Peter de la Billiere in their second visit to Dhahran, an invitation from the *Daily Star* to London's Inn on the Park for the promised Gold Star Awards, and an unforgettable Arabian banquet in honour of the whole detachment, given by Prince Turki bin Nasser bin Abdul al Saud, but the reward they wanted most was to go home.

On 11 March 1991, a 14 Squadron 'four-ship' of Tornados, led by Doug Moule, began the exodus from Dhahran, missing a memorial service there which gave thanks to, and remembered all who had suffered in the war. Held in the gymnasium of the Rezyat Compound, the service was led by Rheindahlen's Padre Clive Parnell-Hopkinson, who had quietly provided much spiritual and practical comfort to the detachment throughout most difficult times; it was attended by Air Chief Marshal Sir Patrick Hine, the UK Joint Commander in Operation Granby.

Prisoners of War, Fg Off Budgie Burgess and Sqn Ldr Bob Ankerson return to Brüggen.
(*RAF Brüggen*)

The show over, Jerry Witts waves farewell to the first of his Tornados leaving Dhahran to
return to Brüggen. (*RAF News*)

Two GR1s, with the necessary support, stayed in Bahrain to maintain a presence in the Gulf but the remaining aircraft, air and groundcrew, returned to Brüggen between the 16 and 19 March. Jerry Witts, who had led the first of some 600 war missions flown by his detachment, had planned to be the last to leave but he was overruled by Cliff Spink who ordered him to go back with his Tornados. These final days in the desert were likened to those at the end of a school term, a not too distant memory for some, as old friends went their various ways again and a very close-knit community dissolved.

Jerry Witts got airborne with his four aircraft from Dhahran at 0930 hours on 16 March; unencumbered by bombs and with scant attention now to the RWR, they climbed through an oily haze before bursting into a bright, clear sky, the Red Sea, Nile, and eventually the coast of France clearly visible. Three uneventful top-ups from their tankers took them into an ever greener and more beautiful Europe as they sped north and descended into the perennial haze of the Clutch. Signalling their return, the arrival over Brüggen was rather lower and faster than usual.

The band was playing 'Those Magnificent Men in their Flying Machines' as canopies opened and gloved hands emerged as if to acknowledge the cheers and applause from a throng of hierarchy, station executives, families and friends. They were home.

The following extracts, taken from a local newspaper, gave an on-the-spot German perspective of another homecoming, this one different but no less emotional. It began with: 'Even the aircraft seem to be nervous today' as excited children, Union Jacks in their hands, craned to see the VC10 approach from the East and trundle to a stop before them. Then came the applause as the black and white flag of the returning 17 Squadron was presented proudly at the door of the transport, the men and women emerging to handshakes all round. Then suntanned men in big hats and red-eyed women cried quietly as they embraced, young children and a few bachelors looking on bewildered as the band played its welcome. An airman and his son would not let go of each other and a navigator saw his three-week-old daughter for the first time, then the beer began to flow. It was an unforgettable scene.

'Arris, the 31 Squadron bear was typical of the returning heroes; he had flown many missions over Baghdad but was very reluctant to talk about it. Jerry Witts explained, "'Arris is the strong and silent type but we know he cares.' True to form 'Arris didn't bat an eyelid; he sat thoughtfully in his corner of the crewroom, still resplendent in full flying kit, watching the world go by. Ice-cool, he had shown no fear over Baghdad, when kidnapped by Canadians (who threatened to send back his ears) or by the nurses at Wegberg – who mooted even worse.

In a war of forty-two long days, Brüggen had been a major player in a Tornado GR1 force of forty-six aircraft, which flew 1,600 operational sorties, dropped 106 JP233s, 4,400 free-fall 1,000lb bombs, and launched 1,100 LGBs and 104 ALARM.

Flt Lt 'Arris returns from a good war – with a spring in his step – flanked by Flt Lt Kevin Baldwin (left) and Wg Cdr Jerry Witts. (*RAF News*)

In his 1998 presentation on Granby and Desert Storm to the RAF Historical Society, Jerry Witts did not pass judgement on Tornado tactics in Desert Storm but he did reflect on some of the lessons learned. He believes that a continued and necessary dedication to Central European low-level tactics obscured the possible need and potential for medium level alternatives in the post-Cold War era of limited conflicts, when sufficient countermeasures might be available to permit such sorties. He attributes the ultimate success of these alternatives in the Gulf War to the inherent flexibility and broad experience levels, including the ability to operate effectively at low level, within the Tornado force. Ideally, these requirements would have been foreseen and the crews better trained in carrying their war loads over long distances supported by AAR, rehearsed in the worst-case scenarios, and then delivered against typical, heavily-defended targets. All this again drew attention to the old maxim once displayed so prominently at Brüggen, that organisation and training in peace should be tuned fully to the needs of war.

Looking back, many reflected on the value of Cold War Tacevals and the repeated rehearsals for them, including those uncomfortable hours in NBC kit and gas masks, in preparing them for this unexpected ordeal in the desert. That said, they were very grateful for some respite from such exercises after having endured 'the real thing'. There was also much praise for the Tornado GR1, for doing all that was expected of it – and more.

It is a comforting facet of human nature that success and good times dominate the memory but many of the author's unofficial inputs from those 'at the sharp end' made it clear that at times it was not all sweetness and light in the Allied camp. Guidance to the aircrew from above was clear from the start: they were to do their best without unnecessary risk, but had everyone read the script? Of course those who do the fighting are often not privy to the 'big picture': the strategies, aims, objectives and constraints, military and political. Also, this type of war had been neither envisaged nor trained for, and the equipment was more suited to a war in the Central Region of Europe, and of course there was the wisdom of hindsight. However, none of this deterred some from arguing that the particularly hazardous JP233 campaign, while justified at the outset, went on too long. Medium level dumb bombing had to be accepted as an alternative but steep dive attacks, while more accurate than level or dive/level attacks from 15,000 feet, were hardly conducive to high survival rates. Many found it hard to accept the reasons why medium level LGB procedures had not been developed earlier in the UK, and the Pavespike/Paveway force deployed more expeditiously. There was also a feeling among increasingly tired fliers that remote authorities did not appreciate fully the workloads, sleep deprivation and aircraft problems on the flight line, and that there was too much micro-management from above. Of course, no war in history has ever been without mistake and, despite these frustrations, the boys from Brüggen believed that they had done their best.

No further attempt is made here to plead what should have been or might have been, analyse the tactics and achievements of the air war in the Gulf war or portray the moods, apprehensions, natural fears and elations in what was, to date, the most dramatic period of Brüggen's history. Suffice it to record again the admiration of all those who have some inkling of what was involved but did not have to share the traumatic experiences of those Tornado crews as they went about their duties so laudably and effectively. An attempt to add more would be to gild the lily.

Chapter Nine

The Last Ten Years

After the Gulf War great minds could return to the question of the defence needs of a Europe no longer under massive threat from the Soviet Union. This change in the politico-military tapestry would have global implications now that the huge NATO bastions in Europe, manned by the resident nations and incomers from America, Britain and Canada, were no longer required. From one side came national and local demands for drastic reductions in this foreign presence and aircraft noise, while on the other there were pressures to 'bring the boys home', if only to save the enormous costs of keeping these forces and their families on the Continent.

Of course it was not as simple as that. Within the early, euphoric days after 'The Wall' came down there were also great uncertainties, with dire warnings from eminent pundits of potential instability in Eastern Europe and the crumbling Soviet Union. There were statesmen and politicians who saw an enduring value in a North American and British presence on the Continent of Europe, if only as a mark of unity and solidarity. They were joined by the protagonists of NATO, which many believed had done a good job but had more to do; they were most reluctant to see its military arm cut back too far.

There were also practical problems. It would take time to prepare facilities in the UK to accommodate a mass withdrawal of British land and air forces overnight. So, with the principle of force reductions accepted, a reappraisal of military commitments, driven by political and financial imperatives, would be followed by selective cuts and a staged reduction of British forces in Germany.

There were other considerations. The RAF was anxious to phase out its Phantom FGR2s, which were no longer required to share the policing of the airspace in north-west Germany with the USAF, and France, the air defence of which could now be left to the Germans, Dutch and Belgians. Therefore, despite pressure in some NATO quarters for their retention, the FGR2s, together with an RAF Regiment squadron, began the RAF's departure from Germany, and Wildenrath, less its married quarters and some domestic facilities to be used by Brüggen, was handed over to the Germans in 1992. Brüggen then became the main airhead in RAF Germany and the Harrier flight simulator moved to Laarbruch.

The RAF needed to continue realistic low flying, albeit mixed now with some medium level offensive training, but the former would be severely restricted in the 1990s by an embargo (with some exceptions) on flying below 1,000 feet over Germany. This meant that, for routine low flying, much of RAF Germany's strike/ attack force based at Gütersloh, Laarbruch and Brüggen, would spend many largely unproductive flying hours transiting to and from the UK low flying facilities, with exorbitant fuel costs. It made sense, therefore, that with the disbandment, in 1992, of Laarbruch's Tornado strike/attack squadrons (Nos. 15, 16 and 20), and the re-deployment of No. II (AC) Squadron to Marham, RAF Germany's Harrier and helicopter force moved to Laarbruch from Gütersloh when that station was handed over to the British Army in 1993.

With two down and two to go, which station would be the next? Local politics and practicalities again came into play and there were infrastructure and engineering reasons why Laarbruch should survive, but these were heavily outweighed by factors favouring Brüggen (cynics might include the survival of that much-revered golf course), so Laarbruch would close in 1998, its squadrons finding new homes in the UK.

All this impinged increasingly on Brüggen, directly or indirectly, during its last ten years and there was no lasting, post-Cold War stability for the station. Starting in April 1991, with several months of runway refurbishment ahead, 14 Squadron would operate from its site in the south-east of the airfield and 31 Squadron from the old QRA site, both using the southern taxiway for take-offs and landings. No. IX Squadron was detached to Wildenrath and 17 Squadron remained in the Gulf at Muharraq. For the Germany-based Tornados a Fast-Jet Turnround Facility (FJTF) at RAF Leuchars was established for more efficient use of the UK Low Flying System (LFS). This was the turbulent scene when the new C-in-C, Air Marshal 'Sandy' Wilson, arrived in May 1991.

In the coldest, wettest June at Brüggen for thirty-five years, the station rehearsed Operation Shandigan, which allowed Soviet inspectors access to verify that NATO's military equipment did not exceed the scales authorised under the Conventional Forces in Europe (CFE) Treaty. Tony Harrison remained in command for a year after the Gulf War, with much to do yet happy to hand over the station to accounts clerk Jenny Vickers for a day. Jenny had won this prize in a Benevolent Fund Draw and she made the most of it, lunching royally in the officers' mess (to comments on the youth and attractiveness of the new station commander), listening to war stories in 31 Squadron's crewroom (where the hairstyle drew much attention), and disciplined her husband, Corporal Vickers, in a CO's Orderly Room (for an unmentionable offence). In October, the station received the Wilkinson Sword for its support of the Benevolent Fund in its Fiftieth Anniversary of the Battle of Britain Appeal.

Between such brief respites Tony Harrison broke new ground, Brüggen leading the way into the New Management Strategy (NMS). In essence this required the station to take control of its finances, dispensing funds from a given budget 'on broad assumptions' to subordinate budget holders. There were teething troubles and 'vigorous discussions', but under the overall supervision of the budget manager, Higher Executive Officer Simon Mills, and management planner Squadron Leader Gordon Rayfield, this first year of NMS was, in the words of the station commander 'an unqualified success'.

In common with the Brüggen Tornado squadrons, No. 37 (Rapier) Squadron became part of Operations Wing when No. 4 Wing, RAF Regiment, disbanded, and was constantly on the move thereafter. In September 1991, its 125 men deployed *in toto*, half to Belize and half to the Falklands, where the squadron could now expect to spend four months out of every sixteen, at a high state of readiness defending Mount Pleasant. Working and living together in confined conditions, in some very isolated sites, took some getting used to but the initially very frugal conditions continued to improve over the squadron's eight detachments since 1982, with the relative luxury of Portakabins now giving a degree of privacy. The gunners still had to learn how to fend for themselves and for others (one finding it difficult to cook with washing-up liquid). These detachments offered better than usual operational training for 'A' Flight. In live Rapier firings from Hookers' Point, Senior Aircraftsman Jones, Leading Aircraftsman Webster and Leading Aircraftsman Shanks destroyed their twelve feet wingspan targets, while several others scored technical hits. Similarly demanding, the gunners also practised with general-purpose machine guns against Skeet targets in the all-arms air defence role, and enjoyed some success. There were plenty of sporting and leisure activities to keep the squadron fit in body and mind, with participation in the British Forces Falkland Islands March, a two-day walk in the clouds over the Wickham heights, BBQ parties to recover and 'intellectual' quiz nights. On 17 December the flight celebrated 37 Squadron's fortieth birthday with a medieval fancy dress party in the hangar and a champagne reception in the Joint Service Officers' Mess.

Meanwhile, 'B' Flight was helping to protect Belize International Airport, as it had since 1991. Unofficial records say little of this primary role but make much of the squadron's exploits in jungle training and of its many extraneous activities. Jungle patrols, a record eight in all, were high on the agenda, usually on the Guatemalan border to gather information on illegal aliens and drug running operations, or merely to contribute to the 'hearts-and-minds' campaign. One 37 Squadron patrol took to horseback – a sight to behold. Then there was scuba training over one of the largest barrier reefs in the world, windsurfing and sailing, followed by rest and recuperation in such exotic places as Florida, Mexico, Costa Rica and Honduras. Life was not all hard work in the RAF Regiment. Both squadron detachments returned to Brüggen in January 1992.

A victim of its own success and reputation, Brüggen hosted a proliferation of visits from ever more diverse interests. In November 1991, the programme included the C-in-C and Dep Cdr RAF Germany, fifty members of the Dutch '*Onze Luchtmacht*' (Our Air Force), the Officer Commanding, sixteen doctors and nurses from RAF Wegberg, ex-members of the German Afrika Korps, the Chief Joint

Sgt Pete Scott, 37 Squadron RAF Regiment, leads the extraction of a foot patrol in Belize, by RAF Puma helicopter. (*37 Squadron*)

Services Liaison Officer, Director of Military Products, Rolls-Royce, and twenty members of the German Red Cross.

While 17 Squadron and then 14 Squadron basked in the sunshine of a Las Vegas winter on Red Flag, airfield operations at Brüggen remained minimal as work on the runway extended into January 1992.

Down at 431 MU, Propulsion Engineering Squadron completed its Spey engine overhaul programme in February, having serviced 1,221 Buccaneer and Phantom engines since 1973. The squadron hit the headlines again that month when one of its ladies, Tanya Stapley, organised a sponsored aircraft pull to fund special equipment needed by meningococcus meningitis sufferer Llionis Williams. Pulling a 16-ton Tornado the requisite 100 yards in under one minute was a feat in itself, but in this case it was accomplished by the ladies of the station, in yet another example of Brüggen's charitable initiatives and generosity. Perhaps all this was celebrated in 431 MU's Fear Dry Inn, which was given a full face lift in the spring of 1992. A new bar emphasised the German rustic style; the function room now had a dance floor and a stage, and could seat 160 guests in comfort for every social activity; new central heating was installed throughout and there were excellent external facilities with patio, BBQ and children's play area. There was no shortage of places to relax at Brüggen.

On 5 March, after a parade reviewed by the Dep Cdr, Air Vice-Marshal 'Black' Robertson, 52 Field Squadron marched out of Brüggen's life to the sounds of

'Auld Lang Syne'. The squadron had been crucial to the station's survivability and effectiveness in war, its work often rehearsed dramatically during exercises and VIP visits. Its prominence on the sports field and in social activities also made it a very popular, integral part of the station. Proud of their achievements, Captain Steve Black wrote in the *Circuit*: 'We marched off the square in style, with a pride that the RAF will always be envious of.' Perhaps he left the station before the airmen could think of a suitable retort?

As one unit left Brüggen others arrived, including the Command Meteorological Office, RAF Germany's Air Movements Squadron, Freight Distribution Centre, VIP Andover and No. 12 Flight, Army Air Corps (AAC) from Wildenrath.

The station now operated twenty-four hours a day, seven days a week, and in its first full month of operations the Movements Squadron handled 158 aircraft movements, 2,000 passengers and 425,000lb of freight. The Army Air Corps (AAC) arrived from Wildenrath with its four Gazelle helicopters and thirty soldiers, but this uniformed strength was reduced to seven when maintenance support for the flight was handed over to the civilians of Bombardier Services Ltd. The number of workers on the station had now risen to 3,000.

Men from Bombardier putting a Gazelle to bed in Hangar 3, at the end of another busy day for 12 Flight, Army Air Corps, at Brüggen. (*RAF Brüggen*)

THE LAST TEN YEARS

Group Captain Ken Block 'N' Tackle retired from the RAF on 1 April 1992, when the responsibilities of 431 MU's Salvage and Transportation Section were transferred to Support Command. He was pleased with his rapid promotion since enlisting nine years before, but happy to retire into a distinguished group of other mannikins at the Luftwaffe Museum in Hamburg. During his time as the MU's Public Relations Officer he attended twenty-eight crashes, every formal event and beer-call, but was never found the worse for wear at these social occasions. With stiff upper lip, hard outward appearance, glassy eyes but heart of plastic, he was a stickler for protocol and an on-the-spot court martial awaited anyone who transgressed. Attended by OC 431 MU, Wing Commander Al Smith, Ken Block 'N' Tackle was dined-out in Hamburg with proper style.

Speaking to the *RAF News* before he relinquished command of the station to Group Captain Rob Wright in June 1992, Tony Harrison called the performance of all at Brüggen, particularly during the Gulf War, 'Just magnificent, from the unsung heroes who worked long hours in the background, to the crews who flew deep into Iraq time after time.' There would be no argument with that. He also praised the station's German and Dutch workers and paid tribute to friends and neighbours 'outside the wire', who accepted the consequences of having a major airbase on their doorstep.

The demise of the Property Services Agency (PSA) came in 1992, when the station assumed responsibility for the development and upkeep of its estate through the newly established Property Management (PROM) office, thereby replacing the Station Services Flight. Cutting out PSA meant that PROM could deal direct with the *Finanzbauamt*, now the *Staatlichtesbauamt* (SBA), and for minor projects direct with contractors, thus speeding up works services and reducing costs. OC PROM, Squadron Leader Julian Andrews, helped make it all happen. When he arrived at Brüggen in October 1992 work was in hand, under the old system, on the kitchen of the Fear Dry Inn and a shower block, but these jobs were still not finished when he left more than two years later. In the new organisation things would be different, but the challenges were formidable. At one stage PROM had 104 Part 2 services on its books, at a cost of DM28M, in addition to Part 1 works on the Main Access Control Centre (MACC), wing briefing room, air terminal and sergeants' mess. These major projects were managed by RAF Germany but in practical terms much was left to PROM. The air terminal was cost-capped but essential adjuncts, such as the access road, car park and connection to water and power supplies, had been omitted from the original estimates and additional funds had to be found from other sources or by judicious accounting. The car park's interlocking blocks were bedded on environmentally friendly, recycled ground glass rather than sand, to improve drainage at low cost and with no risk of weeds, the whole impressive complex being completed in 163 days. This successful introduction of PROM would be followed, in January 1993, by the formation of an Office of Management and Budget (OMB), which provided a framework for planning and financing to enable the delegation of tasks, budget, responsibility and authority to cost centres, effectively completing the implementation of the NMS. The station population now totalled 6,600, comprising 250 officers, 2,300 other ranks, a civilian workforce of 450 and 3,600 dependants.

No. 37 Squadron was in the Hebrides again for an MPC in 1992, the *Circuit* telling of the road journey through Holland (courtesy of the Dutch police), the ferry trip (with a coachload of schoolgirls and the Lincoln Gilbert and Sullivan Society) and of roaring through the UK (which incurred the interest of the Grampian police). Tall stories followed of fish that got away, sailing in force eight gales, inept horse-riding, rock climbing and avalanches, hillwalking in the rain and 'gamesmanship' in golf. Only at the end was it noted that 'the missile firings were one of the most successful ever, with zero operator errors, no equipment faults and an optical hit on a Falconette'. Life was interesting on 37 Squadron.

With the Brüggen Tornado squadrons now employed in Operation Jural, the RAF's contribution to the Coalition's Operation Southern Watch, 14 Squadron flew to Dhahran in November to help monitor the 'No-Fly Zone' (NFZ) in Southern Iraq. No longer the 'alone, unarmed and unafraid' reconnaissance missions of old, TIALD-capable Tornados could also, from 1994, have Vicon camera pods fitted for surveillance from medium level, with guns and Sidewinder missiles for self-protection. For added security, they would fly within force packages which might involve E-3 Airborne Early Warning (AEW) and EC-135 electronic intelligence gathering aircraft, F-15 Eagles for fighter cover, EF-111 and F-16 aircraft for SEAD support. The Vicon cameras enabled panoramic area cover and high resolution imagery of specific targets with the simplicity of old-fashioned black and white wet-film photography, hundreds of feet of which could be processed and analysed rapidly and efficiently after landing, within the Reconnaissance Intelligence Centre (RIC). Not for them the problems facing those remaining at Brüggen that winter, when the snow and ice teams struggled to do their job without the de-icing chemicals now banned by the Germans as being 'environmentally unfriendly'.

Consistent with the drawdown in RAF Germany, 431 MU was a victim of 'Options For Change'. Wing Commander Al Smith commanded the disbandment parade, reviewed by the Deputy Commander on 3 December and Tornados of IX Squadron overflew in salute as General Timm, German Air Force, presented the unit with a '*Fahnenband*' (battle honour) to mark the closure of another British unit on German soil. The piecemeal rundown of the unit, and transfer of some tasks to the station, then gathered pace; Al Smith handed over to Squadron Leader H.D. Davies on 4 February, the unit disbanding finally on 31 March. In forty years at Brüggen, first as a GEP then an MU, the unit had given invaluable, highly specialised professional support to RAF Germany and the station, while contributing greatly to their myriad charities, social and sporting activities.

In welcoming 1993, during which the station would celebrate forty years' service, Rob Wright thanked everyone for all they had done at work and play, in true Brüggen spirit, and did forecast another busy year of change. He looked ahead to the first Taceval since the Gulf War, the seventy-fifth anniversary of the RAF, the demise of RAF Germany and 2ATAF and the assumption of command by HQ 2 Group. As C-in-C, Air Marshal Sir Sandy Wilson would preside over these historic events, mindful of their political, practical and psychological implications. Accordingly, he invited the Parliamentary Under Secretary of State for Defence, the Air Member for Personnel and others to address the first ever RAF Germany Wives' Conference in the Crossbow Club at Brüggen in March.

RAF Germany, the last of the overseas Commands, ceased to exist at 2359 hours on 1 April 1993, the RAF's seventy-fifth birthday, and in his farewell address Sir Sandy said: 'For over thirty-four years, the squadrons of RAF Germany have had a reputation for professionalism in NATO which is second to none. Everyone who has served, or continues to serve with the RAF in Germany can be proud of their contribution to European defence and deterrence. You have truly earned the "Keepers of the Peace" epitaph.' The final act was a parade at Brüggen on 21 April, attended by many former C-in-Cs, after which Sir Sandy and Lady Wilson departed, not by station train as had been the tradition, but by VIP Andover. So ended an era. HQ 2 Group took over the premises thus vacated at Rheindahlen, with the AOC, Air Vice-Marshal Black Robertson commanding the RAF units staying in Germany as part of NATO's Rapid Reaction Force (Air) (RRF (Air)).

The station commander, Gp Capt Rob Wright, and Mrs Wright, bid farewell to the last C-in-C, RAF Germany, AM Sir 'Sandy' Wilson and Lady Wilson, at Brüggen on 1 April 1993. (*Sandy Wilson*)

The long awaited Taceval, the last in the Cold War style, took place on 4-6 May, NATO having yet to develop an alternative strategy to match the changed European order, or any commensurate way of testing a unit's capability. Despite the now unrealistic scenario, most of the required skills were still relevant for any conflict and Brüggen had no problem rising to the challenge. The exercise was deemed 'an outstanding success', with the award of '1's for Operations and Survival to Operate, with a '2' for Support, the NATO team notably impressed by the 'very knowledgeable and enthusiastic battle staff' in the COC. As a result, the station earned a CINCENT Certificate of Commendation, the first to be awarded since the end of the Cold War. It was presented to Brüggen by the Deputy C-in-C, AFCENT, Air Marshal Sir Michael Stear in December.

Tragedy struck in June when a IX Squadron Tornado collided with a civilian helicopter on pipeline inspection near Kendal in the Lake District; the Tornado was able to land safely, but the crew of the helicopter was killed. The exhaustive investigation which followed laid no blame on the aircrews but recommended that the Civil Aviation Authority and MOD continue to seek improvements in deconfliction procedures for civil and military aircraft operating at low level.

The new air terminal at Brüggen was opened formally by the AOC during his annual formal inspection of the station on 30 June 1993. This impressive facility could, simultaneously, handle an aircraft arriving and departing with more than 200 passengers. The throughput now included a daily shuttle from Northolt, RAF Germany's VIP Andover, two weekly trooping flights by Britannia Airways, the very popular Welfare Charter Flights 'Brüggen Air' (Stansted and return for £95) and a host of transport and other visiting aircraft. Movements Squadron, commanded by Squadron Leader

The whole station is represented at the presentation of CINCENT's Certificate of Commendation to Gp Capt Wright by Deputy CINCENT, AM Sir Michael Stear, in December 1993. (*RAF Brüggen*)

RAF Brüggen's new Air Terminal, opened formally on 30 June 1993. (*RAF Brüggen*)

Chris Hewat, was soon processing 4,000 passengers a month while Cargo Handling Flight, run by Warrant Officer Bill Kearney, dealt with one million pounds of air cargo, including accompanied baggage, in addition to half as much again in surface freight. An automated palletisation system removed much of the pain of 'humping and dumping', allowing up to forty pallets to be on the move at any one time. Little was it known then how all this would be put to the test on several occasions before the end of the century.

By now, IX Squadron had taken over the development of tactics for the employment of ALARM missiles, begun by 20 Squadron during the Gulf War, with airborne training enhanced by clearance to carry drill rounds. In the Cold War, area suppression was envisaged along a corridor to be used by attack packages, each ALARM within multiple firings seeking specified emitters. The emphasis was now on rapid response, out-of-area operations and 'on call tasking', using target of known location (TKL) tactics and different delivery modes against radars already identified and pinpointed, typically by Luftwaffe Electronic Combat Reconnaissance (ECR) Tornados. For its work with ALARM, IX Squadron would be presented with the Wilkinson Sword in 1995.

Meanwhile, 14 Squadron had begun specialising in TIALD, which had also made its operational debut in the Gulf War and continued in use there in the aftermath, Wing Commander Frank Turner, OC 14 Squadron, and navigator Flight

Lieutenant Stephen Beardmore flying the first sortie with the pod at Brüggen on 19 August 1993. TIALD enabled Tornado to designate LGBs from high and low levels, with better accuracy than had been possible with the Pavespike designator, and for some reconnaissance tasks, by day and night.

Combined Air Operations (COMAO) were now routine for all the flying squadrons. In July 1993, ten Brüggen Tornados and four Harriers from Laarbruch flew low-level over Holland, climbed into the new North Sea instrumented range (ACMI) for combat with Coningsby-based Tornado F3s, before refuelling from VC10 tankers. The attack package then descended to low-level, through an F3 combat air patrol (CAP), to carry out a simulated attack on RAF Kinloss before taking on fuel again from the VC10s for their return to Germany. Two months later, the Tornados dropped live 1,000lb bombs at Grafenwoehr Range in Bavaria, in a COMAO with USAF F-15s, Belgian F-16s and Canadian F-18s. These were high-value sorties.

The summer brought more evidence of the new relationship between East and West. Slovak MiGs, Albatros and AN-16 aircraft dropped in at Brüggen on the way to the Fairford Airshow; a Slovak team reported a 'very successful' CFE inspection of the station; the USAF began dismantling its 'Big Ears' aerial in the south-west corner of the airfield and a fire-damaged 17 Squadron Tornado returned from Deci to Brüggen in a Russian Antonov 124 'Condor'. This huge aircraft, with a take-off weight of 893,000lb, would become a frequent visitor.

Now a frequent visitor to Brüggen, the huge Antonov 124 'Condor', had to remain on the ORP for loading and unloading. Evidence of rapid runway repair exercises can be seen on the taxiway in front of 31 Squadron (top). (*RAF Brüggen*)

262

With all that had been achieved in 1993, and a reduced flying target set for 1994, MOD sensed economies, and a Manpower and Vehicle Audit produced a case for reducing Brüggen's establishment by 170 engineering posts, eighty-nine of them in Engineering and Supply Wing. This would take effect between April and October 1994, impacting heavily on workloads at all levels.

In OC 17 Squadron's New Year's message from Dhahran, where his squadron had taken over Operation Jural duties, Iain McNicoll wrote, 'There has been nothing dull or routine about the way in which 17(F) Squadron spent 1993 and I am sure that 1994 is not going to be boring. At year's end we find ourselves part of the coalition policing the NFZ in Southern Iraq, in providing the aircrew and first line groundcrew on this three month rotation. The work is hard and there are few days off, with flying operations which can take place at any time of the day or night. The groundcrew work twelve hour shifts and a flying sortie, as part of a package, can last for over three hours, with at least one hour spent over visibly war-torn Iraq.' This was Brüggen's new 'war', its officers and other ranks making the best of it. None wanted to be away from home at this holiday time but there was plenty to keep them occupied at work and (non-alcoholic) play. Iain McNicoll himself flew in a four-ship formation over Iraq on Christmas Day, before returning to the Khobar Towers accommodation for a Christmas BBQ (with a difference!) and a volleyball match. On New Year's Day 1994 he was delivering live, TIALD-designated LGBs on Udairi Range in Kuwait, his navigator, Flight Lieutenant Dave Coombes, successfully guiding both their bombs and those of their No. 2 (who had a TIALD failure) on to a wrecked Iraqi armoured vehicle.

Back at home, at a poignant sunset ceremony on 20 May, a single Tornado overflew the officers' mess annual reception and the legendary tree which had become the source of so many tales. Now it was officers from 14 Squadron who took up residence in its natural cover on many a Friday night beer-call, providing target practice for rival squadrons with hoses and fire extinguishers.

Wing Commander Stu Peach took over IX Squadron in May 1994, just as the manpower cuts were beginning to bite, but the squadron itself was well-prepared for Exercise Distant Thunder in Alaska. This COMAO included operational low flying (OLF) over realistic field targets, numerous electronic threats and opportunities to deliver 1,000lb bombs in loft and laydown modes. Such exercises now involved the Franco/British Air Group, and were being held as far afield as North America, Spain, Turkey, the Far East and Australasia. In September 1994, 17 Squadron Brüggen Stanival and elements of Nos. IX and 31 Squadrons went to Singapore, the aircraft using AAR but also staging at Akrotiri in Cyprus, Seeb in Oman and Colombo in Sri Lanka. There they put the Five Power Defence Agreement Integrated Air Defence System to the test in untypical visibilities of

The legendary tree behind the Officers' Mess, host to many an informal soiree, bears witness to a more formal celebration on The Queen's Birthday, 20 May 1994. (*RAF Brüggen*)

2,000-3,000 metres, caused by forest fires in Indonesia. Familiarisation with the different battle management and control arrangements was invaluable and the development of a standing Mobility Operations Order for Brüggen's role in the new RRF(Air) concept would stand the wing in good stead through the second half of the decade.

Of course, no amount of training or preparation, however realistic, can generate the many forms of nervous tension and apprehension in war. The author would not dare to venture into this very private world, but he found one overriding concern among those who had been to war, and a powerful motivator in itself, that being a determination not to let the team down by any personal failings.

Those at Brüggen in June and July 1994 may remember two unique and impressive sights. First came a fly-past of twenty-four helicopters to mark the activation of the Multinational Division (Central), then an armada of aircraft from former adversaries: TU134s, MiG21s, SU22s, SU25s, AN26, MiG29s, L29s, L59s, Hip and Hind helicopters, again refuelling at Brüggen en route to Fairford. For their arrival and departure ATC and the airfield support services had to be – and were – at their very best.

Friends again. Czech Air Force MiG29 and Royal Air Force Tornado meet at Brüggen.
(*RAF Brüggen*)

Taken in 1994, this is believed to be the first official photograph of Brüggen's Station Fire
Service in its 40 year's history: always ready but perhaps often taken too much for granted.
(*RAF Brüggen*)

No. 37 Squadron was now preparing for Rapier 2000, Field Standard 'C' (FSC).
The roof of a custom-built hangar for the new equipment was completed in July
with a 'Richtfest', the ancient German tradition equivalent to 'topping out' in the
UK. There would be testing times ahead for the squadron.

Group Captain Glenn Torpy took command of the station in October, as
tensions in the Gulf increased and 14 Squadron aircrew, having escaped from
Brüggen after spawning a galaxy of new offspring, helped to identify Iraqi troop
movements below the 32nd parallel with its fast-developing expertise in TIALD
and Vicon operations, the latter now producing very useful imagery. Then, in a
bilateral agreement with the Americans (Operation Driver), Brüggen reinforced
its Jural detachment at Dhahran with six more Tornados, drawn from throughout
the wing.

To signal IX Squadron's Eightieth Anniversary on 8 December, the *Brüggen
Circuit* carried the story and an evocative picture of one of its Wellington bombers

Perhaps taking squadron 'togetherness' a little far, seven of 14 Squadron's officers became proud fathers in the spring of 1994. (Back, L to R): Sqn Ldr Mike Napier, Wg Cdr Tom Boyle, Flt Lt Steve Lloyd. (Front, L to R): Flt Lts Nigel Cookson, Nigel Crennell, Gerry Cepelak, Nick Maunder. (*RAF Brüggen*)

from Honington in 1940, which carried the motto: 'There's always bloody something'. In a weekend of remembrance in November, squadron members old and new celebrated this milestone and the part played by the squadron in sinking the *Tirpitz*, on 12 November 1944. Nose art on a Tornado, carrying the motif 'Still Going Strong', brought back memories of that carried by Lancaster 'J' on that historic raid.

After the departure of Russian forces, it was possible to fly into eastern Germany. Squadron Leader John Scholtens was one of the first to do so, on 6 January 1995, his last sortie as executive officer with No 31 Squadron. Leading a pair of Tornados, he and his pilot, Squadron Leader Ed Smith, had a grandstand view from 1,000 feet (much higher than they or any RAF crew had ever anticipated in war) of the ground they had learned by heart in the Cold War. John takes up the story: 'As we crossed the Deconfliction Zone on a misty winter's day into a land covered with light snow, nervous tension and an eerie silence took hold; there were no radio calls, no tell-tale signals on our RWR and little evidence of Warsaw Pact equipment on the ground, yet we flew on in silence with bated breath for a full five minutes into that once forbidden land; it was like a spring had snapped on the mighty Soviet war machine. We flew over the now disused Zerbst and Wittstock airfields, passed close to Brandenburg, Neuruppin and Altengrabow airfields and within thirty miles of Berlin. The once proud base of Zerbst, which had concentrated NATO minds for so many years, now lay abandoned, a sad sight with HAS doors ajar or wide open and no sign of life. A feeling of great elation engulfed us as we realised the enormity of what had gone before – with this first-hand evidence that it was truly over.' What better way for John to end his second tour at Brüggen than with such a memorable flight, before a posting to the Directorate of Public Relations, MOD, as a wing commander. Later, Brüggen Tornados carried out an airfield attack on another of its primary targets in the Cold War, Laage, now an active NATO base, and engaged in simulated combat with the airfield's MiG29s of the new Luftwaffe.

On 6 January 1995, Sqn Ldr John Scholtens, on his last sortie with 31 Squadron leading a pair of Tornados, took a close look at Zerbst, Wittstock, Brandenburg, Neuruppin and Altengrabow air bases, in the recently hostile East Germany. It was now truly over. (*John Scholtens Collection*)

THE LAST TEN YEARS

On 25 January 1995, haggis was on the menu at the officers' mess for Burns Night. In a frantic hunt and dash from its native Scotland, Squadron Leader Davie Paton and Flight Lieutenant Iain Cosens of 14 Squadron collected the beast from Mr McQuilton, butcher of Leuchars, and flew it with all speed to the rich and famous at Brüggen. There it was met on landing by head chef Flight Sergeant Stephens, whisked into the pot and, with due ceremony, served first to the station commander, who pronounced it to be 'of the finest quality and taste'.

The last Andover shuttle flight between Brüggen and Northolt took place on 31 March, and was celebrated in the customary manner by respective station commanders, members of 32 Squadron and the movements staff at Brüggen.

The last Andover 'Shuttle' between RAF Germany and the UK, left Brüggen on 31 March 1995. (*Brüggen Philatelic Club*)

In May 1995, Brüggen had its first Taceval in the RRF (Air) role. The preparation phase led to a simulated off-base deployment, vacant IX Squadron and the old QRA sites representing a Forward Operating Base (FOB), from which day and night operations were flown. Again showing the way in NATO, the station was awarded a most commendable mix of '1's and '2's for resources and performance in all phases, under the headings Operations, Support and Survival to Operate.

On 26-28 May 1995, 17 Squadron, with many former members, celebrated its Eightieth Anniversary. The formal parade and a sunset ceremony, commanded by Iain McNicol and reviewed by Air Chief Marshal Sir Patrick Hine (a former CO), were enhanced by fly-pasts of 17 Squadron Tornados and a Spitfire from the Battle of Britain Memorial Flight, the latter to commemorate the squadron's former glories in Burma during the Second World War. The squadron displayed its Standard for the first time with nine Battle Honours, the limit of eight having been waived to allow the Gulf War Battle Honour to be added. With this dispensation applying to all four flying squadrons at Brüggen, they paraded their Standards together, to provide a unique photograph of thirty-six Battle Honours.

17 (F) Squadron's 80th Anniversary, May 1995. (L to R) Air Cdre Andy Griffin (ex-CO), Mr Donald Healey (ex-member), ACM Sir Patrick Hine (ex-CO) and Lady Hine watch a Spitfire from the BBMF. (*RAF Brüggen*)

June was a month for fly-pasts. No. 14 Squadron obliged at Ramstein for AAFCE's Annual Reception; a diamond of sixteen Brüggen Tornados, led by Glenn Torpy, overflew Buckingham Palace on the Queen's Birthday; and 14 Squadron performed again at Brunssum for AFCENT's Queen's Birthday Reception. For all this effort, at a time of severe engine and manpower shortages, when aircraft were also being modified to take the Vicon cameras, Glenn made special mention of the superb station engineering support.

To rationalise Brüggen's education facilities and optimise classroom space, it was all change for many of the 800 children educated on the station at the end of the summer term. Barnes Wallis School closed, making its premises available to Bader School in the autumn term, while Cheshire School would be affected only by a small change in its children's age range.

No. 37 Squadron returned from its ninth tour in the Falklands in October 1995 after one of the coldest spells there in living memory, with snow falling almost every day for nine weeks. Rapier equipment and gunners survived these extreme conditions, albeit with the latter facing a serious risk of hypothermia and frostbite as they manned the sites twenty-four hours a day. In this very operational setting

Gp Capt Glenn Torpy at the head of Nos. IX, 14, 17 and 31 Squadron Standards, all uniquely bearing nine Battle Honours. (*RAF Brüggen*)

the MPC and visitor demonstrations were reported to be 'realistic and interesting', with some spectacular firings and several direct hits.

Also in October, 14 Squadron went to Marine Corps Air Station (MCAS) Yuma, for Exercise Arid Thunder, in which they practised OLF and precisely timed co-ordinated attacks, delivering a total of 140 live BL755 Mk1 CBUs in laydown or shallow dive profiles on the Arizona weapons ranges. This was followed by Exercise Scorpion Wind, a USMC air defence exercise involving 100 aircraft from twenty units; in which the Tornados, accompanied by USN, USMC Harriers and ECM aircraft, attacked strongly defended targets. The squadron, led by its CO, Wing Commander Tom Boyle, was the first foreign unit to take part in this Marine Corps equivalent of Red Flag, in which the actions of all participants were monitored on the ground for definitive debriefings. The mission profiles and tactics were found to be very similar to those used by the RAF, in an exercise which was 'as close as it gets to the real thing' and an outing from Brüggen which was 'definitely 14 Squadron's good deal of the year'. Not to be outdone, 17 Squadron followed 14 Squadron at Yuma for the final phase of Exercise 'Arid Thunder', while IX Squadron celebrated the presentation of the Wilkinson Sword by CAS, awarded for all its hard work with ALARM.

Another Brüggen first, when 14 Squadron joined the US Marine Corps at Yuma, Arizona for Exercise Arid Thunder in October 1995. OC 14 Squadron Tom Boyle and the Brüggen station commander Glenn Torpy present Lt Col Jim Flock, of the F-18 host squadron, with a memento of their visit. (*RAF Germany*)

On 2 November 1995, CAS, ACM Sir Michael Graydon, presented IX Squadron with the Wilkinson Sword for its work with ALARM. The Standard is borne by Flt Lt Steve Freeman, the Sword by Flt Lt John Brooker. Escort to the Sword is Sgt Eddy Smith. (*RAF Brüggen*)

At the end of 1995, NATO began to deploy 60,000 troops to Bosnia to monitor the ceasefire brought about by the Dayton Peace Agreement and Brüggen, with its new facilities, was a major emplaning point for part of the UK and NATO military contribution to the Implementation Force (IFOR). During two weeks in December, with some help from other units, Brüggen dispatched 150 Hercules sorties, with 570 passengers, 256 vehicles and 830 tonnes of freight to Sarajevo, Split and Zagreb, and more would follow. Air movements, air traffic, engineering and catering staffs were all involved and, with temperatures regularly below freezing, Supply Squadron had to issue vast quantities of cold weather equipment for the 24-hour-a-day operation, together with some 30,000 litres of Clearway to keep the airfield open. This first operational deployment of NATO's multi-nation Allied Rapid Reaction Corps (ARRC), with Germany having not committed its forces to overseas operations since the Second World War, attracted much attention from the international media, and for its part Brüggen could be justly proud of a job well done.

It was not only the warriors who were taking to the air; at 0600 hours on 12 December, seventy-one children left the air terminal for Lapland to the sound of festive music played by the station band. Met at Rovaneimi by beautiful and friendly Lap ladies in traditional costumes, the sledge was drawn by reindeer to Santa's village. There, everyone was fed and watered until Father Christmas joined them from across a snow-covered and floodlit river to present each one with a reindeer bell to remember a truly magical day. Meanwhile, back at Brüggen, the pre-Christmas festivities were in full swing.

Brüggen children visit Santa in Lapland. (*Brüggen Circuit*)

Sgt Paul Hilton built this Christmas Grotto first in 17 Squadron in 1993, then, for many years to follow, in Cheshire School and the Crossbow Club. (*Iain McNicoll*)

1996 started badly, with three serious accidents. In January, Tornado ZD846 crashed near Münster, its Italian exchange pilot, Captain Andrea Spinelli, and his navigator, Flight Lieutenant Chris Donovan ejecting safely. In February, ZD789 caught fire soon after take-off but recovered to Brüggen for a successful approach-end cable engagement, and in the same month Stu Peach and his pilot, Squadron Leader Nigel Risdale, had to eject from ZD845 during an air test; both suffered minor injuries and were hospitalised at Wegberg.

OC IX Squadron, Wg Cdr Stu Peach, recovering after his ejection from ZD845 in February 1996, has his audience spellbound during a visit by AOC 1 Group, AVM John Day. (*RAF Brüggen*)

When HQ 2 Group disbanded at Rheindahlen on 1 April 1996, Brüggen became part of No. 1 Group in the UK, with certain responsibilities for those RAF units and personnel remaining in Germany. To reflect this greater role, the station commander became the Senior RAF Officer (Germany) at 1-star level, Glenn Torpy promoted to air commodore *in situ*.

3 BAD Bracht, Explosives Maintenance and Storage Section, which served Brüggen so well, closed in March 1996. (*RAF Brüggen*)

With the demise of 431 MU, responsibility for RAF Germany's Maintenance and Storage Section at 3 BAD, Bracht, was transferred to Brüggen's Engineering and Supply Wing. The unit was heavily involved in out-loading for the Gulf War in 1990 and an unprecedented 11,122 cu metres of weapons to the UK after the Conventional Weapons Logistic Support Study in 1995, before disbanding on 4 March 1996.

No. 37 Squadron became operational with Rapier FSC in 1996. This new equipment comprised a surveillance radar to identify and allocate targets, a tracker radar for all-weather automatic target and missile tracking and fire units mounting eight ready-to-fire missiles. The missile itself flew faster and further than its predecessor and did not need a direct hit to destroy the target. The squadron strength was reduced to six fire units and 108 men, but its overall capability was greatly increased. One FSC fire unit could engage two targets simultaneously in every type of weather, against heavy ECM and in NBC conditions. With the latest sensor and digital technology, it was effective against high speed targets at low or high level, cruise missiles, remotely piloted vehicles and 'pop-up' helicopters. The squadron had no trouble with the conversion programme, finding the new equipment simple to operate and maintain;

it could now make a greater contribution to the peacetime COMAOs, TAMs and the TLP taking place as far afield as Portugal, Norway and the UK.

As a result of the terrorist bombing of the Khobar Towers accommodation complex at Dhahran in June 1996, which killed nineteen American servicemen but left IX Squadron unscathed, the Jural detachments, now each reduced to two months, moved to the Prince Sultan Air Base at Al Kharj, ('Al's Garage)', south of Riyadh in Saudi Arabia. Inside a perimeter fence stretching 140 miles, Al's Garage was a more remote, less well-established desert airfield the size of the Isle of Wight. At 1,600 feet above sea level the temperatures ranged from 120°F by day to freezing point at night, hotter but less humid than Dhahran and a far cry from the climate and creature comforts of West Germany.

17 Squadron 'Blackhand' Tornado in the desert at Al Kharj. (*RAF News*)

At Al's Garage the men from Brüggen lived in tents, but tents with a difference; these were double-skinned, timber-floored, electrically lit, air-conditioned, ten-man tents, with efficient air-locked entrances to keep out sand and heat and plenty of TV and books to pass the time away. With great effort and enterprise they were improved by adding DIY 'Gazebo' annexes, made from materials 'found' locally. This American-style 'Harvest Falcon Housing Area', or 'tent city', accommodated 4,500 Americans, 237 British and 150 French men and women. Sleep was not easy, with transport aircraft coming and going at all hours of the day and night.

With constant noise and sand everywhere, working conditions were difficult; groundcrew had to work long and hard (without air conditioning) to keep six Tornados on the line, while the aircrew were committed to protracted planning and re-planning, but yet, as some said, 'it was all strangely rewarding'. Corporal

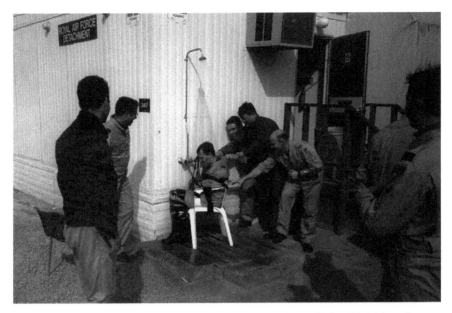

Flt Lt Nick Maunder takes an involuntary shower after his last flight with 31 Squadron at Al Kharj. (*31 Squadron*)

Fred Perry from Brüggen's General Engineering Flight (GEF), remembers that in temperatures of 50°C spanners which were too hot to touch were put into a fridge to cool down. Chief Technician Paul Malley remembers that when a digital thermometer on the 17 Squadron flight line reached 115°F, 'it made a sort of croaking sound and packed in – but the limeys went on working'. The one hundred or so British vehicles suffered too, with sand penetrating everywhere and oil drops baking into cement; everything had to be 'battened down, blanked, bunged and kept clean'. In the Supply Flight, Sergeant Skip Perryman, running a multi-million pound inventory, recalls that twelve hour shifts were the norm, but that they sometimes stretched to sixteen hours. General administration, which depended so much on communications and computers, was very difficult at first, but typical British improvisation invariably came to the rescue and nowhere was this more true and more important than in the catering provided by the RAF's Mobile Catering Support Unit. OC Jural Support Wing, Wing Commander Davie Paton, said of the caterers: 'They really have been magnificent, no praise can be high enough', and this was echoed by all. Locally employed Bangladeshi cooks will be remembered for their 'fantastic' curries and invitations to the British mess hall were much sought after. Praise too, for the Air Support Squadron RE, from Waterbeach, of whom Davie Paton said, 'If they haven't got it and can't get it they'll make it out of something.'

277

Improvisation was also the name of the game when it came to sport. With their own version of the Ryder Cup in mind, British and American golfers pitted their energies, wits and expertise in their own version at Al Kharj, one vast sand bunker. In seven days they cut out a course which comprised five holes named: 'Bunker Hill', 'Pebble Beach', 'Alamein', 'Golf War' and 'The Mother of All Holes'; redundant bed pans were used as holes, chalk marked the out of bounds and painted stones simulated trees. Sad to relate, the British team of twenty, which included eleven men from 31 Squadron, lost by twenty-one points to nineteen.

In September 1996, with more political unease in the Gulf, eight more Brüggen Tornados were placed at seventy-two hours readiness, but they were not needed. Then came the welcome news that UK squadrons were to take their turn on Operations Jural and Warden. Warden was the British contribution to Operation Northern Watch, the equivalent of Southern Watch, but for surveillance over north Iraq it was mounted from the more comfortable American-style base at Incirlik in Turkey.

Air Commodore Nigel Maddox took over the station from Glenn Torpy in November 1996, and the gunners of 37 Squadron had a particularly welcome VIP visit in the summer by Miss World, who had clearly heard of their reputation and readily found time to include them in her busy schedule. At the end of the year, with their expertise in the infantry role, they acted as the 'hunter force' in the escape and evasion phase of the aircrews' winter survival course at Bad Kohlgrub. The potential escapees did not realise that their 'enemies', incognito on 'basic winter training' nearby, were listening in as they discussed their plans and intentions none too covertly over large steins of Bavarian beer in the local bars, but on the following occasion they were glad to have the versatile gunners in the field with them.

It happened on a night in March 1997, when an RAF Puma crashed during the initial deployment phase. From a distance of 400 metres Senior Aircraftsman Hamilton, one of the hunter force, saw the rotors of the helicopter strike a tree while aborting a landing. The pilot and another crew member were badly hurt but the loadmaster was catapulted out of the aircraft without serious injury and the passengers in the rear were largely unscathed. With great presence of mind, and no little strength, the gunners extricated the injured from the cockpit but the pilot succumbed later to his injuries. For their immediate and effective reaction, 37 Squadron's Corporals Mark Coogan and Al Cullen and SAC Rea, would be awarded Commendations in the 1998 New Year's Honours and Awards.

In 1997, with globe-trotting all the fashion, the Brüggen Bears became the first RAF Rugby Football Club (RFC) to visit the Republic of South Africa. A public relations spin-off began when the team provided new balls and coaching for 200 boys and girls in the township of Mamelodi, some of whom had walked six kilometres to be there and none of whom had boots. In nearby Pretoria, training and playing in 70°F, at an altitude of 6,000 feet, was hard work but the team acquitted

Miss World, in the capable hands of No. 37 Squadron, RAF Regiment – but under the watchful eye of their OC, Sqn Ldr Balshaw (far right).

itself well, losing to a South African Defence Force Select team by only 23-10 and excelling thereafter in the ever-present and highly-active social intercourse. The Bears also did well against Hoedspruit, the South African Air Force champions, despite giving away more than two stone a man in the pack, and were unlucky to go down 23-18. Impressed, Hoedspruit presented the Bears with their pride and joy, a stuffed Warthog head, but bureaucracy and customs regulations prevented the team from bringing their trophy back to Brüggen. The tour culminated in a meeting with the British Lions at one of their training sessions, after which Flight Lieutenant Douglas Potter, the officer in charge, summed it all up with: 'We saw all sides of an exciting, beautiful and wild country, played some hard and skilful rugby and made some wonderful friends; hopefully we left a trail of goodwill for others to follow.'

When the author returned to the Bears' club-house in 2000 he found it largely unchanged since his time with the club in 1978, the ghosts of past players and their songs easily imagined. The much-vaunted Warthog head was still awaiting an entry visa.

Turning from Bears to orphan elephants and rhinos, in a heart-warming international rescue which showed that a little help can go a long way, Brüggen Movements Squadron arranged for the RAF to fly used boots and uniforms donated by the German military to the David Sheldrick Wildlife Trust in Kenya.

In colder climes, Brüggen's Corporal Michelle Coy continued to excel as the driver of GB1, Britain's No. 1 Women's two-place bobsleigh. The 1996/97 season in Canada started well for Michelle and Cheryl Done, her brakewoman from Laarbruch, and they went on to win the first British Women's Championships at Winterberg in January. For the Brüggen men, Corporal Graham Richardson drove into second place and serious contention for the 1998 Olympic team, in both two and four-man bobsleigh classes. At work and play, Brüggen was showing the flag internationally.

Trophies galore: Brüggen Bears RFC Clubhouse – little changed over many years.
(*Author*)

Bears of a different hue, typifying the many charitable projects undertaken at Brüggen – this one benefitting 'Children in Need'. (*RAF Brüggen*)

Brüggen's Michelle Coy and her brakewoman Cheryl from Laarbruch: Britain's No. 1 Bobsleigh team. (*Brüggen Circuit*)

Providing the background music at dining-in nights, festivals, shows and fêtes, the Brüggen Voluntary Band had been entertaining the station since it was formed under the direction of Chief Technician Howard Bartlett in the mid-1970s; he was followed by Chief Technician George Geddes, Sergeant John Hunter and most recently by Mr Matthew Hall. They had to work hard to encourage, train and assemble the players in suitable rehearsal rooms, hence their nomadic rovings between Wildenrath, Rheindahlen and finally Brüggen, where they found a home in Barrack Block 88. Increasingly, the band held a wide variety of 'stand alone' concerts including 'The Last Night of the Proms', its formidable repertoire evident again on 26 April 1997 when it presented 'Viva Hollywood', a nostalgic collection of music of all kinds from stage and screen.

Back at work, Wing Commander Bob McAlpine led IX Squadron into the long daylight hours of an Alaskan summer for Exercise Cope Thunder 97-03. At Eielson AFB, the nine Tornados flew COMAOs with USAF and USN aircraft, the RAF groundcrew achieving excellent serviceability in far from ideal conditions. The squadron derived great benefit from flying over this unfamiliar terrain at low-level, with ALARM and inert 1,000lb bombs, working with USN EA-6B Prowlers and monitored by the Yukon Measurement and Debriefing System.

IX Squadron show the way in Exercise Cope Thunder, Alaska, June 1997. (*RAF News*)

With so many of the breadwinners away from Brüggen for much of the time, increasing attention was being paid to the spiritual, welfare and practical needs of those who remained behind. To that end a 'Chaplaincy Team' formed in 1997, brought together the CofE, RC and CSFC padres in a Chaplaincy and Welfare Centre accommodated in a small bungalow behind SHQ. Then there were the health visitors, who formed only one part of the community health services operating in the Brüggen area but who deserve mention for the comfort they gave to many. Qualified nurses with special training in child health and development, health promotion and education, they were always ready to listen and advise, supporting and helping everyone, young or old, married or single, in all situations. Welfare remained high on the agenda at Brüggen.

Chaplaincy Team, 1997: Sqn Ldrs Andrew Jolly, Adrian Gatrill and John Daly.
(*RAF Brüggen*)

In August, OC 17 Squadron, Wing Commander James Kirkpatrick, led five of his officers deep into Russia to revive an association begun in the Second World War at Monchegorsk Air Base, south of Murmansk, in what was believed to have been the first visit by RAF front line aircrew to an operational Russian fighter base since the end of the Cold War. In 1941, elements of 17 Squadron had been part of No. 151 (Hurricane) Wing which was sent to assist the Russians against the Germans, and five squadron veterans were included in this party to meet their Russian counterparts. Throughout the visit the British party was treated to a succession of lavish dinners, washed down by endless quantities of vodka, in sessions which lasted up to five hours but what struck the visitors most was the similarity between RAF and post-communist Russian air force attitudes on all things professional and domestic. One spokesman opined, 'If you taught them English and put them in an RAF uniform it would be difficult to tell the difference.' Brüggen was no longer potentially at war with these men who had come out from behind the Iron Curtain.

With Iraq threatening Kuwait again in 1998, Brüggen was brought to a high state of readiness and reacted at once when Operation Bolton was initiated at 1600 hours on Friday, 6 February (always at beer call time!). Between 8 and 12 February, twenty-four transport aircraft, including a Russian Antonov on contract, plied between Brüggen and Kuwait with 243 passengers, 700,000lb of baggage and freight and ten vehicles, Movements Squadron turning round each aircraft within two hours. Their destination, and that of eight Tornados from 14 Squadron, was Ali Al Salem airfield in Kuwait, a mere sixty miles from the border with Iraq, which still bore the marks of allied precision bombing to rid Kuwait of the Iraqis in 1991. Five days after they had been alerted at Brüggen, 14 Squadron was flying missions from Ali Al Salem in support of Operation Jural, the first RAF unit ready, if necessary, to drop the Paveway 3, a 2000lb LGB with, as one writer put it, 'cutting edge technology employed from a tent in an old hangar'. Later, OC 14 Squadron, Wing Commander Peter Rycroft, commented: 'Being ready to fly combat missions gave us all a cutting edge, a focus for both aircrew and groundcrew which was outstanding.' Flying Officer Darren Arch, who achieved combat ready status during the operation, added, 'Everything I learned in my training suddenly made sense.'

The base had been activated by a team from Strike Command led by 14 Squadron veteran Wing Commander Tom Boyle, with the 400-strong British detachment commanded by Group Captain Mal Prissick, another experienced Tornado pilot; this was a very professional team. Included among the many support elements, hitherto unmentioned, was 14 Squadron's Sergeant Creedy and his three safety equipment specialists – the 'squippers'. It was their job to ensure that parachutes, lifejackets, helmets, masks, inner and outer clothing fitted and functioned perfectly, with constant cleaning, sewing, servicing and testing essential. Fitting a new helmet might take an hour and getting it wrong could leave a pilot or navigator in agony shortly into a flight, and that would not help to win war. Everyone had a part to play and the squippers invariably got it right. A significant deterrent force was now in place in another waiting game.

Ready for anything. Sidewinder AAMs being prepared at Ali Al Salem. (*RAF News*)

Within five days of being alerted at Brüggen, 14 Squadron was flying operational missions (these with Vicon cameras) from Ali Al Salem airfield in Kuwait. (*RAF News*)

The GR1s at Brüggen and deployed on Operational Bolton were already a powerful force but on 23 February 1998 the Tornado GR4 made its debut at Brüggen in what Air Commodore Nigel Maddox described as 'a quantum jump in both avionics and weapons systems, which will allow the Tornado to be a truly all-weather aircraft'.

This Tornado update included a new, multi-function pilot's cockpit display, improved defensive aids, a weapons bus to control the release of new smart weapons, Forward Looking Infra Red (FLIR), TIALD integration, a Global Position System (GPS) and a video recording facility to assist debriefings. Thus the GR4 would assume a more covert mantle than its predecessor and it was appropriate that the first of these aircraft should go to IX Squadron, with its bat motif. Perhaps it was no accident that the squadron was commanded at this time by Wing Commander Bob McAlpine, a Tornado veteran of the Gulf War and MOD project officer for the mid-life update. The GR4 was not, however, immediately compatible with TIALD, a primary requirement for current Gulf operations, so GR1s would remain in service until the necessary modifications had been completed.

Much work continued behind the scenes at Brüggen, often unnoticed and unrewarded, men and women beavering away at their particular specialisations but all subscribing to the effectiveness and way of life on the station. There was metal worker Herr Creusen and fitter Herr Hillen, both of whom belonged to PROM's directly employed labour force, but their skills did not go unnoticed. With many hours of painstaking work using special tools, they produced the unique and ornate fireguard on which the badges of the station and four flying squadrons were mounted, for presentation to VIPs who visited the station. Wherever these artefacts adorned and endured in high places throughout the world, Brüggen would be remembered.

The first Tornado GR4 arrives at Brüggen, heralding a 'quantum jump in both avionics and weapons systems'. (*Brüggen Circuit*)

Back at Brüggen, IX, 17 and 31 Squadrons show off their weapons: ALARM, Paveway LGBs, 'dumb' 1,000lb bombs and Sidewinders. (*RAF News*)

When Nos. 60 and 32 Squadrons ceased their Andover shuttle service between Brüggen and Northolt in March 1995, the role was taken over by the civilian firm Air Swift, and in 1996 by Air Kilroe. The service came to an end finally in March 1998, with Captain Martin Holloway, at the controls of a Jetstream 31, making the last flight.

Also in March, RAF Germany gave up its nuclear strike role, Flight Lieutenant Harry Charlton, Brüggen's Weapon Training Supervisor, organising several functions to mark the event. These culminated in a memorable dining-out night at which the guest of honour was the Assistant Chief of Air Staff, Air Vice-Marshal Jock Stirrup. Surrounded by a collage of photographs and artefacts, reminders of the RAF's strike history, another honoured guest appeared for the last time, a 600 Medium Capacity (inert) nuclear bomb, which sat quietly in the corner of the ante room while many stories were told of the part it played in deterring war, and the anguish it had sometimes caused its minders. The menu for the evening came in a Combat Mission Folder, annotated with initial points (IPs) on target maps and containing the all-important black eye patch (to protect one eye against nuclear glare!). The meal was washed down with 'Atomale', a special brew for the evening, which roused one-time harbingers of Armageddon to rhetoric in the particular vernacular of their trade, in many Cold War stories. That they were never called to their task was a mark of the success of deterrence – Brüggen's very *raison d'être*.

Flight Lieutenant Robin Chisholm, Wing Electronics Warfare Officer (WEWO), recalls how eerie it felt entering the COC on the morning after the night before, through a security cell now deserted where it had been so heavily

This Brüggen 'special weapon', now a thing of the past, rests in peace in 31 Squadron's extended crewroom – seen through the hole that Willie Luys made in 1986.
(*RAF Brüggen*)

Sqn Ldr Peter Cartright, Senior Operations Officer, rides into retirement astride the bomb on which he was a specialist. (*RAF Brüggen*)

manned only the day before, the inner sanctum now open for all to see. The bombs themselves were whisked away, covertly into the night, and into history, but some training rounds took up residence in squadron crewrooms, where they were treated with some reverence at first before being ignored as nothing more than a piece of the past.

On 17 September, the RAF was on the Noorderplas Lake, Roermond, for Exercise 'Grote Slinger' ('Big Pendulum' in Dutch). A big yellow RAF Sea King search and rescue helicopter deployed from the UK for this exercise to re-qualify forty aircrew from Brüggen and Laarbruch in life raft and wet-winching drills. This time and money saving alternative to training in the UK, inter alia providing the Dutch with a free demonstration of the RAF at work, was organised by Squadron Leader Bill Davies, Station Navigation Officer, assisted by Squadron Leader Martin Wistow, Station Flight Safety Officer. All went well until the latter, supervising the safety boats, decided to test the underwater capabilities of the management radio, but it says much for this equipment that it worked perfectly when recovered from the bottom of the lake.

Emphasising 'togetherness' in sport and social events, Brüggen's Dutch and German neighbours were always much in evidence at the RAF Germany Golf Club on the station. The author recalls flying down from RAF Oldenburg, North Germany, forty years before, when the course was in its infancy and almost deserted. Now, it had a multi-national membership, the car parks were invariably

RAF Germany Golf Club Manager, Ron Powell, with part of his half-million Deutschemarks win. (*Ron Powell*)

full, 140 days a year were committed to golf society events and it was a venue for many RAF Championships. To its manager Ron Powell, 1997 had been a special year; he won half-a-million Deutschemarks (£160,000) on the German lottery, had his second heart by-pass and reduced his handicap from eight to six, not necessarily in that order. It is not known whether his big win was seen in the same light as a golfer's 'hole in one', with drinks all-round, but a brand new Jaguar Sovereign arrived on the scene and it seemed that with Ron continuing to work at his hobby he was having his cake and eating it.

One of the oldest recreational institutions at Brüggen ceased trading in 1998 when the Malcolm Club, the source of many tales of the past, handed over its premises to the YMCA. The new establishment, run by Eileen Gilchrist then remained open to the end, providing a comfortable, all-ranks meeting place for meals and refreshment; it was staffed by British dependants and with all the goods in its shop coming direct from the UK, it was in effect a 'little UK'.

In 1998, it was IX Squadron which flew the 20,000th hour (in 4,700 missions) on Operation Jural, then in its sixth year, and the Tornados went to war again in a controversial, short-lived campaign against Iraq. In response to Saddam Hussein's continued obstruction of UN weapons inspections, and his on-going refusal to comply with Security Council resolutions, the US and UK alone agreed on a programme of airstrikes. On 11 November, US bombers were already airborne and British Tornados were only two hours from take-off when Saddam climbed down and pledged to resume co-operation with the UN. In the uneasy peace which followed the two allies threatened action without further warning if Iraq reneged on this latest undertaking. When it was clear that it had done so, pre-planned strikes were launched on 16 December, amid world-wide concern, in Operation Desert Fox. Brüggen aircrew were not involved but 12 Squadron flew twenty-eight sorties from Ali Al Salem airfield, Kuwait, without loss, in a Tornado force which included aircraft from the wing.

Well-versed with the station and its roles from his previous tour at Brüggen, Air Commodore Iain McNicoll took over from Nigel Maddox in December 1998, to find the station in very good heart but with much still to be done. Agreed increases in engineering manpower had yet to materialise and experience levels were now becoming a matter of concern; there was a shortage of TIALD and Skyshadow pods for training, delivery of GR4 was behind schedule, as were updates to its software, all of which combined to drastically reduce overall aircraft availability. It was, therefore, to Brüggen's great credit that much of the flying task was still being achieved.

In February 1999, the GR1s at Al Kharj were replaced by Tornado F3s, while those at Ali Al Salem, at which future Brüggen detachments would be based, continued, when necessary, to carry out offensive missions in addition to surveillance duties. In the same month, elements of the ARRC began to deploy to Macedonia for Operation Agricola, setting the pace for what was to be a very busy year for the station. In the first six weeks of Agricola eight Hercules (based at Brüggen) supported by Belfast, Antonov and Ilyushin transport aircraft, moved 500 personnel, 165 vehicles and 650 tons of freight – and more would follow.

OC 31 Squadron, Wing Commander Robbie Low, has reflected on changes in the role of the RAF in Germany, and the Tornado force in particular, since the Cold War ended. As a first tourist and already a qualified weapons instructor (QWI) at Laarbruch from 1983 to 1989, his flying had consisted of repetitious low-level work in simulated attack and strike profiles largely within Germany's low flying system. Much of his time had been devoted to the study and rehearsal of contingency plans for an all-out war in Europe, within the pre-planned nuclear programme and QRA commitment. Life became more interesting and demanding as new training opportunities and exercises were introduced to exploit the Tornado's night/all-weather capability and its JP233 runway cratering and airfield denial weapon, but low-level operations remained the norm.

The end of the Cold War and Gulf experience changed all that. Medium level weapons deliveries were developed as alternatives to, and to supplement low-level operations. JP233 was discarded (the mines becoming politically unacceptable) as greater attention was paid to the employment of TIALD-designated LGBs, with the development of tactics and the weapons system for their more effective use from medium level. Henceforth, the choice of options on the day would depend on the circumstances, the opposition expected and the availability of airborne warning and control systems (AWACS), electronic countermeasures (ECM), fighters, et al. Tornado aircrew now had to be ready for any exigency.

Out-of-area operations and other potential conflicts in Europe demanded skills other than those rehearsed during the Cold War. Rapid deployment and long range, heavyweight sorties called for proficiency in AAR by day and night, in all weathers. Medium level operations and a paucity of assets meant that Tornado crews had to be ready to operate with aircraft from other squadrons and nations, in mutual confidence and on standard procedures, within different battle management systems and host nation rules. The increasingly ambitious, worldwide and diverse COMAO programme recognised these requirements.

Experienced and new crews had to cope with all this additional training and a massive increase in transit flying, including the need for RAF Germany crews to fly regularly to the UK for their low flying with little if any increase in the overall flying hours allocated. In 1999, Robbie Low averaged sixteen hours a month, his crews only a few hours more, so it was greatly to the credit of contemporary Tornado men that they should acquit themselves so well in versatility and adaptability. Operation Engadine would provide plenty of evidence that they did just that.

On 28 March 1999, the station went to twenty-four hour manning, all leave was cancelled and security increased ten-fold as anti-war demonstrations in nearby Düsseldorf accompanied increasing tensions in the Balkans. The Rambouillet Accord had failed to secure peace in the region and increasing evidence of human suffering called for a tougher stance against Serbian 'ethnic-cleansing'. It was all hands to the pump, with flying operations and engineering support centred on 14 Squadron, its squadron commander, Wing Commander Tim Anderson and his executive officers at the helm. The squadron PBF was optimised for the purpose (secure communications etc.) by GEF within twenty-four hours, while TIALD, Boz and Skyshadow pods appeared as if by magic to join the LGBs and Sidewinder missiles being prepared for up-loading on to the Tornados. This was serious business.

The 4 April 1999 was an Easter Sunday, and it was on that night, in a first for any unit in Germany since the Second World War, that Brüggen dispatched six Tornados against Serbian military and infrastructure targets in the former Yugoslavia. Thus, the station began its contribution to Operation Allied Force in Operation Engadine, the bombers refuelling several times from VC10 and Tristar tankers in sorties lasting up to eight hours. Sensibly, the VC10s of 101 Squadron had deployed to Brüggen from Brize Norton to enable continuous planning and liaison with the Tornados and to accompany them throughout their long missions. This resulted in a very strong professional and social bond between these two elements of the force and the VC10 crews soon made themselves at home in a very different habitat for them, adopting that section of the officers' mess bar vacated by the outgoing 17 Squadron. In the words of one of the crews, this transition to war had gone 'worryingly smoothly', but Brüggen had been practising for years and could turn its hand to anything.

A Paveway LGB being prepared at Brüggen, for dispatch direct to Kosovo in Operation Engadine, April 1999. (*HQSC/RAF News*)

Not knowing how long the operation would last, to mitigate the effects of the 7-8 hour operational missions and allow time for essential rest, training and extraneous activities, Tim Anderson introduced a four-day cycle. The first day was devoted to preparation for a sortie on the second night, and this was followed by two days for debriefing, administration and rest before the cycle started again. Every mission demanded complete co-ordination and integration with the other components of the force package, remote from each other but brought together by state-of-the-art communications. Intelligence was derived from NATO and national AWACS, ECM by EA6B Prowlers, HARM SEAD by F-16s, ground attack by F-18s and Tornados, and fighter cover by F-15s and F-16s. Particularly with hindsight, there were inevitable questions as to the efficacy of intelligence, targeting and weapons employment, with much debate on the pros and cons of committing 'dumb' bombs from medium level and the well-proven but little used ALARM, again underlining the crucial importance of all aspects of battle management to mission effectiveness.

The evening farewells to wives and families can only be imagined; one pilot spoke of seeing his wife off to the UK just before he climbed aboard his Tornado for Kosovo; likewise another left his quarters at the same time as his wife went off for an evening of bridge. At about 2200 hours the telltale whine of VC10 engines signalled the start of another hard day's night for many; no one knew what was in store and emotions ran high. Take-offs were at about 2300 hours, with scenes strangely reminiscent of Second World War airfields as executives and others gathered in the control tower or the meteorological office and groundcrew perched on the revetments, all to watch pensively as the first tankers, each carrying 80 tons of fuel, lumbered off a runway none-too-long for them. They were followed by the equally well-laden Tornados, then a peace of sorts descended on the airfield.

A Brüggen 'package' comprised two sections of three Tornados, all aircraft carrying TIALD, Paveway LGBs, Boz and Skyshadow, Sidewinder AAMs and loaded Mausers; some crews were equipped with Night Vision Goggles (NVG). Tanker support was provided by three VC10s (one acting as a spare). The outbound leg could take up to four hours with the first refuelling taking place off the French Rivera, followed by a 'top-up' before entering the target area. Weather permitting, the LGBs would then be released at about 20,000 feet, out of range of the most intensive AAA but not the SAMs. Because TIALD had to 'see' its assigned target many missions were aborted because of unsuitable weather. No. 31 Squadron reported that all its Engadine sorties were engaged by either SAM or AAA (or both), pilots often having to drop external fuel tanks and take evasive action. Many crews spoke of their first experience of coming under fire as more surreal than terrifying, pin-points of light chasing them through the night, seemingly innocuous but of course potentially lethal. That said, they soon gained a healthy respect for the Serbian gunners, with the adrenalin build-up peaking in hostile airspace following weapons release or when the mission was aborted, after which most spoke of feeling very tired as they began their long return trip to Brüggen, with more AAR and perhaps poor weather or aircraft emergencies with which to contend.

Stories of heavyweight AAR and interplay between the Tornados, VC10 and Tristar tankers could occupy a full chapter, telling of man-made and natural incidents often in concert with thunder and lightning in generally far from ideal weather conditions. At 20,000 feet and an indicated airspeed of 300 knots, closing in on the refuelling drogue at a critical 2-3 knots of overtake, in the dark and often in and out of cloud, needed every concentration and crew co-operation. However, the underlying theme was of the great mutual respect between all the players, including the invisible controllers in the air and on the ground, in a dimension of air operations which would have been inconceivable in the Cold War.

The relief of all concerned, of the crews in the cockpits, their families and groundcrew, the executives and support staff, when all the crews returned safely to Brüggen throughout Engadine was palatable. The deeply-felt support of the local German and Dutch employees on the station and neighbours 'outside the wire' was much appreciated. One German lady, perhaps taking a cue from a famous broadcast during the Falklands War, wrote that she 'counted them all out and counted them all back'.

CAS, ACM Sir Richard Johns, flanked by the Station Commander and OC 14 Squadron, in the 14 Squadron site at the height of Operation Engadine. (*RAF Brüggen*)

The crews often arrived back at about 5am, at which time the whole station was ready, willing and able to meet their every need. The officers' mess was often the venue for informal debriefings between bomber and tanker crews, with a can of beer or two to unwind. Breakfast became dinner and the mess staff worked irregular, unsocial hours, willingly and silently when the crews took to their beds.

A more elaborate fillet steak and champagne breakfast followed the last of some 130 missions (an average of six sorties/crew) mounted from Brüggen on 29 May. Tim Anderson, the station commander and Air Commodore Vaughan Morris, from the Combined Air Operations Centre at Vicenza, congratulated everyone on the station involved in Engadine, while signed squadron prints were exchanged with OC 101 (VC10 Tanker) Squadron, Wing Commander Ian Elliot.

By now, NATO had gained air superiority and inflicted severe damage on Serbian military assets and supporting infrastructure, all greatly impeding Serbian activity in Kosovo. However, more was to come; the whole Brüggen operation, with a mix of twelve Tornados and twenty-four crews from IX and 31 Squadrons, then moved to Solenzara, a French base on the island of Corsica. Wing Commander Greg Bagwell, OC IX Squadron and overall detachment commander, welcomed the greater efficiency inherent in this move but now there were too many NATO assets chasing too few targets and hostilities were almost over. The few missions flown were very much shorter, involving only one or two air refuellings, and gone were the psychological implications of mounting operations from the family base. The two squadrons now flew as separate entities, IX Squadron greatly frustrated by weather problems but 31 Squadron was able to fire ALARMs. The commander of the 450-strong RAF detachment at Solenzara was Group Captain Jerry Witts, the ex-31 squadron commander of Gulf fame, now taking time out from commanding RAF Northolt. He praised the generous co-operation of the French, which enabled the force to become operational and ready for tasking on 1 June, three days after the arrival of the first aircraft from Brüggen.

Throughout the campaign, even during the move to Solenzara, the Brüggen Wing maintained the four-day cycle and, other than those cancelled by weather, flew all the missions with which it was tasked. No. 14 Squadron, which had spearheaded Operation Bolton a year before and spent so much time recently at Ali Al Salem, flew some sixty per cent of the missions, achieving a very high success rate, its engineers working twelve hours a day, seven days a week. Again, Brüggen had been in the vanguard of this campaign, but there would be no NATO Kosovo medal for its support personnel, they did not satisfy the eligibility criteria!

A healthy rivalry had existed between the Brüggen squadrons throughout the operation, with sparring and spoofing rife whenever there was an opportunity. At the end of play, IX Squadron, perhaps with the connivance of Jerry Witts, arranged for a signal to 31 Squadron advising them that they would be returning to Brüggen in a seven day trip by sea. Understandably, this was greeted with dismay until the ruse was rumbled and the victims were aboard their Hercules heading for home. Then, to rub salt into the wound, their arrival at Brüggen went almost unnoticed

IX and 31 Squadrons carried out bombing missions over Kosovo from Solenzara, Sardinia, in Operation Engadine, June 1999. (*31 Squadron*)

in the middle of the night, whereas IX Squadron flew the Tornados back to a very proper welcome during the day.

Spare a thought now for the families of those who were involved elsewhere, in one way or another with Bolton, Engadine, or the many other commitments of the time, and for those who were responsible for their welfare. One such man was OC Personnel Management Squadron, Squadron Leader Johnston Calder, who commented to the *RAF News* that the much-vaunted 'peace dividend' had led to a 'stress dividend' for some of those families, underlining the importance of their welfare to operational effectiveness. With many of Brüggen's personnel on forty-eight hour standby, and spending six months of every year away from home, ever more attention had to be paid to those left behind, especially the recently arrived, newly married, or those with young children. Much depended on the service's legendary self-help within unit 'families', but with many more wives working there were increasing demands on organisations such as SSAFA, Homestart, the HIVE, health visitors, wives' clubs, medical staff, youth services, and of course the padres. Johnston wrote, 'I gained a privileged insight into the resilience of RAF families and their can-cope, can-manage attitude, the value of a collective spirit with everyone pulling together is obvious to anyone who has worked here over recent years.' Brüggen looked after its own.

Writing for all in the *Brüggen Circuit*, OC 14 Squadron, Wing Commander Tim Anderson, stressed that Engadine had been a team effort, providing 'a healthy dollop of glue to bond us together, from right across the station and from all ranks and trades in common purpose; we are now very much a battle-hardened air force.' Tim would be awarded a DSO for his part in the campaign.

Among the messing staff who cared so loyally for those at the sharp end during this war, and indeed throughout many years before and after, were Hannelore Kentopf, Rudi and Annie Krul, Fred Jordan, Ron, Hannelore Beer and Bert de Vries. Hannelore Kentopf, a native of Elmpt, had served behind the bar in the officers' mess since 1960 and took her turn when the crews returned from Kosovo. She remembers wild days in the different climate of the Cold War and saw rather quieter social patterns emerge from changes in the station's role since then. For her, 'The best days were from the early 1980s to the mid-'90s, especially with IX Squadron on some extremely lively Friday nights; it was not unusual to come in on Saturday morning and find people sleeping in the bar, but I have enjoyed all my years here enormously, the people have been so friendly.' Such natural pleasure from those who served helped greatly to make the lifestyles at Brüggen what they were.

Ever discreet, Hannelore Kentopf saw it all from the bar in the officers' mess, from 1960 until the end. (*Hannelore Kentopf*)

From Echt in Holland, came Rudi and Annie Krul, both of whom had been involved in catering at the sergeants' mess since the 1960s. Annie has fond memories of serving Princess Margaret, Prince Philip and Diana, Princess of Wales, as well as many Government ministers; she clearly enjoyed working for the RAF, was awarded an AOC's Commendation in 2000 and stayed on to the end.

Rudi and Annie Krul worked in the sergeants' mess from 1960, Annie rewarded with Commendations in 1991 and 2000. (*Sergeants' Mess*)

An ex-chief technician at Brüggen, Fred Jordan became a stalwart behind the sergeants' mess bar for twenty-five years, always able to remember his regular customers and their preferred tipple. Awarded a C-in-C's Commendation before dying of cancer in 1997, the bar was later dedicated to him.

After retiring from the RAF at Brüggen, Fred Jordan served as a barman in the sergeants' mess, receiving a C-in-C's Commendation for his 25 years of excellent service there in February 1997, shortly before he died of cancer. (*RAF Brüggen*)

National serviceman Ron Beer married another Hannelore when he returned to Brüggen as a civilian, thereafter both of them serving the officers' mess well, quietly and courteously until it closed. Bert de Vries started work in the mess as a barman in 1969 and progressed to mess supervisor. He remembers 213 Squadron going to Kuwait and riotous summer balls in the '70s which demanded a collective staff effort for up to thirty-six hours non-stop. He saw the big tree behind the mess grow to host many a party, and watched it cruelly wreathed in rings of fire when struck by lightning, split in two and finally succumb to the axe for the safety of all. It was he and Ron Beer who built the barbecue at the rear of the mess, in one of their many enterprising initiatives. Bert was also properly recognised for his part in the efficient running of the mess, with the award of a BEM in 1993, the medal presented by the AOC 2 Group, Air Vice-Marshal 'Black' Robertson.

Bert de Vries began work in the officers' mess as a barman in 1969 and became a supervisor. He was presented with a BEM in 1993, by AOC 2 Group, AVM 'Black' Robertson. (*RAF Brüggen*)

Such loyalty and sense of duty among the staff was legion throughout the station, Brüggen's Catering Squadron being another unit mentioned regularly in official records and the *Circuit* for its all-important contribution to the well-being and therefore operational effectiveness of those in its care. The improvement in facilities, service and fare over the years and throughout the station is thus well documented. Less well known is how essential flexibility was introduced in the mid-1970s when the squadrons dispersed permanently to the four corners of the airfield and it became necessary both to reduce travelling time and exposure to hostile activity in exercise and war. Derek Charles, then the warrant officer in charge of the airmen's mess and later the civilian manager of the Brüggen Bowl, remembers that they improvised six units, each of six cookers powered by propane gas, from sixty cooking sets made redundant at RAF Hullavington. These units, each supervised by a corporal cook, would be sent out to the four flying squadrons, 431 MU and the MT Section, but not without some risk. He recalls that when one of the gas bottles blew a leak, the warrant officer in charge of the fire section, in a sight to behold, contained the problem and rode with great courage astride the offending cylinder while it was towed on a trolley to Hill 60 to be rendered harmless.

Thereafter, and especially during the last ten years, Catering Squadron continued to respond readily to many unexpected, diverse and often dramatic surges in demand. Despite considerable turbulence and the continuing need to support all the station activities while so many of its number were detached out-of-area, the squadron, under Squadron Leader John Kelly and Warrant Officer Grimshaw, won the Strike Command Catering Trophy in 1997 and 1998.

Also in 1998, it won the Jolliffe Trophy 'for the best standard of both cuisine and service' in the RAF, and in the Combined Services Catering Competition, Senior Aircraftswoman Clare Williams was the first woman to become RAF Senior

The RAF Culinary Team 1998 award winners (L to R) SAC Wayne Hunt, SAC Pete Dunn, SAC Clare Williams and SAC 'Scouse' Woods. (*RAF Brüggen*)

Chef of the Year and win a bronze medal, Brüggen's Senior Aircraftsmen Wayne Hunt, Pete Dunn and 'Scouse' Woods joining her on the list of winners.

Neither was Brüggen's Engineering and Supply Wing, although severely stretched, ever found wanting. While supporting Operation Agricola, the engineers had to cope with some 5,000 hours of extra work generated by the introduction of Tornado GR4, on-going modifications to the GR1, RB199 engine production, and Operation Engadine. For its part, Supply Squadron deployed a large support group to Solenzara and doubled its usual monthly turnover of aviation fuel. MT Flight also rose to the occasion while continuing to provide those routine services so often taken for granted; it won the RAF and Defence Road Safety Rose Bowls in 1998 and 1999, was judged to have made the best contribution to road safety within the UK Armed Forces in the MOD Tri-Service Competition, and won the Strike Command Trophy in 1999. While all this was going on, three hundred personnel were trained to operate the new Logistics Information Technology System (LITS), which went 'live' in October 1999. The wing as a whole had also assisted with the closure of Laarbruch and reallocation of its resources. It had been a busy time for the engineers and suppliers.

So it was for Air Traffic Control Squadron, which won the Cossor Trophy for its overall efficiency in trying circumstances. Despite a much increased workload and the departure of seventy per cent of its validated controllers, the squadron continued to operate fully effectively, with an unblemished safety record in a complex and congested Düsseldorf West Sector. It too coped admirably with the twenty-four hour operations demanded by Agricola and Engadine, with movements on the airfield complicated by the size of the Antonov 124, which had to be loaded, off-loaded and parked on the Operational Readiness Platform (ORP) at the end of each runway. There was often tension in the control tower when non-NATO aircraft, their crews unfamiliar with local procedures, had language difficulties, were recovering short of fuel or had emergencies, but the controllers were up to it and continued to remain on top of their many mundane tasks. Not many people would know that they were responsible for the length of the grass on the airfield, which had to be more than 150mm high (to discourage birds foraging for worms) and less than 200mm (to deny cover for foxes and rabbits). Then there was the very variable runway braking action, which had to be measured regularly with a Mu-meter towed behind a Land Rover at 40 mph, it being rather more accurate than 'belting down the runway, slamming on the anchors and seeing how long it took to stop'. The arrester cables and barriers had to be rigged correctly and all movement areas cleared of anything which might cause foreign object damage (FOD). All these things were attended to rigorously and continuously, making Brüggen's ATC Squadron a worthy winner of the trophy.

Last but not least, there was the Met Office, weather forecasts being critical to safe and effective training and combat operations, typically in the Kosovo campaign, where talk boxes were used for routine operations. Very detailed, face-to-face briefings were resumed during this conflict, both for the crews and the

Neville Simmons, Senior Met Officer RAF Brüggen, and his staff, were presented with the prestigious Houghton Trophy by the station commander, for their invaluable contribution to the success of Operation Engadine. (*RAF Brüggen*)

decision-makers, and the recipients listened well. As a result of their excellent efforts, Brüggen Met Office was awarded the prestigious Houghton Trophy.

Brüggen's participation in the Kosovo campaign brought the Duke of York, the Prime Minister, Defence Secretary and Minister for the Armed Forces to Brüggen, all of whom were lavish in their plaudits. The Right Honourable George Robertson commented: 'RAF Brüggen is doing a great job for the country and for European law and order. These missions are far from risk-free but our crews are brave, disciplined and professional and I am delighted to place on record just how much we value their efforts.' The station commander, Iain McNicoll, who flew on several operational missions himself in Tornado and VC10 aircraft, added, 'After an initial period of understandable apprehension among the crews before the first mission, morale among the squadrons became very upbeat.' There was no doubt of that.

In a major speech on 29 September 1999, CAS, Air Chief Marshal Sir Richard Johns, said that the air campaign had been a decisive element in the operation to bring peace to Kosovo. He claimed that when such joint operations were considered, air power, while no panacea, would usually be the primary instrument of initial reaction because it could be deployed and withdrawn quickly, demanding less human and material commitment to achieve political objectives, while involving fewer political risks. In Engadine, Brüggen had done much to support this view.

An official report on the Kosovo air campaign: *Kosovo – Lessons from the Crisis*, issued more than a year later, confirmed its success but underlined the need for all-weather PGMs, compatible air-to-air communications, improved EW and SEAD measures. Statistics were produced to refute criticism in *Flight International* and a BBC 'Today' programme, that the RAF's bombing performance in Kosovo was the worst in its recent history. For Brüggen aircraft, all weapons released were precision guided, with a 'hit rate' of some seventy per cent.

Engadine put paid to many of the domestic events and activities planned for that spring of 1999, most regrettably those due to mark the disbandment of No. 17 Squadron. A casualty of the Strategic Defence Review, the squadron's run-down had begun before the crisis developed and many of its personnel then found themselves switched in haste to other Tornado units. The squadron marched into history with its Standard on 31 March, after a simple service in St. Andrews Church attended by those who were left, a few ex-members and many friends from other units on the station. A 'dining-out' was held in the Oranjerie Hotel, Roermond, at which Air Commodore John Houghton, a former CO, was guest of honour. The Squadron Standard was laid up at Cranwell in July 1999.

Brüggen also said farewell to its 'heavy fleet' vehicles in April. The oldest unit on the station, No. 2 MT (Det) was born of No. 317 MT Squadron, which arrived at Brüggen in April 1953, and was later absorbed into 431 MU for the recovery and salvage of RAF and Army aircraft in northern Europe and for RAF freight distribution in Germany. These tasks would now be undertaken by No. 2 MT Squadron from RAF Stafford.

Again because of Kosovo, the annual Brüggen 10 Race was postponed until 22 September, a day on which temperatures reached 30°C, the highest temperature recorded in that month for twenty-six years. Notwithstanding the conditions, 1,000 runners took part; Andrea Whitcombe broke the ladies' record, Simon Bell won the men's race and Brüggen took the team prize. The highlight of the day, however, was provided by 37 Squadron's Senior Aircraftsman Andy Hall; he completed a full marathon on the registration hangar's treadmill in just over four hours and, after fifty minutes' rest, ran the Brüggen 10 in a most impressive time. This feat was all the more amazing because Andy had suffered a stroke three years earlier, leaving his memory and speech impaired and the left side of his body paralysed. Prospects for a full recovery seemed very poor, but six months later he returned to his squadron and began intensive preparation for this race, to generate funds for the Stroke Foundation. When the author spoke to the now Corporal Andy Hall in September 2000 he found him fit and well, still exercising strenuously and working hard for the charity which had served him so well in his time of need. He believed his recovery in mind and body was in no small way due to the Regiment's fitness ethic (and because his wife was a nurse). Andy epitomised the spirit of Brüggen.

37 Squadron's Andy Hall, stroke victim, avid supporter of the Stroke Foundation and star
of 1999's Brüggen 10 Road Race, congratulated by station commander Iain McNicoll.
(*RAF Brüggen*)

Fired by the success of their great adventure in South Africa in 1997, the Bears RFC
went to Australia in 1999, Dougie Potter again being a leading light. There they
won two of three games against strong civilian and army teams, and at one match,
unexpected support from local Albanian refugees, anxious to show their gratitude
to the RAF for its efforts over Kosovo, may have helped the Bears win 14-3.

One of the many international events in which Brüggen always played its part
and excelled, was the Nijmegen March. So it was in 1999, at the eighty-third of these
annual meetings that fifteen men from 37 Squadron, carrying fully-loaded bergens
and led by Flying Officer Conrad Allen, completed the final twenty-five leg in the
excellent time of six hours and fifty minutes, forty-five minutes ahead of the next team
to finish. Since the norm was about eight hours, with twelve hours not unusual, this
was an outstanding feat of stamina, training and teamwork which brought great and
visible credit to the team, the squadron, and to Brüggen. In 2000, 37 Squadron would
go for another record, with thirty-one marchers, the largest military team to date.

On an unseasonably cold and wet day in June 1999, as the station began to return
to a degree of normality, Brüggen ladies braved another of their Ground Defence
Training Days, organised to give them some idea of what their men had to go through.
Dressed in olive green, webbing and steel helmets, armed and 'cammed up', they
looked ready for anything. However, some might come to remember the old soldier's

Dressed to kill. Annually, Brüggen ladies got a chance to sample what their men went through in their Ground Defence Training. (*RAF Brüggen*)

advice never to volunteer for anything, when they were confronted with the gory sight of a crash victim (who would probably have died), a target to be shot at (a cardboard menace which would probably have survived), ropes not made for walking across water, tents which would not erect, a major fire which would not go out and the ultimate torture of abseiling. Afterwards, fortified by much post-exercise liquid refreshment, the war stories began and the day was deemed to have been a great success.

The ladies were in action again throughout a special week in September, when the station took part in a SSAFA 'Big Brew'. Held every two years to boost funds for needy ex-servicemen and their families, volunteers made tea on a massive scale for neighbours, friends and anyone passing by, in return for donations to SSAFA. The 1999 Big Brew was as successful as ever.

Other charity initiatives – and there were many of them – were more strenuous. Striding along the flooded banks of the Mosel, suffering swollen feet, blisters and the temptation of 'weinstuben', sponsored Brüggen walkers raised a great deal of money for cancer research. In 1998, Brüggen had topped the charity leagues for the second year running. Thereafter, having been at war in 1999, its fundraising might have suffered, but this was not the case, the Station Charities Committee alone disbursing DM175,000.

There was, however, very sad news that year, when 31 Squadron pilot, Flight Lieutenant Dick Wright, and his navigator, Flight Lieutenant Sean Casabayo of XV(R) Squadron, were killed when their Tornado crashed in Northumberland during a QWI Course at Lossiemouth. In its tribute, 31 Squadron laid on a very moving military funeral at Dick's village church near Cosford, a four-ship of Tornados overflying in a last salute during the interment.

Having lost its responsibility for the security and release of nuclear weapons, the strength of Brüggen's security squadron dropped from over 300 to some eighty men and women. However, with the demise of HQ RAF Germany and then HQ 2 Group, the squadron picked up the residual policing of RAF interests in north-west Europe, including escort duties for unusual loads, which took it to Italy, the south of France and up to the port of Hamburg. General Duties Flight now included the all-important station warrant officer and an army of directly employed labourers.

With crime prevention on the station and in the local area now top of the agenda, the RAF Police and the local German authorities were specifically targeting hooliganism, vandalism and domestic violence. Drinking, often to celebrate a homecoming, remained a problem but, with continuous warnings and more alternatives to the use of private cars laid on, the number of drink/drive cases, on and off base, and vehicle offences generally, reduced significantly in Brüggen's final years. The Police Club, one of thirty-two known bars on the station, still thrived in 1999, but the old interplay between the RAF Regiment and the Security Squadron, which had often filled the cells, was now history.

The measures adopted to minimise the consequences of excessive alcohol led to some interesting stories. A 'taxi fund' held in the guardroom for hapless revellers who were unable to pay their fares was perhaps not intended for homeward trips from as far away as Amsterdam, but it was in Amsterdam that one victim of cruel humour found himself on his stag night after his friends had placed him on a train in a semi-conscious state. There, in the dead of night without shoes and in trousers borrowed from a Dutch sympathiser, he persuaded a taxi driver that the RAF police would pay for his safe return and three hours later put the guardroom to the test. Payment was made, but not before Warrant Officer Rawle, known for his persuasive manner, rounded up the six culprits and took DM100 off each to pay the driver and reward him with a handsome tip. Those who had had a little too much to drink might try to get a ride home in an RAF police car on routine patrol, but this did not mean that their troubles were over. It was Warrant Officer Rawle himself who picked up one airman from his comfortable resting place in a ditch and delivered him, against his will, to the door of his married quarter. There his wife treated him, and the whole married patch, to her views on his behaviour.

There was no let-up from these day-to-day routines despite the massive increase in security measures required by Operation Engadine, demands on the

Security Squadron during anti-war demonstrations, commensurate media interest and various incidents on the station. On Saturday evening, 24 April, the squadron helped to mitigate the effects of a major fire in 14 Squadron's barrack block, Corporal Suzanne Cobbett, RAF Police, being one of the first on the spot, calling for assistance and initiating an emergency evacuation. With a paucity of fire-fighting resources (due to flying operations), but in a copybook operation helped by personal initiatives, the RAF police team, headed by Sergeant Bowen, soon established control, forced entry to and removed adjacent vehicles and generally secured the area, thus helping to limit what might have been a major crisis. The station support services (supply, accounts, messing, launderette and SIF etc.), and many individuals, then rallied to help those who suffered as a consequence of the fire. For their professionalism and courage, Sergeant Bowen, Corporals Cobbett, Keogh, Morgan and Churchill, were awarded the Provost Marshal's Commendation.

Seeking enlightenment from all sources, the author visited the sergeants' mess in 1999 to find it much changed since his last visit in the mid-1970s. Between 1991 and 1993, major works services had transformed the mess, now catering for 600 members, with some sixty living-in. The lounge was greatly extended and refurbished, facilities for the ladies much improved, a new heating and lighting system installed and the accommodation blocks renovated. The mess, then managed by Warrant Officer Lloyd, was the usual hive of activity before one of the

Contemporary living. The anteroom in the refurbished Sergeants' Mess. (*RAF News*)

three formal balls a year, and it was heartening to conclude that the old traditions, disciplines and rituals remained largely unchanged. The practice of inviting senior corporals to gain an insight into life in the sergeants' mess had been laudably maintained. The corporals, once deprived of their club, now had their own facility, over which they exercised some control, under overall NAAFI management.

The *Brüggen Circuit*, which kept the station so well up-to-date on events, requirements and opportunities on and off base, celebrated its thirtieth birthday in the autumn of 1999. A team of three ladies, all dependants, produced some 2,000 copies of the fifty-six page magazine every month for eleven months of the year (February being devoted to the annual station handbook). With dynamic advertising (fifty per cent of the content useful in itself), the enterprise was largely self-funding, albeit with nominal contributions from all officers and sergeants and a subsidy from the SIF. The success of the *Circuit* depended on the resourcefulness, determination and personal skills of the team, particularly their ability to obtain the inputs needed to render a useful and attractive product. The magazine did, however, have its ups and downs; in the mid-90s it survived a period in the doldrums to become even more successful and self-sustaining, and there is clear evidence of this in its thirtieth anniversary celebration and millennium editions. The *Brüggen Circuit* has made a really valuable contribution to the quality of life within the station community.

At Ali Al Salem, formations of four mutually-supporting GR1s, with their external support packages, continued to mount Vicon, TIALD and Paveway missions, on pre-planned and airborne tasking in the reconnaissance and/or attack roles. They were

IX Sqn, led by Wg Cdr Greg Bagwell, at Ali Al Salem, 1999. (*RAF News*)

ready for anything and, with two-month detachments and improving facilities, life was now bearable if tedious. Writing home, one man reported plenty of opportunities to keep the weight down with running, or the weights, in the gym, playing squash, football or basketball, but that 'mountains of cookies, crisps, chocolates and other goodies' remained very tempting. He also reported the dangers in forays to Kuwait City: 'The Kuwaitis' night technique for crossing a motorway is to turn off their lights, attack it at ninety degrees as fast as they can and then swerve into the lane they want. If they can't make it they drive down the fast lane the wrong way looking for a place to cross.' By comparison, missions over Iraq were a piece of cake.

Brüggen had plenty to celebrate at the turn of the century; 1999 had been an outstanding year and it was no surprise when it was awarded the coveted Stainforth Trophy, awarded annually to the station judged to have achieved the best overall performance in Strike Command. Brüggen was in fine fettle to greet the new millennium.

Anglo-American training had notched up another 'first' on Operation Bolton in January 2000, when 31 Squadron GR1s provided highly successful medium level TIALD designation for Hellfire missiles, fired from USAF AH-64A Apache helicopters at low-level over the Udairi Range in Kuwait.

Brüggen Tornados used TIALD to designate Paveway LGBs launched from USAF Apache helicopters over Udairi Range in Kuwait, 1999. (*RAF News*)

The globe-trotting continued, with IX Squadron going to Savannah, Georgia, in February for an air-to-surface combat and identification evaluation training (ASCIET) exercise, with US naval and air forces. They operated within an instrumented range against ex-Soviet equipments, one of their objectives being to evaluate means of avoiding 'blue-on-blue' fratricide. They also found time to relax but OC IX Squadron denies that unofficial driving on the Daytona Sands racing circuit was banned during their time because of over-zealous role changes on the part of some of his pilots in their hired cars.

In the limelight again, 37 Squadron became top shots at Bisley in the RAF Regiment's Millennium Meeting, with honours and trophies too numerous to list. The squadron spent the first months of 2000 in the Falklands, where Senior Aircraftsman 'Jock' Connor was rewarded with a trip in a Tornado for being the squadron's 'Top Rapier Operator 1999'. With plenty of missiles and targets to play with in good weather, an MPC at Bertha's Beach went well, with VIPs and other guests witnessing the squadron at its best. Secretary of State, Geoffrey Hoon, showed that there was nothing to it by hitting a target with his first shot. But not everything went well: one missile couldn't be bothered to fly and ploughed spectacularly into the beach, giving much pleasure to the guests if not the hosts. The next also behaved badly, to cheers and calls for more, while the one remaining round began to fizz and smoke on its launcher, causing the VIPs to take cover rather rapidly behind a convenient Portakabin. Off-duty, everyone was kept busy with the 'Sweat-athon', which simulated the 8,286-mile trip from the Falklands to Brüggen, in a mixture of running (Mount Pleasant to Stanley), rowing (to Argentina and later across the Atlantic), cycling (through South America and across the Sahara to Gibraltar) and swimming across the Straits of Gibraltar into Europe before cycling to Brüggen. The trip took eleven days, twelve hours and twenty minutes, the whole detachment taking part in thirty minute shifts on the equipment, twenty-four hours a day. It is not surprising that, in the words of one participant: 'By the end of it most of us were walking in a funny way.' The event raised some £7,000 for 'Hope and Homes for Children'.

That winter, Brüggen's (and the UK's first) World Cup skeleton bobsleigh winner, Flight Lieutenant Alex Hamilton, staked her claim to a place in the 2002 Olympics by winning the event in the Goodwill Games at Lake Placid, USA. Hurtling down conventional bobsleigh tracks, at very low level and speeds of 80 mph is sport for the very brave but Alex was not the only woman at Brüggen to show the way. Senior Aircraftswoman Rachel Keen was chosen to represent Britain in the similarly challenging luge event, likened to 'sliding down Olympic bobsleigh tracks on a tea tray at 60 mph, steered by the merest movement of the body'. Bravo to Brüggen's ladies.

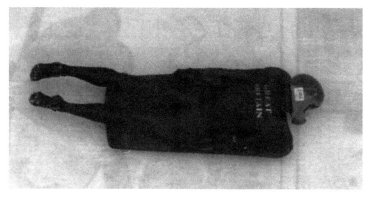

British Bobsleigh Champion, Flt Lt Alex Hamilton, on the run. (*RAF News*)

On 25 March, IX Squadron took part in a moving wreath-laying ceremony in Poland, to commemorate one of its wartime pilots shot after escaping from Stalag Luft 3 in 1944, and whose body now lies in a military cemetery in Poznan. Pilot Officer 'Cookie' Long's helmet was found and preserved by a Polish farmer after he had baled out from his stricken Wellington bomber and returned it to the squadron in 1998. A cherished piece of heritage, the leather helmet flew aboard IX Squadron Tornados during the Balkans campaign and with OC IX Squadron when he led four Tornados over the ceremony at Poznan. It now flies with the squadron's junior pilot.

IX Squadron's heritage. Sqn Ldr Steve Kinnaird with Plt Off 'Cookie' Long's 1942 flying helmet. (*RAF News*)

The annual ceremony to commemorate the loss of Allied aircrew and Dutch Resistance workers in Roermond took place on 6 April 2000. This was another memorable day for its key figure, resistance fighter Anja van Leyssen, when she received an honorary MBE for her devotion to the cause from the UK Ambassador to the Netherlands, Dame Rosemary Spencer.

RAF Brüggen entertains Anja van Leyssen, GC, MBE on her 80th birthday. (Seated, left) Ursula Anderson (wife of Stn Cdr); (L to R, standing) Sqn Ldr Peter D'Ardenne (PMC), Wg Cdr Julian Andrews (OC Admin Wg), Marguerite Reith (Dutch Liaison Officer), Flt Lt Lynnette Bolton (ASO). (*Brüggen Circuit*)

Another milestone was passed on 4 April 2000 when the last JP233, once a primary weapon in the GR1's Cold War arsenal and used during the Gulf War, was ceremonially outloaded from Wulfen storage area by Brüggen armourers, helped by the station commander. When the weapon was conceived several decades before, it might have been expected to be delivered to East Germany by air, but now it rumbled towards Leipzig by train, for disposal by a one-time East German civilian firm.

Air Cdre Iain McNicoll bids farewell to Brüggen's last JP233 – ironically off to end its days in eastern Germany – by rail. (*RAF Brüggen*)

Short of a real war, 14 Squadron went for a less painful alternative in Green Flag COMAOs of eighty aircraft on EW and OLF training at Nellis AFB in July 2000, the hottest time in Nevada's year. Despite temperatures often above 38°C and no sun shelters for the aircraft, with careful management of the twelve hour working days and taxi/take-off times, air-conditioned crew buses and plenty of chilled water, men and machines survived and prospered.

Also in July, 31 Squadron flew six Tornados to Darwin to take part in the Australian air defence Exercise Pitch Black, the squadron's first major exercise overseas with the GR4. The Tornados, together with Singaporean F-16s and RF-5s, carried out offensive missions against targets defended by Australian and USMC F-18s (deployed from Japan). The *RAF News* reported that the exercise area included tropical coastlines and azure seas, muddy, crocodile-infested estuaries and the semi-desert of the outback 'providing an interesting set of survival challenges should any of the crews have to bale out'. Accordingly, the aircrew were issued with pistols to give them 'a sporting chance' against the salt water crocodiles but were not heartened to hear from a local guide that 'the noise of the pistol might, at best, only scare a "salty"'. The squadron was accommodated in what was described as a 'backpackers motel', downtown Darwin, but at the height of the tourist season there were no complaints. The exercise was an instructive experience for all.

Then 31 Squadron flew the six Tornados to RAAF Edinburgh, Adelaide, where IX Squadron, supported by BAe and the RAF's ALARM Support Authority, carried out live firings of ALARM over the Woomera Range, in Exercise 'Dingo Dart'. In this first peacetime overland (day only) firings, RAF Sentry E-3D aircraft located the radar emissions to trigger the missiles and, with only two days of preparations before a three day firing programme, ten of the twelve available missiles were launched successfully. The exercise produced definitive data to confirm the effectiveness of ALARM in the modes employed.

No. IX Squadron took the Tornados back to Germany in stages; from Darwin to Singapore, across the South China Sea to Sri Lanka, on to Cyprus via Muscat – and then home. They were off again in October to Ali Al Salem, where Operation Bolton was still providing good opportunities to practise Vicon and TIALD skills.

In September 2000, Iain McNicoll handed over the station to Tim Anderson, promoted to group captain after commanding 14 Squadron. The new station commander was soon made more aware of the potential pitfalls facing the unwary in matters of protocol when he was visited in his office by a gentleman unknown to him, dressed in combat kit and bearing the rank of colonel in the Royal Engineers. The visitor had no name tag and did not introduce himself, but it was reasonable for Tim to suppose that this was the commander of a visiting detachment of sappers, at Brüggen for the annual rehearsal of their airfield maintenance duties. The guest seated himself, exchanged pleasantries and left before anyone realised that he was a serving air vice-marshal, with responsibilities for Brüggen, but was there on this occasion as the honorary colonel of the visiting territorial army regiment.

Gp Capt Tim Anderson could not wait to get rid of Air Cdre Iain McNicoll, as the station changes hands on 6 September 2000. (*RAF Brüggen*)

In September, 31 Squadron went to Goose Bay for Western Vortex, where Robbie Low led a four-ship fly-past to commemorate the sixtieth anniversary of the Battle of Britain and flew his last sortie with the squadron before handing over to Wing Commander 'Paddy' Teakle. The three squadrons were now concentrating on electro-optical (EO) training with NVGs and FLIR, to provide an alternative to the use of tell-tale TFR at low level.

On 14 December 2000, the Brüggen Wing held its final inter-squadron bombing competition. This demanding exercise called for a timed recce run, followed by a first run attack (which included a dynamic manoeuvre to achieve a prescribed line of attack), three further bombing passes and a strafe run, before terminating with a precisely timed break into the circuit back at Brüggen. No. IX Squadron carried the day, 14 Squadron coming second and providing the winning crew. Perhaps it was a pity that a combat phase had not been included, 31 Squadron having honed these skills in combat against No. 20 Squadron Harriers earlier in the month.

On 20 December, 14 Squadron ended its run of fifty-five years in Germany, its final three-ship formation overflying the station in salute as it flew to its new home in Lossiemouth. The great 'march out' had begun.

Exercising his prerogative as station commander, Gp Capt Tim Anderson flew his last sortie in a fully armed 14 Squadron Tornado on 14 Dec 00, with OC Ops Wg Cdr John Scholtens as navigator, before the squadron flew off to its new home at Lossiemouth on 20 December. (*RAF Brüggen*)

Flt Lt Eric Androvani, the 14 Squadron snake, followed his minders to
Lossiemouth, by means not divulged. (*14 Squadron*)

Chapter Ten

Marching Out

In his message to the station at the beginning of 2001, Group Captain Tim Anderson was very positive, but he did add a well-timed, cautionary note: 'There is no doubt that there is an increasing likelihood today for our people to question their lot. In several areas they have legitimate concerns while in others they fall prey to the ever-present crewroom lawyers and doom-merchants. It behoves us all in the command chain, at all levels, to champion their legitimate causes, while disabusing them of ill thought through and unfounded perceptions. That task, and the dividing line between the two, is perhaps more difficult to grasp than ever.' He had set the tone for the final act.

The station chaplains added their bit in the *Brüggen Circuit*, prophesying that 2001 would have its high and low points and that, of course, 'One day the removal men will come and this wonderful experience will have come to an end.' They

'One day the removal men will come.' A giant C17 helps the RAF move out of Brüggen – from an airfield already almost deserted. (*RAF Brüggen*)

exhorted all to make the best of what time remained – and the people of Brüggen got the message.

"Dad rang. He said he has now arranged the march-out for tomorrow instead of next week."

(Bruggen Circuit)

Unlike some RAF stations no longer required in Germany, which were handed back to HM Defence Estates for disposal to the Federal authorities, Gütersloh and Brüggen were destined for 'continued British national use' by the British Army.

The phased withdrawal from the station was planned and monitored in detail by the Brüggen Drawdown Team (BDT), which was set up on the station in October 1998. It was headed by Squadron Leader Martin Evans, an administrative officer and ex-National Health Service manager. The team included an engineering officer, Flight Lieutenant Alex Elliott, who had the necessary prerequisite of a Third Degree Black Belt in Tae Kwon Do, a supply officer, Flight Lieutenant Paul Haggett, with an equally essential sense of humour, and an admin/personnel specialist, Sergeant Steve Farrar. They drew up a drawdown work plan based on a Gantt chart, effectively a flow chart of inter-linked activities which would guide each unit through the necessary drawdown actions until handover to the army in March 2002.

Typically, the BDT identified those redundant assets (rubb hangars, metal presses etc.) to be returned to the UK, and others (HAS management cabins, bulk fuel tanks, runway repair aggregate, scrap metal etc.) to be disposed of locally. Their plans also covered transfer of all residual responsibilities for the 800 or so RAF personnel remaining scattered around the Continent in NATO HQs, embassies, exchange postings et al.

Vacant possession. The grass now grows long on a redundant weapons storage site.
(*Michael Mortimer*)

Not including the disbandment of 17 Squadron in March 1999, 14 Squadron was the first major departing unit to benefit from the BDT's efforts, lessons from this move proving invaluable in the greater exodus to follow. It became apparent that planning, by a nominated project officer for each wing and squadron, should begin eighteen months ahead of departure, and that the disposal of unwanted equipment, assessment of hazardous waste requirements and 100% inventory checks should be carried out with at least six months to go. However, the drawdown had to be effected in tandem with continued operational and training commitments, and adequate resources had to remain in place for the station to fulfil its main operating base functions until flying ceased in October 2001. How different this was from the shock treatment meted out to the four Hunter squadrons at Brüggen in 1957, which called for their complete disbandment within a very few weeks. The difference, at least in part, was of course due to the complexity of the contemporary task and the myriad health and safety, environmental and federal regulations.

On the template developed from 14 Squadron's experience at Lossiemouth, the BDT recommended measures to ensure that Marham and Wittering were ready, as far as was reasonable, to receive their ex-Brüggen squadrons. These squadrons sent their representatives ahead to supervise building projects, and properly constituted advance parties were deployed before the arrival of main bodies. Few details seemed to escape attention, down to the curtailment of postings to Brüggen critically close to the move, the establishment of separate squadron budgets at the new units, correct transfer of numerous documents (many sensitive or otherwise classified) detailed actions for the rear party and co-ordination of household removals. This 'marching out' was no movement 'on the hoof' and personal inconvenience was minimised in the sympathetic consideration given by all support personnel at Brüggen and the receiving units.

The departure of the RAF from Brüggen was viewed with very mixed feelings within the surrounding communities. Few would miss the aircraft noise, which at times since 1953 had been near intolerable for some, but equally there were property developers who welcomed the release of land for building within the soon to be defunct noise/potential hazard 'footprint'. Everyone would find their new military neighbours different, with fewer army families and more single servicemen bringing changes in domestic and social patterns. Some 800 hirings in Elmpt and Brüggen would be handed back to the German Federal Authorities, and the new incumbents would generally have less earning power, manifest in fewer expensive cars and more motor cycles.

Of great concern, when the army took over, was a drastic reduction in the number of posts remaining for the 300 loyal civilian employees on the station. Some 140 posts in the HQ at Rheindahlen, vacated by well qualified, English speaking dependants of servicemen and women from RAF Brüggen, offered little comfort, because pay scales at Rheindahlen were considerably less than those at Brüggen. Accordingly, every effort was made by the station and the civilian works councils to ameliorate this regrettable consequence of the move, by seeking the best available employment opportunities for those made redundant.

Martin Evans was also President of the Service Institute Fund (SIF), with daunting responsibilities for collecting, banking and distributing non-public funds and running non-public services. To illustrate the spending power of the largely married RAF community, he had been able to expect a rebate from purchases at the Handelshof wholesale outlet to render DM20K for the SIF annually, that being 1% of the spend there by families in a typical year. This had been but one source of income within a £10M annual turnover; others included contributions from personal subscriptions, Haircraft, Launderette, the Kart Club, tax-free shopping, Travel Shop, and many other activities. While continuing to disburse monies for just causes on the station during the drawdown, Martin had now to turn his attention to the disposal of such SIF facilities as the Gun Club, Launderette and Brüggen Bowl, ideally by direct sales to the army, and what was to be done with the Golf Club?

The RAF's Central Services Institute Fund, administered at RAF Innsworth for the benefit of the service as a whole, had foreseen a legacy accruing from Brüggen's closure and a large part of the station's non-public funds had been earmarked to that end perhaps, inter alia, to prevent too much money being spent on the farewell celebrations. In fact, the station's official liability to the Central

Fund was DM186K but the fund had hoped for DM300K and was very pleasantly surprised when DM500K was handed over voluntarily in July 2001, with the prospect of a similar amount to follow.

During his research, the author was treated to a demonstration of the economy transport promoted by the BDT (which acted also as a rapid-escape, physical training and stress-relief machine), but thought it unlikely that the unicycle would replace the profusion of sleek sports cars which were now being readied to grace the roads of Norfolk.

Involved in many careful balancing acts, OC Brüggen Drawdown Team, Sqn Ldr Martin Evans, on his 'alternative transport'. (*Sarah Evans*)

Brüggen's Engineering and Supply Wing had no future. As an entity it would, as with all support wings in Germany before it, now fade into history; it had excelled in its many diverse jobs but all too rarely had they been trumpeted. Much had already been done to prepare for the end but it was now up to Wing Commander Paul Ridge, who took over from Rob Ryder in the summer of 2000, to finish the job.

Brüggen's nuclear weapons had gone, and 1 April 2001 saw the demise of the Armament Engineering Squadron, the last by that name in the RAF, as its duties were absorbed into the Mechanical Engineering (Air) Squadron. However, the RAF's once biggest Cold War bastion and Tornado base, from whence, within the last two years, a virtual war had been waged with conventional weapons, had much to dispose of, and this was down to Supply Squadron. Initially, it was thought that some of the remaining thirty-day war reserve stocks and weapons might best be taken away by rail, using the link between the station and the Bundesbahn main line at Arsbeck, but this foundered on the costs of reactivating the line and the availability of alternative options. With great initiative and financial acumen, supply and movements staffs made use of tri-service Distribution and Storage Defence Agency trucks and RAF transport aircraft, which might otherwise have returned to the UK empty or with space available and purloined Royal Logistics Corps transport after the cancellation of a military exercise. In their death throes, Supply Squadron and Movements Squadron were at their best.

The same could be said of the other squadrons on the wing, which, with progressively reducing manpower, were required to dispose of their stores and equipment without prejudicing planned operations and possible contingencies; it was a careful balancing act. Also, Brüggen had the lead in Tornado GR4 engineering, typically with the TIALD/avionics interface within the accelerated enhancement package. By the beginning of 2001, usually with a much reduced aircraft availability below the nominal establishment of twenty-four aircraft, due to external modification and trials programmes, the two remaining squadrons would be lucky to start the flying day with six aircraft on the line. The run-down was complicated further by the squadrons' nomadic existence, in which there was no let-up in 2001; this in itself imposed additional strain on resources, but the station continued to support detachments with additional manpower as required. Paul was lavish in his praise for the British Aerospace 'Rep', Ronnie MacIndoe, who over ten years had worked in the background but with the confidence of all, a thorough knowledge of the Tornado and tireless enterprise, Ronnie contributed much to the wing's strenuous efforts to get the best out of dwindling assets in difficult circumstances.

Every unit on the station was making its own arrangements, comprehensive and in great detail, well in advance of redeployment or disposal, the issue in February of Administrative Order No. 01/ 01, detailing the closure of the Security Squadron and transfer of responsibilities, being typical. Under the command of Squadron Leader Peter D'Ardenne, security had to be maintained during the drawdown on base, at Wildenrath, Bracht and as far away as Hannover Airport, pending progressive handover to the Royal Military Police (RMP). In addition, squadron duties in support of station administration and handover procedures were defined in detail. Most importantly, every consideration was given to drafting plots for squadron personnel, and transferring the police dogs to Sennelager.

In March, thirty-four officers and 113 groundcrew of 31 Squadron were back in Nevada for another Exercise Red Flag, the first in which the Tornado GR4 had participated and in which a non-USAF officer, Group Captain Tim Anderson, was nominated as a force commander. In day and night phases, much good work was done with EO devices, TIALD and Paveway LGBs, the GR4s performing impeccably throughout the two-week exercise. Indeed, they were the only aircraft in the 'friendly' force not to be targeted successfully by the defending SAMs. An altogether excellent exercise. The squadron then had two weeks' block leave at Brüggen before working up for a Western Vortex exercise at Goose Bay in June. It was all go.

In February and March, 37 Squadron had been exercising in a very different climate. With special dispensation from the host country's Foot and Mouth restrictions, the squadron deployed to Northern Norway, around Bardufoss airfield, with ninety-two men, five Rapier Fire Units and full support, on Exercise Joint Winter 2001. There, after invaluable cold weather survival training for all, the self-sufficient fire units dispersed to remote hill-top locations for best overall

Meanwhile, life goes on. In March 2001, 31 Squadron introduced Tornado GR4 to Red Flag in Nevada. (*RAF News*)

cover, where they remained fully operational at all times for ten days while the whole system went through the full gamut of operational scenarios. The exercise included a squadron Staneval, in which many real-time problems rendered paper injects largely unnecessary. Highly realistic airborne targets were provided by RAF Tornados and RNoAF F-16s, while on the ground, Norwegian Special Forces proved to be a formidable foe. Making best use of compacted snow, the gunners survived well in temperatures ranging from +4° to -40°, albeit with hard lessons learned; one observed that it could have been worse; they could have been at Spadeadam! The Norwegians had been good to them. The squadron returned to Brüggen during April, with just enough time to recover from these exertions before departing in May for another tour in the Falklands.

Brüggen and the RAF relinquished responsibility for Nordhorn Range to the German Air Force in March 2001. Highly competent, if invisible, British voices had run the range since 1946, initially for the RAF but then for use by all NATO forces, making it the busiest weapons range in Western Europe. As a mark of enduring co-operation and friendship, the last commanding officer, Squadron Leader John Gresham, presented Stadt Nordhorn's Bürgermeister, Herr Husemann, with an English oak tree, which they planted together in front of the town's Rathaus.

The dentists also said their farewells to Brüggen in style, on a weekend of professional (sic) and social reflections in March. At a formal dinner, the usual display of silver artefacts were replaced, rather sadistically, by an old pedal drill 'rendered toothless' to ensure that it was not brought back into play in the less formal festivities which followed.

By now, all the social, sporting and charitable activities were winding down, but not without many a final flourish. Among them, the Fun Kart Club held

37 Squadron, RAF Regiment, on Arctic survival training in Norway – March 2001. (*37 Squadron*)

37 Squadron – ready for anything. Exercise Joint Winter 2001, Norway. (*37 Squadron*)

a twenty-four hour Charity Challenge, in which MT excelled in the driving but PROM raised the most money, adding to a big cheque for SSAFA. Not to be outdone, 255 'powerwalkers' completed 10km in three laps of the Brüggen domestic site, to make a major contribution to Breast Cancer Care, and the Skidmore Trophy Tournament was also held for the last time at Brüggen (to be hosted next by RAF Coltishall). In memory of Brüggen 'supplier' and sportsman, Warrant Officer Peter Skidmore, who died in 1978, it was right that this special seven-a-side soccer competition against the Command suppliers should be won by Brüggen.

Then there was the last RAF-organised 'Brüggen 10' road race, held on 28 April 2001. First staged in 1980, with a field of ninety competitors, this heavily sponsored event grew in every respect, up to 1,500 competitors with varying degrees of the serious and not so serious intents, again promoting a wide network of international friendships while generating vast sums of money for British, German and Dutch charities. Over the years, military and civilian men, women and children, from many nations, braved temperatures from -2°C to +31°C, completing the course in times ranging from fifty minutes to three hours. The sponsors, runners, marshals and armies of helpers, all deserving great credit.

The 'powerwalkers' of Brüggen ready to do their bit for Breast Cancer Care.
(*RAF Brüggen*)

... as were the runners in this last 'Brüggen 10', 28 April 2001, dedicated to a variety of charities. (*RAF Brüggen*)

Willie Luys, central to the race administration, ran his seventeenth race in 2001, a race in which Squadron Leader John Kelly led the whole of his Catering Squadron and the officer-in-charge, Squadron Leader Kenny Grant, carried a ceremonial scroll bearing a challenge to the British Army to 'uphold the values and traditions of the Brüggen 10'. Time would tell.

Willie Luys, the run's veteran organiser and runner, passes a water stop. Would this be his last 'Brüggen 10'? (*RAF Brüggen*)

The Brüggen Bears RFC decided to celebrate their demise at home and away. In May, twenty-five of their members attended the International Benidorm Rugby Sevens, aimed at 'developing individual and group skills, promoting initiative, communication, teamwork and leadership qualities', and by all accounts there was plenty in evidence. Wing Commander Julian Andrews, the Club's President, went along to add some decorum – but seemingly failed to do so. The team may not have achieved the highest accolade on the field but it came home with sore heads held high and a message from the organisers 'that they were one of the clubs they would most like to see again in Benidorm'.

The Bears' final fling, 4-5 June, involved 220 guests, among them many ex-Bears from far-flung parts of the world, first at a meet-and-greet which extended through Friday evening to 0530 on Saturday morning, and then a spectacular, formal dinner dance on the Saturday which lasted just as long. A game of sorts was played in between, the veterans prevailing against the present incumbents, the legendary Kenny Brockless (from the author's time) playing against his son, the present officer i/c, Flight Lieutenant Kenny Brockless. Julian Andrews was on hand again, this time to administer a concoction called 'Blood' – purported to be life-saving but which turned out to be more life-threatening. On Sunday an auction of artefacts, collected over the life of this most famous RAF Rugby Football Club, raised DM1,700 for charity, bringing its final season's contribution to the Birmingham Childrens' Hospice to DM6,700. To Brockless junior must go the lion's share of the credit for the huge success of this memorable event.

Game over. Players young and old (Brockless Snr. ever at the centre), tolerant wives and loyal supporters, during their long, last weekend at Brüggen. (*RAF Brüggen*)

The Formal Farewell to the 'Last and Best' of RAF Brüggen took place on 15-17 June, beginning, in fine weather, with a parade of all station units reviewed by CAS, Air Chief Marshal Sir Peter Squire, and Lieutenant General Walter Jertz, Commander of German Air Force Tactical Command North, as Tornados flew over in salute. General Jertz then presented '*Fahnenbänder*' (battle honours) to the station and its last operational squadrons, and in his address praised the efforts of RAF airmen and women who had contributed so much in Germany to keeping the peace, saying: 'Today brings to an end a history and tradition which could not have been more successful.' The celebrations then began in earnest, with a Guest Night in the officers' mess attended by the VIPs and twenty-three former station commanders, while many less formal activities took place elsewhere on the station.

The weather also blessed a highly successful 'Families Day' on the Saturday, which included demonstrations by the Queen's Colour Squadron, the Falcons parachute display team and a 'role demonstration' by the station's own aircraft. A multitude of displays and fun stalls catered for all and raised more money for charity. The weekend ended with a service in St. Nicholas Church, followed by a reception in the sergeants' mess.

CAS, ACM Sir Peter Squire, on the dais at RAF Brüggen's final parade, 15 June 2001.
(*RAF Brüggen*)

Wg Cdr John Scholtens accepts Brüggen's '*Fahnenband*' from Lt Gen Walter Jertz, Commander of the German Air Force Tactical Command North. (*HQ PTC PR*)

The last salute. Four Brüggen Tornados overfly the Farewell parade. (*Jochen Ewald*)

VIPs, former station commanders and their ladies, guests at Brüggen's Farewell Guest Night in the officers' mess. (*RAF Brüggen*)

RAF Brüggen, photographed by a member of the RAF's Falcons Parachute Display Team, dropping in on the station's last Families Day, 16 June 2001. (*RAF Falcons*)

The author, with Frau Sandra Gillmeister at the Brüggen Families Day History Desk.
(*Jochen Ewald*)

Ask me another! The station commander, OC Admin Wing and Chief Clerk, never short of answers, at the Families Day BFBS Quiz. (*RAF Brüggen*)

The 'BOBS' (L to R) John Cossey, Bill Cartwright, Geoff Marshall, Ken Milner, Ken Smith, 'Jesse' James, Pete Prince, 'Speedy' Crow, Tony Turner and Gerry Dwyer, veterans of Brüggen's 55 Wing, RAF Regiment, visit the station. (*Gerry Dwyer*)

Some of the men who started it all and who were there at the end. Retired officers of the RAF's Airfield Construction Branch, and their ladies, stayed at the Klimp Hotel, Brüggen Village, for the farewell events. (L to R) Les and Norma Rowe, Jack and Marion Taylor; Muriel and Sid Geoghegan; Jack Campling. (*Jack Campling*)

The staff of the *Brüggen Circuit*, circa 2000: (L-R) Micky Evans-Mooren, Dianna Jenkins and Helen Williams (Editor). (*Brüggen Circuit*)

There to enjoy this spectacular farewell were small contingents from units which, from way back, had helped make Brüggen what it was. Through the *RAF News*, Bob Knight, one of fifteen 'heavy truckers' from 317 MT Squadron of the 1950s, praised 'the smart and courteous NCOs' who acted as their escorts, and all those who 'worked so hard to make it such a memorable occasion'. Frank Leeson, on behalf of a similar number of ex-aircrew from 213 (Canberra) Squadron, spoke of their pleasure at being included in the celebrations, particularly at an informal reception in their old hangar 'which made us feel very much at home'. Then there was the self-styled 'BOBS' (Brüggen Old Boys Society), in reality a small group of veterans from the station's 55 Wing, RAF Regiment in the mid-1950s. They too revelled in the nostalgia of this celebration.

However, the most poignant reunion of all was surely that of officers from the Airfield Construction Branch who, before that final weekend, were treated to an exclusive tour of the station by 'a very attentive' Flight Lieutenant Lynnette Bolton, the Air Staff Officer. Sight of the installations and facilities they had helped create, which had stood the test of time and of which they could be justly proud, brought memories flooding back. They drove through the main site, so much the

In a 'diamond nine' formation, IX(B) Squadron depart RAF Brüggen for RAF Marham on 17 July 2001. (*RAF Brüggen*)

OC Ops Wing, John Scholtens waves farewell to OC 31 Squadron, Wg Cdr Paddy Teakle, as he leads his squadron to RAF Marham on 21 August. (*RAF Brüggen*)

Station Commander Tim Anderson and his deputy, Wg Cdr John Scholtens, fly out the last Tornado from Brüggen, 4 September 2001. (*RAF Brüggen*)

Bringing up the rear, 37 Squadron, RAF Regiment, was the last operational squadron to leave Brüggen in October 2001. (*12 Flight AAC/Crown*)

same yet so different, crossed the runway which started with a pole at either end, followed the road which had drifted mysteriously towards the 'reserve hospital' and came to the end of the line; that now dormant railway from Arsbeck. It had all started with them.

The *Brüggen Circuit* shut up shop in June, after thirty-three years of admirable service. The outgoing editor, Helen Williams, to whom the author is greatly indebted, wrote for all in her gratitude to the advertisers, publishers (ARS of Roermond), contributors, distributors and of course the office staff, all of whom were crucial to keeping the magazine alive, and the station so well-informed.

Newly promoted Group Captain Greg Bagwell led a IX(B) Squadron diamond-nine formation from Brüggen to Marham on 17 July 2001; Wing Commander Paddy Teakle followed with his 31 Squadron Tornados on 21 August and the station commander, Group Captain Tim Anderson, with his OC Ops Wg John Scholtens, flew the last Tornado out of Brüggen on 4 September. Aircraft noise abated, save for residual air traffic helping with this final act until Air Traffic Control closed in October, leaving only ghostly memories of aircraft past, to remind those who remained behind of what had been. By the end of the month 37 Squadron, RAF Regiment, had also departed to RAF Wittering, and it was all but over.

Epilogue

Wing Commander Julian Andrews took command of RAF Brüggen on 16 November 2001, with much left to do before the station could be handed over to the army in the following March. Health and safety imperatives, together with statutory obligations to local authorities, demanded that work on the station's infrastructure, including 'quality of life' enhancements, continued. So it was that patios and flue-liners of married quarters were replaced, sewers relined, drainage improved, double glazing and automated fire alarms fitted. The beneficiary would be 1 Signals Brigade, and the reincarnation would come in the form of Javelin Barracks, named after the Brigade insignia, but a reminder that the aircraft of that name started its life in Germany at Brüggen some forty-five years earlier. Other memories were upheld by Willie Luys and those local nationals taken on by the army for their expertise in running this great base. So some things may continue as before, albeit under a new flag, and Willie Luys may not have run his last Brüggen 10.

In the penultimate edition of the *Brüggen Circuit*, OC Engineering and Supply Wing, Paul Ridge, answered his own question: 'Why is Brüggen so different?', with: 'What makes Brüggen the jewel in the crown is the people', and ended with: 'In time the memories of Brüggen will fade, but the least we can do as individuals is to ensure that the spirit lives on.'

Amen to that.

Appendix One

RAF Brüggen

Station Commanders

Group Captain	W.V. Crawford-Compton DSO DFC	May 53–Dec 55
	A.G. Dudgeon CBE DFC	Dec 55–Oct 57
	C.D. Tomalin OBE DFC AFC	Oct 57–Dec 59
	E.D. Crew DSO DFC	Dec 59–Oct 62
	I.G. Broom DSO DFC AFC	Oct 62–Nov 64
	E.B. Sismore DSO DFC AFC	Nov 64–Apr 66
	C.D.A. Browne DFC	Apr 66–Jan 68
	D.C.A. Lloyd	Jan 68–Apr 70
	J.B. Curtiss	Apr 70–Aug 72
	D. Harcourt-Smith DFC	Aug 72–Jul 74
	P.R. Harding	Jul 74–Jan 76
	J.R. Walker AFC	Jan 76–Jan 78
	G.C. Williams AFC	Jan 78–Dec 79
	P.P.W. Taylor AFC ADC	Dec 79–Dec 81
	C.J. Thomson AFC	Dec 81–Dec 83
	J.K. Sim OBE AFC	Dec 83–Dec 85
	J.E. Houghton AFC	Dec 85–Nov 87
	R.H. Goodall AFC	Nov 87–Dec 89
	A.J. Harrison CBE	Dec 89–Jun 92
	R.A. Wright AFC	Jun 92–Oct 94
	G.L. Torpy DSO BSc	Oct 94–Apr 96
Air Commodore	G.L. Torpy DSO BSc	Apr 96–Nov 96
	N.D.A. Maddox	Nov 96–Dec 98
	W. McNicoll CBE BSc	Dec 98–Sep 01
Group Captain	T.M. Anderson DSO MA	Sep 00–Nov 01
Wing Commander	J.R. Andrews MA	Nov 01–Mar 02

Appendix Two

RAF Brüggen
Resident Operational Squadrons and Aircraft

Diary of Events

Jan 53	85 and 89 Sqns, RAF Regiment (Bofors L40/60) arrive
Jul 53	112 Sqn (Vampire FB5s) arrives from RAF Jever
Aug 53	130 Sqn (Vampire FB5s) reforms at Brüggen
Jan 54	112 and 130 Sqns begin converting to FGA Sabre F4s
Jul 55	67 and 71 Sqns (FGA Sabre F4) arrive from RAF Wildenrath
Jan 56	67, 130, 112 and 71 Sqns begin converting to FGA Hunter F4
May 57	67, 130, 112 and 71 Sqns disband
Jun 57	80 Sqn (Canberra PR7s) arrives from RAF Laarbruch
Jul 57	87 Sqn (Meteor NF11s) arrives from RAF Wahn and converts to Javelins
Aug 57	213 Sqn (Canberra B(I)6s) arrives from RAF Ahlhorn
Oct 57	85 and 89 Sqns, RAF Regiment, disband
Jan 61	87 Sqn disbands
Sep 69	80 Sqn disbands
Dec 69	213 Sqn disbands
Jun 70	14 Sqn begins to re-form with FBSA Phantom FGR2
Aug 70	17(F) Sqn begins to re-form with FBSA Phantom FGR2
Dec 70	II(AC) Sqn begins to re-form with Recce Phantom FGR2
Jan 71	'A' Flight, 25 Sqn (Bloodhound SAM) operational at Brüggen
Apr 71	II(AC) Sqn moves to RAF Laarbruch
Aug 71	31 Sqn begins to re-form with FBSA Phantom FGR2
Mar 75	14 Sqn begins converting to FBSA Jaguar GR1
Apr 75	17(F) Sqn begins converting to FBSA Jaguar GR1
Jan 76	31 Sqn begins converting to FBSA Jaguar GR1
Jan 76	66 Sqn, RAF Regiment, arrives with L40/70 Bofors LAA Guns
Apr 76	66 Sqn re-named 37 Sqn, equipped with Rapier SAM
Mar 77	20 Sqn reforms at Brüggen with FBSA Jaguar GR1
Mar 83	25 Sqn returns to UK
Jun 84	20 Sqn disbands – re-forms with Tornado GR1 at RAF Laarbruch
Nov 84	31 Sqn begins converting to FBSA Tornado GR1
Mar 85	17(F) Sqn begins converting to FBSA Tornado GR1
Nov 85	14 Sqn begins converting to FBSA Tornado GR1
Oct 86	IX(B) Sqn arrives from RAF Honington with FBSA Tornado GR1

Mar 99 17(F) Sqn disbands
Dec 00 14 Sqn moves to RAF Lossiemouth
Jul 01   IX(B) Sqn moves to RAF Marham
Aug 01 31 Sqn moves to RAF Marham
Oct 01   37 Sqn, RAF Regiment, moves to RAF Wittering
Mar 02 RAF Brüggen becomes Javelin Barracks

Bibliography

Armitage, Michael: *The Royal Air Force – An Illustrated History*; Arms & Armour

Bendell, Anthony 'Bugs': *Never in Anger*; Orion

Burns, Michael: *McDonnell Douglas Phantom II*; Osprey Air Combat

Fairbairn, Tony: *Action Stations Overseas*; Patrick Stephens

Franks, Norman: *First in the Indian Skies*

Hall, Ian: *Tornado Times*; No. 2 Group PRU

Lake, Jon: *Operation Desert Fox*; Aircraft Illustrated, March 1999

Lee, ACM Sir David: *The RAF in Germany 1945–1978*

Leeson, Frank: *The Hornet Strikes, The Story of No. 213 Squadron*; Air Britain

Onderwater, Hans: *Second to None*; Airlife

RAF Historical Society Journal No. 20

Spooner, Tony: *Clean Sweep*; Crecy

Index

AAC, 12 Flt, 256
AAR, 200, 208, 224–7, 230, 251, 265, 291, 294
ACB, 6, 12–14, 16, 18–19
ACMI, 166, 193, 217, 262
Adelburger, Frau, 12
Adour (engine), 134, 138, 176, 209
ADR, 213
Agricola, Operation, 290–1, 302
Ahlhorn, RAF, 21, 32, 53–5, 139
Aiken, AVM J.A.C., 85
Air Kilroe, 287
Air Swift, 287
Air Terminal, 167, 257, 260, 273
Akin, Fg Off, 36
Akrotiri, RAF, 62, 185, 265
Al Kharj (Airfield), 276–8, 290
Al Khobar, 229
Al Nimran Hotel, 229
ALARM, 239, 249, 261, 271, 282, 293, 315
Ali Al Salem (Airfield), 284, 290, 295, 309, 315
Allen, Fg Off Conrad, 305
Allied Force, Operation, 292
Allison, Wg Cdr Dennis, 110
Alliss, Peter, 207
Allisstone, Sqn Ldr Mike, 82–3
Anderson, Fg Off B.M., 73
Anderson, Flt Lt Jim, 85, 90
Anderson, Flt Lt/Wg Cdr/Gp Capt Tim, 204, 292–3, 295–7, 315, 318, 324, 338
Andover (aircraft), 269, 287
Andrews, Flt Lt Derek, 99

Andrews, Sqn Ldr/Wg Cdr Julian, 257, 328–9, 339
Andrews, Cpl Paul, 155–6
Androvani, Flt Lt Eric, 205
Ankerson, Sqn Ldr Bob, 238, 241, 247
Anne, HRH The Princess, 97, 173
APC, 22, 32, 34–6, 39–40, 42–3, 60, 62, 103, 109, 130, 138, 157, 166, 188–9, 208, 214
Arber, Fg Off Alan, 12–13, 17
Arid Thunder, Exercise, 271
Arm Eng Sqn, 204
Armitage, AVM/ACM Sir Michael, 164
ARRC, 273, 290
'Arris Arriatis, 189
Arthur, Wg Cdr Peter, 138, 142, 164
ASCIET, 310
ASM, 121–2, 129
Astra Cinema, 13, 33, 154, 173, 198
ATC, 30–1, 38, 78, 98, 185, 220, 265, 302
ATF, 194, 224, 227, 231
Ault, Wg Cdr John, 166

Backhouse, SAC, 182
Bad Kohlgrub, 32, 79, 109, 192, 278
Bader, Gp Capt Douglas/School, 123, 270
Bagwell, Wg Cdr/Gp Capt Greg, 295, 338
Bahrain, 221–4, 226–7, 240, 249
Baldwin, Flt Lt Kevin, 250
Ball, Flt Lt 'Raz', 77, 111, 128
Band, Voluntary/RAF Germany, 192, 198, 282

Bandon, AM The Earl of, 49

Banjo, 184

Barker, Flt Lt Ron, 7

Barnard Trophy, 182

Barnes Wallis School, 270

Baron, Wg Cdr David, 170, 177, 180

Barrow, Flt Lt John, 166, 180

Bartlett, CT Howard, 282

Baxter, SAC, 109

BDR, 142–3

BDT, 319–22

Beamish, Sgt, 164

Beardmore, Flt Lt Stephen, 262

Bears RFC, 118–19, 151, 168, 180,
    278–81, 305, 328–9

Beasant, Flt Lt Norman, 137

Beer, Ron, 297, 299–300

Belize, 254–5

Bell, Fg Off/Wg Cdr 'Tinkle', 43,
    46–7, 49, 122, 131

Bendell, Plt Off 'Bugs', 41–2, 47

Benevolent Fund, 143, 173, 202, 253

Big Brew, 306

Big Ears, 262

Birch, Wg Cdr David, 143, 168

BL755, 93, 222, 224, 271

Black, Capt Steve, 256

Black Eagle Camp, 183

Block 'N' Tackle, Gp Capt, 257

Bloodhound (SAM), 90, 96–7,
    122, 139, 178

BOBS, 335

Bodo RnoAF, 170

Bogg, Wg Cdr Dick, 189–90,
    194, 202

Bolton, Flt Lt Lynnette, 335

Bolton, Wg Cdr John, 189

Bolton, Operation, 284–5, 295–6,
    310, 315

Bombardier Services, 256

Booth, Roy, 103

Bowen, Sgt, 308

Boyle, Wg Cdr Tom, 271, 284

Boz (chaff dispenser), 188, 190,
    229, 292–3

Bracht, 3 BAD, 69, 123, 275, 324

Brackenbury, Wg Cdr Ian, 198

Brakewell, Flt Lt, 59

Bremner, Fg Off Colin, 158

Bretherton, Ron, 136

Bridges, Miss, 118

Broadbent, Sqn Ldr Mike, 134

Broadhurst, AM Sir Harry/Trophy,
    25, 171

Brockless, Kenny, 329

Brockzetel (SOC), 62

Brookes, Flt Lt Mike, 158, 161

Broom, Gp Capt I.G., 75, 78

Brown, Cpl Charlie, 227

Brown, Sqn Ldr/Wg Cdr Eddie,
    51, 56, 59, 61

Brown, Flt Lt Nick, 118

Brown, Flt Lt Norman, 177

Brown, Flt Lt Robin, 43, 46, 49

Browne, Gp Capt C.D.A., 79

Brown, the Rev R.R., 138

Brüggen 10 (road race), 218, 304,
    326–7, 339

Brüggen Air, 260, 290

Brüggen Bowl, 198, 301, 321

Brüggen Circuit, 84–5, 112, 118, 127,
    143, 160–1, 170, 178, 182, 188, 202,
    205, 209, 211–12, 216, 236, 240,
    267, 296, 309, 318, 339

Bruno, Airdog, 155–6

Bryant, Wg Cdr/AVM Derek,
    111, 196–7

Buccaneer (aircraft), 239, 243, 255

Buckland, Flt Lt Neil, 158

Bull, Frau, 80

Burgess, Flt Lt 'Budgie', 238, 247

Burns Night, 92, 168–9, 269

Buxton, Operation, 225

Byrne, Sqn Ldr B.N., 36

Cagliari, 189, 214–15
Cairns, Flt Lt 'Jock', 98
Calder, Sqn Ldr Johnston, 296
Cameron, ACM Sir Neil, 142
Campbell, Flt Lt Archie, 75
Campbell, Wg Cdr Ian, 62
Campling, Fg Off Jack, 15–16
Canberra (aircraft), xi, 51–3, 58, 62–4,
    66, 71–5, 77–85, 90–1, 93–4, 103,
    130, 136, 142–4, 151, 187, 198, 216
Carlyle, FS 'Geordie', 137
Carrey, Flt Lt Dick, xiv, 52, 60–2
Carte Blanche, Exercise, 17, 34
Carter, Sqn Ldr Doug, 221
Carver, Tom, 235
Carvosso, Flt Lt Ken, 166
Casabayo, Flt Lt Sean, 307
Cassell, Fg Off Dennis, 30
Cassidy, Father, 172
Catering Squadron, 77, 300–301, 327
Cathie, Flt Lt John, 170
CFE, 253, 262
Chandler, Wg Cdr John, xiv,
    209, 221, 225
Chandler, Wg Cdr Mike, 84, 90
Chaplaincy Team, 283
Charles, Derek, 198, 300
Charlton, Flt Lt Harry, 287
Chater, Sqn Ldr Joe, 17
Cherry, Sqn Ldr, 36
Cheseldene-Culley, Fg Off, 227
Cheshire, Gp Capt Leonard/School,
    123, 181, 216, 270
Chick, Flt Lt John, xiv, 26, 30, 38
Chisholm, Flt Lt Robin, 287
Christie, Flt Lt, 7
Churchill, Cpl, 308
Clark, Sgt William, 77
Clarke, Flt Lt, 56
Clutch Radar, 176
Cobbett, Cpl Suzanne, 308
Colley, Sqn Ldr 'Tam', 74

Collins, Wg Cdr Tony, 180
COMAO, 231, 262–3, 276, 282, 291, 314
Compton, Fg Off Clive, xiv, 68
Coningsby, RAF, 93–4, 96, 262
Connor, SAC Jock, 311
Conran-Smith, D.R., 139
Coogan, Cpl Mark, 278
Coombes, Flt Lt Dave, 263
Cooper, Flt Lt, 61
Cooper, WO Vic, 191
Cope Thunder, Exercise, 282
Copping, Cpl Bob, xiv, 34–5, 41
Corbitt, Flt Lt Alleyn, 210
Corderoy, Graham, 117
Coronet, Exercise, 21
Cosbie-Ross, SAC, 138
Cosens, Flt Lt Iain, 269
Cosgrove, Flt Lt John, 125
Cossor Trophy, 220, 302
Coulson, Flt Lt Doug, 18
Coutts, Sqn Ldr Dick, 143
Cowper, Flt Lt Jenny, 145–6
Cox Hotel, 212–13
Coy, Cpl Michelle, 280
Crawford-Compton, Gp Capt Bill,
    20, 38
Creedy, Sgt, 284
Creek Scope, Exercise, 118
Creer, Wg Cdr Bob, xiv, 6
Creusen, Herr, 286
Crew, Gp Capt Eddie, xiv, 62, 65, 68, 75
Crossbow Club, 121, 160, 189, 195, 259
Cullen, Cpl Al, 278
Curtiss, Gp Capt John, xiv, 91–3, 96,
    98–9, 101, 110
D'Ardenne, Sqn Ldr Peter, 324
Darbyshire, The Rev, 138
Darrel, Maj, 138
Davies, Sqn Ldr Bill, 289
Davies, Sqn Ldr H.D., 258
Day, Flt Lt Nigel, 138
Day, Sqn Ldr Peter, 171

de la Billiere, Gen Sir Peter, 247

de Vries, Bert, 297, 299–300

Decimomannu/Deci, 103, 185

Dedman, Sgt Ron, 21

Demery, Flt Lt Nigel, 176

Dempsey, SAC, 182

Dent, Flt Lt Norman, 234, 247

Der Adler KG, 115–17, 160, 214

Desert Fox, Operation, 290

Desert Shield, Operation, 221

Desert Storm, Operation, 235, 250

Devon (aircraft), 10

Dhahran (Airfield), 227, 229–36, 238–40, 242, 244, 246–9, 258, 263, 266, 276

Diana, Princess of Wales, 298

Dickson, MRAF Sir William, 17

Dineen, Sqn Ldr Mike, 190

Dingle, Plt Off, 23, 180

Dingo Dart, Exercise, 315

Distant Thunder, Exercise, 263

Donderberg, 125, 160, 202

Done, Cheryl, 280

Donovan, Flt Lt C.J., 274

Dove-Dixon, Fg Off Kim, 190

Downs, Flt Lt Dick, 194

Driver, Operation, 266

Du Crosses, Elbert, 167, 205

Dudgeon, Gp Capt Tony, xiv, 38, 51, 55

Duffy, Flt Lt Kieren, 234, 247

Duncan Trophy, 62

Dunlop, Wg Cdr Pete, 202, 215

Dunn, SAC Pete, 302

Durham, Wg Cdr Ed, xiv, 151

ECM, 29, 97, 134, 158, 188, 221, 229, 231, 238, 243, 271, 275, 291, 293

Edinburgh, HRH the Duke, 58, 178

Edwards, Sqn Ldr Dave, 68

Edwards, Wg Cdr Ted, 171

Eielson AFB, 282

El Adem, RAF, 64, 72

Elizabeth, HM The Queen, xi, 13, 78, 110, 123, 270

Elliot, Wg Cdr Ian, 295

Elliott, Flt Lt Alex, 319

Elmpt/Elmpter Wald, 1–6, 74, 85, 92, 98, 106, 112, 115, 170, 181, 191, 202, 216, 297, 321

Eng and Supply Wg, 131, 143, 174, 180, 198

Engadine, Operation, 291–6, 302–304, 307

Engineering Efficiency Trophy, 109, 198, 210

EOD, 153, 179, 202, 204

Europa Club, 92

Evans, Flt Lt 'Chick', 75

Evans, Wg Cdr Ivor, 227, 234

Evans, Sqn Ldr Martin, 319, 321

Everett, Fg Off Johnny, 15

F.95 (camera), 52, 74, 102

F-84 Thunderjet (aircraft), 19, 24–5, 27, 29, 31, 60

Fahnenband, 258, 330

Falkland Islands, xi, 182, 193, 198, 221, 254, 270, 294, 311, 325

Farrar, Sgt Steve, 319

Fassberg Air Base, 4, 144, 178

Fear Dry Inn, 144, 164, 257

Fenning, Fg Off Ray, 64

Ferguson, Wg Cdr 'Alfy', 200, 207

Field, WO Jeff, 189–90

FLIR, 286, 316

Florennes, BAF, 21, 61, 111, 210

Floydd, Sqn Ldr Bill, xiv, 139, 149, 164

Fluggies, Gaststatte, 213

Flying Eagle, Exercise, 194

Forstmeister, 110, 140, 203

Foster, AM Sir Robert, 10–11, 73, 172, 200, 207, 210, 215

Foulkes, Flt Lt, 46

Foxley-Norris, AM Sir Christopher, 86, 97–8, 172, 197

Frame, Flt Lt Peter, 40, 42

Freeman, SAC, 182

Freeman, Sqn Ldr 'Taff', 111–12
Freight Distribution Centre, 256
Froggatt, Fg Off Dave, 173
Fürstenfeldbruck Air Base, 63, 168
Geddes, CT George, 282
GEF, 277, 292
Geilenkirchen, RAF, 31–2, 34, 48–9, 62
General Duties Flight, 307
Geoghegan, Flt Lt Sid, xiv, 15
GEP, 15, 29, 61, 63, 69, 258
Gerrard, Flt Lt Tim, 156, 166
Gibb, Sqn Ldr Graham, 104
Gibson, Wg Cdr Mike, xiv, 140–1, 164
Gilchrist, Eileen, 290
Gill, Wg Cdr L.W.G., 52
Gillies, Flt Lt Stuart, 238
Gisbertz, Herr, 184
Gloucester, HRH the Duke/
    Duchess, 44, 63
Golf Course/Club, xi, 15–16, 19, 98,
    110, 140, 156, 168, 207, 253, 258,
    289, 321
Goodall, Gp Capt 'Rocky', 207–210,
    226, 340
Goodman, Flt Lt Peter, 118
Goose Bay, 193–4, 208, 215, 221, 225,
    316, 324
Gopher Dram, Exercise, 215
Gordon, Wg Cdr Keith, 164
GPS, 286
Granby, Operation, 221, 224–5, 227–8,
    230, 243, 247, 250
Grant, Sqn Ldr Kenny, 327
Gray, Sqn Ldr Mike, 156, 162
Greaves, Cpl, 72
Green Flag, Exercise, 208, 314
Gregory, Sqn Ldr Tony, 94
Greig, Wg Cdr Jim, 164, 168
Gresham, Sqn Ldr John, 325
Grieve, Flt Lt Alan, 210
Griffin, SAC, 168

Griffin, Sqn Ldr/Wg Cdr Andy,
    165, 192
Griffiths, Sqn Ldr Duncan, 134
Griffiths, Sqn Ldr Pete, 180
Griggs, Flt Lt Steve, xiv,
    157, 176–7
Grimshaw, WO, 301
Grote Slinger, Exercise, 289
Ground Liaison Section, 34
Grout, Flt Lt Wally, 194
Grumbridge, Fg Off G.G., 85
Grypink, Father, 92
Gulf War, xiii, 176, 221–53, 257, 259,
    261, 269, 275, 286, 313
Gütersloh, RAF, 4, 78, 92, 94, 98,
    101–102, 105, 139, 253, 319
Gutjahr, Herr, 184
Haggett, Flt Lt, 319
Hale, FS, 90
Halfacree, Flt Lt Ken, 79
Hall, SAC/Cpl Andy, 304
Hall, Flt Lt/Wg Cdr Ian, xiv,
    140, 142, 194
Hall, Matthew, 282
Hallmark, Exercise, 165
Halt Fair, Exercise, 146
Hamilton, Flt Lt Alex, 311
Hamilton, SAC, 278
Hanbury, Sqn Ldr Terry, 82
Hanks, Mr, 138
Hannah, Flt Lt Bill, xiv, 7
Hanson, Flt Lt Don, xiv, 7–15
Harcourt-Smith, Gp Capt David,
    110, 113–14, 118
Harding, AVM Peter, 133, 219
Harding, Gp Capt Peter, 114,
    118–20, 122–4
Hare, Fg Off John, xiv, 51–2, 71
Harfield, Sgt, 182
Hercules (aircraft), 171, 221, 229,
    272, 291, 295

Harrison, Gp Capt Tony, 216, 218, 242, 253, 257

Hartree, Sqn Ldr Bill, 227

Hastings, Flt Lt 'Sharky', 43

Hattersley, Fg Off David, xiv, 19

Hawkins, Maj, 181

Hayr, Air Cdre Ken, 161

Heavy Fleet, 304

Hebrides, Outer, 6, 75, 138

Hegarty, Sqn Ldr Frank, 24, 42

Hellyer, Fg Off, 73

Henderson, Wg Cdr David, xiv, 180

Hendry, Sqn Ldr Les, 229

Henlow Shield, 85

Hewat, Sqn Ldr Chris, 261

Hewitt, Cpl, 210

Hill 60, xi, 32, 41, 213, 301

Hill, Flt Lt Jon, 203

Hill, Steve, 185

Hillen, Herr, 286

Hindley, Sqn Ldr Mick, 134

Hine, Wg Cdr Derek, 121

Hine, Wg Cdr/Gp Capt/ACM Sir 'Paddy', xiv, 94, 97, 103, 109, 120, 130, 192, 230, 247, 269

Hive, 296

Hoffman, Herr Adolf, 8

Holmes, Sqn Ldr C.J., 22, 43

Homestart, 215, 296

Honey, Plt Off/Sqn Ldr Bob, xiv, 43, 47–8, 94–5, 101

Hoon, Rt Hon Geoffrey, 311

Horning, Gay, 103

Houghton Trophy, 303

Houghton, Wg Cdr/Gp Capt/Air Cdre John, xiv, 157, 161, 165–6, 197–8, 202, 205, 207, 304, 340

Howard, Fg Off/Wg Cdr Richard, xiv, 64, 157, 166, 171

Hubble, Padre Ray, 162

Hudson, SAC Michael, xiv, 33

Hulse, Flt Lt Frank, xiv, 17–18

Humphreyson, Wg Cdr Roy, 137, 157

Hunt, SAC Wayne, 302

Hunter (aircraft), xi, 38–43, 46, 48, 53, 60, 62, 72, 94, 98, 102, 105, 130

Hunter, Sgt John, 282

Hurry, Wg Cdr John, 61

Hutchinson, Flt Lt Les, xiv, 21, 27

IFOR, 272

IRLS, 98–9, 101

Irving, Wg Cdr Nial, 204–205

Jaguar (aircraft), xi–xii, 111, 121, 123, 125, 128–9, 134–5, 137, 139–43, 145–9, 151–2, 154, 156–8, 161–2, 164–5, 167–8, 170–2, 174, 176–80, 184–6, 188–9, 191–2, 197–8, 204, 209, 211, 225, 239, 290, 341

Jalibah (airfield), 237, 244

Javelin (aircraft), 52–4, 58–62, 64, 339

Jeffs, Mr, 38

Jenkins, Fg Off, 32

Jennings, Sqn Ldr Bill, 7, 11, 13

Jertz, Lt Gen Walter, 330–1

Jever, RAF, 4, 21, 139, 165, 168, 341

Jewell, Flt Lt Jimmy, 49

Johns, Wg Cdr Johnny, 20, 23, 38–9

Johns, ACM Sir Richard, 294, 303

Johnson, Gp Capt Johnny, 13

Joint Winter, Exercise, 324–5

Jolliffe Trophy, 301

Jones SAC, 254

Jones, Cpl Bob, xiv, 27, 34

Jones, Sqn Ldr Derek, 206

Jones, Sqn Ldr Ed, 165, 167

Jones, Flt Lt Lee, 42, 48

Jones, Tex, 165–6

Jordan, Fred, 297–9

JP233, 188, 224, 227, 230, 232, 235, 237, 244, 251, 291 313–14

Jural, Operation, 258, 263, 266, 276–8, 284, 290

Kaalk, Mijnheer, 168

Keane, Flt Lt Mike, 120

Kearney, WO Bill, 261
Keen, SAC Rachel, 311
Kelly, Sqn Ldr John, 301, 327
Kent, HRH The Duke, 61, 63
Kentopf, Hannelore, 297
Kenvyn, Flt Lt Ian, 171
Keogh, Cpl, 308
Khobar Towers, 263, 276
King, Cpl David, xiv, 78
Kipness, Maj (USAF), 100, 122
Kirkpatrick, Wg Cdr James, 284
Kirkpatrick, Flt Lt Willie, 161, 170
Kitwood, Fg Off Eric, 21
Knight, Bob, xiv, 235
Kosovo, xi, 292, 293, 295, 296,
    297, 302–305
Krul, Rudie and Annie, 297–8
Kuwait, 66, 67, 221–2, 225, 235, 244,
    263, 284–5, 290, 299, 310
Laage (airfield), 268
Laarbruch, RAF, 31, 45–6, 49, 51, 75,
    82, 85, 96, 98, 99, 101, 103, 123,
    138, 176, 186, 207, 209, 215, 227,
    244, 252–3, 262, 280, 281, 289,
    291, 302, 341
LABS, viii, 54, 58, 74–5, 79
Lamb, Wg Cdr G.C., 59
Lang, Herr Josef, 52
Lapland, 273
Las Vegas, 158, 193, 255
Laser Guided Bomb/LGB, xiii, 171,
    177, 239–40, 241, 243–4, 251,
    284, 292
Lawton, Sqn Ldr Mike, 215
Lees, Sir Ronald, 77
Leeson, Fg Off Frank, xiv, 63, 335
Leigh, Venessa, 178
Levitt, Wg Cdr Tony, 205–206
Lightning (aircraft), 94, 121, 130
Lionheart, Exercise, 190
Lloyd, Flt Lt Steve, 204, 267
Lloyd, Gp Capt Tim, xiv, 82, 89–91

Lloyd, WO, 308
Lone Ranger, Exercise, 64, 72
Long, Plt Off 'Cookie', 312
Lossiemouth, RAF, 157, 166, 171, 200,
    307, 316–17, 320, 342
Lovett, Wg Cdr Malcolm, xiv, 178
Low, Wg Cdr Robbie, 291, 316
Ludwig, Herr, 127
Luys, Willie, 100, 129, 196, 202, 218,
    288, 327–8, 339
Maastricht (War HQ), 152
MACC, 257
MacIndoe, Ronnie, 323
Maddox, Air Cdre Nigel, xiv, 278, 285,
    290, 340
Maina, Lt Mike RN, xi, 41–2, 48–9
Maitland, Fg Off P.J., 72
Major, Rt Hon John, 234, 243, 247
Malcolm Club, 96, 181, 218, 290
Mallet Blow, Exercise, 212
Malley, CT Paul, 277
Mansfield, Fg Off Roger, 30, 32, 46
Maple Flag, Exercise, 212
Margaret, HRH The Princess, 26, 32,
    76–7, 125–7, 208, 298
Marham, RAF, 225, 253, 320, 336,
    338, 342
Martin, AM Sir Harold, 101
Mason, Flt Lt Sam, 137
Massie, Wg Cdr Gordon, 122, 151
Matthias, Herr, 156
Mauser (cannon), 188, 229
Mayer, SAC, 182
MCAG, 138, 181, 196, 198–9, 207
McAlpine, Wg Cdr Bob, 282, 286
McCarthy, Flt Lt, 56
McDade, SAC, 109
McGinty (the goat), 204–205, 214
McIntyre, Flt Lt, 73
McLeod, Wg Cdr Grant, 192, 204
McNicoll, Wg Cdr/Air Cdre Iain, xiv,
    263, 290, 303, 305, 314–15, 340

Mejor, Sqn Ldr, 23, 39
Menzies, WO, 135–6
Met (Office/Men), 113, 302–303
Meteor (aircraft), 16, 21, 32, 52–3, 60, 62, 341
Meuwissen, Mijnheer, 157
MFPU, 51, 63, 75, 79
MiG (aircraft), 23, 26, 227
Miles, Cpl 'Pop', xiv–xv, 26–7, 31
Miller, Wg Cdr 'Dusty', 234
Mills, HEO Simon, 254
Milne, Plt Off, 56
Milsom, Fg Off Dick, xiv, 80, 83
Mitchell, Wg Cdr Frank, xiv, 164, 166–7, 169–70, 173–4, 184
Moloney, Flt Lt, 203
Monte Carlo, Exercise, 21
Morgan, Cpl, 217, 308
Morgan, Flt Lt Jeff, 146, 171
Morgan, Flt Lt Pete, 109
Morris, Wg Cdr/Air Cdre Vaughan, 209, 221, 223, 234, 295
Morrison, J.T., 168
Morrison, Fg Off 'Murph', xiv, 51, 71
Moule, Sqn Ldr Doug, 227, 247
Movements Squadron, 256, 260, 280, 284, 323
MPC, 107, 138, 182, 207, 210, 212, 217, 258, 271, 311
MT Flight, 136, 176, 302
MTSU, 33
MU, 33, 69–70, 78, 82–3, 85, 104, 110, 116, 123, 138, 142–4, 148, 153, 156, 164, 176, 179–81, 194, 209, 213, 242, 255, 257–8, 275, 301, 304
Mudaysis (airfield), 235
Muharraq (airfield), 221–2, 226, 240, 253
Mullen, Flt Lt 'Paddy', 176–7
Mumford, Wg Cdr Anthony, xiv, 121, 126, 129, 136, 139
Murray, Sqn Ldr Rob, 171

Myles, Mary, 242
NAAFI, 27, 85, 96, 118, 120, 155, 309
Naidoo, Fg Off, 72
Nash, Wg Cdr Terry, xiv, 137, 146, 157
Nattrass, Flt Lt Trevor, 107
NAVWASS, 134, 158, 165, 181
Needham, Flt Lt David, 172
Neil, Flt Lt Frank, 208
Nellis Air Force Base, 157–8, 193, 314
Nettley, Wg Cdr R.E.W., 79
New, Flt Lt Pete, 156
News, RAF, xiv, 75, 111, 113, 158, 176, 180, 235, 257, 314
Newstead, Mavis, xiv, 96
NFZ, 258, 263
Nicol, Wg Cdr Ben, xiv, 149, 153, 159
Nijmegen Marches, 305
NMS, 253–4, 258
Noble, Richard, 192
Nordhorn, RAF, 60, 62, 72–4, 80, 103, 107–108, 148, 154, 161–2, 166, 325
Northern Watch, Operation, 278
NVG, 231, 235, 293, 316
Offord, Wg Cdr Ray, 83, 85
OLF, 158, 225, 227, 263, 271, 314
OMB, 257
Onze Luchtmacht, 254
Options for Change, 218, 258
Ord, Wg Cdr George, 114–15, 120
Ormrod, Wg Cdr 'Wally', 110
O'Shea, Flt Lt John, 208
Osborne, Flt Lt Clive, 137
Otterburn Range, 212
Overloon Museum, 136
Palin, AM Sir Roger, 213
Parashot, Exercise, 149
Parkinson, Sqn Ldr Tom, 166
Parnell-Hopkinson, Padre, 247
Parr, Sqn Ldr Jerry, 192
Parry-Evans, AM Sir David, 200
Passfield, Flt Lt Ray, 81
Paton, Sqn Ldr Davie, 267, 277

Patriot (SAM), 48, 55, 96, 99, 131, 139, 150–1, 158, 235–8, 244, 293, 324, 341

Pavespike (designator), 158, 177, 239–40, 251, 262

PBX, 29, 217

Peach, Wg Cdr Stu, 263, 274

Pearson, Fg Off Tony, xiv, 71

Penn, Fg Off Tim, 145

Perestroika, 219

Perfect, Sqn Ldr Tony, 220

Perry, Cpl Fred, 277

Perryman, Sgt 'Skip', 277

Peters, Cpl Tech Jim, xiv, 61, 63, 65, 69

PGMs, 134, 239

Phantom (aircraft), xi, 90, 93–6, 98–9, 101–103, 105–107, 109–14, 118–23, 125, 128–30, 134, 151, 174, 176–7, 185, 191, 204, 212, 252, 255, 341

Phoenix Gliding Club, 162

Phillips, Wg Cdr David, 37, 187

Phipps, Mick, 115, 117

Picnic, Exercise, 55

Pitch Black, Exercise, 314

Pixley, Sqn Ldr Ray, 16–17

Plumbe, Flt Lt David, 172

Pollington, Flt Lt David, 104, 109

Pollock, Sqn Ldr Neil, xiv, 122–3, 150–1

Porter, Plt Off Arthur, xiv, 7–8, 10, 12

Potter, Flt Lt Doug, 279, 305

Powell, Sqn Ldr Derek, 165

Powell, Ron, 289–290

Prissick, Gp Capt Mal, 284

PROM, xi, 218, 257, 326

Propulsion Engineering Squadron, 255

PSA, 93, 100, 138, 194, 204, 218, 257

PSI, 33, 196

Puddick, Dulcie, 96

Pugh, Wg Cdr David, 143

Pye, Flt Lt Ken, 61

Pym, John, 184

QRA, 58, 64, 75, 80, 90, 105–107, 118, 129, 137–8, 140, 156, 165, 197, 200–202, 246, 253, 269, 291

Quicktrain, Exercise, 82, 94

Rand, Master Nav, 58

Rapier (SAM), 99, 111, 121, 128, 138, 178, 182–3, 207, 254, 266, 270, 275, 311, 324, 341

Rawle, WO, 307

Rayfield, Sqn Ldr Gordon, 254

RB199 (engine), 176, 302

Red Flag, Exercise, 157–8, 171–2, 180, 194, 212, 239, 255, 271, 324

Redley, Sqn Ldr Trevor, 16–17

Rezyat Apartments, 235

RIC, 258

Richardson, Cpl Graham, 280

Richardson, Wg Cdr K.R., 74

Richtfest, 266

Ridge, Wg Cdr Paul, 323, 339

Rimmer, Flt Lt Bill, 166

Riyadh, 221, 225, 230, 232, 246–7, 276

Robertshaw, Flt Lt Ken, 85

Robertson, AVM 'Black', 255, 259, 300

Robertson, Rt Hon George, 303

Robertson, Flt Lt Tom, xiv, 74

Robinshaw, Lt Alec, xiv, 18

Rogers, Fg Off Gary, 146–7

Rooum, Gp Capt John, 230

Rorkes Drift, Exercise, 211

Rose, Cpl Bill, xiv, 52, 59

Rosefield, Flt Lt Laurie, 73

Rosenmontag, 33, 48, 116, 119

Roseveare, Sqn Ldr Ken, 95

Roubroeks, Jan, 241

Round Robin, Exercise, 64

Rowe, Fg Off Les, xiv, 15, 334

Royal Flush, Exercise, 61–2, 74–6, 79, 82–5

RRF (Air), 259, 265, 269

RRR, 153, 165

Risdale, Sqn Ldr Nigel, 274
Rusling, Sqn Ldr Nick, 171
RWR, 193, 236–7, 249, 268
Rycroft, Wg Cdr Peter, 284
Sabben, Wg Cdr J.M.H., 176
Sabre, 16, 23–7, 30–2, 34, 36–9, 167
   F-86, 21
Salmond (competition), 62, 76, 79,
   84–6, 111, 113, 128, 134–6, 142,
   200, 207, 209, 215
Samouelle, Wg Cdr 'Sammy', 110
Sandys, Rt Hon Duncan, 48, 58–9
Sassoon (competition), 56–7, 63,
   79, 82–3
Scholtens, Sqn Ldr/Wg Cdr John,
   267–8, 316, 331, 336, 338
Schützenfest, 107, 156
Scorpion Wind, Exercise, 271
Scud (missile), 233, 236, 238, 244
SEAD, ix, 239, 258, 293, 304
Searle, Wg Cdr, 78
Security Squadron, 139, 149, 171, 191,
   307–308, 324
Seidenthal, Herr Willy, 80
Seymore, Sqn Ldr H.D.M., 14
Shaibah (airfield), 237
Shandigan, Operation, 253
Shanks, SAC, 254
Sharjah, RAF, 66–8
Sheldrick, David, 280
Sheraton Hotel, 222–3
SHORAD, 121, 131
Short, Wg Cdr Frank, 205–206
Shucksmith, Fg Off, 48
Sidewinder (AAM), 174–7, 188, 193,
   229, 258, 285, 292–3
SIF, 196, 308–309, 321
Signals Regiment, No. 21, 34
Signals Unit, No. 11 (Det), 28–9
Sim, Wg Cdr/Gp Capt Joe, 157, 161,
   166, 170, 185, 187, 189, 191, 197

Simpson, Wg Cdr R.C., 76
Simulator, Flight, 62, 91, 114,
   191, 252
Sinclair, Sqn Ldr Martin, 168
Sinker, Fg Off, 79
Sismore, Gp Capt Ted, 78
Skidmore Trophy, 326
Skyshadow (ECM), 188, 229, 238,
   290, 292–3
SLAR, 98, 101
Smerdon, Sqn Ldr Dick, xiv, 52
Smith, SAC Mel, xiv
Smith, Fg Off Mike, 36, 82–3
Smith, Flt Lt 'Smudge', 210
Smith, Sqn Ldr Ed, 267, 272
Smith, Wg Cdr Al, 242, 257–8
Solenzara, 295–6, 302
Southern Watch, Operation, 258, 278
Spadeadam, 193, 212, 325
Sparrow (AAM), 93
Spey (engine), 93, 106, 120, 138,
   176, 255
Spinelli, Capt Andrea, 274
Spink, Fg Off David, xiv, 21
Spink, Gp Capt Cliff, 233, 235, 249
Spotswood, ACM Sir Denis, 114
Sprent, Wg Cdr Chris, 104, 109, 113
Squadrons (Flying):
   II(AC), 341
   IX(B), 336, 338, 341–2
   13: 227, 235
   14: 93–4, 100, 103, 105–107, 111,
      118, 120–4, 126, 128–9, 134–5,
      137, 139, 142, 144, 149, 154,
      157, 161, 168, 170–1, 174–80,
      184–5, 188–9, 192, 197, 200,
      202–205, 208–210, 212, 215–17,
      221–3, 227, 234–5, 243, 247,
      253, 255, 258, 261, 263, 266–7,
      269–72, 284–5, 292, 294–6, 308,
      314–17, 320, 341–2

17: 94–5, 98, 100, 103, 105, 108, 111, 113–15, 120–1, 125, 129, 137, 142, 157–8, 161, 165, 168, 170, 172, 179, 184–5, 192, 197, 199, 204–205, 207–208, 214, 216, 225, 227, 234, 236, 249, 253, 255, 262–3, 269–71, 273, 276–7, 284, 287, 292, 304, 320, 341–2
19: 92
20: 139–42, 157, 164, 167, 169–71, 173, 178, 184, 186, 198, 205, 227, 239, 253, 261, 316, 341
25: 96–7, 122–3, 139, 150–1, 180, 341
31, 85, 103–104, 106–107, 109, 111–13, 118, 129–30, 137–8, 142, 144–7, 156–7, 171, 178–9, 184, 187–90, 192–4, 202, 204–205, 207–208, 212, 215–16, 221, 225–7, 229, 232, 234, 239–41, 249, 253, 258, 262–3, 267–9, 271, 277–8, 287–8, 291, 293, 295–6, 307, 310, 314–16, 324, 326, 338, 341–2
32: 269, 287
67: 34, 36–7, 40–1, 43, 45–9, 341
71: 34–6, 40–1, 45, 48–9, 71, 341
80: 51–2, 55–8, 61–6, 68, 72, 74–6, 79, 81–5, 341
87: 51–4, 58–62, 64 341
92: 92, 94
96: 21
101: 292
112: 13, 21–8, 32–4, 36, 39–40, 42–3, 45–6, 48–9, 341
130: 21–3, 26–7, 31–4, 36, 39–40, 45, 49, 341
213: 51, 53, 55–7, 59, 62–4, 66–70, 72–6, 79–90, 216, 299, 335, 341
(ACB), 6, 12–14, 16, 18–19
    5004, 14–19

(RAF Regiment):
    37, 128, 138, 149–50, 182–3, 193, 195–6, 200, 207, 210–11, 217, 254–5, 258, 266, 270, 278–9, 304–305, 311, 324–5, 337–8, 341–2
66: 128, 138, 341–2
85: 20, 341
89: 20, 341
(RE):
    52 Field, 165, 194, 213, 219, 255
(MT):
    317, 29, 235, 304
Squire, ACM Sir Peter, 330
SSAFA, 160, 191, 218, 242, 296, 306, 326
St Andrews Church, 304
St Nicholas Church, 69, 330
Stainforth Trophy, 310
Staneval, 152–3, 156, 177, 325
Stanning, Flt Lt Peter, 58
Stansfield, Wg Cdr Brian, 79
Stapley, Tanya, 255
Stead, Flt Lt Brian, 98, 100
Stear, Wg Cdr/AM Sir Michael, 120, 123, 125, 260
Stephens, FS, 269
Stirrup, AVM 'Jock', 287
Stockdale, Wg Cdr George, 120
Stockton, Flt Lt Ian, 236
Stonor, Wg Cdr Tom, 130, 220
Strangled Sonata, Exercise, 161–2
Strategic Defence Review, 304
Stronghold, Exercise, 43
Stubbins, SAC, 109
Sturley, Wg Cdr Phil, 209
Stutard, Fg Off Jim, 111
Supply Squadron, 69, 164, 273, 302, 323
Sutton, Wg Cdr/AVM John, 93, 148

Sweat-athon, 311

Sylt, RAF, 22, 32, 34, 36, 39–40, 42–4, 46, 60

Tabuk (Airfield), 225, 227, 239, 243

Taceval, xi, 75, 79, 82, 84, 86, 96, 103–104, 110, 130–1, 133, 138, 142, 147–8, 150–5, 170, 174, 185–6, 189, 191, 193, 211, 215, 251, 259–60, 269

Tallil (airfield), 237

TAM, 79, 111, 114, 171, 276

Taylor, Flt Lt Bill, xiv, 143

Taylor, Gp Capt Peter, 166, 172–3

TBC, 157, 171

Teakle, Wg Cdr 'Paddy', 316, 336, 338

Tew, Sqn Ldr Doug, 156

TFR, 188, 316

Thatcher, Rt Hon Mrs, 127, 179

Thomson, Gp Capt John, 173–4, 179, 181, 185

Thompson, Sqn Ldr 'Thump', 73

Thorn, Flt Lt Tim, 102

Threadgould, Wg Cdr Al, 227

Thrift Shop, 117–18, 218

TIALD, 239, 243, 258, 261–3, 266, 286, 290–3, 309–10, 315, 323–4

Timm, Gen., 258

Tirpitz, 200, 267

Tilsley, Flt Lt Eric, 83

TLP, 168, 276

Tomalin, Gp Capt C.D., 55, 340

Torpy, Wg Cdr/Gp Capt/Air Cdre Glenn, 227, 266, 270–2, 274, 278, 340

Travers-Smith, Fg Off Ian, 95

Tristar (aircraft), 224, 226, 292, 294

Turner, Sqn Ldr Dick, 205–206

Turner, Flt Lt/Wg Cdr Frank, xiv, 154, 261

TWM, 118, 130

Ubee, AVM Dick, 60

Udem, SOC, 61–2

Valentine, Sqn Ldr Michael, 182–3

Valley, RAF, 107, 193, 212

Vampire (aircraft), 10, 13, 21–2, 31, 45, 60, 93, 139, 341

Van Leyssen, Anja, 206–207, 313

Vantage, Operation, 66

VC10 (aircraft), 208, 215, 221–2, 224–5, 240, 249, 262, 292–5, 303

Vickers, Jenny, 253

Vicon (camera), 258, 266, 270, 285, 309, 315

Victor (aircraft), 84, 169, 226

Vincent, Sid, 166

Vine, Sqn Ldr Arthur, 111–12, 114, 204

Vulcan (cannon), 93, 106, 198

Wahn, RAF, 20, 44, 47, 52, 341

Walker, Sqn Ldr Ivor, 204

Walker, Gp Capt John, 132–3, 146–9, 151, 158, 174

Walmsley, Sqn Ldr Hugh, 37

Warden, Operation, 278

Watchdogs (Film), 155–6

Watson, Flt Lt Jock, 125

Webster, LAC, 254

Wegberg, RAF, 1, 14, 32, 35, 61, 81, 117, 144, 160, 190, 249, 254, 274

Wells, Flt Lt Tony, 66

Western Vortex, Exercise, 193–4, 208, 217, 316, 324

Wet Feet, Exercise, 45

Wharmby, Wg Cdr Dick, 184

Whitcombe, Andrea, 304

White, AVM Alan, 180, 187

White, Wg Cdr Andy, 215

Whitehouse, Fg Off Johnny, 15

Whitfield, Sqn Ldr/Wg Cdr Joe, 170, 192, 197, 205–206, 209

Whittaker, Wg Cdr Ivan, 68

Wickrath, 96, 160

Wildenrath, RAF, 7, 10, 13, 24, 26, 29, 31, 33–5, 44, 60, 66, 75, 82, 89–90, 94, 96, 120, 139, 144, 161–2, 173–4, 176, 189, 204, 252–3, 256, 282, 324, 341

Wilkinson, Fg Off N.J., 85

Wilkinson Sword, 114, 253, 261, 271–2

Williams, Gp Capt Graham, xv, 151, 155–7, 161–2, 166

Williams, Helen, 335, 338

Williams, SAC Clare, 301

Williams, Wg Cdr Del, xiv, 118, 174, 180–1,

Williamson, Flt Lt/MRAF Sir Keith, xv, 50, 178

Willis, Fg Off Ted, xv, 17–18

Wilmshurst-Smith, Fg Off Simon, xv, 146

Wilson, Cpl Mike, 164

Wilson, Flt Lt Ken, 73, 76

Wilson, Sqn Ldr A.R., 43

Wilson, Sqn Ldr/AM/ACM Sir 'Sandy', xv, 98–102, 130, 253, 259

Wingate, Flt Lt Bruce, 47

Wings:
    4 Wg: 131
    55 Wg: 20, 32, 45, 55, 334–5
    135 Wg: 24, 34, 38, 45, 47, 49
    5357 Wg: 6–8, 11, 13–14, 17–19

Wistow, Flt Lt/Sqn Ldr Martin, 191, 289

Whittingham, Flt Lt Jerry, 170

Witts, Wg Cdr/Gp Capt Jerry, xv, 215, 225–7, 229, 234–5, 239, 248–50, 295

Wives' Club, 114–15, 127, 149, 296

Wolstenholm, Denis, 116

Wood, Flt Lt John, 151

Woodgate, Flt Lt Len, 136

Woodham, Flt Lt Peter, 60 62

Woodroffe, Flt Lt Eric, 206

Woodruff, Fg Off, 32

Woods, SAC 'Scouse', 301–302

Wool Shop, 160, 218–19

Woolston, Plt Off Geoff, xv, 7, 12–13

Wratten, Sqn Ldr/AVM/ACM Sir William, xv, 94–5, 97–8, 103, 225, 230, 246

Wright, Fg Off P.H.F., 72

Wright, Flt Lt Dick, 307

Wright, Flt Lt Steve, 208

Wright, Wg Cdr/Gp Capt Rob, xv, 207, 215–16, 257–60

Yaffie, 168

YMCA, 290

York, HRH The Duke of, 303

Yuma, MCAS, 271–2

Zerbst (airfield), 268